A CULTURAL HISTORY OF TRAGEDY

VOLUME 3

A Cultural History of Tragedy
General Editor: Rebecca Bushnell

Volume 1
A Cultural History of Tragedy in Antiquity
Edited by Emily Wilson

Volume 2
A Cultural History of Tragedy in the Middle Ages
Edited by Jody Enders, Theresa Coletti, John T. Sebastian, and Carol Symes

Volume 3
A Cultural History of Tragedy in the Early Modern Age
Edited by Naomi Conn Liebler

Volume 4
A Cultural History of Tragedy in the Age of Enlightenment
Edited by Mitchell Greenberg

Volume 5
A Cultural History of Tragedy in the Age of Empire
Edited by Michael Gamer and Diego Saglia

Volume 6
A Cultural History of Tragedy in the Modern Age
Edited by Jennifer Wallace

A CULTURAL HISTORY
OF TRAGEDY

IN THE EARLY MODERN AGE

VOLUME 3

Edited by Naomi Conn Liebler

BLOOMSBURY ACADEMIC
LONDON • NEW YORK • OXFORD • NEW DELHI • SYDNEY

BLOOMSBURY ACADEMIC
Bloomsbury Publishing Plc
50 Bedford Square, London, WC1B 3DP, UK
1385 Broadway, New York, NY 10018, USA
29 Earlsfort Terrace, Dublin 2, Ireland

BLOOMSBURY, BLOOMSBURY ACADEMIC and the Diana logo are trademarks of
Bloomsbury Publishing Plc

First published in hardback in Great Britain 2020
This paperback edition 2023

Copyright © Naomi Conn Liebler and contributors, 2020

Naomi Liebler and contributors have asserted their right under the Copyright, Designs and
Patents Act, 1988, to be identified as the Authors of this work.

Series design by Raven Design

Cover image: Elisabetta Sirani - Portia wounding her thigh © Historic Images / Alamy Stock Photo

All rights reserved. No part of this publication may be reproduced or transmitted
in any form or by any means, electronic or mechanical, including photocopying,
recording, or any information storage or retrieval system, without prior permission
in writing from the publishers.

Bloomsbury Publishing Plc does not have any control over, or responsibility for, any
third-party websites referred to or in this book. All internet addresses given in this
book were correct at the time of going to press. The author and publisher regret
any inconvenience caused if addresses have changed or sites have ceased to
exist, but can accept no responsibility for any such changes.

A catalogue record for this book is available from the British Library.

A catalog record for this book is available from the Library of Congress.

ISBN: HB: 978-1-4742-8796-8
Set: 978-1-4742-8814-9
PB: 978-1-3504-1678-9
PB Set: 978-1-3504-1692-5

Series: The Cultural Histories Series

Typeset by RefineCatch Limited, Bungay, Suffolk
Printed and bound in Great Britain

To find out more about our authors and books visit www.bloomsbury.com
and sign up for our newsletters.

CONTENTS

LIST OF ILLUSTRATIONS	vi
NOTES ON CONTRIBUTORS	vii
SERIES PREFACE	ix
Introduction: Defining the Elephant Naomi Conn Liebler	1
1 Forms and Media: Remediating Tragedy in Print and Performance Rebecca Bushnell	15
2 Sites of Performance and Circulation: Mobile Memes in Renaissance Tragedy Bruce R. Smith	31
3 Communities of Production and Consumption: Networks and Publics of a European Genre András Kiséry	55
4 Philosophy and Social Theory: Murdered Majesty: The Stuarts in Tragedy and *Trauerspiel* Richard Wilson	71
5 Religion, Ritual and Myth: Continuity and Change Paul Innes	83
6 Politics of City and Nation: Tragic Politics: Drama and the City in Early Modern Europe Ivan Lupić	97
7 Society and Family: "The Deed's Creature": Family and Gender in English Renaissance Tragedy Coppélia Kahn	111
8 Gender and Sexuality: Undoing the Tragic Subject Goran Stanivukovic	129
NOTES	147
BIBLIOGRAPHY	181
INDEX	204

ILLUSTRATIONS

INTRODUCTION

0.1 *Blind monks examining an elephant*, an ukiyo-e print by Hanabusa Itchō (1652–1724).   1
0.2 The Wheel of Fortune, a miniature from the *Consolation of Philosophy* by Boethius, fifteenth century.   6

CHAPTER 1

1.1 Title page woodcut for *The Tragicall History of the Life and Death of Doctor Faustus*, as printed in 1616.   16
1.2 Ballad woodcut of Dr. Faustus, "Just judgment of God shew'd upon Dr. John Faustus" (1640?).   17
1.3 Detail of a miniature of the Wheel of Fortune with a crowned king at the top, from John Lydgate's *Troy Book* and *The Siege of Thebes* (c. 1457).   21
1.4 Title page illustration of *The lamentable and true tragedy of Master Arden of Feversham in Kent* (1633).   28
1.5 The ballad of "The complaint and lamentation of Mistresse Arden of/ Feversham in Kent, who for the loue of one Mosbie, hired certaine Ruffians/and Villaines most cruelly to murder her Husband."   29

CHAPTER 2

2.1 Studiolo of Federico III da Montefeltro (built 1473–6), Palazzo Ducale, Urbino Alinari.   33
2.2 Portrait of Seneca the Younger by Joos van Wassenhove (c. 1475).   34
2.3 Ruins of the Theater of Marcellus, Rome, from Giovanni Battista de' Cavalieri, *Antiquarum Statusam Urbis Romae* (1585).   38
2.4 Andrea Palladio (designer), Teatro Olimpico (built 1580–5).   46
2.5 Georges Buffequin, design for production of Pierre du Ryer, *Clitophon* (c. 1630).   47
2.6 *Corral* theater, Almagro (built 1628, restored 1953–4).   49
2.7 Salomon Savery (engraver), interior of Schouwburg, Amsterdam.   52

CHAPTER 6

6.1 "Massacre of Alberico da Romano's family," by Giovanni Demin, 1849–50.   100
6.2 "Eteocles and Polynices fighting against each other outside Thebes." Verona, fifteenth century. Tempera on wood.   106

NOTES ON CONTRIBUTORS

Rebecca Bushnell is the School of Arts and Sciences Board of Advisors Emerita Professor of English at the University of Pennsylvania. Her books include *Prophesying Tragedy: Sign and Voice in Sophocles' Theban Plays*; *Tragedies of Tyrants: Political Thought and Theater in The English Renaissance*; *A Culture of Teaching: Early Modern Humanism in Theory and Practice*; and *Green Desire: Imagining Early Modern English Gardens*. She has also published *A Companion to Tragedy* and *Tragedy: A Short Introduction*. Her most recent book is *Tragic Time, Choice, and Consequences in Drama, Film, and Videogames: The Future in The Instant*. Professor Bushnell has received an ACLS research fellowship and the Lindback Award for Distinguished Teaching, as well as an NEH grant for Teaching with Technology. Professor Bushnell served as Associate Dean for the Humanities in the School of Arts and Sciences from 1998 to 2003, Dean of the College of Arts and Sciences from 2003 to 2004, and Dean of the School of Arts and Sciences from 2005 to 2013. She also served as president of the Shakespeare Association of America.

Paul Innes is Professor of English in the Department of Languages and Literature, United Arab Emirates University, Al Ain. He has published widely on Shakespeare and Critical Theory, and has worked at the Universities of Warsaw, Edinburgh, Strathclyde, and Glasgow. His primary academic interests are in Shakespeare Studies and Critical Theory. His major publications are *Shakespeare's Roman Plays* (2015); *Epic* (2013); *Class and Society in Shakespeare* (Bloomsbury, 2007); *Shakespeare: The Barriers Removed* (2005); and *Shakespeare and the English Renaissance Sonnet: Verses of Feigning Love* (1997).

Coppélia Kahn is Professor Emerita of English and Gender Studies at Brown University. She also taught at Wesleyan University and the University of Massachusetts, Amherst. She is the author of *Man's Estate: Masculine Identity in Shakespeare* (1981) and *Roman Shakespeare: Warriors, Wounds, and Women* (1997), and co-editor of six collections of essays, most recently, *Celebrating Shakespeare: Commemoration and Cultural Memory* (2015) with Clara Calvo. She has written widely on feminist theory, Shakespeare, Renaissance drama, and Shakespeare as cultural icon.

András Kiséry is Associate Professor of English at The City College of New York (CUNY). He is author of *Hamlet's Moment: Drama and Political Knowledge in Early Modern England* (2016) and co-editor of *Formal Matters: Reading the Materials of English Renaissance Literature* (2013), and *Worlds of Hungarian Writing: National Literature as Intercultural Exchange* (2016). He is now working on two longer projects, about early modern English literature and the European book trade, and about the birth of media studies in early-twentieth-century sociology, history, and philology.

Naomi Conn Liebler is Professor of English and University Distinguished Scholar at Montclair State University. She has held fellowships from the Southeastern Institute for Medieval and Renaissance Studies at Duke University, three National Endowment for the

Humanities Summer Seminar grants and two short-term Research Fellowships from the Folger Shakespeare Library, and has also served as a Trustee of the Shakespeare Association of America. She is the author of *Shakespeare's Festive Tragedy: the Ritual Foundations of Genre* (1995); co-editor of *Tragedy*, a theory reader (1998); editor of *The Female Tragic Hero in English Renaissance Drama* (2002) and of *Early Modern Prose Fiction: the Cultural Politics of Reading* (2007). She is working on a book about representations of old age in Shakespeare and other early modern dramatists.

Ivan Lupić is Professor in the Departments of English and Croatian in the University of Rijeka, Croatia. His most recent book, devoted to questions of counsel and subjectivity in early modern English drama, is forthcoming under the title *Subjects of Advice: Drama and Counsel from More to Shakespeare*. He is currently working on two new book projects. One, called *Shakespeare and the End of Editing*, considers the history of Shakespeare editing in the context of manuscript studies as an interdisciplinary field; the other, provisionally titled *The Illyrian Renaissance*, asks how cultural changes initiated in the Italian peninsula enabled dialogues across languages, and how some aspects of the Italian Renaissance can be rethought if considered from the multilingual perspective of the European borderlands. He has published widely in fields ranging from Shakespeare translation and contemporary reception to scribal culture, book history, and comparative literary studies.

Bruce R. Smith, Dean's Professor of English and Theatre at the University of Southern California, is the author of seven books on Shakespeare, including *Ancient Scripts and Modern Experience on the English Stage, 1500–1700* (1988; rpt. and e-book 2014) and *Shakespeare | Cut: Rethinking Cutwork in an Age of Distraction* (2016). He is also the General Editor of *The Cambridge Guide to the Worlds of Shakespeare* (2016; digital edition 2019). His chapter on "Renaissance Color across Media" appears in the Renaissance volume of *A Cultural History of Color* (Bloomsbury).

Goran Stanivukovic is Professor of English at Saint Mary's University, Nova Scotia. He is the author of, most recently, *Knights in Arms: Prose Romance, Masculinity and Eastern Mediterranean Trade in Early Modern England, 1565–1655* (2016) and of *Tragedies of the English Renaissance* (with J. Cameron, 2018), and the editor of *Queer Shakespeare: Desire and Sexuality* (Bloomsbury, hb. 2016, pb. 2018).

Richard Wilson is Emeritus Sir Peter Hall Professor of Shakespeare Studies at Kingston University. He was previously Plumer Fellow at St. Anne's College, Oxford, Professor of Renaissance Studies at Lancaster University and Professor of English Literature at Cardiff University. His many books include *Worldly Shakespeare: The Theatre of Our Good Will* (2016); *Shakespeare and Continental Philosophy* (2014); *Free Will: Art and Power on Shakespeare's Stage* (2013); *Shakespeare in French Theory: King of Shadows* (2007); *Secret Shakespeare: Studies in theatre, religion and resistance* (2004); and *Will Power: Essays on Shakespearean Authority* (1993). He is currently completing *Modern Friends: Shakespeare's Fascist Followers*.

SERIES PREFACE

A cultural history of tragedy faces a daunting task: how to address tragedy's influence on Western culture while describing how complex and changing historical conditions have shaped it over two and a half millennia. This is the first study with such an extensive scope, investigating tragedy's long-lived cultural impact and accounting for its material, social, political, and philosophical dimensions.

Since antiquity, tragedy has appeared in a myriad of forms, reinvented in every age. It has been performed as opera, dance, film, and television as well as live theater. From the beginning, concepts of tragedy have also surfaced in other literary genres such as narrative poetry and novels, as well as in non-literary forms, including journalism, visual art, and photography. Tragedy never appears in a vacuum: the conditions of performance and production and its communal functions always affect its form and meaning. Tragedy has never belonged solely to elite culture, and who creates and consumes these forms of tragedy also makes a difference. Not only has the status of tragedy's producers—the writers, actors, artists, and performers—evolved over time, but so has the nature of the audiences, viewers, and readers as well, all significantly affecting tragedy's aesthetic and social impact.

Tragedy also does more than simply represent or perform human catastrophe or suffering; it is a mode of thought, a way of figuring the human condition as a whole. Philosophers and social and cultural theorists from Plato to Lacan have long pondered the idea of the tragic, while in turn literary models have influenced philosophy, social thought, and psychoanalysis. Tragedy has always had a complex relationship with religion and ritual practices, both complementing and conflicting with religious orthodoxies concerning fate, the power of the gods, and the meaning of suffering. At the same time, since its earliest staging in fifth-century Athens as a civic as well as religious event, tragedy has both echoed and challenged relationships of power and political events in societies experiencing conflict or change.

While tragedy in all its versions has thus profoundly tapped into broad social, intellectual, and political movements, it has often represented those themes through individual experiences, ranging from the titanic sufferings of princes to the sorrows of ordinary men and women. While tragedy's themes of ambition, authority, transgression, and rebellion are grounded in religion and politics, its plots often play out through family relationships that both mirror and conflict with social and political norms. When tragedy thus engages familial and personal themes, it often involves tensions of gender and sexuality. Sexuality is a powerful driver of tragic catastrophe, when desire is granted its own kind of fatal power.

As with other *Cultural History* series, here the story of tragedy writ large is divided into volumes covering six historical periods from antiquity to modernity. Although the boundaries between those time are necessarily fluid, the volumes are divided as follows: 1. Antiquity (500 BCE–1000 CE); 2. Middle Ages (1000–1400); 3. Early Modern Age (1400–1650); 4. Age of Enlightenment (1650–1800); 5. Age of Empire (1800–1920), and 6. Modern Age (1920–present). While such a history naturally focuses on Western culture and history, at the end it also touches on tragedy's later post-colonial adaptations, which put its fundamentally Western concerns in a global context. Each volume has its own introduction by an editor or co-editors presenting an original and provocative vision of tragedy's manifestations in one historical era. Each volume also covers the same eight topics as the others in the *Cultural History*: forms and media; sites of performance and circulation; communities of production and consumption; philosophy and social theory; religion, ritual, and myth; politics of city and nation; society and family; and gender and sexuality. Readers may thus follow one topic over a wide historical span, or they may focus on all dimensions of tragedy in one period. Either way they read, they will be able to appreciate the power of tragedy to shape our understanding of human experience, and in turn, how tragedy has changed over time, both reflecting and challenging historical conditions.

Rebecca Bushnell, University of Pennsylvania, General Editor

Introduction

Defining the Elephant[1]

NAOMI CONN LIEBLER

A number of Eastern traditions—Hindu, Jain, Buddhist, Sufi, Baha'i—share a parable about a group of blind men who come upon an elephant. Each man, touching a different part of the animal's body, insists that the beast *is* the single part he touches: tusk, hide, tail, ear, leg, trunk. Needless to say, they disagree vehemently in their definitions—even, in the Japanese illustration by Hanabusa Itchō (1652–1724), coming to blows (Figure 0.1). Informed only by the specific experience of the body available to him but confident in his synecdoche, each man understands the whole by the part he has got hold of.[2]

This parable of diverse perceptions underpins and complicates our understanding—early modern as well as modern—of the phenomenon of literary tragedy. For better or worse, there seems to be very little agreement today or indeed in the Renaissance about just what this genre is, what it entails, what forms it takes—that is, how we would know

FIGURE 0.1: *Blind monks examining an elephant*, an ukiyo-e print by Hanabusa Itchō (1652–1724). Wikimedia Commons.

it if we got hold of one of its body parts. Scholars trained in the European humanistic critical traditions beginning in the nineteenth century, especially those drawn to powerful effect by Hegel and Nietzsche, write about tragedy mainly as a philosophical discourse located in romance, epic, and prose narrative as well as drama; mid-twentieth-century and post-war critics—Walter Benjamin, Lucien Goldmann, Carl Schmitt among others—tried to make sense of a world whose "sense" seemed to be diminishing exponentially in their own time, and in order to do so, drew in literary, philosophical, and historical references from early modernity.[3] Still others, leaning particularly toward the classical traditions of Greek tragedy and specifically Aristotelian distinctions, identify tragedy as a dramatic genre, a kind of fiction performed by actors on a stage. However we define the elephant, it is clear that many, *many* scholars, critics, philosophers, students, teachers, and lexicographers worldwide still debate with passion and "urgency"[4] what it does and why it still does it in the twenty-first century—why we read the old forms; why we will persist in creating new hybridized forms reciprocally influencing each other; why we continue to read texts and attend performances in these forms for heroes we can admire, despise, or even dismiss. Perhaps that is one reason for the persistence of an energetic debate about what it *was* (to use Blair Hoxby's formulation),[5] when and why it still exists, and who owns it (and who misappropriates its label, as modern media often do when headlines define any regrettable outcome as "tragedy"). However we choose to undertake the debate, or even if we choose to ignore it, it seems clear that, like Keats' Romantic-classical urn, the container and its inscriptions can still "tease us out of thought."

For all the modern and postmodern wrangling with this elephant's parts, we still begin with Aristotle, our second earliest-known wrangler (after Plato). I like to think that there was a question that Aristotle wanted to answer in undertaking the checklist of qualities outlined in the *Poetics*, which translators and interpreters have debated ever since. Gerald Else has claimed persuasively that the *Poetics* sprang from Aristotle's desire to prove that Plato, his teacher at the Academy, was wrong to ban poets from his fictional Republic on the grounds that poets lie:

> The banishment of the poets is justified by two main accusations, the one ideological, the other moral, which are rehearsed in Book 10 of the *Republic*: (1) they are *imitators* of things, at two removes from reality, and (2) they cater to our emotions, i.e., the un- and anti-rational part of our nature, especially in its tendencies to *pity* and *fear*.
>
> When Aristotle came to the Academy to begin his studies in 367, the charge against the poets and its two crucial points, "imitation" and "pity and fear," were already, as we should say, a part of the historical record (the *Republic* was written in the 370s). It is no accident that these very concepts, "imitation" and "pity and fear," are at the heart of the *Poetics*. At the end of his renewed attack on the poets . . . Plato invites anybody who is equipped and minded to do so to step up to the bar and defend poetry. The *Poetics* is a brief for that defense.[6]

It is worth noting as well the wisdom of Stephen Halliwell's observations that "The place of tragedy in Athenian culture had evidently produced ideas about the genre and its standards long before Aristotle's arrival in the city," and that "the *Poetics*, which mentions a number of works first performed during Aristotle's own lifetime, would hardly have taken the form that it does if its author had not felt that at least some of the ideals of tragic drama were continuing possibilities in the poetry of his own day."[7]

Halliwell's spotlight on the word "ideals" is meaningful. The "ideal," with its implications of the extraordinary and often the impossible, is understood in the early modern world as beyond the reach of human beings, "which indeede subsisteth, but it is resident above this world" (the *Oxford English Dictionary* cites this 1578 translation of L. Daneau's *Wonderful Woorkmanship of World*); similarly, in Walton's translation of Boethius' *Consolation of Philosophy*, it is said that "Intelligence . . . judgeth after all that is in man, / As he hath in the example ideal / Conceived what no other may nor can."[8] The ideal is thus understood to be not human, *supra*-human, and therefore outside the social.

In this sense, the protagonists of plays we have come to call "tragedies" are seen as at once human enough to be recognized—that is, they are neither divine nor demonic, but instead represent a kind of distillation of whatever their cultures recognize by the word "human"—and simultaneously special, *idealized* versions of the human. As Ophelia says of Hamlet, they are "Th'expectation and rose of the fair state, / The glass of fashion and the mould of form, / Th'observed of all observers" (3.1.151–3).[9] Peerless, they are often isolated, even when surrounded by others. The circumstances in which their choices are made are difficult, and those choices are not often applauded. And yet we think of them, rightly, as tragic *heroes*. To arrive at this label we need to follow not only the precepts but also, to some extent, the practices of Aristotle; we proceed, again as in *Hamlet*, with Polonius—himself an avid student of dramatic genres—"by indirections [to] find directions out" (2.1.63). We will remember his invariably ridiculed but also perennially imitated effort to identify discrete categories of dramatic action when he introduces "The best actors in the world, either for tragedy, comedy, history, pastoral, pastoral-comical, historical-pastoral, scene individable or poem unlimited. Seneca cannot be too heavy, nor Plautus too light for the law of writ and the liberty" (2.2.333–8). In the third Arden edition of the play, Ann Thompson and Neil Taylor follow the second quarto edition of *Hamlet* from 1604, cutting the redundant "tragical-historical, tragical-comical-historical-pastoral" given in the First Folio. We might consider the First Folio excess as testimony to an early modern appetite for definition, catalogue-like inclusiveness, distinction, and an acute sense of the generic hybridity characteristic in plays of this period.[10] Part of what "teases" us in the variegations of Renaissance hybrid tragedies is this paradoxical counter-wish for precision, clarity, a clear path telling us what to like, what to admire, what to fear, what to disdain as we read or watch them.

Such confusion is presented even in the *Poetics*, when Aristotle tells us that tragedy ought, "through a course of pity and fear [to] complet[e] the purification of tragic acts which have those emotional characteristics."[11] Arguably no one has tried harder than Aristotle to explain and catalogue carefully the components of this irritating genre, and yet confusion, or as Stephen Booth called it, "indefinition," endures: "The search for a definition of tragedy has been the most persistent and widespread of all nonreligious quests for definition. I am drawn toward testing the hypothesis that the urge to define tragedy and the urge to define—that is, the urge to have limits—may be more than obviously related . . ."[12] The *Poetics* meticulously guides understanding by naming the plays from which Aristotle derived his *exempla*, which helps to explain what is and isn't tragic. In case we wonder whether any of those assigned tragic qualities and traits would have been perceived by Renaissance readers as persuasive or even instructive, Robert Miola suggests a Renaissance moment when Aristotelian precepts began to be applied specifically back to Greek drama in the reception *Commentarii* (1534) of Joachim Camerarius, where, for perhaps the first time, we see retrospective interpretations of Greek plays according to contemporary understanding of the *Poetics*.[13] More inclusively, Blair Hoxby claims that by 1550, conditions [were] in place for the re-emergence of a full-blown poetics of tragedy. By then Giorgio Valla's translation of Aristotle's *Poetics* had been available for half a century. The works of Aeschylus, Sophocles, Euripides, and Seneca had been circulating in print for three decades or more. And Francesco Robortello's and Vincenzo Maggi's pathbreaking university lectures on the *Poetics* had appeared in print as learned textual commentaries.[14]

There seems now to be little question that the precepts and observations of the *Poetics* were widely available in print and in conversation to the early moderns, at least in Continental universities, as Bruce Smith masterfully traces out in his chapter in this volume. At the same time, we should notice how much of the tragic drama of the period, with minor exceptions such as the severe limitation of the so-called "unities" of time, space, and action, appears to be consistent with Aristotle's ideas of tragic action: dilemma, *hamartía*, heroic agency, responsibility, as I will discuss below. In order to understand Renaissance tragedy, we need to understand its debt, whether by direct access or second-hand influence via translation or exempla, to the *Poetics*.

For all of his diligent empiricism in explaining what tragedy is and does, Aristotle, through no fault of his own, seems to have left us hanging by various threads of cultural contingencies; we experience shifts in the definitions of the meanings of critical terms (e.g., "good" or "moral"), slippages as we move from Greek to English (or any) translation, from prose disputation to dramatic presentation, and transhistorical and intersectional webs of social, legal, political, psychological, and philosophical values and ethics. These relativities are embedded in cultural differences between and sometimes within communities of readers or audiences, signaling how difficult and how nonetheless important it is to know how we are supposed to respond to what we see performed. May we empathize with Macbeth and Timon or admire Coriolanus? *The Spanish Tragedy*'s Hieronimo is demonstrably mad, but what if Hamlet and Titus Andronicus are just faking it? How might this metatheatrical layer change the way we read them and their plays?

Audiences and readers of the period, roughly 1400 to 1650 in Europe and Britain, tackled similar questions, as we can see from even a quick glance at the entries for the word "tragedy" in the *Oxford English Dictionary*. The first meaning given refers not to dramatic or performed genres but to "a medieval narrative or narrative poem, written in an elevated style and dealing with sorrowful or disastrous events, typically the downfall or death of a powerful or important person."[15] Chaucer's *Boece* (*c.* 1380–6), his translation of Boethius' *Consolation of Philosophy* (Figure 0.2), his own *Troilus & Criseyde* (also 1380–6) and the earlier Monk's Tale Prologue from *Canterbury Tales* (1372–80) all offered relatively even-handed advertisements announcing that "Tragedie is to say a certain storie / . . . / Of him that stood in great prosperity, / And is fallen out of high degree / Into misery, and endeth wretchedly" (ll.1973–77).[16] Similarly, *c.* 1425, Lydgate's *Troyes Boke:* "Tragedie, who so list to know, / It beginneth in prosperity, / And endeth ever in adversity; / And it also doth the conquest treat / Of riche kings and of lords great."[17] We see no judgments here, no condemnation or sermonizing. As we might say today, Tragedy "happens"—and mainly to or around those who "beginneth in prosperitie." As the entries move forward in time, some interesting shifts occur: Lydgate's *Minor Poems* (*c.* 1460)— "At funeral feasts men sing tragedies /With woeful ditties of lamentation"[18]— are identified as performances of sorrow, sadness, or sympathy: not yet plays, but sung narratives, and still not yet especially judgmental of their principal characters. This apparent acceptance

INTRODUCTION 5

seems to shift into pointed criticism as we move into the sixteenth century, traceable in successive editions of Lydgate's translations of Boccaccio in the genre that would quickly take over the shape and form of Renaissance tragedy.[19]

More than anyone else of his time, the poet and translator John Lydgate was responsible for popularizing the pattern made famous by Giovanni Boccaccio (1313–75) in *De casibus virorum illustrium (Concerning the falls of famous men)*; some English and French translations add *et feminarum*, perhaps conflating it with another of Boccaccio's popular compilations in the 1360s, *De claris mulieribus* (Concerning famous women). The tales collected in the *De casibus*, compiled between 1355 and 1374, were drawn from classical, biblical, legendary, and mythological sources, all warning of the fall that follows a rise on Fortune's wheel (see Figure 1.3 in Rebecca Bushnell's chapter, this volume, where we also find a deep elaboration of various forms of *de casibus* tragedy in the Renaissance). The title page of Richard Pynson's 1494 edition in English offers an early version of the book's advertisement: "Here beginneth the boke called John Bochas describing the fall of princes princesses [and] other nobles translated into English by John Lydgate monk of the monastery of Saint Edmunds Bury." Pynson's title includes women ("princesses") in its

FIGURE 0.2: The Wheel of Fortune, a miniature from the *Consolation of Philosophy* by Boethius, fifteenth century.

narrative ambit, suggesting a kind of equality in suffering; to all of these, tragedy denotes falling, but not necessarily failing. Judgment is withheld.

In contrast, another English edition printed sixty years later (*c.* 1554) by John Wayland emphasizes the culpability of the fallen, and implies a shift in the assumed intentions of either the printer or the readership he hoped to attract:

> The tragedies, gathered by John Bochas, of all such princes as fell from their estates through the mutability of fortune since the creation of Adam, until his time wherein may be seen *what vices bring men to destruction, with notable warnings how the like may be avoided.* Translated into English by John Lydgate, monk of Burye.[20]

With this shift, tragic tales were advertised as monitory precepts, sermons, or warnings. By the mid-sixteenth century, at least on title pages designed by printers and publishers, tragedy had taken on purpose as a delivery system for judgment, as in Elyot's *Boke named Governour* (1531): "Than shall he in reading tragedies execrate and abhor the intolerable life of tyrants."[21]

An interesting pattern emerges from the diction of these definitions: judgments, assessments, exempla for praise and blame seem to flourish especially in Reformation England. Earlier definitions merely note, without judging or taking sides, that tragedies narrate the hazardous ride on Fortune's wheel, mainly a function of luck or inevitability. Reformation "definitions" seem to emphasize blame, error, culpability: *sin*, which may be an affect of Protestant "reading" more than it is a close translation from the Aristotelian Greek. The tantalizing concept of *error*—temptation and fall, tragic flaw—has been one of the most vexing issues troubling our understanding of tragedy, not *since* Aristotle but rather since we started *translating* Aristotle. In defining the elephant, we understand what fits our specific cultural or personal requirements. In considering Aristotle's idea of *hamartía*, our perceptions of the tragic hero hinge upon how we read that word. For Gerald Else, *hamartía* happens "not thanks to wickedness but because of some mistake of great weight and consequence, by a man such as we have described or else on the good rather than the bad side."[22] Halliwell translates *hamartía* as "a certain fallibility," a potential or capacity for slippage; the hero is "one who falls into affliction not because of evil and wickedness, but because of" this fallibility. Halliwell's Aristotle is noticeably humane, compassionate, even sympathetic to these protagonists "who have suffered or committed terrible deeds."[23] Kenneth Telford's 1960 translation follows a similar vein; his tragic hero is "the sort of man who ... changes to misfortune, not because of badness or wickedness, but because of some mistake, he being a man held in high opinion and of good fortune, e.g. Oedipus, or Thyestes, and notable men of such families."[24] But Telford's edition of this translation provides a crucial clarification in a footnote that commands our attention if we really want to understand this central concept: he defines *hamartía* as "literally, a missing of the mark," and reminds us that "as Aristotle himself indicates throughout chapter 14, [*hamartía*] is an action, not a suffering or a flaw of character."[25] Perhaps we have overlooked this active verb significance for practical reasons of fluid translation: it seems easier to speak of *hamartía* as something we *have* or *embody*, innately or congenitally, and are therefore stuck with, like a blot or stain, or a birthmark. If it is understood as something we *do*, the element of choice enters the equation, and the hero has agency and responsibility in that choosing. As a single word carried into English usage, *hamartía* "feels" easier to use as a noun rather than as a verb. But in that case we lose altogether the notion of option, of dilemma, and with it the perception of agency and responsibility. It would then be nearly impossible to explain why a tragic protagonist takes the action she or he takes except out of insanity, demonic possession, or utter incivility. We often refer to characters who act that way as villains, or perhaps victims, but not heroes.

Although we recognize the derivation of *hamartía* as an active verb form ("missing the mark," or sometimes "he missed the mark"), and thus as the core of Aristotle's definition of tragedy as "the imitation, not of men but of action or life," whose "plot, therefore, is the principle and, as it were, the soul of tragedy, while characters are second,"[26] a remarkable persistence remains among some readers to see these "heroes" as, at best, incompetents. This is often charged to Hamlet who, as one long-lived critical tradition has it, cannot make up his mind despite knowing what he must do, and saying so, as early as the conversation with his father's ghost in Act 1, scene 5; as another tradition has it, he also "thinks too much," as if committing a triple crime (homicide–regicide–kin-killing) ought to be undertaken without a great deal of thought and perhaps better evidence than the word of a ghost. Sometimes these "heroes" are branded greedy, power-mad ingrates like Brutus or Macbeth, arch-criminals to begin with. But as Kenneth Muir immortally reminded readers of his introduction to the first Arden *Macbeth*,

> [O]nly the morally complacent could witness a good performance of *Macbeth* without an uneasy feeling that if they had been so tempted they might conceivably have so fallen. We cannot divide the world into potential murderers and those who are not. It consists of imperfect human beings, more or less ignorant of their own selves, and not knowing (though they have been told often enough) the way to be happy. If they commit evil it is because they hope thereby to avoid another evil, which seems to them for the moment to be worse, or to obtain another good, which seems attractive if only because it is not in their possession.[27]

The critical tradition of finding fault with and in Renaissance tragic heroes stumbles when it confronts Romeo and Juliet, or Cleopatra, or John Webster's Duchess of Malfi, who *do* know the way to be happy but are prevented by relatives or circumstances that will not allow them to live. Here we come to one of the major challenges in understanding tragedy whether classical or early modern: we seem to have great difficulty seeing in these protagonists what Aristotle saw (again in Halliwell's translation): "first and foremost that the characters be good ... where speech or action exhibits the nature of an ethical choice ... [and] that the characters be appropriate" and "better than ourselves,"[28] or, as noted earlier in this Introduction, "ideal." Bernard Knox explained that the persistent critical idea that the protagonist (reminding us that the Greeks did not use the term "tragic hero") must be *worse* than us serves a thematic morality that would keep audiences and readers from attempting anything extraordinary in their own lives: "The modern concept of tragic drama takes for granted the existence of a single central character, whose action and suffering are the focal point of the play .... It was natural that Aristotle should make such an assumption, because his point of view on tragedy is primarily ethical, and the problem of moral choice is most clearly and economically presented in this way."[29] It is not surprising that readers and audiences since Sophocles should think that tragedy is the story of a single figure whether seen as misguided or "appropriate"; most of the Greek tragedies that have come down to us are named for a single eponymous individual, or occasionally for a small family of individuals.

English Renaissance drama generally followed suit, mainly from the examples in Thomas Newton's Seneca,[30] and trained its gaze narrowly upon the predicaments, actions, and reactions of those individuals. It is easy to think, then, that these tragedies are all about these single individuals, which conclusion would allow us to disengage ourselves from their circumstances and their choices; ignoring Muir's cautionary words about Macbeth, we are certain that *we* surely would make better choices. And since these characters are also shown at odds with their communities, critics have tended to see them as non-conformist, errant, and isolated figures who cannot get along with others, who act impulsively (Hamlet's deliberations notwithstanding) or selfishly, and whose consequent deaths are not only their own faults but are fitting punishments for their solitary lives. As Leslie Fiedler eloquently put it, "The image of man in art—precisely when it is most magnificently portrayed—is the image of failure. There is no way out."[31]

However we feel tempted to judge or "assess" them, the protagonists of the Renaissance plays we have come to call "tragedies" are profoundly human, and typically isolated, even when surrounded by others.[32] The circumstances in which their choices are made are difficult, and those choices are not often applauded. It's important to remember that these "character traits," if we can call them that, are *what tragedy performs.* They are not mistakes made while the protagonist fumbles around looking for a "better" way to be.[33] As Gordon Braden observes, "Such impulses on the Greek stage have to contend with more than personal scruples or individual opposition; a diffused communal reality, involved in the tragic passion but also existing outside it and capable of surviving it, can be felt as part of the dramatic medium itself."[34] It's important to take up Braden's reminder that the characters on these stages—Greek, Roman, or Renaissance—are drawn as they are to exemplify, not to assess, something significant about the human condition, and isolation in the performance of the Aristotelian "action having significance" is central to its impact.

Seneca's model for the Renaissance, via Newton's *Tenne Tragedies*, pointed the way to understanding tragedy as the action of individual characters that fall or fail and generally bring down their communities or nations with them. Only the *Troas* and the *Thebais* denote collective protagonists. The others are the usual and familiar suspects: Hercules (*Furens* and *Œtæus*), Thyestes, Hippolytus, Œdipus, Medea, Agamemnon, Octavia. Not by their singular titles, but arguably in their content, we can recognize in the cases of Shakespeare and his contemporaries that great effort is taken in each tragedy to locate the "blame" for at least the shared responsibility on the community, the family, or the nation.[35] It really does take a village—or some larger social entity—to make a tragedy, and it is for that village-as-audience, except in the rare instances of "closet drama," that these plays are performed. As the plays make clear, those larger entities incorporate our narrowly focused-upon protagonists and the cohort of survivors who outlive them in the plays. In Shakespeare's tragedies we hear in the final lines regret for the deaths of the protagonists (e.g., *Romeo and Juliet, Julius Caesar, Hamlet, Othello, King Lear, Coriolanus, Timon*), and the culpability of their survivors who share both the blame and the glory for these and similar magnificent figures, running a gamut from Cambyses to Coriolanus, from Hieronimo to Hamlet to the Duchess of Malfi, who (in accord with Fiedler's precept), precisely when they are most magnificent, go down—magnificently—in flames.

The essays in this volume are divided in scope between those centered on English drama and those looking beyond England to the Continent. England has long been considered the epicenter of Western tragedy in the Renaissance. For many people, this Western tradition is exemplified preeminently by Shakespeare (and within his example, by *Hamlet*) and a handful of others; for this reason most of the contributors to this volume (as well as this Introduction) have, by profession and predilection, written about what is most familiar to them. On the other hand, several of the essays in this volume open the conversation about the relationship between English and Continental tragedy. Smith's wide geographical and chronological coverage reminds us that tragedy has always been a multicultural enterprise; in contrast to our present moment when studying the drama of each nation is often contained within a narrowly specialized cultural and linguistic category (e.g., German theater, or Spanish *siglo de oro* drama, or French Enlightenment studies), audiences as well as scholars and students in the Renaissance were often able to move back and forth, via commerce, leisure travel, and letters from abroad, among a range of theatrical languages. We will see the same idea developed in a quite different way in Ivan Lupić's and András Kiséry's discussions of drama that was once considered, in anglophone scholarship of the period, confined to studies of English, French, Italian, Spanish, and German sources. To these Lupić adds Croatian material and traces its relation to the more conventionally known classical and English texts. Through his focus on versions of the legend of Sophonisba, Kiséry gives us a brief glimpse into Hungarian connections to Renaissance tragedy. The wide circulation of the genre enfolded and reciprocally informed countless iterations and deliveries. This happened offstage as well, when perceptions of tragedy, taken from such works as Hermann the German's thrice-removed "Latin translation of Averroës' gloss on the Greek text in 1256," were understood "as a species of logic rather than a performed poetic art."[36] Although scholarship on these forms requires a host of printed texts to illustrate the points it makes, it can be helpful to remember that performance—spoken, sung, recited—allowed for circulation and re-circulation in ways that books and manuscripts could not do. But as Kiséry traces out in his chapter on "Communities of Production and Consumption," universities across Europe, particularly at Wittenberg and Vienna, were responsible—through curricula, lectures, informal exchange, and vernacular as well as Latin texts—for producing and preserving tragedies that anglophone scholarship would likely never have known. As he shows using the example of versions of *Sophonisba*, performances and lectures, discussions, and tourism itself both created and reflected an international theater-going community sharing, as they do even now, "an emerging theatrical scene" of English, French, Italian, and Spanish theatergoers engaged with dramatic material in other than commercial theater spaces.

Cultural history, I would argue, is not quite the same thing as *literary* history, since theater existed off the page long before it was reified in print. And like any other history, it has its own history and maps that record it. The summaries I have been considering here constitute mainly an elite tradition, dependent for reception on an audience's or reader's Latin or Greek literacy, familiarity with figures out of classical mythology and legend, and similar exposures to a curricular, learned tradition.[37] Regarding English tragedy, by the early days of Queen Elizabeth's reign, another category of tragedy developed and flourished, influenced by Senecan rhetoric and dramatic style, but written in English by and for courtiers and university masters, deriving their material from other classical sources such as Herodotus, as in the case of Thomas Preston's (attributed) *Cambises, King of Persia* (entered in the Stationers' Register in 1569/70) or, to even greater success, Thomas Sackville and Thomas Norton's *Gorboduc* (acted 1561/2 at the Christmas festivities of the Inner Temple and again at Whitehall before Queen Elizabeth), which, while Senecan in rhetorical style and structure, nevertheless derived from a specifically English resource, Geoffrey of Monmouth's *Historia Regum Britanniæ*, and according to scholarly tradition, was meant specifically as a cautionary *exemplum* for the queen to impress upon her the dangers of civil war facing her nation should she fail to designate her successor in time. Though still the product of university-trained professionals (Sackville was Anne Boleyn's cousin-once-removed and a contributor to *The Mirror for Magistrates*, but ultimately left off literature to take up a career in politics and public service; Norton was a successful member of the Inner Temple and a three-time member of Parliament),[38] with *Gorboduc* we see, for perhaps the first time, an English play based on English source material and meant to tutor an English monarch regarding her moral and political obligation to her people. Its Senecan style notwithstanding, *Gorboduc*, an early entry in the development of politically relevant theater, marks a moment when English tragedy claims its audience for its own urgent agenda.

Between the close adherence to classical styles and structures and the emergence of Shakespeare, Marlowe, Jonson, Marston, Webster, Massinger, Beaumont, Fletcher, and Ford—the great age of Elizabethan and Jacobean tragedy—another traceable "map" appeared, perhaps something like a scavenger map, informed with less deliberation and more de facto practice. It appeared to be unfamiliar with classical origins, translations, adaptations, and other signs of direct inheritance; instead it takes us through a relatively unweeded garden of biblical and folkloric trajectories that, even without knowable exposures to Aristotelian pathways, nonetheless presents an unmistakable sense of the tragic that does not depend upon precepts, unities, and similar assessment rubrics. These are often referred to, in British studies at least, as the "Native Tradition," recognizing that even authors and audiences without Latin, Greek, or for that matter without much written English, participated actively and passionately in the creation of drama and other forms that offer up the purgation associated with the tragic genre. These forms, commonly known now as craft or mystery plays and the slightly later morality plays, are so intricately hybridized that even the more "tragic" among them—the Wakefield *Crucifixion* and *Mactatio Abel* (*The Killing of Abel*, sometimes called *The First Murder*)[39]— are laced with humor that softens their tragic narratives. These are the collections, generally agreed to have been performed in the early to mid-fifteenth century in medieval and early modern market towns, to which farmers and craftspeople would travel for as much as fifty miles to sell their wares, hire new help, stock in supplies that they could not produce or procure locally, and when the bartering was done, there was theater— public, free, and outdoors—to relieve the weariness of travel and trade. This is the kind of theater that Foucault might have imagined in identifying *le savoir des gens*: "subjugated knowledges [plural] ... located low down on the hierarchy," technically observant while perceptibly irreverent (though never quite blasphemous), residing in "the specialized areas of erudition as in the disqualified, popular knowledge."[40] Scholarship on these variously called "cycle," "mystery," or "craft-guild" plays recognizes (without necessarily naming it) a double helix: tragedy's release of the passions of pity and terror and its representations of men and women "good" but no better than we are, echoing the principles outlined in the *Poetics*, on the one hand, and biblical, folkloric, and other non-classical threads on the other. Derived from both Old and New Testaments, performed at various points in the ecclesiastical calendar coincident with market fairs in towns such as York, Chester, Lincoln, Norwich, Coventry, and (most famously) Wakefield, these plays truly belonged to the people, as we can hear most clearly in the opening lines of the *Mactatio Abel* acted by the Glovers' guild of Wakefield, when Cain's servant Pikeharness addresses the assembled audience with a mixture of vulgarity and camaraderie:

> All hail! All hail! Both blithe and glad!
> For here come I, a merry lad!
> Be-peace your din, my master bade,
>   Or else the devil you speed.
> Know you not I come before?
> But he who jangles any more,
> He must blow my black hole-bore,
> Both behind and before,
>   Till his teeth bleed.
> ...
> A good yeoman my master has
>   Full well ye all him ken.
> Begin he with you for to strive,
> Certainly, then must ye never thrive,
> But I swear, by god on life,
>   Some of you are his men.
>
> —1–20[41]

There has been much speculation about the staging of these plays—on pageant carts or in an open field or town square—and about their authorship (the Wakefield plays are credited to a "Master" whose name is lost), and we know even less about the authorship or origins of other cycle plays. But it seems somehow fitting that the household servant of the man who brought homicide and fratricide into the world should express himself so crudely. Whatever else these plays brought home to their audiences, they performed *de casibus* stories not so much of people in high places who fell from grace but something closer to Aristotle's advocacy, stories of men, and sometimes women, no better than we are.

Even when the subject was grim and even more terrifying than that of the *Mactatio Abel*, the Wakefield Master gave his fellow workers due respect, as in the *Crucifixion*, where the Carpenters, here called Torturers, commissioned to build the Cross and crucify Jesus, fully understand the enormity of the task: what if the cross falls or collapses? They debate the best measurements to use, the best way to set up the cross ("let it into the mortise fall / For then it will stand best"), and they endure the dilemma of their awful / awe-full assignment.[42] We are not *told* in these plays how to think about or react to them. The Aristotelian "action having magnitude" is performed, and England has, for the first time, its own native-grown dramatic tragedy.

This is not to say that the Senecan influence disappeared or even faded. The *Mactatio Abel*, resting squarely on biblical narrative, is also an early English experiment in one of the most enduring and popular dramatic forms English and Continental audiences developed throughout the Renaissance: it is, at its core, a Revenge tragedy, and its lines can be traced in such fully developed tragedies based in fratricides as *Hamlet* and *Richard II*.[43] Fredson Bowers' now-classic study of Revenge tragedy on the early modern stage has not yet been superseded, and remains a richly informative and comprehensive text, tracing both a native tradition via Anglo-Saxon remains and the Senecan influence. Bowers was very careful, however, to insist that these traditions, preserved in literary documents and dramatic performances, should not be mistaken for any kind of cultural imperative other than popular tastes. A son's revenge for a murdered father, or a father's for a murdered son (e.g., Kyd's *Spanish Tragedy* and Shakespeare's *Hamlet*), was nowhere codified in law, and certainly not as a "sacred" duty, as Bowers notes; "but that there was no law is of little moment. What is of interest for the attitude of an Elizabethan audience towards a stage-revenger is the fact that it was popularly believed by Elizabethans to exist separately in England or else as a general law governing Western civilization"; however encouraged by a flourishing taste in Italian *novelle*, it was "no part of any Elizabethan code except on the stage."[44] As a cultural phenomenon, then, the authority or drive of textual antecedents is often at least equaled if not overridden by popular tastes, an important reminder that theater, arguably more than any other art form, is a collective achievement shaped by—as much as it also shapes—the tastes, interests, and concerns of the populations for and by whom it is created. Those tastes sustained a lively theatrical trade in Revenge tragedies from Kyd's career through Shakespeare's and Marlowe's during the years of Elizabeth's reign.

While it does not appear ever to have gone out of fashion entirely, Revenge tragedy did ultimately show signs of strain under the (equally strained) insecurities of the Jacobean age: commenting, for example, on Christopher Marlowe's career, Irving Ribner traced an arc that began by "embracing a new challenge to the old orthodoxy" in the *Tamburlaine* plays at the start of this career to a finally "pessimistic statement" in *Dr. Faustus* "of human limitation and frustration," and with it, Marlowe anticipated "the spirit of negation and disillusion which [became] the mark of Jacobean tragedy."[45] Ribner reminds us that Shakespeare and Marlowe were part, but not the whole, of a cultural sweep traceable through the tragedies of the age, the pivot from an Elizabethan sense of human possibility to a Jacobean hopelessness: "Seventeenth-century literature reflects this lack of spiritual certainty in its concern with death, time, and mutability, and in the pervasive spirit of melancholy already fully drawn in Shakespeare's *Hamlet* . . . and surviving in the quiet sadness of Ford's *Broken Heart*."[46] The "spiritual certainties" Ribner has in mind are manifested in culture by negotiations of gender, family structures, and the triple designations of guidance recognized in myth, ritual, and religion, labels that change with the identities cultures assign themselves, as Goran Stanivukovic, Coppélia Kahn, and Paul Innes examine in their respective chapters on "Gender and Sexuality," "Society and Family," and "Religion, Ritual and Myth"—all sites of conflict or conformity in tragedies of every culture and every time period that seem concentrated with particular resonance in the drama of the Renaissance.

Lacking "spiritual certainty," the late Jacobean period as recorded in its tragedy seems to have found a way to release its energy, or its anxiety, in the *fin de siècle* decadence of boundary-pushing versions of Revenge tragedy. Sons and fathers avenging each other no longer seemed to capture the spirit of a missing and perhaps by this time seemingly unavailable "justice." One hallmark of English tragedy in this period is a preponderance of female heroes who manage their own destinies. This is the era of Beaumont and Fletcher's *Maid's Tragedy* (*c.* 1608–11), in which a submissive Melantius is forced to hand over his fiancée Evadne to an amoral (and nameless) king. Lacking any male defender, she devises a way to take care of business herself, tying the king to their bed in what he thinks will be a novel sex game. Having immobilized him, she stabs him to death. Meanwhile, the second female character, Aspatia, chronically depressed from the start of the play, also cannot wait for a male hero to rescue her, and arranges to trick Amintor (who had earlier abandoned her) into killing her by cross-dressing as her own "brother" and provoking him to a duel. Though we don't have the dates of its performances, it seems to have been immensely popular in print, going through seven editions between 1619 and 1661. John Webster's better-known masterpiece, *The Duchess of Malfi* (written *c.* 1611–12), also presents a powerful female agency that prevails over vicious attempts by her own brothers to control her and commandeer her inheritance, a motive which is complicated by one of the brothers, Ferdinand, confessing an auto-incestuous obsession for her. A third example of decadence is generally understood to be the capstone of these boundary-breaking experiments: John Ford's *'Tis Pity She's a Whore* (perf. 1629–33) gives audiences an unapologetically incestuous brother–sister coupling, the subsequent murder of the sister, Annabella, by her brother Giovanni when it is revealed that she is pregnant with his child, and his presentation of her heart skewered on his dagger at a feast intended to celebrate her enforced marriage to one of her suitors.

By the time of *'Tis Pity* we are a very long way from any codified system of justice known to Western Europe, and an even greater distance from Aristotle's hopeful precept of representing "a man like ourselves," let alone an "ideal" version of that man. Whatever it is that these Jacobean extremes represent of the culture that produced them seems to defy any neat mirroring function. Even when rooted in romantic domestic sagas that imagine "revenge" for worse social transgression than a relatively "simple" kin-killing, by the end of the era Revenge tragedy blends with domestic tragedies of marital betrayal to produce a new genre, one that resists definition but never loses its ability to speak to us. The closest cultural "explanation" I have seen for *'Tis Pity* was written in 1938 by Antonin Artaud, a pathologically disillusioned French theorist and performance artist who singled out Ford's play as the only Western example of what he called his *Theater of Cruelty*. For Artaud, theater was like a plague, a created "crisis which is resolved by death or cure . . . ." The "essential theater is like a plague," he argues, "not because it is contagious, but because like the plague it is the revelation, the bringing forth, the exteriorization of a depth of latent cruelty by means of which all the perverse possibilities of the mind, whether of an individual or a people, are localized." Ford's play, he argues, and particularly Annabella, performs its revelation by taking us beyond discursive language in all of its extreme gestures. Its "Cruelty" is not, he insisted, "the cruelty that we can exercise upon each other by hacking at each other's bodies, . . . but the much more terrible and necessary cruelty which things can exercise against us. We are not free. And the sky can still fall on our heads. And the theater has been created to teach us that first of all."[47] It should come as no surprise, then, that in our own time the ways in which these plays "speak" should bend to a different set of cultural pressures—times change, perhaps, but the adaptability of Renaissance tragedy to almost any cultural conversation keeps it lively and alive, as we can see in Richard Wilson's chapter connecting the predicament of the House of Stuart and the laboratory for critical thinking that is *Hamlet,* and the excruciating twentieth-century lessons they inspired in Walter Benjamin's difficulties with Carl Schmitt's service to the Third Reich. Sometimes Renaissance tragedy can transport us a couple of centuries away from grappling with our own dilemmas; sometimes it offers an eerily apt model for how best to grapple. The two hundred and fifty or so years of tragedies we have considered in this volume tell that story legibly and indelibly, in separate parts and pieces that have challenged us to understand, like the elephant-exegetes whose parable opened this introductory chapter, how early modern culture revealed itself both in and on stages.

CHAPTER ONE

Forms and Media

Remediating Tragedy in Print and Performance

REBECCA BUSHNELL

In many histories of early modern tragedy Christopher Marlowe's *Doctor Faustus* marks the beginning of "the era of greatness in Elizabethan tragedy."[1] Enlivened by its spectacular stage business, soaring rhetoric, and cast of devils, princes, and clowns, this play still flourishes in print and performance. But in what other ways would people in sixteenth-century Europe have known about this reputed German necromancer Faust, who sold his soul to the devil for power and knowledge? In 1587 a popular prose account of his adventures circulated in Germany as the *Historia von D. Johann Fausten, dem weitbeschreiten Zauberer und Schwartkünstler* (*The History of Dr. Johann Faust, the Famous Wizard and Black Magician*). While never ceasing to condemn its protagonist, the book vividly depicts enough of Faust's spectacular deeds and grisly death to satisfy a reader seeking sensation. In 1592 "P.F." translated this text into English, and it was printed with the more morally explicit title of *The History of the Damnable Life and Deserved Death of Doctor John Faustus* (hereafter referred to as the "Faust Book"). Before that translation was published, however, in 1589 Faustus' story was apparently already out on the English streets, in print and song, as a broadside ballad on "the Life and Deathe of Doctur Faustus the Great Cunngerer." While scholars cannot agree on when Marlowe first wrote and staged his play, the first recorded performance places it at the Rose Theatre in London on September 30, 1594.[2] The play was not printed until 1604, entering the world as *The Tragicall History of D. Faustus*, by "Ch. Marl": by then the story of Faust was the complex hybrid today of humanist rhetoric, satire, and clowning set in an archaic morality framework that we know today.[3]

The playbook, stage version, ballad, and English Faust Book all had long afterlives in the seventeenth century. The old-fashioned Faust Book remained popular and was reprinted eleven times up until 1700. The 1604 version of *Doctor Faustus* was printed again in 1609 and 1611. In 1616 the play was published with a notoriously very different text featuring much more comic material; this text was reprinted (with more additions) four times thereafter through 1663 (Figure 1.1). A cheap ballad of "The judgment of God shewed upon John Faustus, Doctor of Divinitye" circulated in the mid-seventeenth century, offering Faustus' first-person account of his life and moral self-condemnation (we do not know if it is the same as the 1589 ballad).[4] That broadside did borrow elements of the title woodcut of the 1616 edition of *The Tragicall History of the Life and Death of Doctor Faustus*, and its own conclusion echoes the final scene of the play as we know it (Figure 1.2).[5] By mid-century, the play itself seems to have been so altered with special

FIGURE 1.1: Title page woodcut for *The Tragicall History of the Life and Death of Doctor Faustus*, as printed in 1616; 1624 edition. Copyright the British Library Board.

effects and devils that for many viewers it seemed less a tragedy and more a comedy. In 1697, William Mountfort transformed the story into a farce, *The Life and Death of Dr. Faustus: with the humours of Harlequin and Scaramouche*.[6]

These multiple formats can tell us much about how the "damnable life and deserved death" of Faustus could be experienced differently as a kind of "tragedy" when presented as prose history, ballad, and stage play; it could be a narrative of sensational adventure and prodigies, a morality tale or exemplum, and a spectacle combining rhapsodic poetry, clowning, and special effects. In this multiplicity "Faust" thus constitutes an early example of what is now called "transmedia storytelling." Henry Jenkins defines a transmedia story as one that "unfolds across multiple media platforms, with each new text making a distinctive and valuable contribution to the whole."[7] Twenty-first-century media culture may more systematically or intentionally produce stories across different platforms, but such a process was also at work much earlier, when cheap pamphlets, street ballads, and

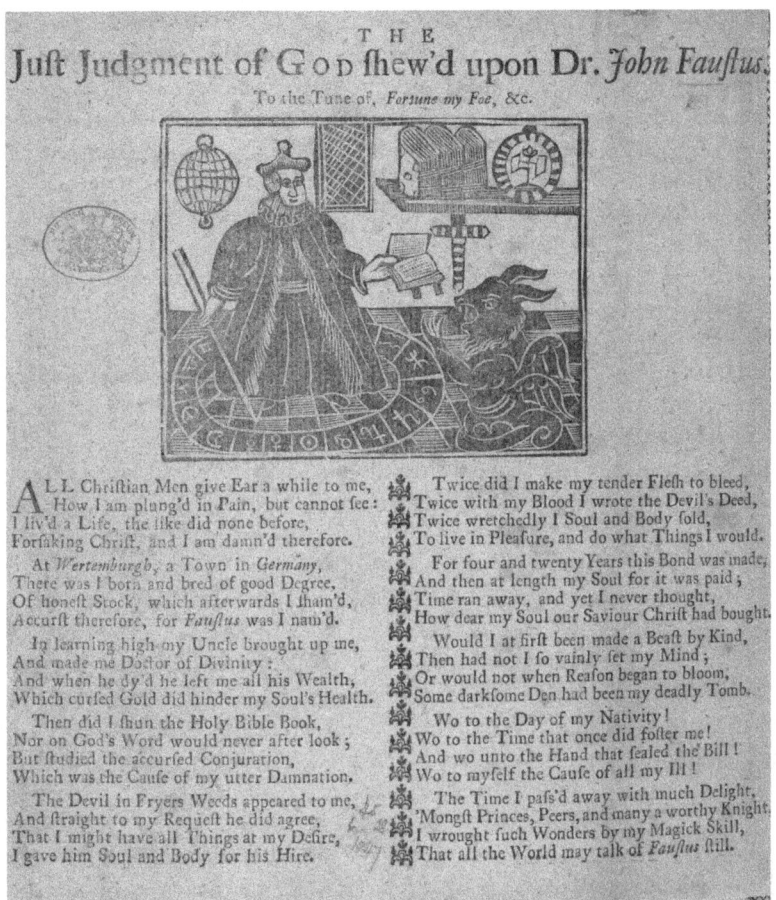

FIGURE 1.2: Ballad woodcut of Dr. Faustus, "Just judgment of God shew'd upon Dr. John Faustus," Roxburghe Ballads. C.20.f.9. p. 280 (1640?). Copyright the British Library Board.

playhouse performances were as much distinct media as film, television, newsprint, or videogames are today. As I have suggested with the example of Faust, at that time, too, recasting of a story always created something distinct, according to what Jenkins describes as "a set of associated 'protocols' or social and cultural practices that have grown up" around a given media format.[8] Pamphlet news, ballads, and stage plays each were associated with different "protocols" and social norms, while they were pitched to distinct if overlapping audiences.

As a form of transmedia storytelling, the proliferation of Faust versions also entails what Jay David Bolter and Richard Grusin have called "remediation." They argue that the transfer of content also entails the "representation of one medium into another"[9]; with remediation, a trace or reference to the earlier medium always remains in the new one. Indeed, for Bolter and Grusin, all media remediate, appropriating "the techniques, forms, and social significance of other media and attempts to rival or refashion them in the name of the real."[10] That is, no medium is pure or identical to itself: it always mimics and rivals other media in re-representing a story.

While recognizing that medieval concepts of tragedy persisted, most histories of tragedy focus on the reappearance and circulation of Greek and Roman classical tragic texts and literary theory that began in late fifteenth- and early sixteenth-century Italy.[11] Classical tragedies then came to the stage, and new tragedies were written and performed in the old style, cross-breeding with vernacular theatrical traditions to produce powerful new hybrids. However, as the whole sweep of this *Cultural History of Tragedy* from antiquity to modernity demonstrates, the concept of tragedy in early modernity cannot be limited to the theater alone. While the erudite humanist circles dedicated to the revival of classical learning and literature wanted to confine tragedy to Greek and Roman models, urban printers wanted a compelling label for any true or fictional story of woe, and tragedy often fit nicely.

Early modern tragedy could be a story arc, a subject matter, a style, and a mode of performance. In the thirteenth century Chaucer ventured a definition of tragedy inherited from late classical authors, glossing Boethius' *Consolation of Philosophy* to declare that "Tragedye is to seyn a dite of prosperite for a tyme, that endeth in wrechidness."[12] At the same time, tragedy suggested a broad category of human crimes and miseries: in his *Poetices* (1561) Julius Caesar Scaliger listed as "the matters of tragedy" such actions as "commands of kings, slaughters, despairs, suicides, exiles, bereavements, parricides, incests, conflagrations, battles, the putting out of eyes, weeping, wailing, bewailing, funerals, eulogies, and dirges."[13] The term "tragedy" could also evoke a grand poetic or theatrical style characterized by expression of pain, heightened emotion, and elevated rhetoric. Some scholars have extended this sense of tragedy beyond theater and poetry: Thomas Puttfarkan argues that both Aristotle's and Quintilian's ideas of tragedy influenced Titian's dramatic paintings, such as those of "Marsyas" or the "Four Great Sinners," with their pathos and "scenes of suffering, cruelty, fear, and horror at the height of their dramatic effect."[14] The invention of opera has been traced back to the Italian humanists who believed that Greek tragedy was entirely sung; early classical scholars of music like Girolamo Mei and Vincenzo Galilei asserted that "the confluence of word and music in ancient tragedy had an affective power lacking in their contemporary drama and music," and believed the new sung drama should do the same.[15]

Scaliger's list of "the matters of tragedy" in fact conflates actions (putting out of eyes, incest, suicides), emotional expressions (weeping, wailing), rites (funerals), and rhetorical genres (eulogies and dirges). This mingling signals that, while Scaliger was writing in the context of Aristotle's *Poetics*, his reconception of tragedy thus embraced multiple forms and genres. The Middle Ages volume of this *Cultural History of Tragedy* amply illustrates the multiplicity of tragic forms and media at that time, including narrative poetry, lamentations, and liturgical, morality, and miracle plays, and these practices and forms had a long afterlife. However, early modernity introduced two new distinct media that transformed the representation of tragedy across Europe: first, print, and then public stage productions in dedicated theatrical spaces. The chapters of this volume address stage performance in much greater detail, so this essay focuses on how the tragic was expressed in a wider range of older forms and new print media as well as theater, all of which borrowed from each other and in so doing expanded the genre in new directions.

The recovery of tragedy as a specific type of drama in the classical tradition began with manuscript transmission, but print dramatically expanded its reach. By the mid-thirteenth century, Seneca's plays had been preserved and were disseminated in manuscript form, and manuscripts of Greek tragedy began to circulate throughout Europe in the fourteenth century. However, the pace accelerated rapidly when Seneca's works were printed in Italy between 1480 and 1490. A Florentine press published four plays of Euripides in 1495, and shortly thereafter Aldus Manutius brought out texts of Sophocles (1502), Euripides (1503), and Aeschylus (1518). As Tanya Pollard notes, "by 1600, there were at least 220 editions of these authors printed in Europe, of which at least 28 were translations into vernacular European languages."[16] The appearance of Greek tragedy in print roughly coincided with the creation of the first classical tragedy written in the vernacular: Gian Giorgio Trissino's *Sofonisba*, modeled on Sophocles' *Antigone* and Euripides' *Alcestis* (it was completed in 1515 but not performed until 1562). The first vernacular imitation of a Senecan tragedy, Giambattista Giraldi Cinthio's *Orbecche*, was produced in Ferrara in 1541.[17]

Equally important were the translation and printing of Aristotle's *Poetics*, which profoundly influenced both the theorizing and composition of staged tragedy. Largely lost to the West throughout the Middle Ages, the *Poetics* was translated into Latin by William of Moerbeke in 1278; the first printed translation was Giorgio Valla's unreliable 1478 Latin version, followed by Alessandro De Pazzi's better one in 1536. But interest in the *Poetics* really took off with Bernardo Segni's Italian translation (1549) and the publication of influential commentaries on the text, including Francesco Robortello's *Explicationes* (1548) and Lodovico Castelvetro's *Poetica d'Aristotele vulgarizzata e sposita* (1570), as well as Julius Caesar Scaliger's interpretive work in his *Poetices* (1561).[18] These translations and apparatuses thus helped to spread the ideas of the *Poetics* across Europe.[19]

While print thus catalyzed the spread of classical models and theories of tragedy, it also fostered new forms of narratives of "woe" hardly classical in subject matter, form, or style. The early European publishing trade catered to a wide audience, when, in Tessa Watt's words, "more people were brought into the reading public," and a wide variety of "stories, images and values permeated the multiple tiers of print society."[20] As my opening example of Faust's story suggests, by the mid-sixteenth century the early publishing industry was omnivorous, absorbing and promoting "tragical histories" in multiple formats: chapbooks, broadsides, and ballads as well as relatively inexpensive playbooks. People of all ranks of society might consume these texts: Roger Chartier has shown how in early modern France "'Popular' literature, 'popular' religion, and 'popular' sociability were ... not radically different from what was read, practiced, or experienced by men and women of other social strata." This was true in many different countries: the literate could experience a continuous rather than strictly differentiated set of "objects, codes of behavior, or cultural motifs" in print.[21]

This chapter is concerned with the remediation of tragic forms in print and on the public stage, where the different media adapted each other while transforming and reframing the subject matter according to their own conventions. The first section explores the transmission of *de casibus* narratives, or stories of the fall of the great, focusing on the influential English collection of first-person complaint poetry, *A Mirror for Magistrates*. There we can see that at the same time that the theater was adapting such poetry, these first-person narratives strove to reproduce the visual effects of the stage. The second section turns to the "convergence" media culture of news pamphlets, ballads, and stage plays representing stories of the crimes and punishment of ordinary people. In both sections, I take my primary examples from the English publishing world, where the archive of examples is both rich and easily accessible through online collections. Some forms might have been specifically English at this time (for example, domestic tragedy), but one could tell a similar story where a comparable print culture generated such multiple media representing tales of woe.

TRAGIC COMPLAINTS

A familiar description of tragedy defines it as a fall from power or glory. Scholars of Renaissance tragedy often point to the few explicit definitions of tragedy that survive from the late Middle Ages, like Chaucer's cited above. In his *Troy Book* John Lydgate elaborated the model:

> But tragedie, who so list to knowe,
> It begynneth in prosperitie,
> And endeth ever in adversity;
> And it also doth the conquest trete
> Of riche kynges and of lordys grete
> Of mighty men and olde conquerouris
> Whiche by fraude of Fortunys schowris
> Ben overcast and whelmed from her glorie.[22]

The Middle Ages volume of this *Cultural History of Tragedy* tells a far more complicated story about the status of tragedy in that period. However, this idea that tragedy entails such falls of kings, great lords, and mighty men from "prosperity" to "wretchedness" does represent a strong through-line from antiquity to early modernity.

The most influential collection of "tragic falls" was Giovanni Boccaccio's *De casibus virorum et feminarum illustrium* (or *The Falls of Famous Men and Women*), written from 1360 to 1364 and revised *c.*1374. Boccaccio's work included hundreds of biographies of biblical, historical, and mythological figures, ranging from Adam up to fourteenth-century princes, all meant to serve as warnings to the "great": Boccaccio asserted that "when our princes see these rulers, old and spent, prostrated by the judgment of God, they will recognize God's power, the shiftiness of Fortune, and their own insecurity."[23] While Boccaccio may have seen himself as composing histories rather than tragedies,[24] the *De casibus* offered abundant examples of the kind of disasters that Chaucer and others had identified as tragic. During the fifteenth and the sixteenth centuries many European writers translated and expanded the *De casibus*, adapting it to their own countries and times. In 1400 Laurent de Premierfait translated it into French as *Du cas des nobles hommes et femmes*, and extended the lives it covered up until his century. In turn, John Lydgate translated Premierfait's text into English as *The Fall of Princes* (1430–40). Whether demonstrating retribution for sin or merely the workings of Fortune (as demonstrated in this image of the Wheel of Fortune included in a manuscript of Lydgate (Figure 1.3), by the mid-fifteenth century such stories were clearly understood as tragedies: Willard Farnham observes that Lydgate "never forgets that he is writing tragedy in the *Fall of Princes*, and besprinkles his pages with that appellation for his work, especially in his envoys."[25]

The best-known early modern English example of *de casibus* literature is *A Mirror for Magistrates*, designed by William Baldwin to take up "Where as Bochas [Boccaccio] lefte, unto this presente time, chiefly of such as Fortune had dalyed with here in this ylande."[26] Much has been written about *A Mirror*'s narratives of disaster as a precedent for the subject matter of Elizabethan tragedy. Farnham sees *A Mirror* developing the idea that tragedy entails "a 'salary of sin' paid here upon earth," "a chartable course whereby man's faults bring him down to ruin."[27] However, its tragedies do include examples of Fortune's fickleness as well as punishment for bad governance and vice. Following Lydgate's example, *A Mirror*'s dedication does insist that the stories that follow exemplify

FORMS AND MEDIA 21

FIGURE 1.3: Detail of a miniature of the wheel of fortune with a crowned king at the top, from John Lydgate's *Troy Book* and *The Siege of Thebes*, with verses by William Cornish, John Skelton, William Peeris and others, England, *c.* 1457 (with later additions). Royal 18 D. ii, f. 30v. Copyright the British Library Board.

God's judgment.[28] However, sometimes the cause of the fall is unclear. For example, Thomas, Earl of Salisbury's death was apparently merely an accident demonstrating "the uncertainty of glory."[29] Baldwin relates how "this strange adventure of the good erle" drove all the assembled storytellers "into a dumpne, inwardly lamenting his woefull destynye": it leads one of them to remark that "This Earle is neyther the first nor the last whom Fortune hath foundered in the heyth of their prosperitye."[30]

A Mirror begins by positing that seven men had gathered to follow Boccaccio and Lydgate by telling the sad stories of "our owne countrey."[31] As Baldwin describes the set-up in his preface:

> To make therefore a state mete for the matter, they al agreed that I shoulde usurp Bochas [Boccaccio's] rowme, and the wretched princes complayne unto me: and tooke upon themselves every man for his parte to be sundrye personages, and in their behalfes to bewayle unto me theyr grevous chaunces, hevy destines, and wofull misfortunes."[32]

The seven men are said to impersonate the dead wretched characters. These "wailings" are linked together by their commenting on the stories and proposing new ones; they thus speak in their own voices as well, albeit channeled through Baldwin's narration.

While invoking Boccaccio and Lydgate, *A Mirror for Magistrates* thus also belongs to the capacious genre of the tragic complaint, a first-person narrative of death and disaster. Stretching back to the laments of classical and biblical texts, and the medieval "*planctus* [wailing], the dirge for the Virgin Mary, the *deploratio* [complaint] and the *lamentatio* [lamentation]," such poetry relating the experience of death and disaster also flourished in Renaissance secular literature and on the stage.[33] Indeed, *A Mirror* significantly differs from Boccaccio's and Lydgate's biographies (while there are some exceptions), insofar as in *A Mirror for Magistrates* all the fallen men and women speak in the first person.[34] Through these voices, these complaints are always inherently dramatic, and in *A Mirror* that effect is amplified.

When the reader is asked to imagine the speakers as ghosts or speaking bodies, these first-person "complaints" of the fallen often hover at the boundary between narrative and performance.[35] As Paul Budra notes, Baldwin and a few other contributors were themselves writing plays at the time and thus were probably "thinking at least in part dramatically."[36] For example, after discussing how to present Richard II's downfall, one of the company asks Baldwin that he should visualize Richard "to be mangled with blew woundes, lying pale and wanne al naked upon the cold stones in Paules church, the people standing round him, and making his mone in this sorte." In the complaint itself, Richard similarly presents himself as a grisly spectacle:

> Behold my hap, see how the sely route
> Do gase upon me, and each to the other saye:
> See where he lieth for whome none late might route. . .
> Behold his woundes, how blew they be about,
> Whych whyle he lived, though never to decay.[37]

At the complaint's conclusion Baldwin relates: "Whan he had ended this so wofull a tragedy, and to all Princes a right wurthy instruction, we paused: having passed through a miserable time full of piteous tragedyes."[38] It is significant that Baldwin thus calls attention to what has just passed as tragedy, when a scene has been evoked both aurally and visually.[39]

These speaking ghosts were thus not only "voiced" by the company, but could also be given a virtual body, as if on stage. At one point, Baldwin describes a storytelling lull, when the group searched the chronicles for tragedies that occurred during Henry VI's reign. He writes that he then became sleepy and an image possessed him:

> But my imagination styll prosecuting this tragicall matter, brought suche a fantasy, me thought there stode before us, a tall mans body full of freshe woundes, but lacking a head, holdyng by the hande a goodlye childe, whose brest was so wounded that his hearte might be seen, his lovely face and eyes disfigured with dropping teares, his heare through horror standing upright, his mercy craving hands all to bemangled, and all his body embrued with his own blood, And whan through the gastfulness of this piteous spectacle, I waxed afeard, and turned awaye my face, me thought there came a shrekyng voice out of the weasande pipe of the headles bodye, saying as foloweth.[40]

This dreadful image leads to the story of Richard Plantagenet, Duke of York and his son, the Earl of Rutland, both killed at the Battle of Wakefield in 1460 (deaths Shakespeare later staged in *Henry VI, Part 3*). Mike Pincombe has commented on how the pathos of these bodies seems designed to evoke both pity and fear: "It is almost as if Baldwin were demonstrating that he could 'do tragedy' if he were granted the right occasion."[41] While classical tragedy might have eschewed such displays, this spectacle of bloody, speaking bodies does echo the gruesome special effects of plays like Thomas Preston's contemporaneous *Lamentable tragedy mixed ful of pleasant mirth, conteyning the life of Cambises King of Persia* (1569). Among other delights, this play features a scene of a man flayed alive and the king's twenty-line death speech delivered after he enters "without a gown, a sword thrust up his side, bleeding."[42]

A Mirror can thus be said to constitute a hybrid form of tragedy: poetic, narrative, and dramatic. As complaint poetry, *A Mirror* and its many analogs surely influenced the development of tragic theater. Wolfgang Clemen has thoroughly explored how European early modern drama adapted the topoi of such dramatic laments, deeply indebted to the vernacular and classical poetic and theatrical traditions.[43] Most recently, Emily Shortslef has argued that the complaint's influence on English theater was "more than merely formal and stylistic," where "tragedy recuperates 'complaining' as a valuable mode of social expression and action."[44] However, as I have suggested, *A Mirror* was already dramatic in nature, insofar as it both developed the voice of the complaint and borrowed from the theater, converging with the stage in the contemporary performance of catastrophe.[45]

TRANSMEDIA TRAGEDY

Although *A Mirror for Magistrates* abounds with princely examples, its world is still more inclusive than its predecessors', stretching to include even a commoner, Jack Cade.[46] While long-standing belief may have stipulated that tragedy concerns only the "great" or those of "high estate," a burgeoning print culture was already feeding an appetite for tales of woe and disaster of all kinds, and not just in the lives of princes. In later sixteenth-century England, complaint poetry itself increasingly concerned persons neither "great" nor historical: for example, in his *A General Rehearsall of Warres (or Churchyard's Choice)* (1579) Thomas Churchyard appends several more common "tragedies" at the end, including "A Pitifull complaint in the maner of a Tragedie, of Seignior Anthonio dell Dondaldoes wife, sometyme in the duke of Florence's Court"; "A heavie matter of an Englishe gentleman and a gentlewoman, in the maner of a Tragedie"; and "A Pirates Tragedies, being a gentleman of verie good house," which shows "the miserable life of a Rover, whose wretched desire of other mens goodes bringes open shame and a violente death."[47]

The extension of tragic complaints to gentlemen and gentlewomen was part of a broader publishing trend promoting tales of woe and violence. In England William Painter's *A Palace of Pleasure* (1566–7) combined both tragic and comic classical and historical tales with stories of non-noble families, which were mined as sources for the stage. Even Ralph Holinshed's *Chronicles* stretched to cover the downfall or death of people other than princes and nobles. Popular in the new market of cheap print were pamphlets, ballads, and broadsides describing notable murders and crimes involving ordinary people. Their context was generally moral instruction, but they surely played to an appetite for sensation: in Peter Lake's words, "The pamphlet narratives themselves were a mixture of the edifying and the titillatory, the admonitory and voyeuristic."[48] In this world, Scaliger's notion of the "matters of tragedy" as "slaughters, despairs, suicides, exiles, bereavements, parricides, incests, conflagrations, battles, the putting out of eyes, weeping, wailing, bewailing, funerals, eulogies, and dirges" was thus not confined either to drama or to the lives of exceptional men and women. Committing a crime or experiencing disaster could make any person both representative and exceptional, and in this sense a tragic persona, even if only for a brief moment of celebrity.

While other countries also witnessed the proliferation of stories of crime and punishment in many forms, England was certainly ahead of its time in promoting serious stage plays focused on topical events.[49] While many have been lost, several tragedies connected to real-life stories of murder and adultery have survived to this day: *A Warning for Fair Women, containing the most tragicall and lamentable murther of Master George Sanders*; *A Yorkshire tragedie, Not so new, as lamentable and true*; and most well-known among them, *The lamentable and true tragedie of M. Arden of Feversham*.[50] These plays are deliberately labeled tragedies, moving the genre directly (in Peter Holbrook's words) "from bloody stories set in far-off or long ago courts and camps (Marlowe's 'stately tent of war') to bloody or serious stories set in the homes of well-to-do, nonaristocratic, modern English."[51]

A Warning for Fair Women's explicitly associates George Sanders' murder with contemporary notions of stage tragedy. The play opens with a contest among the figures of Tragedy, History, and Comedy, where Tragedy is represented as a dominatrix with a whip and a knife. Tragedy claims she

> Must have passions that must move the soule;
> Make the heart heave, and throb within the bosome,
> Extorting tears out of the strictest eyes—
> To racke a thought, and strain it to his forme,
> Until I rap the sences from their course.

In turn, Comedy mocks Tragedy by linking her with Senecan tragic conventions, anticipating a tyrant who "stabs, hangs, impoysons, smothers, cutteth throats," a howling Chorus, and "a filthie whining ghost, /Lapped in some foul sheet, or a leather pelch," who "comes screaming like a pig halfe sticked, /And cries, *Vindicta*, revenge, revenge."

However, after Tragedy drives History and Comedy from the stage, she introduces *this* play as something different:

> My sceane is London, native and your owne.
> I sigh to thinke, my subject too well knowne.
> I am not faind.[52]

Tragedy thus pointedly embraces the "native," the familiar, and the "true" as her subject, in implicit contrast with plays of ghosts and revenge. The induction thus at once sets up the play in terms of conventional expectations of Senecan tragedy yet claims it represents what is actually local and factual. In what follows, the play draws on both modes. It alternates between realistic dialogue echoing its "journalistic" sources and elaborate, bloody dumb shows in which characters interact with allegorical (e.g., Chastity and Lust) and mythological figures (e.g., the Furies) like those that Thomas Norton and Thomas Sackville interpolated in their neo-Senecan tragedy of *Gorboduc* (1561).

A Warning for Fair Women draws on almost two decades worth of prose accounts of this notorious affair. While the play is usually dated to *c.* 1590 (it was printed in 1599),[53] the story is older. In 1573 Captain George Browne killed George Sanders, after he fell passionately in love with Sanders' wife. Browne enlisted the help of a procuress, Mistress Drury, to help him seduce the wife, Anne, and then also relentlessly pursued the murder of her husband. Although Anne's complicity in the plot was unclear, all involved were executed (and Anne eventually confessed). The story's publication history began with the 1573 printing of Arthur Golding's pamphlet, *A Brief discourse of the late murther of master George Saunders of London*.[54] Golding introduces that case as one that has been discussed throughout "the realm," and he insists that it deserves some explication for the reader's moral "amendment"; indeed, most of *A Brief discourse* is given over to Christian advice.[55] Both John Stow and Raphael Holinshed then related the facts of the murder in their respective chronicles, omitting the moralizing and giving the events more the status of historical truth. In 1580, Anthony Munday included the story in his *A view of sundry examples, Reporting many straunge murthers, sundry persons perjured, signes and tokens of Gods anger towards us. What straunge and monstrous children have of late beene borne: and all memorable murthers since the murther of Maister Saunders by George Browne, to this present and bloody murther of Abell Bourne Hosyer, who dwelled in Newgate Market.*" Browne's killing of Sanders thus takes first place as an example of how "the world is bent to all kinds of wickedness" (Munday omits the details of the crime to focus on Browne's cruelty). In this context, the event is only the first of a longer list of crimes and prodigies exemplifying the cosmic disruption of the times, when crime and monstrous births signaled God's wrath at all humankind.

All these media types thus shaped the tragic story of Sanders' murder according their own protocols and aims. In Golding's pamphlet *Brief discourse*, the narrative rests neatly within the moral framework counseling the reader against sin of any kind. In contrast, in the chronicles, the murder and its aftermath are woven into the overall texture of history, demonstrating the extremes of human behavior, but without judgment. Munday's pamphlet presents the crime in a context of apocalyptic thinking about overall human depravity and divine retribution. One can detect all of these elements in *A Warning for Fair Women* itself, in its remediation of its prose analogs, where it blends historical realism and moralizing with bloody dumb shows and stage violence.

At the same time, however, some features of theatrical tragedy were already embedded in the pamphlet narratives and chronicles of crime themselves: the distinction between tragic play text and crime story was not always sharp.[56] For example, in the same year that his ground-breaking *Spanish Tragedy* was published (1592), Thomas Kyd produced his own "true-crime" pamphlet, which often reads much like a play. The book, entitled *The trueth of the most wicked and secret murthering of John Brewen, Goldsmith of London, committed by his owne wife through the provocation of one John Parker whom she loved*, is rich in unmediated dialogue, allowing for the reader to respond as if the scene were being played before them. After the wife Anne has poisoned her husband John Brewen (a process described in elaborate detail), she consorts with her lover John Parker, who incited the murder. Finding she is pregnant, she then begs him to marry her:

> The varlet hearing the great mone shee made unto him was nothing moved therewith, but churlishly answered, shee should not appoint him when to marrie, but if I were so minded (quoth he) I would be twice advised how I did wed with such a strumpet as thy selfe, and then reviled her most shamefully: whereunto shee answered shee had neuer been strumpet but for him, and wo worth [sic] thee (quoth she) that ever I knewe thee, it is thou and no man else that can triumph in my spoyle, and yet now thou refusest to

make amends for thy fault: my loue to thee thou hast sufficiently tried, although I never found any by thee. Out arrant queane (quoth he) thou wouldst marry me to the end thou mightest poyson me as thou didst thy husband, but for that cause I meane to keepe me as long out of thy fingers as I can, and accurst be I if I trust thee or hazard my life in thy hands: why thou arrant beast (quoth shee) what did I then, which thou didst not provoke me to doo, if my husband were poysoned, thou knowest (shameles as thou art) it had never been done but for thee, thou gavest me the poyson, and after thy direction I did minister it unto him, and woe is mee, it was for thy sake I did so cursed a deede.[57]

While we do not know Kyd's source for his account of these events, he surely invented a dramatic dialogue between the two now regretful and spiteful lovers, ready-made for conversion to the stage. Here his moralizing voice does not intervene in the scene.

While crime pamphlets and stage plays were wildly popular, broadside ballads were the most common means of assimilating the "tragic" in popular culture. Ballads circulated everywhere in early modern European cities and towns.[58] Typically, they were both sung on the streets and hawked by peddlers as crudely printed one-sheet handouts. Some 11,000 English broadside ballads dated to the late sixteenth and seventeenth centuries have survived today, but it was likely that millions were printed at the time.[59] They covered all kinds of current events and popular topics, spreading ideas, stories, and news to both literate and illiterate audiences.[60] While they could thus function like the pamphlets in circulating news, they were also tied to plays. Tiffany Stern has argued that ballads were sold near playhouses, complementing stage performances, and she has detected at least sixty play–ballad links, including ballads relaying the plots of *A Yorkshire Tragedy*, *Arden of Faversham*, *Doctor Faustus*, *King Lear*, *Titus Andronicus*, *Romeo and Juliet*, and *The Spanish Tragedy*.[61]

Not surprisingly, crime, unusual death, and punishment were popular topics for the broadside ballads. Searching the online English Broadside Ballad Archive (EBBA) with the term "death" yields 804 ballads. One can also sort the archive using the category of "tragedy," which Samuel Pepys has applied to his own seventeenth-century ballad collection. Pepys labeled 84 ballads as "tragedy"; applying the same search term to the whole EBBA archive today generates 505 hits. That a ballad could be understood as a form of tragedy is evident from many of their titles: for example, "A Lamentable Ballad of the Tragical End of a Gallant Lord and a Vertuous Lady;" "A Tragical Song: Or, Mr. Wil. Montfort, The Famous Actor Unfortunately Killd";[62] and "The Lady Isabella's Tragedy; Or, The Step-Mothers Cruelty."

Because they often used first-person as well as third-person narration, ballads also added to the genre of complaint poetry. John Kerrigan sees ballads and especially songs "featuring heart-sick and abandoned women" linking medieval and early modern practices of literary complaint.[63] Such ballad lamentations were never limited to the "great" and often featured real-life stories: for example, they included "The Murtherers Lamentation: being An Account of John Jewster and William Butler, who were arraign'd and found guilty of the Robbery and Murther of Mrs. Jane Legrand"; or "The Lamentation of Master Pages wife of Plimmouth, who being enforced by her Parents to wed him against her will, did most wickedly consent to his murther, for the love of George Strangwidge; for which fact she suffered death at Barstable in Devonshire. Written with her owne hand a little before her death." The common tune for all such ballads was "Fortune my foe," known as "the hanging tune";[64] that mournful melody suited the story of Mistress Page as much as it did that of Faust.

Just as this essay began with the remediation of Faust's story, it will end with a more capacious example of a "true-crime" transmedia tragedy: the case of Alice Arden's and her lover Mosby's plot to murder her husband Arden of Faversham, produced as a short history in Holinshed's and Stow's *Chronicles*, a ballad sung and peddled in the streets, and a stage tragedy.[65] As Richard Helgerson has noted, the story had a remarkable media afterlife as well, transformed into a puppet show in late eighteenth-century Faversham and a ballet in Sadler's Wells.[66]

By the time that it came to the stage around 1590, Arden's murder in 1551 had already gained a reputation as an exceptional event, worthy of inclusion in histories of the realm. It first appeared in print in Holinshed's *Chronicles of England, Scotland, and Ireland*, in both the 1577 and 1587 editions (it was most likely based on a manuscript version by the antiquarian John Stow).[67] Holinshed introduces the story self-consciously, acknowledging that it differs from the rest of his chronicles. Amid his relating more significant events of the time, he notes:

> About this time there was at Feversham in Kent a gentleman named Arden, most cruellie murthered and slaine by the procurement of his owne wife. The which murther, for the horriblenesse thereof, although otherwise it may seeme to be but a private matter, and therefore as it were impertinent to this historie, I have thought good to set it foorth somewhat at large, having the instructions delivered to me by them, that have used some diligence to gather the true understanding of the circumstances.[68]

We do not know who told him to include the story, which is recounted in a kind of detail unusual for a murder that was not a political assassination.[69] Like Kyd's pamphlet account of the murder of John Brewen, Holinshed's account seems to anticipate a stage version, including patches of dialogue among all the conspirators. While the text itself is relatively neutral in tone, in the 1587 version the history is accompanied by moralizing marginal glosses, commenting on the action unfolding in the text and condemning Alice as an "importunate and bloody-minded strumpet."[70]

As Lena Orlin has established by investigating the historical Arden's life and death, all the print versions of the story refashioned a matter of local politics and property disputes into a tragedy focusing on Alice Arden's role in instigating the murder, in which she became the epitome of female wickedness.[71] Orlin notes that by 1609, Alice had achieved a kind of "mythical stature," when John Rainolds compared her with Clytemnestra and Livia.[72] The stage version appeared in print in 1592 as *The lamentable and true tragedie of M. Arden of Feversham in Kent who was most wickedlye murdered, by the meanes of his disloyall and wanton wyfe, who for the loue she bare to one Mosbie, hyred two desperat ruffins Blackwill and Shakbag, to kill him. Wherin is shewed the great malice and discimulation of a wicked woman, the unsatiable desire of filthie lust and the shamefull end of all murderers*. While the play itself is more morally complex than this description suggests, the text with this devastating title was printed twice in the 1590s, and it was popular enough to be reprinted in 1633. The printer then decorated the title page with a woodcut illustration representing the stabbing (Figure 1.4).

FIGURE 1.4: Title page illustration of *The lamentable and true tragedy of Master Arden of Feversham in Kent* (1633). RB127248. Huntington Library, San Marino, California.

This stage version of Arden's murder took much from Holinshed, both in plot and approach, but then transformed it according to contemporary stage conventions. The playwright did borrow major plot points and scenes from Holinshed, adapting that text's dialogue exchanges and even picking up individual phrases. Catering to the contemporary taste for complex rather than simple theatrical plots, the playwright then layered onto the Mosby–Alice–Arden story a similar love triangle of the painter Clarke and Arden's servants, Michael and Susan. This move extended the scope of "domestic tragedy" to even lower ranks than that of the gentlefolk, while also allowing for the baser characters' behavior to serve as a foil for the main characters.[73] Further, to make up for the absence of links and viewpoint provided in the prose narrative, the playwright created the character of Franklin, Arden's friend and interlocutor. When involved in the plot in this capacity, Franklin has a vested interest in Arden's perspective on the events.[74] However, at the play's end, Franklin does shift into a different role, when he offers the epilogue, pointing to the play's status as "a naked Tragedy,"

> Wherin no filed points are foisted in,
> To make it gracious to the ear or eye.
> For simple truth is gracious enough:
> And needs no other points of glozing stuff.

As a concluding "chorus," Franklin uncharacteristically points to Arden's own culpability in having taken a plot of ground from Dick Reede "by force and violence."[75] Employing the double plot and choric devices, the play's "remediation" of the prose chronicle thus creates multiple refracting perspectives on the events, complicating its moral valence.

About the same time that the play was reprinted in 1633, a black-letter broadside ballad of the story appeared, entitled "the complaint and lamentation of Mistresse Arden of [Fev]ersham in Kent, who for the love of one Mosbie, hired certaine Ruffians [a]nd Villaines most cruelly to murder her Husband; with the fatall end of her and her Associates. To the tune of, Fortune my Foe." It was illustrated with the same woodcut found on the title page of the 1633 playbook (Figure 1.5).[76]

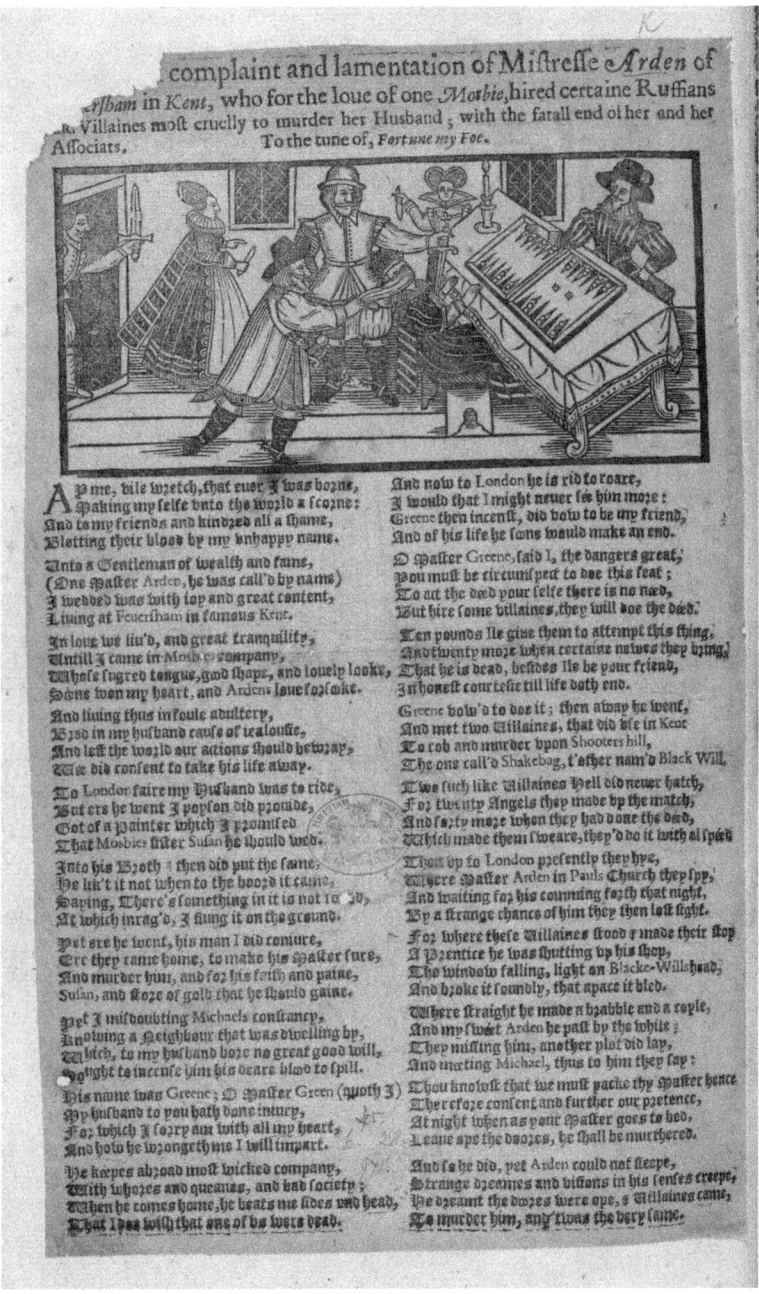

FIGURE 1.5: The ballad of "The complaint and lamentation of Mistresse Arden of/Feversham in Kent, who for the loue of one Mosbie, hired certaine Ruffians/and Villaines most cruelly to murder her Husband," Roxburghe Ballads. C.20.f.9 156–7. Copyright the British Library Board.

Here Alice tells the story, condemning her own deeds in the style of complaint poetry that both relates and comments on the speaker's experience. However, as the addition of the playbook woodcut would suggest, the ballad also incorporates the features of the stage tragedy, interpolating sections of dramatic dialogue in her first-person lament. Further, as the play does, the ballad concludes with an epilogue, shifting to another voice:

> Thus have you heard of Ardens tragedy
> It rests to shew you how the rest did die:
> His wife at Canterbury she was burnt,
> And all her flesh and bones to ashes turned.[77]

In constructing the story for a wide audience, the text thus mixes the representational conventions of first-person lamentation, dramatic dialogue, and choric conclusion. In turn, the woodcut visually evokes the scene of the murder, as it might have been enacted on stage. The conventions of the complaint that focus the reader's/auditor's attention on Alice's experience and the punishment of sin thus operate in tension with the theatrical effects adapted from the play.

As this remediation of Arden's story demonstrates, print culture in England and across Europe both catalyzed a transformation of tragedy as a form of drama and expanded expectation of what could be considered tragic. Print was certainly a key factor in promoting the circulation of classical tragedy and literary theory starting in the fifteenth century, strongly influencing the creation of neoclassical tragedies in circles dedicated to humanist learning and values. However, as the case studies examined here have shown, at the same time, print culture was shifting the conventional tragic narrative of a fall from "prosperity to adversity," or crime and punishment, from the worlds of the aristocracy and learned men and women to the streets and households of the gentry and even common folk. As the following chapters of this volume will demonstrate, moving tragic performance to dedicated public theater spaces required adapting old and new theatrical conventions to serve a wider public. But the integration of ideas of tragedy into different print forms—the pamphlet, chronicle history, playbook complaint poem, and ballad—not only meant that tragedy reached greater audiences, but also that a broader span of real-life, human experience could be conceptualized as tragic. In turn, these different media forms fed off each other, recasting the tragic in terms of their own specific context and conventions, whether moral, historical, spectacular, or merely sensational.

CHAPTER TWO

Sites of Performance and Circulation

Mobile Memes in Renaissance Tragedy[1]

BRUCE R. SMITH

The first performance of an ancient tragedy in Renaissance Europe can be sited with some precision: on a five-foot-high platform in or near the Campo de' Fiori in Rome, in 1486 or perhaps a year before. The play was Seneca's *Phaedra* (better known at the time by the name of its male protagonist, Hippolytus). The actors were colleagues and students of Giulio Pomponio Leto (a.k.a. Julius Pomponius Laetus, 1428–97), whose accomplishments as a Humanist included founding the Accademia Romanum in 1457, writing treatises on Roman antiquities, producing the first scholarly editions of Sallust and Varro, networking with scholars and educators from other parts of Europe, and successfully fighting off charges of sodomy and paganism lodged against him by Pope Paul II. Leto had founded the academy after succeeding Lorenzo Valla, his former teacher, as professor of eloquence in the Gymnasium Romanum.[2]

Our knowledge of the event comes largely from two sources. The first is a letter to Cardinal Raffaele Riario (1461–1521) that Leto's colleague Giovanni Sulpizio da Veroli (a.k.a. Johannes Sulpitius Verulanus, 1440–after 1508?) prefaced to the *editio princeps* of Vitruvius' *De architectura*, which he edited and published in 1486. Cardinal Riario, known to his contemporaries as an enthusiast for Roman antiquities, a supporter of the arts (he is credited with inviting Michelangelo to Rome), and an astute politician, was about to build a new Florentine-inspired palace near the Campo de' Fiori. In his prefatory letter to the cardinal Sulpizio encourages his dedicatee to reconstruct one of Rome's ruined theaters or, better still, to erect a new theater built according to Vitruvius' prescriptions.[3]

The second source is a letter written sixty years after the event, in which Desiderius Erasmus gives his old friend Joost Vroye, a legal scholar at the University of Louvain, a roll call of the Humanists he met during his sojourn in Italy between 1506 and 1509, a list that includes not only Cardinal Riario but Tommaso Inghirami, who as a young man had played Phaedra with such force that he became known thereafter as "Phaedrus," the name by which Erasmus hails him in the letter to Vroye. A Humanist pun was involved in this nickname, since *Phaedrus* is also the name of a dialogue by Plato.[4]

Two repeat performances of *Phaedra* were staged. The first was in a fortified patrician space, the very site of Pomponio's imprisonment by the anti-Humanist Pope Paul II: the

Castel Sant'Angelo. For this second performance a more sympathetic pope, Innocent VIII, was present as chief spectator. A prologue by Sulpizio for the second performance suggests that the audience needed guidance on what they were about to witness: "Something new will appear before you," the Prologue says, "a grave and pitiable happening that will cause every onlooker to leave the playing-place instructed and cautioned."[5] In the mid-1480s "tragedy" as a species of dramatic performance had yet to be acclimatized. For the third performance, in the courtyard of Cardinal Riario's palace, a mock-up of an ancient Roman amphitheater was erected, complete with ranked seating and a gigantic canopy to shade an audience that included "people" as well as persons of honor.

The challenge we face in this chapter on "Sites of Performance and Circulation" is how to account for the establishment, the *grounding*, of this "something new" and its subsequent spread throughout Europe. By 1650, a hundred and sixty years or so after the first performance of Seneca's *Phaedra* in Rome, plays called tragedies were being performed all over Europe, in languages other than Latin, in all sorts of venues, for all sorts of purposes. What happened between 1486 and 1650 has traditionally been told as a story of example and imitation, of sources and adaptations, of transplantation and the colonization of local dramatic forms. It shapes up as a story with a linear plot. It begins in Italy, passes in picaresque vagaries through various cultures and language groups, and ends triumphantly in the plays of Lope de Vega, William Shakespeare, Pierre Corneille, and Jean Racine.

Perhaps in our own cultural moment we can find new, non-linear, non-triumphalist ways of coming at the phenomena of sites and circulation. For a start, we can learn to think of "tragedy" not as a critical construction or a canon of self-contained plays but as a set of "memes," units of imitation that proliferate in human cultures as genes do in tissues. Examples of memes provided by the term's coiner, Richard Dawkins, include "tunes, ideas, catch-phrases, clothes fashions, ways of making pots or of building arches."[6] To which could be added "ways of making plots or of building playhouses." The term *meme* even has an ancient Greek etymology to recommend it: *mimeme* ("that which is imitated"), a by-product of a term with an impeccable academic pedigree, *mimesis*. Circulation becomes, in this model, not a series of authoritative acts but something on the order of sampling and remixing. "Theatergrams" is the term Louise George Clubb has proposed for the way bits and pieces of Italian drama, *commedia dell'arte* in particular, circulated in Renaissance Europe.[7]

Sites for the three performances of Seneca's *Phaedra* in Rome in the mid-1480s can serve as paradigms for the performances of tragedy that followed all over Europe. Each of the three Roman sites had its own *ethos*, in the original Greek sense of "custom, usage, disposition, character."[8] Each site had its own social identity, its own distinctive physical spaces, its own repertory of subjects for dramatic performance, its own staging traditions, its own reasons for wanting to enact this new thing "tragedy." The result, in each site, was a different set of tragic memes. Each ethos was not, however, a self-contained entity. As Leto and his collaborators demonstrate, boundaries between *ethoi* could be crossed, with sometimes startling results. To these three paradigmatic sites for tragedy we need to add a fourth: studies. The Accademia Romana had originally met in Leto's own house. The move into public space was personally and politically significant for Leto—and culturally prescient for tragedy as a phenomenon in sixteenth- and seventeenth-century European culture.

PARADIGM 1: STUDIES

The *studiolo* designed in 1473 for Federico III da Montefeltro in the ducal palace at Urbino (see Figure 2.1) can help us locate the first ethos for the performance of tragedy. Books figure alongside musical and scientific instruments in the illusionistic wood-inlay paneling of the *studiolo*, while Seneca (see Figure 2.2) looks down from the east wall among the writers and thinkers whose portraits line the room. In Joos van Wassenhove's painting, Seneca is shown in an act of reading, not writing, setting an example for the occupants of the room. The ensemble of decorations suggests that the *studiolo* was a place not just for displaying collected treasures and for meditating but for *doing* things.[9]

A *studiolo* in Renaissance Italian was a little *studio*, which John Florio in his *New World of Words* (1598) defines, in terms more capacious than we might expect, as "a study or place to study in, a cabinet, a closet, a university, a college. Also a desk, a standing desk in a school for great books to stand upon."[10] Today we are apt to think of studies as places of solitude and quiet, but the décor of Federico's *studiolo* in Urbino and in the study that Isabella d'Este designed for herself in the Castello San Giorgio in Mantua 1495 with paintings by Botticelli and Mantegna suggest otherwise.[11] By including in his definition of *studio* a standing desk for books, Florio confirms that one of the main activities in Renaissance studies was reading.

FIGURE 2.1: Studiolo of Federico III da Montefeltro (built 1473–6), Palazzo Ducale, Urbino. Alinari via Getty Images.

FIGURE 2.2: Portrait of Seneca the Younger by Joos van Wassenhove (*c.* 1475), for the studiolo, Palazzo Ducale, Urbino, Italy. Now in the Musée du Louvre, Paris. Wikimedia Commons.

For most people today reading is a solitary, passive, and silent activity, but testimony from the Renaissance suggests that reading could also be gregarious, active, and sounded. Jennifer Richards in *Voices and Books in the English Renaissance: A New History of Reading* has amassed evidence that early modern men and women were much more accustomed than we are to reading aloud: to each other as well as to themselves.[12] Recent psychological research cited by Charles Fernyhough in *The Voices Within* indicates that "voices on the page" remain a phenomenon for many readers, even if they are not making audible sounds as they read.[13] When other people are present, a reader *performs* the text at hand, especially if he or she gives different voices to different characters. Agostino Mosti in his memoire of life in Ferrara in the sixteenth century reports that reading of comedies and tragedies and of epic poems by Boiardo and Arisoto (two authors patronized by the d'Este dukes) were social events in courtly circles.[14] "Companionate reading" is the name we might give to events like these. With respect to drama, Renaissance reading practices prompt us to reconsider the conventional distinction between "closet drama" (a nineteenth-century coinage) and drama for performance.[15]

Beyond dedicated private spaces in palaces and houses, a second version of studies as a paradigm for performance of tragedy presents itself in Renaissance academies, schools, colleges, and universities. Florio includes "a university, a college" in his definition of *studio*. In the second half of the fifteenth century and throughout the sixteenth, academies were established all over Italy, some of them with specifically theatrical interests, like the Accademia degl' Intronati in Siena (founded 1525), whose members jointly authored a classical comedy, *Gl'ingannati*, which Shakespeare may have encountered directly for the plot of *Twelfth Night*, a play that had its first recorded performance in an academic setting, the still standing great hall of the Middle Temple in London, in 1602.[16]

The Camerata of Florence (fl. 1573–87), sponsored by Count Giovanni de' Bardi, wanted to restore *melos* to tragedy: the "language that has rhythm and melody" singled out by Aristotle in the *Poetics* (1449.b.30, 1450.b.10, 1450.b.16) as one of tragedy's six basic elements, indeed as "the greatest of the sensuous attractions" of tragedy (1450.b.17).[17] Such a goal was already on the minds of Leto and his collaborators a century earlier. Sulpizio specifies that Leto's students were taught both to act and to sing (*et agere et contare*) Seneca's *Phaedra*.[18] The result of the Camerata's experiments was what is now recognized as the earliest opera: a setting by Ottavio Rinuccini (words) and Jacopo Peri (music) of Ovid's story of Daphne in a syllable-by-syllable musical setting combining the rhythms of speech with melodic cadences in what came to be called *stilo recitativo*. Memes from Ovid proved just as important to Renaissance tragedy as the repertory of stories in Seneca, Sophocles, and Euripides.

Humanist pedagogy, in which reading aloud from Latin texts was central to the curriculum, insured that *reading* Seneca, in the schoolroom as in the private study, was *sounding* Seneca.[19] Erasmus in *De ratione studii* (1511), the blueprint for John Colet's refoundation of St. Paul's School in London in 1509, describes how tragedy should be taught, with special attention to "the representation of place, time, and sometimes action, and the occurrence of heated exchanges, which may be worked out in couplets, single lines, or half-lines."[20] Read aloud and enacted, those "heated exchanges" take on all the more power, even as the young scholars are trained in skills of declamation they will need when they enter public life. The first master of St. Paul's School, the man charged with putting Erasmus' ideas into action, was William Lily, who had studied with Leto in Rome. The Latin lesson in *The Taming of the Shrew* 3.1 offers a comic example of how reading aloud worked in Renaissance schools. It was a small step from reading plays aloud in class to reciting them, with costumes and props, before an audience.[21]

We have a vivid witness to putting on tragedies for pedagogical purposes in Michel de Montaigne's essay "Of the Institution and Education of Children" (1.26), which was likely written in Montaigne's private study, still preserved in a free-standing tower at the Chateau de Montaigne near Bergerac in the Dordogne. Quotations from Montaigne's favorite writers are painted on the beams of the ceiling. Trained to speak Latin from early childhood, Montaigne was sent by his father to the new collège de Guyenne in Bordeaux, presided over from 1534 by André de Gouveia (a.k.a. Andreas Goveanus, 1497–1548), a Portuguese Humanist who had been rector of the college of arts in the University of Paris. By the time Montaigne arrived at the collège de Guyenne about five years later, performances of Latin plays were established features of the curriculum. Montaigne's description, given here in John Florio's English translation of 1603, suggests that performances of Latin tragedies were major events in college life and probably also in the civic life of Bordeaux. "I have undergone and represented the chiefest parts in the Latin tragedies of Buchanan, Guerenti, and of Muret," Montaigne reports;

which in great state were acted and played in our college of Guyenne: wherein Andreas Goveanus our rector principal; who as in all other parts belonging to his charge, was without comparison the chiefest rector of France, and myself (without ostentation be it spoken) was reputed, if not a chief master, yet a principal actor in them.[22]

The Latin tragedies by George Buchanan in which Montaigne acted were probably the biblical play *Baptistes sive Calumnia* (1542) and/or Buchanan's Latin translation of Euripides' *Medea* (1543).[23]

Erasmus laid out his pedagogical paradigms and Buchanan wrote scripts for school productions of classical tragedies before the tumult of the Reformation. Erasmus stayed true to the Catholic faith, but his educational scheme was taken up by Protestant educators. Johannes Strum's Latin gymnasium in Strassburg (founded 1537) was, in the sixteenth century, a famed example. The curriculum included Aristotelian and Horatian poetics and works of Plautus, Terence, Sophocles, and Euripides, plus performances of neo-Latin drama, often on biblical themes.

Reformation principles in action can be observed in Théodore de Bèze's *Abraham sacrifiant*, which was acted in the place de la Palud in Lausanne in 1550. Bèze (a.k.a. Theodore Beza, 1519–1605) had been appointed professor of Greek at the University of Lausanne the year before the performance.[24] Abraham's willingness to sacrifice his son Isaac as told in Genesis chapter 22—a favorite subject in medieval biblical plays—allowed Bèze to combine memes from a variety of sources: Seneca (orations, stichomythia, a chorus of shepherds), religious drama (a presenter opens and closes the play, the characters make their entrances out of a "house" appropriate to Abraham, Satan appears disguised as a monk), comedy (the shepherds are a jovial crew), and worship services (Abraham and Sara make their first appearance singing a hymn and so do the shepherds who accompany Isaac to the sacrifice site). The preface that accompanies *Abraham sacrifiant* catches the mixture of classical/tragic and medieval/comic elements in Bèze's play. "It is partly tragical and partly comical," Bèze explains in Arthur Golding's 1577 English translation: "& therefore I have separated the prologue, & divided the whole into pauses, after the manner of acts in comedies, howbeit without binding of myself thereto. And because it holdeth more of the one than of the other: I thought best to name it a tragedy."[25] The site of the performance of *Abraham sacrifiant*, in Lausanne's place de la Palud, near the city's recently stripped and scoured thirteenth-century cathedral, suggests how civic religious drama of the Middle Ages could be adapted to Reformation purposes. In 1559, with Calvin, Bèze founded the new Geneva academy, a training ground for promotion of Calvinist doctrine.

The Catholic Counter Reformation was just as strong in its zeal for drama, especially in Jesuit schools. The *Ratio atque Institutio Studiorum Societatis Iesu* (1599) enjoins teachers of rhetoric to "assign the writing of some short dramatic episode instead of the usual topic, for example, an eclogue, a scene, or a dialogue, so that the best may afterwards be performed in class, with the roles portioned out to different pupils." Rules for rectors of Jesuit schools are advised that "Tragedies and comedies, which are to be produced only rarely and in Latin, must have a spiritual and edifying theme. Whatever is introduced as an interlude must be in Latin and observe propriety. No female makeup or costume is to be permitted."[26]

A famous example of how Jesuit school drama could function as *propaganda fidei* is the performance of Jakob Bidermann's "Comico-Tragoedia" *Cenodoxus* at the Jesuit college in Munich in 1609. A wide stage erected in the college's lecture theater was lined at the back, in medieval fashion, with booths representing various fictional locations in the play. Since play performances by the college provided the chief dramatic entertainment for the Munich court, an audience of nobles and patrician citizens were present. So powerful was the play's depiction of the damnation of Cenodoxus (Greek for "Vainglory")—an unnamed Humanist doctor of Paris—that fourteen nobles of the Bavarian court were moved to undertake the spiritual exercises of Ignatius Loyola. The actor who played the vainglorious Humanist Cenodoxus not only went on to complete Loyola's exercises; he joined the Society of Jesus and ever after led a pious life. Bidermann, who had written *Cenodoxus* seven years before the play's performance, produced a series of neoclassical tragedies, each with a spiritual program: *Belisarius* (1607), *Macarius Romanus* (1613), *Josephus* (1615), and *Cosmarchia* and *Philemon Martyr* (1618). *Cenodoxus* enjoyed a revival in 1613.[27]

School productions proved to be even more portable than academy-pieces. They could be transported from the lecture hall or refectory to a palace, an open public space, or even a purpose-built theater. A particularly striking example is Étienne Jodelle's *Cléopâtre captive*, often cited as the first classical tragedy in French. Written by the twenty-year-old Jodelle and acted by himself in the title role with some of his friends, the play was performed twice in 1553, first in the presence of Henri II and his court at the hôtel de Reims in Paris and afterwards at the collège de Boncourt in the presence of students as well as "personages of honor." Jodelle was a graduate of the college and had made a place for himself in an artistic academy of sorts, the Pléiade. Étienne Pasquier's account of the second performance of *Cléopâtre captive* in the collège de Boncourt notes that "all the windows were filled like tapestries with an infinity of people of honor, and the court was so crammed with students that the doors to the college disgorged them."[28] Pasquier's reference to the windows suggests that the performance took place outdoors, with students filling the school's courtyard and *personnages d'honneur* looking down from a floor above—an arrangement like the ones that traveling players rigged up in inn yards and town-hall courtyards all over Europe and one that was replicated in the *corrales* theaters of Spain and the amphitheaters of London.

Performances eight years later of the first neoclassical tragedy in English, Thomas Sackville and Thomas Norton's *Gorboduc*, display a merging between Senecan memes and princely auspices. The first performance of *Gorboduc*, a dramatization out of ancient British history with similarities to Shakespeare's *King Lear*, took place in the great hall of the Inner Temple in London, one of the so-called "inns of court" for legal training, during the household's 1561/2 Christmas celebrations. Sackville and Norton, who had done their legal training in the inns, were just beginning their careers as public figures; the actors were gentlemen students from the Inner Temple. A second performance was staged at court in the presence of Queen Elizabeth. Before each act there was music and a mimed "dumb show"—memes taken over from medieval courtly entertainments.

Gorboduc was followed at the inns of court by performances of at least three other tragedies, all of them in the presence of Queen Elizabeth: George Gascoigne and Francis Kinwelmershe's *Jocasta* (Gray's Inn, 1566), an English translation of Ludovico Dolce's *Giocasta* (1547), itself based on Euripides' *Phoenician Women*; a multi-authored adaptation of Dolce's *Gismond of Salerne* (Inner Temple, 1566); and Thomas Hughes' *The Misfortunes of Arthur* (Gray's Inn, 1588).[29] *Gismond of Salerne* is the first English tragedy to be adapted from an Italian *novella*. Particularly at the court of Ferrara, as we shall see, *novelle* supplied a new set of memes for tragedy. As all these instances illustrate, it was in mergings of *ethoi*—and in recombinations of memes from multiple sources—that tragedy found a foothold in European culture. The result was hybrid tragedies combining memes from Seneca with memes from medieval religious plays, Ovid's *Metamorphoses*, national histories, romance narratives, and comedy.

PARADIGM 2: PUBLIC SPACES

With both the Castel Sant'Angelo and Cardinal Riario's palace at their disposal, Leto and Sulpizio nonetheless chose the Campo de' Fiori for the inaugural performance of Seneca's *Phaedra*. Ancient tragedy, they knew, had been a civic event staged in public spaces for audiences of thousands. Mute testimony to that situation loomed in the outer walls of the Theater of Marcellus and the ruins of Pompey's Theater, both situated near the Campo de' Fiori. (See Figure 2.3.)

Public spaces like the Campo de' Fiori were not, it turned out, viable sites for the new dramatic genre tragedy. The reasons are not hard to find: public spaces already had their own dramatic traditions in the form of religious plays, farces, ceremonial entries, and carnival entertainments, and the civic populace had no imaginative investment in the kinds of events that Seneca, Sophocles, and Euripides dramatize. Traditionally, in Italy as elsewhere in Europe, dramatic performances in public spaces like the Campo de' Fiori had been carnival entertainments (*feste, triomfi, farse*) and religious plays (*sacre rappresentazioni*), the latter customarily enacted in some version of the open "place" that Robert Weimann has described, amid *lughi deputati* (literally, "delegated locations") in the form of houses appropriate to different persons in the play and/or to

FIGURE 2.3: Ruins of the Theater of Marcellus, Rome, from Giovanni Battista de' Cavalieri, *Antiquarum Statusam Urbis Romae* (1585). By permission of the Folger Shakespeare Library.

different locations in the fiction. Changes in fictional location were accomplished by the actors' moving from one "delegated location" to another.[30] Two kinds of public-space events did, however, prove amenable to tragic memes: political history and biblical stories.

Albertino Mussato's Latin drama *Ecerinis* (c. 1315), often cited as the first tragedy since Roman times, narrates recent political history: the career and downfall of Ezzelino da Romano (1194–1259), whose atrocities included the killing of several thousand citizens of Padua, making him a modern equivalent of the tyrants in Seneca's recently discovered tragedies, Thyestes in particular. The Paduans celebrated their victory over Ezzelino by passing a law that Mussato's play was to be recited every Christmas in the Palazzo della Ragione with the author in attendance.[31] The gigantic great hall of the palazzo, completed in 1219, measures 81.5 meters by 27 meters (267 feet by 89 feet), a public space if ever there was one.

Mussato's play combines memes from Seneca (chorus, messenger, dramatized horrors) with memes from *sacre rappresentazioni* (the exemplary hero, divine intervention).[32] *Recitare* in Italian, let us recall, can mean, in Florio's definition, both "to read out aloud that others may hear and understand" as well as "to play a comedy or tragedy." The organization of the play lends itself to recitation in the first sense. Speeches spoken by the Messenger and the chorus exceed in length and frequency those assigned to the protagonist Ezzelino. Most major events are narrated by the Messenger, not enacted, and speeches by the chorus are directed to the assembled Paduan audience, even when the fiction is located elsewhere.[33] Thanks to a misinterpretation of a passage in Isidore of Seville's encyclopedic *Etymologiae* (early seventh century CE), medieval readers imagined that plays in ancient Rome had been performed by being read aloud from a pulpit while actors mimed the story below. The idea accorded well with medieval practices: (1) authors entertaining listeners by declaiming from their own works (as Chaucer is shown doing in Corpus Christi College Cambridge MS 61); and (2) mime in all its forms as a component of medieval entertainments.[34]

In public spaces biblical stories also proved amendable to tragic memes, as witness Bèze's *Abraham sacrifant* in Lausanne in 1550, already noted. On one occasion at least Sulpizio's and Leto's desire to perform tragedy in a Roman theater was realized. At Bourges in the department of Cher in the 1530s recently uncovered remains of a Roman theater became the site for a performance of *Les actes des apôtres* (*The Acts of the Apostles*), a series of stories in which death is the frequent denouement.[35] Thomas Coryate in his visit to the remains of the Roman amphitheater in Lyon in 1608 thought about the early Christians who were martyred there and the "no less tragical than copious history of the cruel sufferings" recorded in Eusebius' *Ecclesiastical History*.[36]

In Spain, thanks to the dominance of the Catholic Church, the interplay between native dramatic traditions and Humanist tragedy occurred even earlier and lasted longer, well into the seventeenth century.[37] Lucas Fernández (1474–1542) brought tragic gravitas to the *Auto de la Pasión* (*Play of the Passion*) performed in the cathedral of Salamanca in 1503.[38] More thoroughly Humanist is the *Tragedia Llamada Josefina* (*Tragedy Called Joseph*, published 1535) by Miguel de Carvajal (c. 1495–1578), who wrote for the ducal court of Alba. *Josefina*, complete with five acts, messenger, and chorus, was performed as an *auto sacramental* in a plaza in Carvajal's native Palencia. Later, in 1559, the episode of Joseph and Potiphar's wife landed the play on the Index Librorum Prohibitorum.[39] Pedro Calderón de la Barca (1600–81) combined a career of writing *comedias de tramoyas* for the commercial theater and the court of Filipo IV with writing *autos sacramentales*—more than seventy in all—for the city of Madrid.[40] Calderón's tragedy *Los Cabellos de*

Absalón (*Absalom's Hair*, acted 1634) displays his double-handed expertise in pleasing audiences within two different performance paradigms.

In the course of the sixteenth century tragedy did come to flourish in public spaces, just as Leto and Sulpizio had hoped, albeit not in the particular public spaces they had in mind. Marketplaces, town halls, inn yards, tennis courts: it was into such communal spaces that itinerant actors carried tragic memes. For these traveling troupes mobile memes were more than a metaphor. In the repertories they took from place to place, memes from the new genre of dramatic tragedy were combined with memes from other dramatic traditions (including farces, religious plays, *commedia dell'arte*, and the no less new genre of classical comedy) as well as with memes from other performance modes like music, dancing, fencing, and even puppetry.[41]

In Spain a touring company organized by the actor-manager Lope de Rueda (1509?–65) toured up and down the country from the 1540s, playing in great halls of the nobility but also in inn yards, patios, and plazas for ordinary people. Cervantes, looking back in 1615 on his boyhood experience of seeing Rueda's company perform, confirms another eyewitness in remembering Rueda's makeshift staging arrangements. Planks served for a stage, a curtain pulled by cords hid both the actors' dressing space as well as singers who lacked musical instruments, and costumes and props that included only a few sheepskin tunics, wigs, and beards.[42] Tragic memes (notably the wife condemned to death) figure in one of Rueda's own scripts, *La Comedia Llamada Eufemia*, based on the same tale in Boccaccio (2.9) that supplied the wrongly-suspected-wife plot of *Cymbeline*, but all of Rueda's performances featured comic *pasos* or joke-skits that could be inserted before, during, or after the main play.[43]

In France troupes of actors whose traditional offerings were mystery plays and morality plays were including tragedies and comedies in their repertory in the 1530s. Civic records in Amiens between 1536 and 1567 describe itinerant actors as *joueurs d'histoires, tragedies morales et farces* (players of histories, moral tragedies, and farces), and a license issued in Paris in 1544 to Jehan Anthoine, called *joueur des anticques jeux romains* (player of antique Roman plays). Anthoine hailed from Piedmont on the border between France with Italy and may have brought Italian tragic memes with him.[44] Such shifts in repertory were encouraged in the course of the sixteenth century by suspicions and hostilities about dramatizations from the Bible on the part of both Catholics and Protestants. Tragedies, including three by Garnier (*Les Juives*, *La Troade*, and *Hippolyte*), were included in the offerings of Adrien Talmy's company, who traveled over northern France as well as playing, after 1578, at the hôtel de Bourgogne, the one licensed playhouse in Paris. Itinerant Italian and English troupes also performed there. Records of stage arrangements in Rouen, a particularly vigorous center for drama, suggests that staging arrangements were simple: scripts require no more than a door, a curtain, and a second-tier playing space above the main stage.[45] The hôtel de Bourgogne theater belonged to the Confrérie de la Passion, an association of amateur actors who held an exclusive license for performing religious plays dating back to 1402. No sooner had the confraternity set up their new playhouse in 1548 than the old religious plays, with their admixture of broad comedy and apocryphal non-biblical stories, were forbidden by law. After failing to hold an audience with farces and secular plays, the confraternity started leasing out the playhouse for other performances.

From the 1580s through the middle of the seventeenth century traveling "English Comedians" were a phenomenon all over continental Europe, from Paris to Riga, from Helsinki to Ljubljana, and many points in between.[46] As it happens, the earliest record, from 1585, locates English actors in Denmark, in the courtyard of Elsinore's town hall—a situation that cries out for linkage with the actors who arrive at Kronborg Castle, Elsinore, in *Hamlet*. To judge from the titles associated with English actors in financial records, Polonius' account of the actors' repertory may not be so far-fetched. He calls them "The best actors in the world, either for tragedy, comedy, history, pastoral, pastoral-comical, historical-pastoral, tragical-historical, tragical-comical-historical-pastoral, scene individable or poem unlimited" (2.2.379–82) and mentions Seneca by name. What the First Player proceeds to recite, at Hamlet's request, comes from a classical tragedy on the fall of Troy, in the Senecan mode. What the company performs for the full court in 3.3 is something more current: a love-poisoning tragedy that might have come out of an Italian *novella*. The players' tragedy, as Hamlet sets it up, is proceeded by a music-accompanied dumb show (a meme from mummings) and is interrupted by Hamlet's bawdy asides (a meme from satiric farce). In due course tragedy gives way to out-and-out comedy with the stage direction "*Enter two* CLOWNS, *carrying a spade and a pickaxe*" (SD at 5.1).[47]

The miscellany of memes and modes in *Hamlet* helps us understand the two published repertories of the "English Comedians" in German. *Englische Comedien und Tragedien Sampt dem Pickelhering* (*English Comedies and Tragedies with Pickelherring*, 1620) contains a version of *Titus Andronicus* as well as the exploits of the clown Pickelherring. A play-list from the visit by English players to the Elector of Saxony's court at Dresden in 1626 includes a version of *Hamlet einen Printzen in Dennemark*.[48] What we have in the German printed collections, Pavel Drábek argues, is not corrupt versions of scripts that exist in better condition elsewhere but "records of performance," particular performances in particular local circumstances.[49] To judge from the printed collections and eyewitness accounts, the English actors' repertory included memes from a variety of performance modes, including clowning, music, dancing, and sword-fights as well as tragedy. To German audiences the English actors offered something like the miscellaneous pleasures of the cobbler-Meistersinger Hans Sachs (1494–1576), who counted 61 tragedies among his works, along with carnival plays, biblical plays, and short dramatized jokes (*Schwänke*).[50] To audiences all over Europe—audiences who for the most part did not speak English—"English Comedians" were like the *commedia dell'arte* troupes who also traveled the roads and rivers of the European continent, bringing with them a distinctive style of acting and a distinctive set of memes that transcended local languages. For the "English Comedians" tragedy provided several memes, but their performance style included memes from many other traditions.

PARADIGM 3: PALACES

Originally, the whole project of reviving ancient tragedy was an academic idea. Sulpizio was about to publish a scholarly edition of Vitruvius and perhaps conceived the staging of Seneca's *Phaedra* in a Vitruvian theater as a kind of appendix to his book, if not as a smart publicity move. The Accademia Romana, as we have seen, originally met in Leto's own house, which was full of excavated Roman artifacts. When the likes of Cardinal Riario got involved, these prized artifacts got transferred, figuratively if not literally, into gilt display cases. And so it happened with Seneca's *Phaedrus*. Apparently at Sulpizio's behest, Cardinal Riario took on the project of reviving classical tragedy, and he did it on a grand scale befitting his reputation as politician, patron of the arts, and priest, in descending order of importance. What started out as an academic exercise became an occasion for displaying Riario's cultural capital.[51]

The same appropriation happened in the fifteenth, sixteenth, and seventeenth centuries, first in Italy and then all over Europe, as learned academies were established under noble sponsorship: the Medicis in Florence, the Estense in Ferrara, the Gongazas in Mantua. When academies attempted to bring classical tragedies to the stage, their patrons' cultural capital became even more conspicuous. The more expensive the production of a classical tragedy, the more cast members involved, the longer the performance, the more lavish the sung and danced *intermezzi* between the acts, the grander the effect of magnificence.[52] Hence the relative rarity of such performances. Most of them were one-off affairs. Trissino's *Sophonisba* is an example. This landmark play— the first Italian tragedy to be written on Greek models rather than Seneca—enjoyed only two performances, first in a French translation at Blois in 1556 (six years after Trissino's death) for the court of Marie de' Medici and Henri II, and then in 1562 in a production at Vicenza designed by Andrea Palladio, whose patrons were members of the Barbaro family.[53]

With respect to patronage and drama there were three ways of arranging things: (1) the in-house model, whereby patrons maintained musicians, writers, and painters for their own use; (2) the internship model whereby patrons "rewarded" the on-demand services of academic authors and actors; and (3) the outsourcing model whereby patrons hired professional actors to put on plays for them.

The first model is exemplified in the career of the Spanish poet, musician, playwright, and actor Juan del Encina (1468?–1529). Thanks to the close political and cultural ties between Spain and Italy at the end of the fifteenth century (the Kingdom of the Two Sicilies was ruled by the House of Aragon), Encina made multiple journeys between Spain (where he graduated from the University of Salamanca as Doctor of Law, took minor religious orders, and entered the service of the Duke of Alba) and Rome (where he enjoyed the patronage of various popes and cardinals). His dialogic *églogas*, as he called them in deference to his hero Virgil, were all performed by him and his fellow courtiers in princely environments. One of them has been cited as the first tragedy of the Spanish golden age: the *Égloga de Fileno, Zambardo y Cardonio*, in which one of two friends in love with the same woman commits suicide. In Encina's *églogas* memes from Virgil, Ovid, Italian pastoral poetry, and rustics speaking in Salamancan dialect jostle for attention. Multiple printed editions of his works assured readership and performances in both Italy and Spain.[54] In Encina's dramas Italian humanism meets Spanish local color—all within the confines of aristocratic palaces.

Connections of the in-house model with other paradigms of performance characterize the career of Giraldi Cinthio, who plotted a path that led from the study to the palace, from the palace to the theater, and from the theater back to the study. A native of Ferrara, Giraldi held a series of academic appointments at the University of Ferrara, including chair of philosophy and chair of rhetoric. He was also a member of the short-lived Ferrarese literary academy the "Elevati."[55] The d'Este court in Ferrara had been a music and theater center since the late fifteenth century, when Duke Ercole I had sponsored a production of Plautus' *Menaechmi* in a translation by Battista Guarino in the Palazzo del Corte before audiences that reportedly numbered ten thousand.[56] A permanent theater was under construction in the palace's *sala grande* when Ercole I died in 1505—a project that was abandoned by his cash-strapped successor, Alfonso I, but taken up again in 1531. The court poet, Ludovico Ariosto, whose Terence-inspired comedy *I Suppositi* had been acted at court in 1509, took charge of the project. The theater was destroyed by fire the very next year, but Ercole II d'Este, who assumed the dukedom in 1534, proved to be an enthusiastic patron of music and drama, and Giraldi the professor of rhetoric seized the occasion.[57]

Giraldi made his debut as a writer of Italian tragedies in 1541 with *Orbecche*, inspired in part by Seneca's *Thyestes*. The event was sensational, in every sense of the word: Giraldi dared to show what Seneca only describes, production values were high, the standard subjects of Seneca and the Greek tragedians were replaced by love-driven stories out of Boccaccio and Giraldi's own *Gli Ecatommiti* (*The Hundred Tales*, written 1530s, published 1565), and a happy ending was added in *Altile* (1543), setting off a huge academic debate.[58]

The first performance or *Orbecche*, as the printed edition of 1543 proudly records, was in the presence of the duke. It took place not in the duke's palace but in Giraldi's own house. Ariosto's nephew played the title role of Orbecche, the daughter of the Persian king Sulmone, who moves through a revenge plot that would be quite at home on the Jacboean stage in England, complete with a scene in which Orbecche is presented by her father with the corpses of her children and the head of her husband on a silver platter. The circumstances of the play's premiere suggest a *studiolo* recitation, but in his dedication of the printed text Giraldi thanks one of his wealthy young acquaintances, Girolamo Maria Contugo, for paying for construction of a stage. Similar disbursements from the ducal treasury and from students of the Faculty of Law confirm that Giraldi's later tragedies were also staged in his house. There were between-the-acts music by Alfonso della Vivuola (a meme from more miscellaneous court entertainments) and illusionistic perspective scenery by Girolamo da Carpi (a meme from easel paintings). In the printed text Giraldi boasts in the preface that he has restored spectacle to theater after a thousand-year lapse.[59] Strictly speaking, that was not true. Sulpizio, describing the production of *Phaedra* in 1486, praises Cardinal Riario for being the first in modern times to make *picturatae scoenae* ("pictured scenes"). From other sources we know that one of the ways Inghirami made his reputation as "Phaedrus" was to extemporize when part of the scenery fell down during one of the performances.[60]

By 1594 there had been nine editions of *Orbecche*, plus a collected edition of all Giraldi's tragedies. Giraldi's pan-European fame had been assured by the publication of *Gli Ecatommiti* (*The Hundred Tales* 1565, French translation 1584, partial Spanish translation 1590), which provided plots for Cervantes, Shakespeare, and Lope de Vega, among others. A treatise that Giraldi wrote later in the 1540s, *Discorso ovvero lettera intorno al comporre delle commedie*, gives theoretical justifications for his innovations, as do letters that he exchanged with other writers. In writing these treatises and letters Giraldi the courtier-playwright returned to the *studiolo* of Giraldi the professor of rhetoric. In Giraldi's career success, mobility was all.

The internship model of palace tragedy is well documented in England. The earliest record comes not from the court of the realm but from the court of Cardinal Thomas Wolsey, whose acquisitions of titles, houses, and luxury goods made him a rival of his master Henry VIII and a figure comparable to Cardinal Raffaele Riario in Rome. Sometime between 1522 and 1530 boys from St. Paul's School performed "a tragedy of Dido, out of Virgil" for Wolsey's court, perhaps at Hampton Court Palace. Usually assigned to John Rightwise, who had been engaged by John Colet as sub-master of St. Paul's School, this *Dido* has also been attributed to Rightwise's wife Dionysia, who was the daughter of William Lily, who had met Leto in Rome.[61] One of Wolsey's projects for displaying his cultural capital was the establishment of Cardinal's College Oxford (now Christ Church College), where lectures on Greek and Latin authors were to be daily events.[62]

To judge from surviving records, Henry VIII's dramatic tastes were more retro than Wolsey's, running to mummings, morality plays, and masques. Beginning in the 1560s, however, with the accession of Elizabeth I, court financial records include more and more classical subjects being performed by boys from St. Paul's School, the Merchants Taylors' School, the Chapel Royal, and the chapel at Windsor, including *Damon and Pythias* (1565), *Massinissa and Sophonisba* (1565), *Iphigenia* (1571), *Ajax and Ulysses* (1572), *Narcissus* (1572), *Alcmaeon* (1573), *King Xerxes* (1575), *Mucius Scaevola* (1577), *Meleager* (1580), *Scipio Africanus* (1580), and *Pompey* (1581).[63] Add to this list *Cambises King of Persia* by the future Oxford vice-chancellor Thomas Preston (possibly performed at court in 1560), *Gorboduc* (performed by students of the Inner Temple in 1562), *Jocasta* (performed by students from Gray's Inn in 1566), and *Gismond of Salerne* (performed by students of the Inner Temple in 1566), and Elizabeth's management plan for dramatic entertainment is clear enough.

The publication in 1594 of *The Tragedy of Dido Queen of Carthage: Played by the Children of Her Majesty's Chapel. Written by Christopher Marlowe, and Thomas Nashe* signals a transition to the third plan for bringing tragic drama to English royal palaces: the outsourcing model. The title page may imply a performance before Elizabeth Queen of England, but there is no financial record of the customary reward, and the play may have been written or adapted for performance in a rented space in the former Blackfriars priory in the mid-1580s, after the boys' companies had started "rehearsing" their plays for paying customers.[64] In any case, by the 1570s the queen had begun to bring in adult professional actors who plied their art under the titular patronage of courtiers like the Earl of Leicester and the Earl of Worcester.[65] When professional acting companies began to act in permanent playing places and to charge admission, the fiction of their "rehearsing" plays intended for the queen's entertainment was maintained, even as the companies flourished as capitalist enterprises.[66] Cultural capital was now flowing *into* palaces, not *out of* them.

The extended welcomes given to "English Comedians" by Duke Heinrich Julius of Brunswick at Wolfenbüttel in 1592 and by Landgrave Moritz of Hesse-Kassel at Kassel between 1594 and 1613 represent attempts to combine the in-house model with the outsourcing model.[67] Moritz even built a theater for the visiting players, the Ottoneum (1603–9), the first permanent playhouse in Germany, still standing today with a rebuilt interior that serves as the Natural History Museum in Kassel.

PARADIGM 4: THEATERS

The third performance of Seneca's *Phaedra* in the courtyard of Cardinal Riario's palace in 1486 introduces something entirely new: an attempt to recreate an ancient theater, to realize Vitruvius' description of painted scenery, and to people the theater with a civic, socially mixed audience. What Sulpizio really wanted to do in 1486 was persuade Cardinal Riario to reconstruct one of Rome's ruined theaters or, better still, to erect a new theater built according to principles laid out in Vitruvius' *De architectura*. Given the timing, the performances may have been a kind of publicity stunt. If so, the strategy didn't work. The closest the cardinal came to building a Roman theater was to line the courtyard of his new palace with columns plundered from the ruins of Pompey's Theater nearby. In early modern Europe, as William N. West has pointed out, the idea of "theater" preceded any such thing as a material theater. Ancient texts described and alluded to structures that had little or nothing to do with already familiar performance spaces: market places, streets, cathedral precincts, churches, chapels, great halls, inn yards.⁶⁸ Aside from *The Acts of the Apostles* in Bourges there seems to have been remarkably little interest in performing plays within the ruins of Roman theaters that survived all over Europe.⁶⁹

Vitruvius supplied an ideal model, but in fact each locality found its own way to realize the idea of "theater," using elements from local performance sites (including studies, public spaces, and palaces), accommodated to local acting practices, with or without a nod to Vitruvius. The varied results of these local experiments quite literally *shaped* tragedy in different ways. Initially theater-building activity was centered in Italy and took the form of temporary wooden constructions like the one Cardinal Riario erected in his courtyard. The *teatro* in these cases was more an apparatus or grand piece of furniture than a building. An example had already been set by the temporary theater that Leon Battista Alberti erected in a hall of Pope Nicholas V's palace as early as 1452. Franklin J. Hildy credits the temporary Teatro del Campidoglio designed by Giovn Giorgio Cesarini for a Roman festival in 1513 as being the first attempt to build a free-standing theater from the ground up.⁷⁰

Building of permanent theaters followed in Ferrara (1531), Rome (1545), Mantua (1549), Bologna (1550), Siena (1561), Venice (1565), Vicenza (1580), Sabbioneta (1588), and Parma (1618).⁷¹ Of these buildings, three survive today: Andrea Palladio's Teatro Olimpico in Vicenza, Vincenzo Scamozzi's Teatro all'antica in Sabbioneta, and Giovanni Battista Aleotti's Teatro Farnese in Parma. In these buildings *commedia erudita* based on Plautus and Terence was the usual offering, as witness Ariosto's comedy *Cassaria* (1508) in a production that Fabio Finotti credits as being the first in Italy to use perspective scenery, an innovation introduced by the painter Pellegrino da Udine.⁷² The effect of this innovation is described by an eyewitness, Bernardino Prosperi, in a letter to Isabella d'Este:

> But the best part of all these festivities and performances were the scenes involved in the plays, such as the one realized by a certain Master Peregrino . . .; the scene consisted of a street and a perspectival view of land with houses, churches, bell towers, and gardens, rendered with such diversity as to leave the viewer unsatiated; all this contrived with such ingenuity and skill that I doubt it will be discarded but rather preserved for later use.⁷³

Prosperi distinguishes two elements in this description: (1) in the foreground a street, the standard setting for Roman comedy; and (2) in the distance a landscape, a standard feature of Quattrocento painting.

With respect to tragedy, the apogee of such experiments with perspective was reached in Palladio's Teatro Olimpico in Vicenza, which was inaugurated in March 1585 with a production of Orsato Giustiniano's *Edipo tiranno*, "Sophocles' tragedy adapted in the vulgar tongue and recited with most sumptuous setting by the Olympic Academicians in the year 1585," according to the title page of the printed edition which came out the same year.⁷⁴ (See Figure 2.4.) The cast consisted of 108 brilliantly dressed participants, the audience numbered 3,000 (two-thirds of them from out of town), and the performance lasted from 1:30 in the morning until nearly 5:00, allowing candle-power to be added to the conspicuous consumption. After the epic performance of *Edipo tiranno* the Teatro Olimpico stood empty for thirty years, leaving the wood-and-plaster streets of Thebes still in place for twenty-first-century tourists to enjoy.

Vitruvius' comments on the stage in *De architectura* are cryptic. He describes arched doorways with revolving panels—*periaktoi* in Greek, *periacti* in Latin, *periatti* in Italian— that could be changed to indicate changes in fictional location, or perhaps mood.

FIGURE 2.4: Andrea Palladio (designer), Teatro Olimpico (built 1580–5), Vicenza. Bettman via Getty Images.

Scamozzi's scenic design for the Teatro Olimpico manages to combine ancient and modern ideas about "the scene": in place of the revolving panels that Vitruvius mentions, Scamozzi provides three streetscapes diminishing in perspective distance, and he enlarges the central opening in a way that anticipates the proscenium arches that in later theaters came to span the entire stage.

Enveloping actors and audience in the same perspective space, as Finotti observes, creates a different relationship between spectacle and spectators than was usual in medieval drama, which was played against a line or arc of booth-houses appropriate to particular characters or fictional locales.[75] In Weimann's terms, the design of the Teatro Olimpico brings together two distinct senses of theatrical space. With respect to the stage platform, we have both the downstage *platea* (the "place" occupied in common by actors and audiences alike) and the upstage *locus* (the site of the fiction).[76] With respect to geometry, we have both circular space (actors' and audiences' common ground) and linear space (perspective scenery beyond the arches). With respect to mimesis we have both presentation of immediate action (in the *platea*) and *re*-presentation of action from another time and place (in the *locus*).[77] With respect to perception we have both the drawing-toward of *pathos* (commiseration) and the backing-away of *eleos* (fear), especially when Renaissance commentators like Philip Sidney, conflating tragedy with epic, substituted *admiratio* (admiration) for *eleos*.[78] Tragedy in performance is thus made to occupy a kind of middle ground.

Elsewhere in Europe the open-space *platea* model persisted. In Paris the noble, the academic, and the commercial auspices of Renaissance tragedy converged in the hôtel de Bourgogne. The basse court of the former Parisian *hôtel particulieur* of the dukes of

Burgundy housed the collège du Boncourt, where *Cléopâtre captive* had its second performance in 1553. Elsewhere in the structure was the long narrow room fitted out as a playhouse by the Confrérie de la Passion in 1548. Modern estimates based on engravings and drawings describe a space only 31 meters (102 feet) by 13 meters (42 feet), with a simple stage about 13 meters (43 feet) deep, equipped with a small acting space above the main platform. Some of the audience stood on the floor of the pit; others sat in a steep tier of benches at the back or in one of the 38 boxes ranged along the two sides and at the back.[79] The size and the arrangement invited intimate viewing and listening.

Vernacular tragedies like Garnier's *Porcie*, *Cornélie* and *Hippolyte* were performed there in 1573. From 1578 the hôtel de Bourgogne was a venue for performances by various French troupes (Agnan Sarat, Valleran le Conte, Adrien Talmy, Gros-Guillaume, Belleville) as well as by foreign troupes including the *commedia dell'arte* troupe *I Gelosi* and an English company headed by Jean Thays.[80] The circulation of so many troupes, performing so many different kinds of plays in one place, converged in the dominant dramatic genre of the early seventeenth century: tragicomedy. Garnier's late play *Bradamante* (1582), with a storyline from Ariosto, is an early example.

Stage designs by Georges Buffequin for productions at the hôtel de Bourgogne from 1620 to 1640 show how staging arrangements combined the booth-houses of medieval practice with the perspective illusion of Renaissance Italian practice.[81] (See Figure 2.5.) Buffequin's set for Pierre du Ryer's tragicomedy *Clitophon* (*c.* 1630) provides for separate episodes a castle, a grove, a façade with arch and balustrade, and an outcropping of rocks, all organized within a single illusionistic perspective, complete with vanishing point beyond the statue in the arch. Considering that du Ryer's script digests the rambling narrative of Achilles Tatius' romance *Clitophon and Leucippe* into no fewer than 58 scenes, Buffequin's *décor simultané* seems especially ingenious.

FIGURE 2.5: Georges Buffequin, design for production of Pierre du Ryer, *Clitophon*, Hôtel de Bourgogne, Paris (*c.* 1630). Bibliothèque nationale de France, Département des manuscrits, Français 24330. Public domain.

In France, as in Spain and Italy, the route from studies to theaters came via public spaces as well as via palaces. The companies of Valleran, Talmy, and Belleville had all toured the provinces before (and sometimes after) they took up residence at the hôtel de Bourgogne.[82] In Spain, the route to theaters via market places and inn yards was even more direct. As early as the late 1530s itinerant Italian players and Lope de Rueda's company were performing plays that included tragic memes. The result of these makeshift arrangements were the *corrales* theaters of Seville (1574), Madrid (1579, 1582), and other cities, including Toledo, Valencia, Granada, Córdoba, Barcelona, and Valladolid, all of them presenting distinctively Spanish repertories.[83]

Corrales theaters took the itinerant players' inn yards and courtyards and turned them into permanent theaters by claiming the space between existing buildings, erecting a stage at the end farthest from the street, and putting up ranked seating along the sides and at the back above the entrance door. Windows in the adjacent buildings were repurposed as viewing-places (giving elite patrons more privacy). Standing crowded in the yard were *mosqueteros* (literally musketeers, or groundlings as such standees were called in English), who were separated from the stage by railed-off seating for high-paying patrons (the equivalents of the gentlemen who sat right on the stage in London's public theaters). Since the adjacent buildings with their windows were not owned by the acting company, theater-as-public-space incorporated elements of theater-as-private-space. Sizes of *corrales* theaters varied, but dimensions projected by modern scholars for the Corral del Principe in Madrid include a stage 1.5 meters high by eight meters wide by 4.5 meters deep (about 5 feet by 26 feet by 15 feet)—about half the size of the stages of the Fortune Theater and the Globe in London, although elevated the same degree from the ground. The rectangular auditorium/viewing-place held 1,100 to 1,500 people—again about half the size of the London amphitheaters.[84] A small, free-standing *corral* theater from 1628 survives at Almagro, near Ciudad Real. (See Figure 2.6.)

In these evolved inn yards were performed plays that combined memes from classical tragedy, mythology, and history with memes from chivalric romance, patriotic Spanish history, rustic farce, balladry, and religious drama. The plays of Lope de Vega and Calderón de la Barca are signal examples. As early as 1517 Bartolomé de Torres, who, like Encina, circulated in the course of his career between Italy and Spain, defined the emerging Spanish *comedia* as embracing both tragedy and comedy, according to the social station of the protagonists and the status of the plot as historical story or made-up fantasy.[85] Both Lope and Calderón wrote *autos sacramentales* as well as *comedias*, and Lope wrote epic poems, prose fictions, and lyric poems, all of which could be recited in social gatherings. The uneasy relationship of Spanish playwrights to the Latin classics—now flouting the rules, now incorporating classical memes—is summed up by Frederick A. de Armas as "constant conflict between the uses of the ancients and the desire for the new."[86]

Attempts in the 1580s to put "correct" classical tragedy on the public stage largely failed. Cervantes was one of the writers who tried. The Canon in Book 1, Chapter 48, of *Don Quixote* dismisses most plays on the Spanish stage as "notorious fopperies, and things without either head or foot," but singles out (without naming the author) Cervantes' tragedy *Numantia* among plays "made by judicious poets, which both redounded to their infinite fame and renown, and yielded unto these actors abundant gain."[87] Cervantes is being slyly ironic here. Financial and critical failure though it may have been (it was not printed until the eighteenth century), Cervantes' tragedy on the heroic resistance of the Spanish city Numantia to Roman forces nonetheless illustrates the author's thorough familiarity with the staging arrangements in *corrales* theaters. An apron stage, a "within"

FIGURE 2.6: *Corral* theater, Almagro (built 1628, restored 1953–4). Photograph by F.J. Hildy.

behind a curtain, a "below" accessible through one or more trapdoors, an "above" in the form of a raised gallery: these were the equipment for presentational acting that included increasingly spectacular effects but no perspective scenery. Cervantes in *Numantia* knows how to play this space like a musical instrument. The episode in which the spokesman of the Numantians, standing on the gallery above, confronts the Roman army on the stage below turns perhaps fifteen feet into a vast plain outside the city:

> **Corabino** *stands on the battlement, having a white banner on the point of his lance.*
> **Corabino**
>   Ye Romans, say, from my position here
>   Is't possible my voice your ears can reach?
> **Caius Martius**
>   Be pleased to lower it, speak slow and clear,
>   And then right well we'll understand your speech.[88]

The space below the stage is put to use in the big sacrifice scene in which the Numantians discover they are doomed to be defeated by the Romans. Sound effects accompany one augury: "*Under the stage they make a noise with a barrel full of stones, and discharge a rocket*" (41). The scene's climatic moment comes in this stage direction: "*Here enters from under the stage a demon, from the middle of his body upwards, who seizes the lamb and carries it behind. He presently returns again, and scatters and disperses the fire and all the sacrifices*" (43). All that is missing in Cervantes' stage effects are the actual horses called for in other plays.[89] Although attempting to write a classical tragedy on a classical subject, Cervantes introduces memes from *autos sacramentales* when he summons allegorical figures to the stage: "*Enters a damsel, crowned with a mural crown, bearing heraldic castles in her hand, signifying* SPAIN, *and says,* "Thou Heaven, the lofty, vast, serenely grant,/ Who, with thy fructifying powers, has crowned/ With wealth the chiefest part of this my land . . ." (17–18).

In England the route from studies to theaters came via market places and inn yards just as in Spain, though it did involve more detours through palaces. A parliamentary act of 1572 turned traveling players into criminals ("vagabonds") unless they bore a license from a patron bearing a rank no lower than baron. Hence the names of the acting companies active during the reign of Elizabeth. Leicester's Men and Warwick's Men performed often at court during the 1560s, but they also toured. As we have observed, Elizabeth used the outsourcing model for dramatic entertainment. James I at his accession in 1603 attempted to put all acting companies under the control of members of the royal family, in effect turning the actors into royal servants even as they continued to act in public playhouses.[90] This move gave the appearance that James had the means for the in-house model.

When touring professional actors began to perform in more permanent quarters, tragedies and histories with tragic memes were part of the professional actors' stock-in-trade.[91] The first play scheduled for the first free-standing playhouse, at Newington Butts south of London Bridge, in 1567 was a biblical tragedy to be played by Warwick's Men: *The Story of Sampson*.[92] The titles of Shakespeare's earliest printed plays (all of them tragedies and histories with tragic memes) suggest not only the prevalence of tragedy in the repertories of the companies he worked with but also the function of printed texts as cues for purchasers to construct or (if they had seen the play in question) to *re*-construct stage performances as they read the text in their studies:

- *The Most Lamentable Roman Tragedy of Titus Andronicus: As It Was Played by the Right Honorable the Earl of Derby, Earl of Pembroke, and Earl of Sussex Their Servants* (printed 1594)
- *The First Part of the Contention betwixt the Two Famous Houses of York and Lancaster, with the Death of the Good Duke Humphrey: And the Banishment and Death of the Duke of Suffolk, and the Tragical End of the Proud Cardinal of Winchester . . .* (printed 1594)
- *The True Tragedy of Richard Duke of York, and the Death of Good King Henry the Sixth . . . as It Was Sundry Times Acted by the Right Honorable the Earl of Pembroke His Servants* (printed 1595)
- *An Excellent Tragedy of Romeo and Juliet, As It Hath Been Often (with Great Applause) Played Publically, by the Right Honorable the L[ord] of Hunsdon His Servants* (printed 1597)
- *The Tragedy of King Richard the Second. As It Hath Been Publically Acted by the Right Honorable the Lord Chamberlain His Servants* (printed 1597)
- *The Tragedy of Richard the Third . . . As It Hath Been Lately Acted by the Right Honorable the Lord Chamberlain His Servants* (printed 1597).

One play in particular, Thomas Kyd's *The Spanish Tragedy*, illustrates how performance paradigms merged in London's public theaters. As a student in Richard Mulcaster's Humanist curriculum at Merchants Taylors' School in London, Kyd may have been among the students who acted a lost play *Timoclea at the Siege of Thebes* at Queen Elizabeth's court on February 2, 1574.[93] The story, out of Plutarch's life of Alexander, tells how Timoclea, a Theban woman with a reputation for chastity, kills the Thracian officer who has raped her.⁹⁴ Another classical tragedy with a female protagonist, Garnier's *Cornélie*, was translated by Kyd and dedicated to Lady Bridget Fitzwalter, Countess of Sussex, likely as an appeal for patronage. In his dedicatory address "T.K." praises Fitzwalter's "noble and heroic dispositions."⁹⁵ Kyd's preface to *Cornelia* promises that the next summer he will send Fitzwalter a translation of Garnier's *Porcie*. That offering never materialized, perhaps because Kyd died the same year *Cornelia* was first printed. A second printing of Kyd's translation, a year later by a different publisher, retitles the play *Pompey the Great, his Faire Cornelia's Tragedy*, changing the reader's subject position from female to male.

Fitzwalter's husband Robert Radcliffe, fifth Earl of Sussex, was the patron of Sussex's Men, who are credited with performing *Titus Andronicus*.⁹⁶ It is possible that they also performed Kyd's *The Spanish Tragedy* in the 1580s, but the play's first recorded performance was on February 23, 1592 by Lord Strange's Men at the Rose Theater on the South Bank. The same year was printed *The Spanish Tragedy: Containing the Lamentable End of Don Horatio, and Bel-Imperia: with the Pitiful Death of Old Hieronimo*. No fewer than eleven editions followed down to 1633, with additions by the likes of Ben Jonson bringing the tragedy up to date.

The play's visual and verbal excesses became objects of parody almost from the start—there are over a hundred contemporary allusions—but Kyd was a master at remixing tragic memes and using the resources of the new public houses to full effect. Giraldi's meme of revenge drives Kyd's play, and a play-within-the-play evokes not only scholastic drama but a plot that would be a credit to Giraldi. To work revenge on the three political enemies who have murdered his son, Hieronimo proposes that they join him in acting a play. "When in Toledo there I studied," Hieronimo tells them, "It was my chance to write a tragedy—/ See here, my lords—*He shows them a book*." The tragedy was an academic exercise: "It was determined to have been acted/ By gentlemen and scholars too,/ Such as could tell what to speak." Balthazar, one of the enemies about to be drafted into the play, appreciates the shift in paradigm from study to palace: "And now it shall be played by princes and courtiers—/ Such as can tell how to speak."⁹⁷ The final shift in paradigm, from palace to theater, will leave him dead.

The play-within-the-play, "The Tragedy/ Of Suleiman the Turkish Emperor" (4.4.1–2), is reminiscent of Giraldi's *Orbecche* in its eastern setting, female protagonist, thwarted love, and vengeful king/father. In this case, however, the deaths are real, and Hieronimo in the course of the play manages to stab his three enemies before attempting to stage his own Stoic suicide in a 79-line oration—one of many memes in the play from Seneca, who is in fact quoted, in Latin, several times in the script. Kyd puts to adept use all the resources of London's public theaters, including the space "above" (where a figure named Revenge and the ghost of the wronged lover Andrea likely stay throughout to observe the proceedings on the main stage below) and the space "within" (whence a banquet is brought forth and where, perhaps, is located the arbor-prop on which Hieronimo's son is hanged, to be revealed when a curtain over the opening is pulled back as a climax to the play-within-the-play).⁹⁸ In the career of Thomas Kyd we witness the creative convergence of studies, public spaces, palaces, and theaters.

A solution for accommodating the authority of Vitruvius with the exigencies of performance spaces in Spain, France, England, and the Low Countries was found in the early seventeenth century when architects like Inigo Jones designed playhouses that featured classical elements but nonetheless retained affordances of the open stage: making entrances and exits from "within" via two doors in the *scenae frons*, acting on a gallery

FIGURE 2.7: Salomon Savery (engraver), interior of Schouwburg, Amsterdam (built 1637, engraving 1658, nineteenth-century reproduction). Victoria and Albert Museum, London.

"above," and making "discoveries" via a central opening. A design attributed to Jones for an unnamed theater (1616–18), now realized in the Sam Wanamaker Theatre at Shakespeare's Globe in London, is one example.

Another is Jacob van Campen's design for the Schouwburg in Amsterdam, opened in 1638.[99] (See Figure 2.7.) Built on the site of an academy theater, the Schouwburg was ostensibly modeled on the Teatro Olimpico, but Salomon Savery's engraving of the interior shows features of open performance spaces that have been retained: a gallery "above" (apparently supplied with a figured tapestry or curtain) and two doors for entrances and exits. The main features taken over from the Teatro Olimpico are two arches (much less prominent than in Palladio's design) that open onto perspective vistas and the classical entablature of the *scenae frons* and stage surround. A new feature in the Schouwburg—a curtain running the width of the stage, shown pulled back in Savery's image—anticipates the proscenium arch that emerged in the eighteenth century, effectively eliminating the *platea* of public-space acting and turning the play into a representation of events that happened in another time and place.

The production that opened the Schouwburg was Joost van den Vondel's *Gysbreght van Aemstel*, a patriotic tragedy that continued to be performed on New Year's Day in Amsterdam every year down to 1968.[100] In its patriotism Vondel's play is like Shakespeare's *Richard II* and *Richard III*, Cervantes' *Numantia*, and Garnier's *Porcie* (described on the title page as *tragédie françoise . . . propre & convenable pour y voir depeincte la calamite de ce temps* ("French tragedy . . . fit and proper for seeing depicted the calamity of this time").[101]

It took a hundred years and more for Pomponio's and Sulpizio's dream of tragedy in public theaters to be realized. Montaigne, for one, would have been pleased. He concludes his essay "Of the Institution and Education of Children" with an attack on people who condemn dramatic performances. Montaigne argues instead that

> Politic and well-ordered commonwealths, endeavor rather carefully to unite and assemble their citizens together; as in serious offices of devotion, so in honest exercises of recreation. Common society and loving friendship is thereby cherished and increased. And besides, they cannot have more formal and regular pastimes allowed them, than such as are acted and represented in open view of all, and in the presence of the magistrates themselves.

Indeed, princes should pay for play performances and allow theaters to be built in cities: "there is no better way than to allure the affection, and to entice the appetite: otherwise a man shall breed but asses laden with books."[102] We can relieve ourselves of that burden of books by attending to the multiple sites and multiple modes of circulation of Renaissance tragedy in performance.

CHAPTER THREE

Communities of Production and Consumption

Networks and Publics of a European Genre[1]

ANDRÁS KISÉRY

Who wrote, performed, watched, heard, read tragedies in the Renaissance? What characterized the authors, actors, and audiences that were called into being by creating the genre? This chapter suggests that the communities formed around tragic drama before the mid-seventeenth century were fundamentally different from their modern counterparts not only in their makeup, culture, and beliefs, but also in structural terms. In other words, Dryden's suggestion that Renaissance drama was produced by a "Giant Race, before the Flood" reflects not just his sense of artistic belatedness but also the transformation of the social and institutional settings of tragedy across Europe over the turbulent and critical middle years of the seventeenth century.

The features of the antediluvian Renaissance landscape can usefully be identified through their contrast to later developments—this is why this chapter begins by offering a glimpse of the emerging modern culture of tragedy, followed by an overview of some of the main features of its Renaissance equivalent.

The second half of the chapter takes advantage of an important feature of the tragic genre: namely, its tendency to re-use plots across occasions, languages, and cultures. Sets of tragedies are recognizable as not just structurally or thematically similar (as are for example *Bildungsromane* or quest romances), but as dramatizations of the same scenario or myth, as representations of a story that logically, if not actually, precedes all of them. The heuristic value of observing the modifications to a tragic plot over a series of treatments has been shown by scholars as different in outlook as, for example, Hans-Robert Jauss, George Steiner, Christian Biet, Pascale Aebischer, and Ivan Lupić, who explored the historical trajectories of Iphigeneia, Antigone, Oedipus, Cleopatra, and Hecuba, respectively, revealing shifts in literary culture, in the representation of racial difference, in aesthetics, or in political ideas among the iterations of the same plot at various historical moments.[2]

I rely on the travels of the tragic plot of Sophonisba across early modern Europe in constructing a fragmentary, picaresque survey of the social lives of Renaissance tragedy, of the communities, publics, and networks that produced, circulated and enjoyed them, from the early sixteenth to the mid-seventeenth century, from Italy through France and England to Germany.[3] While the itinerary of the princess of Carthage leaves massive territories uncharted (to mention only the most obvious omission, it does not set foot on the Iberian peninsula), it still affords us glimpses of the variety of communities that formed around tragedies in early modern Europe.

The mobility of early modern tragedy, its ability to cross political, geographical, cultural, and social boundaries, and to interconnect the divided parts of Europe through a variety of networks, is my theme in what follows.[4] Tragic drama helped constitute not only national publics and communities, but also a notion and a practiced reality of Europe as a cultural community over the sixteenth and seventeenth centuries, but my aim is to also bring to light the boundaries, the divisions, the discontinuities, the asynchronous development of literature and culture across the world of the Latin alphabet.[5] But first: a glance at what came after the Renaissance.

1663: CORNEILLE'S *SOPHONISBE*

In his preface to his *Sophonisbe*, Pierre Corneille writes about the difficulty and the glory of treating a subject that has already been dramatized by others. His play should be judged by how successfully he distinguishes his from his precursors' versions, finding new dramatic solutions for the same challenges: this, he asserts, is not only how the ancient tragedians worked, with Aeschylus, Sophocles, and Euripides producing competing representations of the death of Clytemnestra, but also how modern authors have written series of successful versions of the tragic plots of Mariamne, Dido, or Cleopatra. Corneille's immediate predecessor was Jean Mairet, whose *Sophonisbe* (1629, first published in 1634) continued to be performed to the end of the seventeenth century and after, and as he points out, Mairet wasn't the first modern writer to write a tragedy about the princess of Carthage, either. Mentioning Trissino and Montchrestien as the precursors of Mairet's *Sophonisbe*, Corneille expresses his hope that the plots of his own *Cid* and *Horace* will also be taken up by others in tragedies that will be as different from his, as his *Sophonisbe* is from Mairet's.[6]

For Corneille, authors of tragedies form diachronic communities, as they explore the dramatic potential of shared plots by using different "ornaments"—each writer emulating his precursors by finding new ways to imagine the same characters' motives and actions.[7] The reason why Corneille discusses his own take on the Sophonisba plot, and with it, his participation in the historical community of the authors of tragedies of Sophonisba, is that the seventeenth-century stage has by this time become the focus of a different, diachronic community and cultural formation: the emerging critical public of French theater. Corneille's preface to the reader was an intervention in the debate about his tragedy which flared up shortly after its first performance in January 1663. Early in February, Jean Donneau de Visé's miscellaneous three-volume *Nouvelles nouvelles* already included a conversation among the members of a fictional salon about two contemporary plays, Molière's *École des femmes* and Corneille's *Sophonisbe*. The *Nouvelles* hadn't even come out when François Hédelin, abbé d'Aubignac, an important theorist of the theater, published his own remarks about *Sophonisbe*, a pamphlet in the form of a letter addressed to the "duchesse de R." Both writers were critical of the play, and both argued that it compares unfavorably to Mairet's. D'Aubignac went to great lengths to advance his opinion as the articulation of the judgment of the more sophisticated part of the play's audience, presenting himself as much an interpreter of the judgment of the audience as a judge. One of the defenses of the play elicited by d'Aubignac's epistle was written, surprisingly, by Donneau de Visé, who now argued that having watched *Sophonisbe* again, he thought it reasonable to change his opinion about it—and launched an at times *ad hominem*, point-by-point rebuttal of d'Aubignac's *Remarques*.[8]

The publication of *Sophonisbe* in March 1663 is Corneille's answer to his critics. In the preface, he defends his decision to work on the theme of an existing play not only by pointing at d'Aubignac's own contribution to a tragedy of Dido, written by Boisrobert only a few years after the success of Scudéry's *Didon*, but also with reference to the historical record that is independent of any dramatic representation. The preference of non-verisimilar historical truth over plausible actions derived from current assumptions about human conduct also serves to justify his supposed transgressions against the expectation of the verisimilitude of character and action. He suggests that if his Sophonisbe is too much of a heroine, and not enough of the lover that "our delicates" would prefer her to be, this is because he is ultimately guided by Livy, not by Mairet, in imagining her.[9] Corneille's response to his critics is thus an intervention in a public debate about critical standards, about the sources, purposes, and limits of dramatic and critical authority.[10]

Tragedy was central to a major shift in the social life of French literature and theater: the process of professionalization and institutionalization that started just as Corneille was launching his career around 1630. After a couple of decades of decline in popularity, tragedy now saw a revival and cultural re-valuation and elevation as a representative genre, subject to public critical judgment, symbolically marked by the appearance of Mairet's *Sophonisbe*, considered as the model of regular tragedy, and the *querelle* surrounding Corneille's *Cid* in 1637, where popular success was pitted against the verdict of learned critics and of the newly founded Académie.[11]

The professionalization of authorship, by which I here simply mean earning a living from selling one's writing, first became possible for the authors of plays. Corneille's claim to being France's first modern author rests on his successful combination of commercial production with cultural prestige. Throughout his career, he strove to balance box office success against critical, academic recognition, and to combine court patronage with income from the publication of his plays, printed individually as well as in carefully compiled and revised collected editions. He was addressing a public understood to be general and plural even as it was becoming more exclusive: he asserted his aim to please the court as well as the people, the ladies in the audience as well as those who accompanied them, seeking common approbation as well as the favorable judgment of the *savants*.[12]

In mid-century Paris, the opinions of the public were both invoked and shaped by an emerging critical scene, a literary public sphere in which fierce debates were conducted about tragedy's ability to please its audiences in pamphlets appearing in rapid succession. Corneille's authorship thus coincides with, and is marked by, the rise of a distinctly new, modern phenomenon, a public that was addressed not only by theater performances but also by a steady flow of publications that discussed and judged these, transforming the experience by mediating it. The published arguments often retained the appearance of originating in private, sociable discussion, offering themselves as simulacra of conversations and letters, inciting their readers to follow their example and engage in similar exchanges. At the same time, these critical debates were also intensely aware of their reach: they sometimes even declared that "all of Paris" or indeed all the provinces were following their altercation, positing and thus conjuring into being a national public of print.[13]

Only the institutionalization of regular commercial playing abstracted the modern theater public from the performance, and gave rise to satirical and polemical reflection on playing and also on playgoing, from performers, audience members, as well as pamphleteers.[14] Across the continent, in addition to such live critical interaction and general print commentary, written critical reflection on individual plays and performances also began to appear. The emergence of criticism as a separate field of activity, and the appearance of the figure of the critic create new conditions for literary and dramatic production,[15] marking the end of the historical scope of the present survey. Such mechanisms of public arbitration served (or strived) to tie locally, institutionally, and socially distinct audiences into the modern literary and theater public of a city, a nation, or even a continent. These imagined vernacular communities both exceeded and transformed empirical audiences, and also helped assimilate academic drama, court entertainment, and commercial theater to one another. Absent such a comprehensive discourse for and about an abstract public that would have governed the uses of tragedy in the Renaissance, we must consider the settings of tragic drama of the sixteenth and early seventeenth centuries in their heterogeneous plurality. Nor is the modern, market-based distinction between cultural producers and consumers applicable across the forms of social life of tragedy in the period. Through the sixteenth and in most places also much of the seventeenth century, drama was usually performed by communities who were their own audience: at court, in schools, as parts of civic entertainments—where those not playing one day might conceivably have done so the next.[16]

RENAISSANCE COMMUNITIES BEFORE 1663

Although the experiences of early modern audiences of tragedies may largely elude our grasp, the scant evidence about actual Renaissance playgoers reveals the absence of hegemonic standards of expectations, the unpredictability and plurality of response, and the importance of personal concerns audiences brought to the play.[17] While many performance spaces were socially exclusive and hierarchical,[18] in the audience of public performances men and women, noblemen and plebeians, Catholics and Protestants, disaffected noblemen and loyal servants of the current regime were standing side by side, watching plays which demanded that they temporarily and hypothetically suspend their confessional, political, and social identities and inhabit unfamiliar perspectives, but also allowed them to explore the implications of complex scenarios for their own position.[19] The realization that on the public stages, Renaissance plays were engaging with a conscious plurality of perspectives is an important complement to performance-oriented readings of tragedies that do not so much reconstruct lived cultural experience as construe responses presumed to be implied by the script.

The heterogeneity and transience of these communities and settings does not amount to complete disjunction and fragmentation, however. While communities could be constituted locally around any given performance or text, the institutions and communities in which tragedies existed formed intersecting networks of experience that spanned most of Western Christendom, crossing political, linguistic, and religious boundaries. Rather than marking a self-enclosed tradition, nationality itself could function as a transnational network in the period. Traditions of early modern performance were habitually described in "national" terms: traveling companies were branded as English, French, Italian, or Spanish players, as indications not only of their language, but also of their playing style. Such national identities were the function not so much of belonging to a bounded cultural community as of trans-continental circulation. Traveling companies were often hired to perform before exclusive court audiences, whereas their public appearances also drew large urban crowds. Wherever they went, they served as models for the local professional companies that would identify as domestic—not least by contrast with these cosmopolitan troupes, which were themselves being domesticated, as they were beginning to play in local languages, and their ranks were filled with local actors.[20]

It would however be a mistake to simply equate the culture of tragedy with theater practices, and an even bigger mistake to confuse the communities that tragedy called into being with professional theater companies and their publics. Before the emergence of the new kind of literary and theatrical public here exemplified by Corneille's moment, tragedy and the theater had an uneasy relationship, a theoretical match that only gradually became a regularly performed reality. The often quite substantial sixteenth-century Italian discussion about the tragic genre and about specific tragedies unfolded at a relatively slow pace, with books responding to books, debating the achievements of tragedies that were themselves primarily experienced as books.[21] The occasional, private, academic performances of tragedies did not have much of an impact on these arguments, not even as pretexts for commentary. Philip Sidney's damning comments about the contemporary English stage, *c*. 1580, as offering "neither right tragedies, nor right comedies" but "mongrel tragi-comedy," and his mention of the Inns of Court play *Gorboduc* as a praiseworthy counter-example, are another reminder of the division between commercial performance and tragic drama, and also of the variety of ways in which academic, civic, courtly, and commercial settings created different connections between textual circulation and performance. We don't know the plays Sidney is objecting to, because very few English commercial plays (i.e., drama that would have been in the repertory of professional players) survive from this period, whereas the formally and politically ambitious *Gorboduc*, which was performed as an occasional entertainment before courtly and academic audiences, survives in three printed editions. Because texts are codified and performance is evanescent, Sidney's attempt to project a single set of literary norms on a varied field of dramatic production has proved remarkably successful.

Plays written for the commercial stage only became a staple of the London book trade shortly after Sidney's lifetime, from the last decade of the sixteenth century on, and even then, stage and print success remained distinct although interrelated. On the one hand, stage success could prompt publication, and it certainly influenced publishers' choices among available play scripts, the majority of which still did not get printed.[22] But on the other, tragic drama that may never have been performed, and certainly not on a commercial stage, continued to circulate in print. In this marketplace of dramatic literature, theatrical failure could even serve as an argument about the distinction of the play text as well as of its readers, using the distance from commercial production as a mark of prestige—its failure could be used to show that it was, as Hamlet puts it, "caviare to the general," a play so sophisticated that only the select few were able to appreciate it.[23] Similarly, when playbooks derived from the scripts of the public stage enjoyed long-term success in a series of new editions, this was not just the function of their continuing presence on the stage, or of a memory of their success there, but also a sign of the existence of an increasingly national reading public of plays that was distinct from (although arguably an extension of) London theater audiences.[24] Although the 1642 closing of the theaters interrupted the production of playbooks, the market started to recover in the 1650s, years before the theaters would have reopened.[25]

The publication of English plays was reflective of a well-established and thriving urban, commercial theater world which around the turn of the seventeenth century is only comparable to the even more prolific Spanish context. England is also exceptional in that we have a lot of information about performance, not least from the print publication of commercial plays. English playbooks frequently advertise their origins in performance by a specific theater company, theater, etc. on their title pages, constituting a rich, if rather skewed (because commercially dominated and London-focused) archive of performance history—whereas in Renaissance France, there is a striking disconnect between performance and publication. William Shakespeare's collected plays, published in 1623, were not only collected and prefaced by his fellow actors, the collection also lists the principal actors who appeared in the plays, linking the texts to their commercial, theatrical origins. By contrast, when Alexandre Hardy, the first professional dramatist in France, published his collection of tragedies in 1624, the book avoided any reference to the plays' previous life in performance, seeking instead to assert Hardy's status as a poet. Whether because he tried to imitate the early seventeenth-century collections of the tragedies of such gentlemen-dramatists as Jodelle, Garnier, or Montchrestien, or because the company was only willing to authorize him to publish plays that were no longer in fashion, Hardy's printed corpus is dominated by tragedies, at the expense of the genres which were considerably more popular on the stage and which also outnumbered tragedies in Hardy's performed output.[26]

Modern anglophone academic research tends to focus on commercially produced vernacular drama, taking Shakespeare's work and its circulation as paradigmatic. This emphasis makes it easy for us to overlook how crucial educational institutions and the study of classical languages were not only for the forms of tragic drama but also for its social life in the early modern period. The origins of tragedy as a modern dramatic genre can be traced to the encounter with classical plays as the textual objects of study in the Renaissance academic context.

Philipp Melanchthon's interest in classical drama meant that he translated Euripides, lectured about the Greek tragedians at the University of Wittenberg, and as part of the educational program, also organized performances of tragedies in his *schola privata*. This multi-faceted exploration of tragic drama was informed by Melanchthon's sentence "Utiliorem post sacrorum bibliorum lectionem esse nullam quam tragoediarum Aeschyli, Euripidis, Sophoclis et Senecae"—other than the Holy Bible, nothing is more useful to read than the tragedies of Aeschylus, Euripides, Sophocles, and Seneca.[27] In the framework of a broadly conceived moral education, ancient tragedy responded especially well to an attention to exemplarity, and tragic sententiousness was particularly amenable to the analytic technique of commonplacing.

The academic reading, translation, and writing of tragedies wove another transnational network. While traveling professional theater companies criss-crossed the densely urbanized zones of the continent, the travels and contacts of scholars also extended to locations outside of these commercial and demographic centers. The humanist model advocated and epitomized by Melanchthon was disseminated not only by his translation of Euripides, his *Cohortatio ad legendas tragoedias et comoedias*, and the prefaces to Winshemius' translations of the tragedies of Sophocles: Melanchthon's Wittenberg students (who came to study there from all over Lutheran central and northern Europe) and the students of Wittenberg-educated professors also helped to circulate his ideas.[28]

Melanchthon's 1545 lectures on the *Electra* were probably attended by Georg Tanner, who became professor of Greek at the University of Vienna in 1557. In his first lecture course, Tanner focused on the *Electra*. Among his Vienna audience was Péter Bornemisza, who would go on to study in Wittenberg and later became a Lutheran bishop. Bornemisza published the first translation of the *Electra* into Hungarian in 1558 under Tanner's influence. To his idiomatic vernacular prose version, Bornemisza attached a brief Latin tract in which he articulates Melanchthon's insights about the play as they were conveyed to him by Tanner. According to Melanchthon's 1545 course description, he intended to use the tragedy of the "politicus" Sophocles as an opportunity to consider the problem whether tyranny is to be patiently endured or resisted. Melanchthon would have wanted his students to follow Chrysothemis rather than Electra, to choose endurance rather than resistance, but in his classroom, students had to deliberate over both characters and both options, and arrive at the right conclusion through a debate.[29] Bornemisza's tract also concludes with this question—which, unlike Melanchthon, he leaves open. While his Latin tract asserts Bornemisza's participation in a European academic universe, the translation itself—and the modifications and elaborations of Sophocles' text, including the introduction of the low comic figure Parasitus—is proposed as a contribution to an emerging vernacular public. It is dedicated to Bornemisza's compatriots at the University of Vienna, young Hungarian noblemen studying there who intended to perform it, presumably as part of the celebrations of Ferdinand's coronation as Holy Roman Emperor.[30]

Latin and vernacular translations of classical and contemporary tragedies played an important role in the creation of a modern European tradition of tragedy. They introduced the genre to new settings, and in the process, they projected and identified new types of publics and communities, although these are now often hard to discern. Later in his life, Bornemisza was the tutor of Bálint Balassi, who became the foremost Hungarian poet of the late sixteenth century. It would be reasonable to assume that Bornemisza discussed Sophocles with his student, although this is impossible to know. A close prose translation of Euripides' *Iphigeneia in Aulis* into Hungarian, which survives in a single fragmentary copy printed in Sibiu (German: Hermannstadt, Hungarian: Nagyszeben), Transylvania between 1575 and 1580, can be attributed to Balassi only tentatively.[31] We also know from a contemporary manuscript note that Balassi was working on a translation of George Buchanan's Latin *Jephthes*, but his version of this tragedy does not survive.[32] We only have his translation of Cristoforo Castelletti's *Amarilli*, a pastoral comedy this soldier-courtier poet titled a "*Beautiful Hungarian Comedy*," dedicating it to the noble women of Transylvania—a clear departure from his tutor's association of classical tragedy with academia.

This association of genres with dedicatees perhaps too neatly captures some of the social and cultural associations of tragic drama in the sixteenth century. While the academic context may seem to associate tragedy with male, homosocial communities, an attention to textual circulation complicates this view considerably. To take the English example: the scripts of England's commercial theater industry were closely linked to performance, and the distance of translation as a literary activity from the professional stage may have been one of the reasons for the significant presence of English women of high status among translators of such tragedies, as well as among the patrons of translations. Lady Lumley's translation of the *Iphigeneia in Aulis* of Euripides via the Latin of Erasmus, Lady Herbert's translation of Garnier's *Antony* (whose female center is Cleopatra, of course), Lady Cary's *Mariam* (possibly inspired by Dolce's *Marianna*) are important participants in a text-based, "literary" tradition that is clearly distinct from the drama written exclusively by male authors for performance by the English professional companies, a tradition that is now more familiar, but which by no means dominated sixteenth- and seventeenth-century Europe.

The thematic focus of classical and of classicizing continental tragedies (the subjects of translation) is another possible reason for the female participation in their production:

tragedy was a genre that stirred up the emotions through the representation of suffering, and one whose protagonists were distinguished as subjects of passion rather than of action.[33] Early modern tragedy understood this distinction as gendered. A glance at the titles reveals a landscape dominated by female protagonists: in contradistinction to our post-Romantic assumptions, for the Renaissance, the paradigmatic tragic figure is not Oedipus or Orestes, and not even Antigone, but Hecuba.[34] Cast and repertory seem to have informed each other: Italian professional companies began to feature female players after 1560. Their often highly skilled actresses distinguished these companies from local comedians, and were also the focal point of the transformation of their repertories, which now also included tragedies starring these divas.[35]

Hamlet's reflections on the effeminacy of suffering and his meditation on Hecuba as a paradigm of tragic passion and sympathy indicate how compelling this gendered model was, even in the English context. But English commercial theater, both in London and on its provincial and continental travels, developed a different model, in sync with the remarkably physical English performance style. In these plays, male agency, and tragic *action* often seems to be the focus of tragic experience. The English commercial stage was a retrograde formation in that its cast also remained all male through the mid-seventeenth century. And although tragic drama became a star vehicle in England as well,[36] the biggest and most spectacular roles of the English stage were written for men: Edward Alleyn was associated with the role of Tamburlaine, and Richard Burbage was remembered as the male lead of some of Shakespeare's greatest tragedies, for example. All the female parts were played by boys apprenticed to the actors. After reaching adolescence and serving their term of indenture, many of these boys continued as adult male actors.[37] Boy actors followed in the wake of the Italian divas as performers of complex and demanding female roles: Shakespeare's Julia and Cleopatra, Webster's Duchess of Malfi and Vittoria Corombona were played by boys who must have been stellar actors, able to hold their own against their adult partners. Nevertheless, due to the culturally anomalous performance practices, in the English professional tragic repertory, the female lead of continental tragedy was largely elipsed by the male hero—Hecuba by Hamlet.[38]

The first tragedian whose work reached the English commercial stage in a translation advertised as such, with the original author's name attached, was Corneille. The performance and publication of Rutter's translation of the *Cid* in 1637 was a one-off that aimed to capitalize on the epoch-making media event of the early-seventeenth-century French literary public sphere, the success and scandal of the Parisian *première* and the *querelle* that followed. Katherine Phillips' translation of *Pompée*, in heroic couplets, was staged in Dublin in 1663. This translation merged the traditions of commercial performance and female authorship, signaling the onset of a new era.

SOPHONISBAS, 1502 TO 1680

In 1502, Galeotto del Carretto wrote a tragedy based on the story of the Carthaginian princess Sophonisba and her two suitors, casting the political problem faced by Carthage into the dramatic form of personal conflict. Carretto's Italian tragedy, like other early humanist examples of the genre, is a dramatization of historical events taking place over many years and in a variety of locations. It is not divided into acts and is explicitly intended for reading. Instead of maintaining a steady focus on the female tragic figure, it adopts the expansive political perspective of its epic and historical sources, Petrarca's *Africa* and Livy.[39] Carretto's *Sophonisba* is not part of the reductively conceived classical canon of Italian Renaissance tragedies, which since the late sixteenth century has been taken to begin with Giangiorgio Trissino's *La Sophonisba*, the play traditionally considered as the first "regular" tragedy, that is, the first tragedy modeled on classical example, and supposedly on Aristotelian principles.[40] Trissino's play also served as the starting point for all *Sophonisba*s written before the turn of the seventeenth century.

Trissino's *Sophonisba* is a learned attempt to reform Italian literature by introducing a Greek model for tragedy. Although he was among the foremost scholars of Greek of his time, Trissino's interests and agenda were also defined by the urgent concerns of a community whose debates he personally engaged in, and with and for whom he was writing at the time. The origins of his play have been traced back to the legendary conversations conducted in the early sixteenth century at the Orti Oricellari, the gardens of the Rucellai family, in Firenze, where Trissino was in discussion with Machiavelli, Bernardo and Giovanni Rucellai, Ludovico Martelli, Alessandro de'Pazzi, Luigi Alamanni, and others, about ancient history, modern politics, and vernacular writing.[41] A series of tragedies that date from the second and third decades of the century, including Giovanni Rucellai's *Rosmunda*, Trissino's *Sophonisba*, Pazzi's *Didone*, Alamanni's translation of the *Antigone*, and Martelli's *Tullia*, are either products of this environment, or echo conversations that originated there: with Rucellai, Trissino even engaged in an amicable contest of reciting lines from their tragedies.[42] These tragedies use their historical subject matter to reflect on the fate of Italy, and of Firenze in particular, at a time of foreign invasions and "alterations of state." Their tight plotting of tragic action in the face of an unpredictable fortune served in turn as a model for contemporary historians.[43]

They also grapple with the challenges and choices involved in putting the vernacular to literary use and approximating tragic verse to contemporary popular speech. In his dedication to Pope Leo X, Trissino talks about choosing the vernacular for his tragedy so that "all the people" can understand it. Their ambition to speak to, or at least imagine, a national public defined by language, prompted an intense debate among sixteenth-century Italian intellectuals about what that language should be like: Trissino, Martelli, Machiavelli, and Pietro Bembo all contributed to the discussion about the "questione della lingua," with Trissino advocating for a supra-regional, "courtly" Italian over the Tuscan dialect widely promoted as the literary language.[44] The textual project of *Sophonisba* is also marked by this concern: its early editions were printed using Trissino's experimental orthography, introducing a set of additional graphemes from the Greek alphabet to reflect current pronunciation more accurately.[45] Trissino's *Sophonisba* is thus a paradigmatic example of the centrality of tragedy, as a representative public genre, to national cultural revivals, and specifically, to efforts to modernize national languages, literatures, and theater, a symbolic role the genre was to play not just in Italy, but until and through the nineteenth century, in many other European countries as well.

Trissino's erudition earned him a job as a diplomat at the pontifical court, and he dedicated his tragedy to the pope. *Sophonisba* became the most reprinted Italian tragedy in the period,[46] an important point of reference for sixteenth-century Italian authors as a cornerstone of the project of tragic writing. In an epilogue attached to the first Italian tragedy to be actually performed in Italy, *Orbecche* (1541), Giovanni Battista Giraldi Cinzio invokes Trissino as the first who brought tragedy to the Arno,[47] while in his prologue to *Marianna*, Lodovico Dolce cites *Sophonisba* and *Orbecche* as his targets of emulation.[48] Literary ambition did not immediately result in theatrical interest: while vernacular comedy on the classical model was acted from the beginning of the century, tragedies only begun to be staged, occasionally, from the 1540s on. The first performance of *Sophonisba* in Italy had to wait until 1562. That year, the Accademia Olimpica, a learned association of Vicenza, decided to perform it in Palladio's temporary theater erected inside the massive hall of the city's Basilica. The elaborate *scenae frons* with one of the central moments of the play, Massinissa handing over the poison to Sophonisba, is represented on a wall painting in Palladio's Teatro Olimpico, built as a permanent structure a decade later, which thus became a monument to its own—as it turned out, short-lived—history as an academic theater.[49] The Accademia Olimpica, which was an antiquarian enterprise that aimed to revive the glory of classical theater, clearly stood out among the hundreds of sixteenth-century Italian academies, but performances staged by learned and aristocratic academies were an important part of the theatrical landscape.

While some of the interests of Trissino and the Orti Oricellari group were alive to the members of the Accademia Olimpica, and thus may have informed their performance in Vicenza, the first staging of Trissino's tragedy, which took place at the French court six years before the Vicenza production, inevitably erased the cultural and political concerns of Italian intellectuals, and refocused the play around new preoccupations for new audiences. Twice in 1556, in February and in April, once as part of the carnival season and once on the occasion of an aristocratic wedding, a French adaptation of *Sophonisbe* was played before King Henri and Catherine de Médicis at Blois. The actors were members of the court: Sophonisba was played by Louise de Clermont-Tallard, the governess of the royal children, who also participated; the prologue and final chorus were delivered by Mary Queen of Scots, herself brought up at the French court, and soon to be married to the heir apparent, the future François II. Surviving records show that the performances were lavish affairs, with 1,500 livres spent on fabrics, among other things.[50]

A contemporary manuscript of the play includes not only a complete list of actors, careful indications of their entrances and exits, but also a preface by Mellin de Saint-Gelais, the court librarian, which reveals that he produced the translation as a joint effort with Jacques Amyot, the tutor of the royal children.[51] The script is mostly in prose, with only the choruses in verse. By cutting some of the speeches considerably, the two humanists adjusted the play to the desired length (three hours total) and to the capacities of the performers, while the young Jean-Antoine de Baïf composed a monologue in alexandrins to serve as an *intermède*. It was not for lack of diligence on their part that Catherine de Médicis was displeased by the result. A genre about tyrants, the fall of kings, and the suffering of the great, tragedy was frequently offered as a mirror to princes, but it was not necessarily a mirror you wanted to look into, or a form in which you wanted to be commemorated. The Queen Mother decided that tragic spectacle brought bad luck to the kingdom, "so she had no more performances of that sort,"[52] preferring Italian *commedia dell'arte* and tragicomedies. These two performances of *Sophonisbe* were the last tragic spectacles performed at the French court for quite a while.[53]

In contrast to the unusually rich manuscript accounts of the tragedy's creation and production, its 1559 printed edition extricates this *Sophonisbe* from the complications of collaboration. As the work is released into commercial circulation as a literary text, only the fact of the performance at Blois is mentioned, the stage directions are removed, the prologue that was written for the occasion is omitted, and the publisher's note only mentions "the principal author," Saint-Gelais.[54]

Mellin de Saint-Gelais' adaptation of *Sophonisbe* is invoked as a precursor in Antoine de Montchrestien's preface to the first edition of his *Sophonisbe*,[55] published almost two generations later, in 1596. *Sophonisbe* was Montchrestien's first play, and it exemplifies the regional embeddedness of tragic drama written by members of the educated bourgeoisie and nobility in Normandy. It was written and published in Caen, the city where Montchrestien studied. In the dedication to the 1596 edition, he thanks Madame de la Verune, the wife of the governor of Caen, for the performance she had made possible[56]—which makes it sound like a private, occasional event, and along with the publication, part of Montchrestien's bid to advance himself within local patronage networks. No information survives about further performances. Although professional French theater troupes performed in a variety of genres, the repertories in the late sixteenth and early seventeenth centuries appear to have been dominated by farces and *sotties*, rather than tragedies.[57] The apparently limited presence of the genre in the repertory seems to be consistent with Montchrestien's emphasis on the value of tragedies as reading matter in the dedications of the 1601 and 1604 Rouen collected editions of his tragedies to the young Prince of Condé.

Montchrestien's links to Normandy are less exceptional than our post-Renaissance assumptions might suggest. In the period, Paris only had one theater building, the hôtel de Bourgogne, owned and rented out by the Fraternity of the Passion, who had been in charge of mystery plays until they were banned in 1548. Theater in the provinces was just as important and probably more vibrant: around 1600, Rouen had three performing venues, used by French as well as English companies. Nor was the printing of plays concentrated in Paris: until the 1620s, Rouen dominated the French market of play publications.[58] Until the mid-seventeenth century, Normandy dominated the production of tragic drama. Corneille's move from Rouen to Paris is emblematic of the shift that ends the geographical diffusion of cultural production characteristic of Renaissance France.[59]

As the published texts of French Renaissance tragedy usually don't reveal much about their life on the stage, it is only from other, scattered evidence that we occasionally learn about their performances by itinerant companies. Although we don't know of further performances of his *Sophonisbe*, contemporary political correspondence suggests that *L'Écossaise*, Montchrestien's tragedy about the death of Mary Queen of Scots, went on to be performed by professional players, outside of his personal networks. We know it was staged in Paris in 1601, in Orléans in 1603, and again in Paris in 1604. These performances worried English diplomats not simply because of the politically sensitive nature of the subject—the play was also available in print, after all—but because of the scandalous affront of *staging* unflattering representations of living persons. Complaints were lodged with French officials about "so lewd an indiscretion," and the actors appear to have been threatened with punishment.[60] Who these players were we don't know, but it is clear that in late sixteenth-century France, their shows reached relatively large and heterogeneous urban audiences, and played an important part in the formation of political publics and political networks, locally as well as internationally.

As Catherine de Medici's reaction to Saint-Gelais' *Sophonisbe* implies, plays on classical and biblical subjects inevitably highlighted the pressures and problems of the contemporary political world. Dramatizations of contemporary political events—like the death of Mary Stuart—also served as a public vehicle for the circulation of current political information, and as such, an important part of a complex mediascape that preceded the rise of the periodical press as the dominant form for the public, commercial dissemination of news. In the anxiety with which political agents viewed the stage we may glimpse a reflection of theater audiences. Across the Channel, we find the Earl of Essex worrying that "the prating tavern haunter speaks of me what he lists; the frantic libeller writes of me what he lists; already they print me and make me speak to the world, and shortly they will play me in what forms they list upon the stage,"[61] thus registering the importance of actors and theater audiences to the constitution of an elusive urban public sphere, and to the constitution of his own honor and political reputation. While the turn of the seventeenth century reverberates with scandalous performances, such direct participation of drama in the public sphere of politics was becoming less characteristic over the course of the seventeenth century. As the stage is replaced by print as the primary public medium for the circulation of news, and as literature is demarcated as a distinct field of production, representations of contemporary politics disappear from the theaters. In a parallel and related development that accords with Norbert Elias' account of the civilizing process,[62] audiences were gradually silenced, disciplined, even disarmed, and new codes of conduct were imposed on them, serving both as social markers and protocols for the exclusion of the unsophisticated.

Cultural sophistication and an engagement with life in a political environment are also key features of the first English *Sophonisba* and its cultural setting. In England, the last decades of the sixteenth century saw the emergence of an urban theater scene driven by competition among several companies settled into repurposed playing spaces and purpose-built amphitheaters. From the 1590s, the London book trade started to publish playbooks directly and explicitly originating on these stages, contributing to the rise of a theater scene where playing, publishing, playgoing, and playreading were intersecting with each other. Each play addressed a public that was conscious of earlier plays and performances, and each play inevitably but often also strategically signaled its position in a field of emerging distinctions among tastes and conventions, among companies, venues, and their audiences. These internal distinctions within the field have allowed critics to hypothetically associate the thematic and stylistic concerns of the plays with company repertories and theater audiences.

This audience has become central to the modern understanding of early modern English drama, a community that has sometimes been elevated by scholars to the status of quasi-mythic co-authorship because of its social diversity and participating engagement with the players.[63] Although women participated in court masques and civic performances, their absence from the commercial and the academic stages meant that—with the possible exception of occasional performances at aristocratic households—they did not perform in tragedies. But while the work of representation on the professional stage was gendered as male, women were a presence at the theaters, both as paying spectators and as workers, part of the complex plurality of the audiences at the big amphitheaters.[64]

Audience members' interaction in a space of watching and being watched further complicated their experience. While recent efforts to imagine the social as well as the physical, spatial, auditory, visual, and even olfactory conditions, the embodied experience of early modern performance and theatergoing have been dominated by an interest in the theater as a space and medium in general, important new work has also allowed us to better understand the implications of genre for theatrical audition, forging a crucial link between literary and performance-oriented study of form and reception.[65]

The amphitheaters were not the only venues where commercial companies appeared, the people attending them not the only kind of audience they addressed. In legal fiction as well as to some extent in practice, commercial performance served as rehearsal and preparation for the company's true calling, which was to entertain the court. The Master of the Revels supervised the scripts intended for court performance; in some periods, his interventions may have been quite extensive, amounting to a form of co-authorship.[66] Professional companies also played at academic venues during holiday celebrations, their performances intersecting with the rich dramatic tradition of the various colleges and other institutions. With the publication of the *Records of Early English Drama* series, theater history has also begun to integrate performance outside of the metropolis, appearances at houses of aristocrats as well as at various provincial venues, into the account of early modern English theater history, recognizing commercial theater as an important part of the cultural landscape of the provinces as well.[67] The actors in *Hamlet*, as a troupe arriving from what must be London at Elsinore castle, at a royal court as if it was any great house in the countryside, rather helpfully blur the distinction between foreign and provincial touring, and remind us of the reach of tragic performance far in excess of the recorded sites and instances.

John Marston wrote *The Wonder of Women: Or The Tragedie of Sophonisba* for the Children of Blackfriars, a company in which he also became a shareholder. Children's companies were an important phenomenon of the culture of early modern English theater, a curious operation that straddled the divide between different types of theatrical culture. Although made up of choirboys from the Cathedral and the royal chapels, they were a commercial operation. They were performing at indoor venues, referred to as "private" playhouses, playing spaces within the city limits that were more comfortable and also more expensive than the capacious suburban open-air amphitheaters of the adult companies. They entertained their smaller, fashionable audience with satirical, topical, or otherwise adventurous drama.

Marston's *Sophonisba*, published in 1606, juxtaposes the exploration of interest and opportunity through the discourse about the reason of state, used by political intriguers, with the neostoic language of endurance voiced by their victims. The complementarity of these two perspectives articulates the unfolding of the tragic conflict of Marston's tragedy, which thus provides an exemplary analytic of the workings of power—not an oppositional critique, but a pragmatic modeling of exigencies and expediencies, of decisions and outcomes, inviting its publics to engage in a form of political commentary on the dramatic action. The two modes of discussion it deploys, the reason of state as the mode of analysis of the world of politics, and neostoicism as the ideology for survival and success in political environments, were important tools in the hands of ambitious young men aspiring to political careers.

The interest of *Sophonisba* (as well as of other boy company plays) in the world of politics is partly motivated by the shared experience of the author and a presumably significant segment of his audience. Marston spent several years at one of the Inns of Court, which provided training in the common law and also served as a finishing school for the gentry. Many a political career began at the Inns, but they were also the center of a trendy urban male subculture—as well as of occasional performances of plays and entertainments.[68] With its political and formal concerns, Marston's drama was clearly defined by the coterie culture characteristic of the Inns and a theater audience immersed in this culture,[69] while in its printed form it also contributed to the commercial dissemination of these styles and preoccupations to a wider public.

Other features of the play establish different connections. Modern scholarship has described the linear structure of *Sophonisba* as un-Marstonian and "Tamburlaine-like"[70] but what feels like a broadly Marlovian poetics might also be informed by the declamatory style of late-sixteenth-century French tragic drama. Nor should this be surprising: unlike tragedies written for the public stages, with their larger casts, adult male stars, and onstage fights and battle scenes, the tragedies in the early-seventeenth-century repertory of boy companies[71] show clear affinities with the drama of Garnier and Montchrestien. Samuel Daniel's *Philotas*, which preceded *Sophonisba* on the Blackfriars stage by two years, is most obviously and directly indebted to that tradition, but *Bussy d'Amboys*, *The Revenge of Bussy d'Amboys*, *The Conspiracy of Biron*, and the *Tragedy of Biron*, George Chapman's four claustrophobic tragedies featuring tormented, soliloquizing heroes are also inflected by it. The boy actor in the role of the suffering heroine aligned Marston's *Sophonisba* with the tradition of pathetic tragedy that was dominant on the continent, with the tragic genre as the medium for representing passion rather than action.

These thematic choices are also suggestive of a theater and an audience that eagerly cultivated anything French and continental. Although Marston's play is not an adaptation of a French play,[72] he is working on a plot that has been made recognizable as a tragic *sujet* by Italian and especially French drama—whether by Montchrestien (who crossed the Channel to England to escape prosecution for dueling just a year before Marston wrote his play) or by Nicolas de Montreux, whose *Sophonisbe* was published in Rouen in 1601. The very existence of Marston's version is therefore an argument against reading English tragic drama as an insular phenomenon, and an indication of the extent to which English readers and writers were aware of continental, and especially French literary production. And while recent French Sophonisbas provide a genealogy for Marston's take on tragic drama, reading the English play against these also highlights the tight, action-packed intrigue plots that distinguished the scripts written for the London stage.

Marston's time at the Middle Temple establishes the social and cultural context his plays address, and it also makes him one of a number of Renaissance dramatists with a legal or administrative background—like Norton and Sackville, the authors of *Gorboduc*, Francis Beaumont, who trained as a lawyer before spending a decade as a professional playwright, Pierre Matthieu, who identified on the title pages of his tragedies as a "doctor of the laws," Robert Garnier, a magistrate whose political tragedies are suffused with the rhetoric of the courtroom,[73] or Pierre Corneille, who could always fall back on his lucrative position as an advocate in Rouen.[74]

Daniel Casper von Lohenstein was another jurist-magistrate-tragedian. His *Sophonisbe* is the last major Silesian tragedy, and perhaps the last major play that belongs to the literary culture of the Renaissance. Written between 1666 and 1669, a few years after Corneille's play, it was addressed to an entirely different audience, and participated in a different world of print. As a result, while Corneille's play appears as a modern theatrical piece intended for polite society, Lohenstein's *Sophonisbe*, with its elaborate dedications, looks more like a piece of learned court poetry. In the absence of multiple companies and theaters competing for large, regular audiences, no critical discussion emerged in Germany in the seventeenth century that could have served as an alternative to the academic discourse in which Renaissance tragedy was born. Lohenstein's work is reviewed, admired, and commended by scholars who praise him in the context of the *historia litteraria* of Germany—the *querelles* fought in French pamphlets and salons are unimaginable in the seventeenth-century central-European literary universe, which is fragmented into smaller local centers, and dominated by the rhythms of scholarly discourse rather than by the more rapid public discussion of journalism. In what constitutes a striking example of the non-contemporaneity of contemporary phenomena, Corneille was firmly located in the new era, in the culture of modernity, whereas Lohenstein ended up being seen as part of the old—and was duly forgotten in the eighteenth century.

Like all authors of *Sophonisba*s, Lohenstein also clearly knew about earlier dramatizations the Sophonisba-*sujet*, and like Marston and Corneille, instead of reworking an earlier version he also turned to historiography for the materials of his own tragedy. But in a remarkable divergence from Marston, Corneille, and all their precursors, when

Lohenstein published his *Sophonisbe* in 1680, he did so in an edition whose one hundred pages of dramatic text are followed by 76 densely printed pages of apparatus citing sources ranging from Livy on the death of Hanno (note to act 1 v. 18) and Strabo on the population of Cyrtha (note to act 1 v. 34) to John Selden on Syrian gods (note to act 1. v. 217), and the *Journal des Sçavans* about the ability of the salamander to withstand fire (note to act 2 v. 496). The apparatus underscores the extent to which tragic form serves as a medium for polymathic learning, addressed to the men of letters of Germany, among whom the tragedies appear to have been in circulation before their print publication.[75]

The play combines careful antiquarian scholarship with the political analysis of the characters' actions in a Tacitean, reason of state modality, focusing on the use and control of passions in government. It is the principle of the preservation of the political community that also necessitates those of Sophonisbe's actions that appear to be in conflict with the principles of ordinary morality. If Corneille's critics complained about his Sophonisbe's de facto bigamy, Lohenstein's public is treated to a scene of Sophonisbe having her sons compete for the honor of being sacrificed to Baal, the winner only to be replaced in the last minute by a captured Roman, who is sacrificed onstage.

It is not only Lohenstein's historical-anthropological exploration of cultural difference that prompts the suspension of the reader's moral judgment of individual actions. The Roman war against Carthage is described early on as an effort to remove the shackles of Moorish domination from Mediterranean regions, from Hispania and Sicily, thus prefiguring the seventeenth-century wars against the Ottoman occupation of Central and South-Eastern Europe. But the triumphalism of this analogy is cancelled out by the play's world-historical focus on the inexorable succession of empires. This is the perspective that becomes explicit when Lohenstein conjures up the ghost of Dido to Sophonisbe, and has her prophetic voice survey the rise of empires, the decline of African power, the conquest of Ottoman Asia and Africa by the next global imperial power, the Europe of the Habsburgs. Not only is this Carthage imagined as the geopolitical competitor of a European empire, a mighty opponent—Lohenstein's anti-tyrannical convictions, his commitment to the civic-republican institutions of the cities of Silesia, under encroaching Habsburg control, make his Sophonisba a figurehead of hopeless yet fearless resistance.[76]

In contrast to the Sophonisbas that descend from Trissino's tragedy, Lohenstein's heroine is an African woman, a Moor. Marston introduced several black characters, but in the familiar sixteenth-century scheme of representation, they are figures of racialized bondage and of moral depravity, servants who provide a contrast to the purity and color-coded Petrarchan beauty of Sophonisba.[77] Lohenstein's approach is strikingly different. In seventeenth-century Silesia, the representation of racial difference on the stage is not motivated by the ideological needs of Western European colonization, but by the politics of Central European imperialism. The pre-Christian setting also suspends the religious logic of racial difference: it is the clash between continental empires that find their signifier in skin color. Seventeenth-century writers and players of Sophonisba are thus both symptomatic of the emergence of an imagined community of modern Europe, and actively setting the terms of that community.

Lohenstein's tragedies embody the politically oriented historical learning that provides training to state servants—and they did not only serve this function in print, but also on the stage. The first known performance of *Sophonisbe* took place in May 1669, at the Magdalena Gymnasium, one of the two Protestant high schools of the city of Breslau (present day Wrocław), the school where Lohenstein also graduated before leaving for his legal studies and travels. As there was no university in Silesia, the gymnasia were the centers of the intellectual life of the city and the region. Public rhetorical exercises—*acti scholastici*—became a regular part of the academic year around the time the young Lohenstein entered gymnasium, and he participated in them between 1646 and 1651. *Actiones theatrales* were also regularly staged: Lohenstein's first tragedy, *Ibrahim Bassa*, was written in his last year, and was performed by his schoolmates. School performances were by necessity transvestite—like Marston's, Lohenstein's Sophonisbe was also a boy, a condition Lohenstein exploited through cross-dressing-based intrigue.[78]

Such Protestant school drama emerged at the intersection of the two largest European networks of theater performance. Jesuit schools were the most important cultural competitors of Breslau's Protestant schools, and Jesuit theater was a major influence on their culture of performance. By the end of the sixteenth century, the Jesuits took over much of the secondary education in Europe, and the children of the elites of Catholic countries, from Spain and France to Poland and Hungary, were educated almost exclusively in the hundreds of colleges they maintained. Theater was the defining cultural medium of the Society, which used comedies, tragedies, and martyr plays as pedagogical and propaganda tools. The sheer number of performances in this extensive transnational network made Jesuit theater the single most pervasive theatrical phenomenon of the early modern period, the theater people were most likely, and in several regions of Europe, only able to experience.

Although the Breslau school stage never became professionalized like the London children's companies, it also intersected with the theater of English traveling companies. The plays of such central figures of an emerging vernacular academic-literary canon as Gryphius and Lohenstein were staged at the same large public halls that also hosted English companies, and performed to the same audience of city and state bureaucrats, local patricians and nobility, fellow students and their families, and others, generating a considerable sum in entrance fees for the gymnasiasts. Little surprise that schoolmasters were hostile to traveling players: they viewed them as competition.[79] While a standard trope of anti-theatrical commentary was to complain about the professional players being common, rude, and ignorant, a bunch of ruffians playing to the rabble, the majority of actors employed by the professional traveling companies were in fact gymnasium- and some of them even university-educated.[80] Such academic complaints against professional actors were partly symptoms of how close the two performance traditions were at this point, how much their audiences and even offerings coincided. The same year as the first recorded performance of Lohenstein's *Sophonisbe*, the diary of a senator of the city of Danzig (Gdańsk) describes a performance of another play by Lohenstein, *Ibrahim Bassa*, by the commercial troupe led by Carl Andreas Paulsen, at that city's fencing school, which also served as the city's public theater.[81] In Danzig, English players appeared from 1587, and performed at the "fencing school" from its opening around 1612 to around 1660, when they were finally superseded by German companies. The public of Lohenstein's tragedy in Danzig was thus called into existence by the frequent visits of English troupes at this important hub of the Baltic trade.[82] But as we have seen throughout this chapter, participation in such networks was only one of the ways in which early modern tragic drama created communities and publics that exceeded its immediate audience.

CHAPTER FOUR

Philosophy and Social Theory

Murdered Majesty: The Stuarts in Tragedy and Trauerspiel

RICHARD WILSON

"I think they are making a scaffold to make me play the last scene of the Tragedy": when she heard carpenters at work in Fotheringay Castle, where she would be beheaded, Mary Stuart prepared for her "supreme moment of tragedy" with the confidence that, as she told her judges, "the theatre of the world is wider than the realm of England."[1] The Queen of Scots had likened herself to the histrionic Richard II; and it was because "we princes are set as it were on stages, in sight and view of all the world," Queen Elizabeth explained to Parliament, that this royal rival hesitated for ten weeks before signing her death warrant.[2] So, in an age when power was either constituted in "celebrations of royal glory" or in "violence visited upon the enemies of that glory," Mary's eventual execution, on February 8, 1587, collapsed those dual modes of spectacle into a new kind of *theatrum mundi*, where the old drama of "the cease of majesty" (*Hamlet*, 3.3.15) would be recast, to display both of "The King's Two Bodies": as subject *and* object, tyrant and martyr.[3] Scholars notice that in later editions of *Basilikon Doron*, his advice to his own heir, the doomed Prince Henry, her son James VI and I therefore corrected his mother's "true old saying," that a king is "set on a scaffold," to insist that a king is "set on a *stage*"; as if to avert the danger he "must have felt to be inherent in the royal drama."[4] James Stuart's attempts to insulate his family romance from the tragic genre did not save Mary's only other grandson, Charles I, however, from following her on January 30, 1649 to the place of execution:

> That thence the royal actor borne
> The tragic scaffold might adorn:
> While round the armed bands
> Did clap their bloody hands.[5]

"Is my hair well?" Charles asked his executioner; perhaps mindful how his grandmother's "polled" gray head had been exposed when her wig came off in the axman's hand.[6] Andrew Marvell's tribute to Mary's grandson, as an actor *born* to adorn "the tragic scaffold," thus chimes with reports that he had imagined "his truest kingdom was the stage," and studied his Shakespeare Folio for its "sad stories of the deaths of kings" (*Richard II*, 3.2.131). Then, like those characters in "the beautiful theatre of the old order" raised "to some scaffold, there to lose their heads" (*Richard III*, 4.4.229), Charles stepped out of Whitehall Palace into his own "lamentable tragedy" with "the same unconcernedness" as he had shown performing there "on a masque night."[7] So, critics have lately come to view Shakespeare's tragic drama as a "great eclipse" of monarchy, when by making "Proud majesty a subject" (4.1.242) of audience approval, and deconsecrating the Lord's anointed, "tragedy made it possible to decapitate him."[8] Shakespeare initiated "a custom for kings to lose their heads," as Michel Foucault put it.[9] the impact of tragedy on the Stuarts is therefore well attested.[10] Less attention has been given to the impact of the Stuarts on tragedy. Yet Marvell's testimony that Charles never "called the gods" to vindicate his divine right implies the witnesses to "that memorable scene" were divided between royalists mourning a Christ-like martyr, and republicans applauding the death of a tyrant, like the spectators of some ancient drama:[11]

> A bleeding head, where they begun,
> Did fright the architects to run.
> And yet by that the state
> Foresaw its happy fate.[12]

Contemporary pictures of the Stuart executions illustrate the opposed reactions Marvell registers, with officials oblivious to Mary's distraught maids, or to women depicted miscarrying in "fright" at Charles' decapitation. That division highlights divergent concepts of tragedy, as if the meaning of the genre is being revised to reflect the two faces of this family. Classically, "mere suffering can never be tragic."[13] Yet as Julian Young relates in *The Philosophy of Tragedy*, there was always a problem with Aristotle's theory that tragedy originates in some human flaw, and that a play about an innocent victim will not generate the essential catharsis of pity and terror, because it is "simply shocking." And Christianity makes it even harder "to understand why shock should *exclude* fear and pity," when "Christian art and emotionalism is devoted to grieving for crucified Christ."[14] In *The Pathos of the Real*, Robert Buch similarly contends that Christianity short-circuits tragedy, which no longer stages triumph over suffering, but suffering as a "protest against the ways of the world."[15] The extent to which that dramaturgical turn was keyed to the fall of the House of Stuart is suggested by the earliest play about the disastrous dynasty, *Maria Stuarta Tragoedia*, a Latin school text of 1589, which ends with a gruesome tableau in which James cradles "his mother's headless, bleeding neck," recalling how often he had hung from it, as her ghost tells him to rejoice, "for she has won the heavenly crown of a martyr."[16]

In Jean de Bordes' *Maria Stuarta* James arrives too late to save his mother, "and bursts out in grief at the barbarity of the English heretics." The king is converted to Catholicism by the ghost, yet returns to Scotland, "leaving England to the punishment of God."[17] That anti-climax suggests how Mary's death framed what Shakespeare termed *the question*, posed by the revenge tragedies produced in Catholic circles after 1587, of "whether to suffer / The slings and arrows of outrageous fortune," like some tortured saint, "Or to take arms against a sea of troubles" (*Hamlet*, 3.1.60–1), with an avenging armada. The subtitle of a lost *Tragedia della Regina di Scozia* by the celebrated Dominican friar Tommaso Campanella implies a militant answer: "For Spain Against England." But devised for Jesuit seminarians in Milan, *Maria Stuarta* instead initiated a suicidal program that embraced "the slings and arrows" with the masochism of a Saint Sebastian. This included the *Stuarta Tragoedia* penned in 1593 by Adrien Roulers, professor of rhetoric at the Benedictine college in Douai, a haven for Elizabethan exiles. Given that venue, it is no surprise that the ghost in Roulers' play belongs to Henry VIII, rising from Hell to confess the horrors caused "by his incestuous and adulterous union with his daughter," Anne Boleyn, and by their "Jezebel" bastard Elizabeth.[18] This specter comes hot from Seneca. Yet what is arresting is how, for all the "motive and cue for passion" (2.2.538) in these Baroque teaching aids, such as the victim's bleeding head flaunted by her butchers in Roulers' play, the waiting game they bequeath to modern drama concerns the *hesitation* of an avenger who by "thinking too precisely on th'event" (4.4.9), "Did nothing" (2.2.462).

Elizabeth called Mary "the daughter of debate."[19] But if these college plays "configure the tragic paradigm" so that the disembodied head or headless torso "becomes a spur to revenge," the quandary they had to finesse was that outside student debates *nothing happened*.[20] So, while his inertia drew this "John-a-dreams" (545) ever closer to the English throne, what James did *not* do impacted on tragic form as much as what their killers inflicted on his child and parent. The duplicity clouding the Queen of Scots thickened, for instance, in rewrites of one play about his mother scholars think James read, *Escossoise, ou le Desastre Tragedie*, initially drafted by Antoine de Montchrestien about 1597. An adviser to France's Huguenots, Montchrestien was aware of the Protestant character assassination of Mary as Duessa in Spenser's *Faerie Queene*, for which the king wanted the poet "tried and punished."[21] But he had also absorbed Montaigne's dismay that "the fairest Queen," whose followers worshiped her as "higher than God," was dispatched by her jailers as "no better than a carter"; and the result is a drama that echoes the essayist's "disbelief in either" party.[22] Thus, even its Elizabeth learns compassion, as she shifts from saying, in effect, "'twere well / It were done quickly" (*Macbeth*, 1.7.1), to issuing, in later versions, a futile stay of execution. Montchrestien was voicing the skepticism of *politique* moderates in Europe's wars of religion; a middle way Shakespeare adopted, with ambivalent glances at Mary's fate in *Richard II* and *King John*. By the time James was presented with it in 1604, the new king of England thus had "a story that exonerates both his mothers," as equally hopeless.[23] But the paradoxical outcome of this weak power was a drama of the power of weakness:

> This realm has witnessed more than once its monarchs die
> In ways that brought more glory to the kingly race,
> And much disgrace to the rejoicing, guilty throng.
> What wonder is it, then, if yet another mob
> Increases with my corpse the count of slaughtered kings
> Of English blood? Is't not the English custom
> To hold the blood of Kings of very little worth?
> They've spilt it lightly, and trimmed like crazy reapers
> All branches of the trunk that were, because of birth,
> Entitled to demand the right to rule this realm.[24]

In such lamentations, Joost van den Vondel's *Mary Stuart, or Tortured Majesty* racks up the passive aggression of martyrdom by counterpointing the violence of the "mob" against the queen's helplessness, for "she dies as a sacrificial lamb, as Jesus did."[25] The author admitted "Aristotle's laws of the theatre hardly allow a character so completely innocent"; but explained how his "solution was to shroud Stuart's innocence with the fog of contemporary gossip, slander, and evil, so her Christian and royal virtues shine forth even brighter."[26] Critics infer that Vondel was in fact articulating his own conflicted position at the time of writing in 1646, as a Catholic convert in the Protestant Netherlands, while affirming the royal prerogative to impose a religious truce, like Henri IV's Edict of Nantes, which the vanquished Charles had "consummately failed" to uphold.[27] In pleading for "helpless right" he was following Mary's earlier Dutch hagiographer, Jacob Zevecotius, whose *Maria Stuarta*, printed with a Greek setting in 1623, reflected its author's contrary conversion to Protestantism, through a heroine ecstatic to exchange the "false world" of her "lost crown" for an "eternal one" in heaven.[28] The fact that this anti-Aristotelian drama could thus be turned to either a Catholic or Protestant perspective was indicative of the "irenic desire to have done with schism."[29] But as tragedians looked to the fatal platform erected for the hapless House of Stuart, all they seemed to see was a "broken, hopeless history," and the funereal *theatrum mundi* Hamlet pictured as "a sterile promontory":[30]

> . . . this brave o'erhanging, this majestical roof
> fretted with golden fire—why, it appears no other thing to me
> than a foul and pestilent congregation of vapours.
>
> —*Hamlet*, 2.2.291–3

"A sterile promontory": that was how Walter Benjamin viewed the entire genre of Trauerspiel composed in the wake of the Stuart cataclysm. In his 1925 book *The Origin of German Tragic Drama* the Marxist critic argued that the genre abreacted in its very name (from the German for sorrow—*trauer*—and play—*spiel*) the collective trauma caused by watching "the seventeenth-century ruler, the summit of creation, erupting into madness like a volcano and destroying himself and his entire court" (64).[31] To Benjamin, "The death of Hamlet, which has no more in common with tragic death than the Prince himself has with Ajax" in the Greek tragedy by Sophocles, is the icy peak of the *Trauerspiel*, and "for this reason alone it is worthy of its creator: Hamlet wants to breathe in the suffocating air of fate in one deep breath. He wants to die by some accident . . . Whereas tragedy ends with a decision, the essence of the *Trauerspiel*" is an "appeal of the kind that martyrs utter" against fate (130). Shakespeare's drama of "the not quite dead" thus presages an entire genre of "Winter Fruit," like *The Famous Tragedy of King Charles*, rushed out in London in 1649, which derives "enigmatic satisfaction" in marking the "subjection of man to fate" (133):[32]

> What is a man,
> If his chief good and market of his time
> Be but to sleep and feed?—A beast, no more.
> Sure, he that made us with such large discourse,
> Looking before and after, gave us not
> That capability and god-like reason
> To fust in us unused.
>
> —*Hamlet*, 4.4.33–9

Benjamin never cites Freud's theory that melancholy symptomizes a failure to mourn.[33] But his comparison of *Hamlet* to Dürer's *Melancholia* situates the play in a Reformation Europe riven by "Wittenberg and the protest against it": Luther's denial of prayers for the dead and the Counter Reformation crusade to restore them. Thus, action was "deprived of all value," he writes, when "something new arose: an empty world" (133). Critics have come around to the idea that Shakespeare's great drama of the undead does record the "mixed signals" of this crisis of faith, with a Protestant Prince haunted by a Ghost crying for remembrance from a Catholic Purgatory.[34] But Benjamin specifically relates this *horror vacui* to the Thirty Years' War, when states were torn by schism, and the ruler who held "history in his hand like a scepter" (59), could take sides only by force, like "the hellish Pyrrhus" (2.2.443) of legend.³⁵ What makes *Hamlet* so resonant of the Baroque, then, is how it protracts a prince's indecision into "the rhythm of a constant pause," suspending his hesitation between passivity and aggression in the uncanny "witching time of night" (3.2.358) Benjamin calls "the midnight hour of the *Trauerspiel*" (129), when the violence needed to seize power with "such bitter business as the day / Would quake to look on" (361–2), only deepens the "stasis of melancholy."³⁶ Nietzsche had written how Hamlet found it laughable to be "expected to repair a world which is out of joint," once he had stared into the void.³⁷ Benjamin counters that by invoking "the divinity that shapes our ends" (5.2.10), and the "special providence in the fall of the sparrow" (158), Shakespeare is attending to this stalled "interim" (73) as an "anticipatory deadline," a dialectical *caesura* or interregnum on the eve of a revolutionary decision:³⁸

> So, as a painted tyrant, Pyrrhus stood
> And, like a neutral to his will and matter,
> Did nothing.
> —*Hamlet*, 2.2.460–2

While pondering the deadlock in *Hamlet*, Benjamin had studied Carl Schmitt's *Political Theology*, with its brutal maxim that "Sovereign is he who decides on the exception," because the exception to the rule "is analogous to the miracle," and makes the king like God.³⁹ The Catholic lawyer was urging the ministers of Germany's Weimar Republic to act like Charles' nemesis, Oliver Cromwell, and govern by emergency decree. Yet whether by design or not, Benjamin took Schmitt to mean that fear of tyranny "makes it the most important function of the prince to avert this" outcome.⁴⁰ He was extrapolating that aversion from plays by Baroque German writers such as Andreas Gryphius, which all portrayed the sovereign in the likeness of a Stuart, as an abortive absolutist, who should be "responsible for proclaiming a state of emergency," but instead reveals how "he is incapable of making a decision," and so becomes a mere victim of "bloody terror": "He is the lord of creatures, but he remains a creature" (85). In Gryphius' *Murdered Majesty: Charles Stuart*, the "sublime status" of God's vicar on one hand, and his "infamous futility on the other," thus interact in "a manner unsurpassed" in incoherence. For with this *Trauerspiel* of 1657, the author "had no hesitation in explicitly endowing" the beheaded king with the halo bestowed in German engravings that sanctified "Carolus der Märtyrer" as the Lord's representative, Benjamin noted (67). Yet in contrast to the absolutist Vondel, Gryphius also showed how the criminal negligence of his earthly reign meant Charles' finest stage was indeed the grave, where the king's natural body would be wholly decomposed:⁴¹

> "He leaves us his body as a pledge of final good will," says the daughter of Charles Stuart about her father, who for his part did not forget to request that it be embalmed. Seen from the point of view of death, the product of the corpse is life. It is not only in the loss of limbs, not only in the changes of the aging body, but in all the processes of elimination and purification that everything corpse-like falls away from the body piece by piece. It is no accident that precisely nails and hair, which are cut away as dead matter from the living body, continue to grow on the corpse. There is in the physis, in the memory itself, a memento mori; the obsession of the men of the baroque with

death would be quite unthinkable if it were only a question of thinking about the end of their lives.

—212

In *The Famous Tragedy* Charles only appears at the end, as a corpse. Gryphius likewise foresaw how the royal martyr would return as an Anglican saint, with his organs "transplanted" as relics.[42] Thus, this Stuart is "a radical stoic," in Benjamin's book, "for whom the struggle for the crown" is an "occasion to prove himself in torture and death" (67). That death drive, flagged in the title of *Guilty Innocence: Mary Stuart* by Gryphius' imitator August Adolf von Haugwitz, reflected the context in which these *Trauerspiele* were written, the havoc created by one Stuart decision with global consequences: the acceptance, on September 28, 1619, by James' son-in-law, Friedrich V of the Rhineland, of the crown of Bohemia. As a Protestant star, the prince was offered Bohemia by its Reformers, in defiance of the Catholic Habsburgs, but on the assumption James would arm his daughter Elizabeth and her husband in a plot that dated from their London wedding in 1613, for which Shakespeare wished a happy Bohemian ending in *The Winter's Tale*. As Frances Yates recounted, it was "a great tragedy of misunderstanding," as "James stood for peace at all costs; he wanted to achieve this by marrying his children to opposite sides"; but he remained "incapable of taking decisions," and so failed to act like a king. Thus, "Europe rushed on, unguided and confused, into the Thirty Years War." The historian wondered "what plays were staged by the English players" for "the Shakespearean pair" in Prague, as they waited in vain for rescue.[43] So, it may be significant that the company manager, Robert Browne, is known to have repeatedly programmed *Hamlet*, which he may even have commissioned for the company's continental tours.[44]

Gryphius, who based his comedy about the *Meistersinger* contest, *Herr Peter Squintz*, on the actor Peter Quince in *A Midsummer Night's Dream*, wrote his *Trauerspiele* in the train of the Stuarts during their wandering exile, which began with Frederick's crushing defeat in 1620, and ejection from the Rhineland. Abandoned by James, the "Winter King and Queen" fled to what the playwright William Davenant called a "hospital for kings" in the Hague, where Gryphius became an agent for their daughter Elizabeth, just as she was quizzing Descartes about "the disasters her family suffered at the hands of Providence."[45] The philosopher told the princess these "tragedies" were "more glorious, fortunate and sweet" than those of "common men."[46] Yet "Seeing our whole fatherland is buried in ashes and converted into a theatre of vanity, my aim is to represent the mutability of all human affairs," Gryphius demurred.[47] So it seems apt that his name was Greif. He grieved at seeing Henrietta Maria arrive in France, after her husband Charles was imprisoned. But whether presenting a deposed emperor in *Leo Arminius* or a martyred queen in *Katherine of Georgia*, he was grieving as much for the mayhem they caused as for these royals themselves. No wonder Benjamin sensed "a fundamental uncertainty" in *Carolus Stuardus* "as to whether this is a drama of tyranny or martyrdom" (73). He was evidently taken by Fortinbras' eulogy that Hamlet would have "proved most royally" (5.2.342) as such a decider. But as though suddenly aware of its authoritarian drift, he shut down his discussion of Shakespeare by returning the Prince to the "sterile promontory" of the martyred House of Stuart, and the "zone of indeterminacy" that is the space of "sovereign indecision":[48]

For the *Trauerspiel* Hamlet alone is a spectator by the grace of God; but he cannot find satisfaction in what he sees enacted, only in his own fate. His life, the exemplary object of his mourning, points, before its extinction, to the Christian providence in whose bosom his mournful images are transformed into a blessed existence. Only in a princely life such as this is melancholy redeemed, by being confronted with itself. The rest is silence.

—158

It took a quarter century for Schmitt to reply to Benjamin's book on *Hamlet* and the *Trauerspiel*, and to boast how this Marxist Jew had "expressed his gratitude to me in a personal letter" (62). During that dark time he rose to be "Hitler's crown jurist," as the legal enabler of the dictatorship that forced Benjamin into exile and suicide.[49] So, when his own *Hamlet or Hecuba* was belatedly translated into English in 2009, it was a disturbing reminder of the part played by Shakespeare's tragedy in debates about relations between intellectuals and power in Germany, "ever since the work was adapted as *Der bestrafte Brudermord* soon after its first appearance."[50] Schmitt's argument, that in *Hamlet* the paralysis of the avenger "stems from the contemporary historical presence of Mary Stuart's son" in an identical impasse, and that this "Hamletization" finds "a suitable explanation only in James" (25–6), accords with theater historians who see in the plays "a *caveat Rex*."[51] But critics scorn his sleuthing as a "simple minded" and "primitive" historicism.[52] They deduce that the theory in fact reflected the Nazi resolution "to shake off the role of Hamlet in favor of becoming Fortinbras, freeing the national spirit from Shakespearean tragedy."[53] For there is a glaring parallel between the attorney's predicament over "a regime based upon murder" and the Prince's dilemma concerning "bitter business" to be done under cover of the dark. *Hamlet or Hecuba* is indeed a key to "the most impressive defense of Nazism ever devised."[54] But what is not sufficiently recognized is how it was Benjamin's ghost that beckoned Schmitt back to the benighted Stuart battlements to observe the dawn of modern tragedy.

Once *Hamlet or Hecuba* is viewed as a riposte to *The Origin of German Tragic Drama* that book itself appears as a logical sequel to Schmitt's early book *Dictatorship*. For there the "Winter King and Queen" are depicted as the unwitting catalysts of the "iron constitution" of dictatorship that so excited Benjamin's messianic fantasies, when James' betrayal of Frederick ushers in Wallenstein's reign of terror, as Charles' abjection propels Cromwell's Protectorate. So, if Schmitt turned to *Hamlet* after he lost his own access to power, and was barred from office in 1945, he had already devoted half his magnum opus to the age of Shakespeare, and the other to explaining its relevance to modern Germany. *Dictatorship*, which was translated into English only in 2014, makes it clear why these Weimar intellectuals were fixated on the Stuarts, and why *Hamlet* became for them a supreme "discussion of the state of emergency" (65). Benjamin based his fatalistic reading, that instead of a royal decision, Hamlet passively submits to "the suffocating air of fate," on a mistranslation of the Prince's joke about the lethal duel as an athletic exercise: "'tis the breathing time of day with me, let / the foils be brought" (5.2.129). But the Jewish thinker was projecting his own 1921 "Critique of Violence," which attempted to distinguish bloodless divine violence from bloody political violence, when he claimed Shakespeare was "striking Christian sparks" by deflecting the avenger towards the "blessed existence" that "Christian providence" promises martyrs who passively endure their "slings and arrows" (158).[55] Schmitt's delayed reaction to that mystical disarmament of the play was the more dismissive coming from a Catholic:

> *Hamlet* is not Christian in any specific sense, and even the famous passage concerning providence and the fall of the sparrow that Benjamin invokes does not alter the fact.

> Perhaps it escaped Benjamin's attention that Hamlet speaks of a "special providence," whereby we already enter into theological controversies . . . At this point Hamlet stands between Catholicism and Protestantism . . . Shakespeare's drama is no longer Christian.
>
> —61–2

Schmitt's objection that "What can be called Christian" in *Hamlet* "has passed through James, the son of Mary, who was completely caught up in the confessional struggle" between Catholicism and Protestantism, situates the Stuarts as collateral victims of an epochal clash of England and Europe (61). For unlike Benjamin's melancholy mourners, Schmitt's Shakespeare accepts the sacrifice when "baser nature comes / Between the pass and fell incensèd points / Of mighty opposites" (5.2.61–3). In fact, "only eight of seventeen rulers of the Stuart name reached the age of fifty," the attorney records (27). On this count, the "unhappy Stuart lineage" has equivalent status for modern tragedy to the House of Atreus in Greek drama, where Orestes and Oedipus are also "figures from a living myth that are introduced into the tragedy from an external present" (46). Yet "the fate of the Atreidae does not affect us as deeply as that of the unhappy Stuarts," according to this geopolitical critique, because the Scottish line was not only "shattered by European religious schism" (52) but crushed between the armies of the continental states and the warships of an England primed for "departure from a terrestrial to a maritime existence" (65). All Schmitt's ideas about the existential antagonism of friend and enemy, land and sea, war and peace, debate and decision, play and seriousness, sacred and secular, and art and power, together with his paranoia about the Anglo-Saxons as the Germans' fraternal foes, are thus condensed into the terse last pages of his Shakespeare book, where his conflictual theory of tragedy reads like a prediction of the breakdown of our own twenty-first-century world order:

> It was precisely in this century from 1588 to 1688 that the island of England withdrew from the European continent. . . Following the lead, first of seafarers and pirates, then of trading companies, England participated in the land appropriation of a New World and carried out the maritime appropriation of the world's oceans. . . The Stuart dynasty was not fated to foresee any of this [because] the Stuarts grasped neither the sovereign state of the European continent nor the transition to a maritime existence that England achieved during their reign. Thus they disappeared from the stage of world history as the great appropriation of the sea was decided and a new global order found its documentary recognition.
>
> —64–5

To Schmitt, the theorist of "great spaces," *Hamlet* is a tragedy because it expresses the realpolitik of Shakespeare's own piratical existence, when "life was still ungrounded and elementary – not yet incorporated into the strict framework of the sovereign state" (41), with its neutralizing project of "peace, security, and order" (63). Schmitt's cartoon of an exceptionalist buccaneering England that was "coarse and elementary, barbaric," and never signed up to European civilization, is in the style of Voltaire, whose caricature of the Bard as a "drunken savage" he approves. The difference, however, is that for Hitler's attorney such brigandage is what defines the freebooting Elizabethan as a truly tragic dramatist, in contrast to tame Parisian "comedians" like Racine and Corneille, with their "legalistic unity of action, time, and place" (41). That was why "the German of the *Sturm und Drang* invoked Shakespeare," rather than these neoclassicists, and the reason Goethe "delivered his fabulous speech" excoriating "all French *Trauerspiele*," with their fake "Greek armor," as kitsch "parodies of themselves." If Nazi Germany had become "as barbaric as Tudor England," the architect of its permanent state of emergency seems to imply, it would not only have produced great tragedy, but achieved a final solution to its age-old problem of *Lebensraum* (63–4).

For the Nazi lawyer, authentic tragedy accrues "surplus value" from some "ineluctable reality" that is "externally given, imposed and unavoidable." It encodes the "entanglement of indisputably real people" in "real events" (45). Thus, the "terrible reality" that "shimmers through the masks and costumes" of *Hamlet* is the likeness of Gertrude to the Queen of Scots, who had similarly married the Earl of Bothwell, the suspected murderer of her husband and James' father, Henry Stuart, Lord Darnley. According to Schmitt, the original audience "was convinced" of Mary's guilt (18), which thereby constituted an *intrusion* of real time into the fictive time of the play. And it is true that the real-life Polonius Lord Burghley listed "detestable acts committed" by the Stuarts as reasons why James was "unacceptable to the people of England," and that these "horrible deeds" of "cruelty and mortal hatred" included the assassination of the king's father, murder of his regent, and slaying of his grandfather.[56] *Hamlet* therefore "incorporated the many violent deaths surrounding James" via a strategy of "distantiation," Schmitt writes, by "pretending to be about something very different from what is really at stake." The purpose of this "insulating layer" was to prevent "the fire of real life from consuming itself."[57] The meaning of that phrase is itself opaque, and complicates the critic's depreciation of the aesthetic. But it is hard not to detect the implied analogy between Schmitt and Shakespeare, as authors compelled to "timidly maneuver" around an "unalterable reality" of state violence, the "mute rock" on which their projects smashed, "sending the foam of genuine tragedy rushing to the surface" (45).

What Benjamin and Schmitt share is a notion of tragic Stuart drama as a "shroud to cover the horror of the execution of one sovereign by another."[58] So, like the dumb show that precedes "The Mousetrap," Shakespeare appears to share "a realm of human innocence" with his Player, but he is in fact a prisoner of his "barbaric and elemental" time, which "breaks into the time of the play" like the iceberg that sank the *Titanic* (45). Sovereign, in this special pleading, is the audience of courtiers, whose "concrete presence" (35) at the Globe dictates to the captive writer, because it is in the know about crimes he evades out of "political considerations" (48). *Hamlet* can thus legitimate Schmitt's own "jump beyond the limits of legality," for there is a parallel, he insinuates, between the "national emergency" that destroyed the Weimar Republic and the "crisis and catastrophe" that devoured the Stuarts.[59] What the book never mentions is that the initiated would also know how James became Elizabeth's heir by conniving in the killing of his real mother, and so climbing over the dead bodies of *both* his parents:

> . . . so, after Pyrrhus' pause,
> A rousèd vengeance sets him new a-work;
> And never did the Cyclops' hammers fall
> On Mars his armour, forged for proof eterne,
> With less remorse than Pyrrhus' bleeding sword
> Now falls on Priam.
>
> —*Hamlet*, 2.2.467–72

Schmitt's activist reading of *Hamlet*, as a tragedy in which Shakespeare endorsed the cruel necessity of "the expulsion of the Stuarts" from "the stage of history" (62), cries out to be viewed in light of his own refusal to disavow genocide or submit to denazification. For "What is Mary to him, or he to Mary?" we might ask. When he shrugs that "Many things are sad. One can weep for many things" (45), but Hamlet "does not weep for Hecuba" (42), it is therefore important to remember that this conveyancer of the camps "never made a single statement admitting his complicity in the crimes of the Third Reich, nor did he ever express any empathy for its victims."[60] In fact, one can only guess what the old Nazi made of the Player's portrait of Hamlet's favorite mass murderer, "With blood of fathers, mothers, daughters, sons, / Baked and impasted," as "senseless Ilium, / Seeming to feel his blow, with flaming top / Stoops to his base" (2.2.132–56). These lines echo Marlowe's about Pyrrhus burning Troy's "topless towers."[61] But as Richard Marienstras pointed out in his searing 2001 introduction to Shakespearean tragedy, after Auschwitz any such allusion to the Trojan holocaust signified the Shoah.[62] For post-war readers, the "bloodboltered shambles" in *Hamlet* had become the "forecast of the concentration camp" that James Joyce said it would.[63] And the callousness with which the Black Prince insists the "sudden death" to which he condemns his university friends Rosencrantz and Guildenstern is "not near my conscience" (5.2.47–59) does seem to match the cold-blooded realism with which Schmitt's Stuart-centered concept of tragedy "distantiates" the "casual slaughter" (326) of history's truly "innocent victims."[64]

There is a chilling passage in *Hamlet or Hecuba* when James' most "intelligent defender" is said to be "Isaak Disraeli, the father of the famous Benjamin," who argued that if the king had won a battle "he would be as respected as Frederick the Great" (29). This sneer at Jewish intellectuals suggests that in Schmitt's mind the self-styled *Rex Pacificus*, who "destroyed the sacred substance of the kingdom by indulging in endless disputation," rather than fighting "on a field of historical action," stands for Weimar's politicians, the beneficiaries of a similar wartime stab in the back. Thus, Shakespeare devised his play to urge his royal patron "not to squander the divine right in reflections and discussions," just as Schmitt prodded Hindenburg to rule by diktat. But only at the Globe, in the shape of Hamlet, could the misbegotten James "die like a king," in this retelling.[65] Here Schmitt was giving the tragedy a protagonist who acts as decisively as the "warlike" pirates he encounters (4.6.13), when he affirms that Fortinbras "has my dying voice" in the "election" of a successor (5.2.297–8). This "election" is said to affirm "the old blood right" of monarchy; but more importantly for Hitler's solicitor, it prefigures the arbitrary fiat by which Cromwell nominated his son Richard to succeed him, subject to "the acclamation of the attendant masses" (58–9). For Schmitt, Hamlet became the great decider. The Fascist ideologue is thereby co-opting Shakespeare to his lifelong campaign for plebiscitary dictatorship, as a form of "direct democracy" that "can express the will of the people" better than the "gruesome comic fantasy" of parliament.[66]

As "The soldiers' music and the rites of war / Speak loudly for him" (343–4), Schmitt's Siegfried-like Hamlet finally attains tragic status, as the mythic mobilizer of a militarized *völk*. So, the stakes could not be higher, as philosopher Roberto Esposito explains: "The end of sovereignty, sanctioned by the revolutionary fall of the royal head, was simply an act in a process" that reduces "human beings to things," and it is this reification that makes democracies vulnerable to surrogates of "the absent sovereignty," of which "Fascism represents the most aggressive form."[67] In his 2011 book *The Royal Remains* Eric Santner therefore spells out the ramifications of such a revanchism for understanding how Shakespearean tragedy dramatizes in its very overload the "fundamental impasse" that "putting the People in place of the King cannot ultimately be done."[68]

The "too-muchness" of Shakespeare's play functions as a sort of archive that registers a fundamental mutation in the body politic . . . It is thus for very good reason that the time of *Hamlet* was a period when the doctrine of the King's Two Bodies had reached a sort of crisis point, which became decisive for the future of the institution of kingship over the next centuries. It is these mutations that allowed for the execution of Charles I and of Louis XVI when the "People" asserted themselves, and came to embody the head of their own body politic.[69]

For Santner, Shakespeare's tragedies expose the catch in the incarnational idea that "the King never dies," which is that the "sublimity and horror of the pompous body of the king do not disappear from the world once the place of the royal personage has been emptied," but return "in a world without kings but only 'People' and their leaders," with the populism of the Terror and the pogrom.[70] The "bare life" to which humanity is degraded in *Hamlet, King Lear*, or *Macbeth* is here said to illustrate the analysis developed by Giorgio Agamben out of Schmitt and Foucault, that "the camp is the space that is opened when the state of exception begins to become the rule" through the *biopolitics* that is the mode of power after kings.[71] Or, as the French theorist lectured, "Shakespearean tragedy dwells on the wound . . . inflicted on the body of the kingdom when kings die violent deaths," because this "modern kind of theatre" foreshadows the "governmentality" of extralegal "Hitlerian nights, of the Night of the Long Knives."[72]

Kantorowicz's "study of medieval political theology" has been taken to be an antidote to Schmitt.[73] Because it was associated with his genuflecting 1927 bestseller on the Hohenstaufen emperor Frederick II, the work had for long been dismissed by Shakespeareans as yet another legitimation of the *Führerprinzip*.[74] But Kantorowicz's 1957 book now appears to have "inverted Schmitt's political theology," as here the doctrine of the incarnation is said to be "a liberating fiction" that sanctifies the office above its holder. Whereas the Nazi jurist invested the dictator with divine power, Kantorowicz is therefore felt to have "restored the emancipatory function of law: to create fictions that remove man" from such absolutism.[75] For while Schmitt stressed the *theology* in "political theology," and the real *presence* of the king's corporeal body, Kantorowicz came in the second half of his interrupted career, spent as a Jewish exile in Oxford, Berkeley, and Princeton, to valorize the *political* or *representative* body of the corporation. So, in his account, Macbeth's intimation that his life is "but a walking shadow, a poor player" (*Macbeth*, 5.5.23) condensed the revolutionary revelation that "the 'head' of the body politic which, after all, was a mortal individual man, was of minor importance as compared to the immortal body corporate." *Capital* authority was never to be confused with that of the *capo*, as Schmitt termed Wallenstein, the incumbent head of state, "That struts and frets his hour upon the stage, / And then is heard no more" (24–5).[76]

"Show his eyes and grieve his heart, / Come like shadows, so depart": when Macbeth's Witches posed "A show of eight kings" before James, at a gala performance in 1606, the "last with a glass" reflected into his face the sovereign's signature metaphor of the mirror as a "Crystal through which you may see the heart of your King."[77] But this eighth Stuart was the Medusa-like mother *James had helped to murder*. So, as they "conjure up the uncanny ghostly procession" of a line that stretches "to the crack of doom" (4.1.126–33), Kantorowicz observes, these Witches do the same as English lawyers, by projecting the Crown as a "mystical person," whose present head is disposable in the onward march of "the immortal body."[78] No wonder, then, that Macbeth exclaims, "Thy crown sears my eyeballs!" (128); for like the looking-glass the king shatters in *Richard II*, Mary's mirror flashes the mortal message to the monarch that "A brittle glory shineth in this face. / As brittle as the glory is the face" (4.1.277). By repeatedly rehearsing the scenario of the killing of the king, Shakespeare's historical tragedies thereby memorialize the moral that "Uneasy lies the head that wears the crown" (*2 Henry IV*, 3.1.31). Thus, far from deifying the Stuart dynasty, the doctrine that "The body is with the King, but the King is not with the body. The King is a thing . . . of nothing" (*Hamlet*, 4.2.25), would be sharpened in these plays into the legal weapon to cut off the uneasy head of James' son, when the regicides pushed to its logical conclusion what Kantorowicz describes as "that most unpleasant idea of the violent separation of the King's Two Bodies":

> Without those distinctions. . . it would have been impossible for Parliament to summon, in the name of Charles I, King body politic, the armies which were to fight the same Charles I, king body natural . . . Nor can the fiction of the King's Two Bodies be thought of apart from the events when Parliament succeeded in trying "Charles Stuart" for high treason, and finally in executing solely the king's body natural without doing irreparable harm to the King's body politic—in contradistinction with the events in France, in 1793.[79]

The entire critique of Shakespearean tragedy depends, in *The King's Two Bodies*, on the distinction Kantorowicz draws between the guillotining of Louis XVI and the separation of the Crown from the head of Charles I. But here the historian's own disturbing ambivalence towards authoritarianism supplies a lesson in the problem Shakespearean tragedy poses, about the difficulty of making a "due decision," when "strokes arbitrate" such "unsure hopes" (*Macbeth*, 5.4.17–20), and this must give us pause. For after the Nazis had dismissed him from his university post, Kantorowicz declared that in such a state of emergency individuals are unimportant, since "'the empire transcends the individual,' and I would be the last one to contradict that."[80] "When I think of what lies ahead for Germany that Jew thing is not so important," shrugged the biographer of Frederick II.[81] Likewise, Benjamin thought *Hamlet* "positively demands" a dictatorship; and Schmitt heard in James' saying that a king is "set on a stage," a surrender to the "huge machine" of modern statehood.[82] Kantorowicz saw that submission in Shakespeare's metaphor of the monarch as "a mockery king of snow, / Standing before the sun. . . To melt away" (*Richard II*, 4.1.260–2); which he viewed as a premonition of "England's revolutionary history," and "the Martyrdom of the Blessed King Charles I." This royal "sun-imagery reflects the splendor of the catastrophe," he wrote.[83] But as Andreas Höfele remarks in his book *No Hamlets*, "a much more sinister sun rises" from Kantorowicz's account of the transit "from sun to sun" (50) in Shakespeare.[84] For the authority behind this interpretation was a 1939 edition of *Richard II*, where the editor John Dover Wilson had specifically noted how "the sun-image dominates the play as the swastika dominates the Nazi gathering."[85]

CHAPTER FIVE

Religion, Ritual and Myth

Continuity and Change

PAUL INNES

Religion, ritual, and myth are so intertwined in this period that it is often difficult to differentiate among them. One person's religion can be another's myth or superstition, particularly in a climate of constant change, reformation, and sectarian warfare, and familiar later modern concepts such as the separation of church and state simply do not exist in early modern Europe. In England, socially contested connections such as that between the monarch and the established church can produce far-ranging ramifications, so much so that it can be almost impossible at times to separate religious matters from the political.[1]

Tragedy as a form is especially sensitive to waves of socio-political upheaval, and many factors play a part. The status of the tragic protagonist as a personage of high social standing renders the role pivotal in negotiating such difficult and changing terrain.[2] In addition, the vexed relationship between the stage and the authorities flavors not just the writing of a text as dramatic script but the specific circumstances under which it is performed. The dynamic that results is not simply a reflective correspondence between socially produced religious anxieties and the drama; instead, plays often manage and even contribute actively to the various debates. A case in point is the reception of Middleton's satirical comedy *A Game At Chess* (1624), an intervention in its own right in the political row over a potential Spanish match for the heir to the throne.[3] Here Middleton is simply applying a formula for stage success that is derived from a whole host of other comedies and tragedies set in Catholic countries such as Spain and Italy, from Kyd's Elizabethan play *The Spanish Tragedy* (c. 1587) through to the Jacobean vogue for complex multiple plotlines in similar locations. *The Duchess of Malfi* (c. 1612) and *The White Devil* (1612) by John Webster, *The Changeling* (1622) by Middleton and Rowley, *The Revenger's Tragedy* (1606) by Middleton and Tourneur, and Middleton's own *Women Beware Women* (c. 1623) are all inflected by religious and social conflict, especially in terms of their consumption by English metropolitan audiences. A taste for salacious details projected onto other cultures, especially Catholic ones, results at one level in the emergence of well-known stage stereotypes such as the Machiavel and malcontent.[4] Figures like these, however, are symptoms of a fundamental anxiety about religion and politics, and this is just in terms of internal Western European Christian faction-fighting.[5] The situation becomes even more complex when taking into account representations of other religions such as Islam or Judaism, however hazily conceived they may be.

Religion shades over into ritual because of still-fresh cultural memories of a very recent shared Catholic past. This is only to be expected, since the rites of the old religion permeated society for such a long time. The response of the dramatists is again complexly multi-faceted. For example, there is the aspiring man who reaches too far in the form of Marlowe's Faustus, who enacts a series of perverse magical rituals that parody conventional Christian practices. This play could be interpreted as a liminal or transitional text, one that very precisely dramatizes a serious problem of religious faith during the movement from Roman Catholicism to Anglicanism in England: how does one manage the traditional figure of the devil in this situation? Moreover, some of the plays move well beyond Christianity to imagine how the rituals of other religions might have been performed. The Roman past provides just such an opportunity, which is unsurprising given the weight attached to its historical and cultural status. The action in Shakespeare's *Titus Andronicus* (*c*. 1592) is driven by the patrician general's sacrifice of Alarbus, the eldest son of the Queen of the Goths, at the tomb of his own deceased sons. The execution of Alarbus is carried out when he is dragged by the surviving sons of Titus down through the trapdoor in the middle of the stage, a very precise use of the underworld associations derived from a long tradition of medieval drama. Similar points could be made about the function of the stage trapdoor elsewhere in the same play, when Demetrius and Chiron throw the body of Bassianus into a pit in 2.3, followed almost immediately with Quintus and Martius Andronicus falling into the same dank hole. *Hamlet* (1599) makes even more use of the understage location at key moments, underscoring the relationship between the trapdoor and the underworld as visual and auditory reminders of that play's obsession with the earth and what is beneath it. The Ghost shouts up at Hamlet (1.5.151), leading to what a later culture would call a metatheatrical moment when Hamlet refers to "this fellow in the cellarage" a couple of lines later (1.5.153). More famously, the graveyard scene (5.1) functions entirely by focusing attention on the trapdoor, with the dark comedy of the gravediggers, the appearance of Ophelia's funeral cortege, and the physical struggle between Hamlet and Laertes in what is supposed to be the space for Ophelia's coffin. This trapdoor location is also presumably how the hellmouth that swallows Faustus in Marlowe's play is raised onto the stage floor so that he can be cast into it in a physical enactment of his damnation.[6]

Perhaps even more importantly, tragedy itself has a socially important ritual function. C.L. Barber established a critical definition of the social function of Shakespearean comedy as a form of ritual in the late 1950s.[7] However, from the inception of the Athenian dramatic festivals, the association between comedy and tragedy has often been a very close one.[8] Emphasis upon their common social origin gained prominence with the publication of René Girard's book *Violence and the Sacred* in 1977.[9] His book reasserted the ritualistic functions of tragedy, and with hindsight could be seen as a major part of what might be termed an anthropological turn in literary historical studies.[10] In some instances this has linked with a materialist emphasis on ritual as both potentially constitutive of the social order, and also subversive.[11] Situating tragedy within the overall context of the social milieu within which it is produced and performed, these works analyze the ways in which its various constitutive elements work to purge the system originally defined by Aristotle. In particular, the cathartic function of the tragic protagonist as scapegoat comes in for a great deal of attention, linked with Aristotle's concept of *catharsis*, which is often understood as a socially dynamic function as well as an individual one; in this respect a tragic sacrifice is necessary for the dramatic resolution to take place.[12]

Just as religion can shade over into ritual in early modern drama, both can impinge upon the terrain of myth. Broadly speaking, two main aspects can be most easily recognized. The first follows on logically enough from the social rituals associated in the first instance with comedy, and this is the area of folklore, or, more precisely, what might be termed medieval myth. In tragedy, this can take the form of figures such as the Weird Sisters in *Macbeth* (1606), who have been variously interpreted. They can be seen as devilish or satanic, which is certainly the most easily available set of meanings in Shakespeare's period, especially given the reference to King James' own witch-hunts in Scotland. They could also be described as descendants of something like the Norns from Norse mythology, or their Greek equivalents, the Fates. At any rate, they certainly combine elements from all of these strands of myth and folklore.[13] Northrop Frye is often mentioned as the major figure in a movement to locate Shakespeare's comedies in a pattern of folklore and mythic remembrance.[14] His emergence was almost contemporaneous with the publication in 1965 in Western Europe of the Polish academic Jan Kott's highly influential book *Shakespeare Our Contemporary*, with its profound effect on productions of Shakespeare.[15] Kott's work is notable for the ways in which it suggests that an almost Jungian mythic unconscious lies underneath all of Shakespeare's plays; it was also immensely important in providing a treatment of folklore elements that could be useful for productions of Shakespeare's tragedies.

The second area of correspondence between religion and ritual on the one hand and myth on the other comes in the form of direct references or allusions to classical Western myth, usually in the form of short scenes within plays.[16] Even so, there is a further element to myth in early modern drama, and that is how tragedy in particular can function as a form of myth-making in its own right. This is especially notable in plays where the sacrifice, to use a Girardian vocabulary, results in a newly re-established social order. In effect, plays such as Shakespeare's *Coriolanus* (1608) or *Antony and Cleopatra* (1606) reconstitute the Roman state by means of a foundation myth. In the case of *Coriolanus*, his death can be seen as the necessary prelude to the emergence of the mixed constitution of the Roman Republic, while the destruction of Antony and Cleopatra heralds the new era of the Roman Empire.[17] Classical history and myth are accordingly intermingled, and the result, at least in the case of *Antony and Cleopatra*, is a play whose figures have attained a mythic status all of their own, especially given the afterlife of Cleopatra.

RELIGION

Marlowe begins *Dr Faustus* with a set-piece scene that is typical of his staging practice. The protagonist speaks a soliloquy in which he runs through various types of learning, from the humanities and medicine through to law, dismissing each in turn. He then comes to the Christian religion:

> When all is done, divinity is best;
> Jerome's Bible, Faustus, view it well.
> *Stipendium peccati, mors est*. Ha! *Stipendium, etc.*,
> The reward of sin is death? That's hard.
> *Si peccasse, negamus, fallimur, et nulla est in nobis veritas.*
> If we say that we have no sin
> We deceive ourselves, and there is no truth in us.
> Why then belike we must sin,
> And so consequently die.
> Ay, we must die, an everlasting death.

What doctrine call you this: *Che sera, sera.*
"What will be, shall be." Divinity, adieu!

—1.1.37–48

As with the other forms of learning, Faustus reacts against this one, noting that it is a hard doctrine. However, his decision is not simply predicated upon the difficulty of the Christian life; lurking beneath his rhetorical display is a specific type of Protestant teaching, that of Calvinist predestination.[18] His learning and knowledge of Latin permit him to be able to read Jerome's bible for himself, without needing any mediator such as a priest. Despite his supposedly great knowledge, he reacts against the Bible emotionally, and what this moment stages is the "aspiring man's" inability to move fully beyond the sphere of the emotions. He dissects the injunction against sin with forensic precision, choosing to rely upon one type of Christian doctrine to rationalize his predisposition to pleasure. One of the most disconcerting aspects of this play is the uses to which Faustus puts the power he gains via his infernal pact; they all seem rather pointless and mundane, and Mephistopheles quite rightly realizes that the best way to keep Faustus in his power is to distract him constantly with fresh entertainment.[19] Indeed, the soliloquy points to this propensity from the outset, with Faustus employing an inverted logic of heavenly necromantic books, an oxymoron that fits well with his inability to move beyond his desires. This initial scene therefore concentrates in extreme form a whole series of religious issues, and the figure of Faustus serves almost as a metonym for a whole range of crucial contemporary debates between Catholic and Protestant, different kinds of Protestantism, and ultimately between reason and belief.

All of these issues provide fertile ground for tragedy in this period, because of the ways in which they contradict and conflict with one another. Many plays directly take advantage of the potential afforded by religious issues to construct the necessary tragic dilemma that drives their plot devices. However, dramatists have to be very careful here because they are dealing with such explosive material, which explains why Shakespeare, for example, never uses the term "Bible," preferring the more neutral "book" in plays such as *All Is True* (1613; more commonly known as *Henry VIII*). English playwrights take advantage of their audiences' fascination with the supposed excesses of Catholic cultures to investigate various facets of religious debate. Many early modern tragedies are set in recognizably accessible locations such as Spain, Italy, or France, and not simply because of the availability of source material in the form of novellas or recent events. The geographical displacement technique enables the plays to dramatize the ways in which supposedly Christian personages of high social standing nevertheless act in ways that are represented as utterly corrupt.

Many of Marlowe's plays, for example, are saturated with imagery and characters who break the boundaries of what might be considered normal behavior, precisely because they are located at the edge of what is possible. In this respect, the horrific events of *The Massacre at Paris* (1593), despite the rather fragmentary nature of the text that has survived, demonstrate an early modern English fascination with the "Machiavellian" dealings of the French royalty and nobility. It is almost as though a cultural obsession with this type of behavior is driven by a need to focus upon as many sordid details as possible, because the context of Catholic piety is so much in contradiction with the doings of the various characters. This fascination carries through to later plays such as Cyril Tourneur's *The Atheist's Tragedy* (c. 1607), which is not so much about religion in and of itself; rather, what is explored is the contradiction between a fundamentally religious society on the one hand and the actions of one of its most highly placed members on the other.

Plays do not always draw attention to themselves in this way, however; rather than advertising aspects of religion in their titles so as to seduce potential playgoers, they often incorporate religious elements into what are otherwise secular plotlines. This is not simply a way of adding local flavor; it can often be incorporated in ways that subtly foreshadow later plot developments. An example comes right at the beginning of *The Changeling* by Middleton and Rowley:

> 'Twas in the temple where I first beheld her,
> And now again the same. What omen yet
> Follows of that? None but imaginary:
> Why should my hopes or fate be timorous?
> The place is holy, so is my intent:
> I love her beauties to the holy purpose,
> And that, methinks, admits comparison
> With man's first creation, the place blest,
> And is his right home back, if he achieve it.
> The church hath first begun our interview,
> And that's the place must join us into one
> So there's beginning, and perfection too.
>
> —1.1.1–12

As with *Dr Faustus*, this play begins in soliloquy; unlike the earlier play, the speech is relatively short. It is also delivered by one of several of the more important characters in a play that is structured more by the ensemble than by means of a single main protagonist. It would be tempting to suggest a generational difference here between Elizabethan and Jacobean drama, but of course many of the plays from the earlier part of the period require large numbers of characters. What does seem to be Jacobean here, though (the play was first performed in 1622, although it was not published until 1653), is the breathy hint of corruption in the subtle linkage between "temple" and "church." Even though Alsemero directly describes himself in morally upright terms to the audience, his Spanish Catholic culture is undermined by its association with a pagan past. Beatrice-Joanna is about to come on and say to the audience how much she is attracted to him, and the force of her desire is what will propel the action of the play. Alsemero's use of the word "interview" mingles a sense of their mutual perception of each other, but the play goes on to demonstrate that his freedom to act upon his desire as a man is entirely different from the options open to Beatrice-Joanna as a woman circumscribed by the patriarchal will of her father.[20] A sense of idolatry lingers around Alsemero's initial description of her, layering the male gaze with unsettling associations of problematic Catholic imagery for the English Protestant audience. A very specific cultural logic is at work here, one that can be seen in other texts from the early modern period such as the figure of Archimago in Book One of Spenser's *The Faerie Queene* (Book One was initially published in 1590). The conflation of Catholicism and idolatry with a negative representation of paganism leads, in the case of Spenser's sprawling romance, to a characterization that is strikingly similar in its connotations to that of Faustus in Marlowe's play.

The Friar in Shakespeare's *Romeo and Juliet* (1595) is by contrast seemingly benign, at least on the surface, as he tries to help the two lovers, and it is hardly his fault that his instructions to the exiled Romeo end up lost in transit.[21] However, openly anti-Catholic prejudice can take an even more extreme form in Jacobean drama when cardinals take the stage. The phlegmatic Cardinal in Webster's *The Duchess of Malfi* kills his mistress Julia by getting her to kiss a bible smeared with poison (5.2.272) and his counterpart Cardinal Monticelso in *The White Devil*, also by John Webster, is very much a Renaissance prince who becomes Pope. Excessive details such as poison-by-Bible are the stock-in-trade of the successful Jacobean tragedian, and such emblematic details constitute a concentrated visual representation of the cultures being enacted and produced for the London stage.

The uses of religion become rather imprecise when it comes to non-Christian characters. Othello's religion seems to be a relatively minor part of his situation, which is much more fully one of cultural alienation. One would expect a perhaps more rounded representation of his Islamic faith because he is Moorish, but in fact he seems to inhabit a much more liminal world reminiscent of the outrageous tales of travelers. This is especially true of his rhetorical description of how he won Desdemona (1.3.129–70), as well as his fanciful tales about the handkerchief that comes to emblematize his jealousy (3.4.57–70). In other words, his "otherness" is racial and cultural first and foremost, rather than religious, and his tragedy is produced by an inability to comprehend the insinuations of Iago for what they are.[22] This places Othello on the receiving end of a typical stage Machiavel's manipulations, in much the same way as occurs in other plays set in the Catholic world.

What this suggests, of course, is that early modern English playwrights mostly had a very nebulous knowledge of religions other than Christianity, at least for the most part. As with Othello, Aaron in *Titus Andronicus* is represented as Moorish, but quite what this means in the context of a play set in the mid-to-late Roman Empire is at best unclear. In fact, the play is extremely inexact and inconsistent with regard to religion throughout, moving from the sacrifice of Alarbus at the beginning through to the moment when Lucius Andronicus is presented with Aaron as a prisoner by one of the Goths:

> Renowned Lucius, from our troops I strayed
> To gaze upon a ruinous monastery,
> And as I earnestly did fix mine eye
> Upon the wasted building, suddenly
> I heard a child cry underneath a wall.
>
> —5.1.20–4

Lucius is in the process of returning to Rome at the head of a Gothic army loyal to himself, and here one of the soldiers says that he wanted to be a tourist. This seems rather strange because it plays against the stereotype of the marauding Goths; after all, they would go on to sack Rome in a later generation. The ruins to which he refers are more a part of early modern England than the scenery of the Roman Empire, especially in a period before Christianity became the official religion of the Roman state. This peculiar moment is both odd and specific, being loaded with all sorts of cultural associations derived from the recent religious past of Shakespeare's England, and the anachronism seems rather unsettling. However, what matters for Shakespeare's audiences is that the past is made familiar by means of recognizable description, and this seems much more important than historical accuracy as such.[23]

Unlike these previous examples, Jewish figures tend to be presented in a much more forthright manner, at least insofar as attention is focused on their culture and religion. Shakespeare's Shylock has often been turned into something of a tragic protagonist, which is hardly surprising given the history of the twentieth century in particular. Such maneuvers, however, raise the issue of how the English viewed Judaism in the early modern period, particularly since there were relatively few well-known Jewish figures in the country at all.[24] Representations such as that of Barabas in Marlowe's *The Jew of Malta* (c. 1589) are therefore based on a paucity of direct information, and so can be considered more of a displaced imagining of possibilities. This is borne out by the way that Marlowe's play is introduced by the ghost of Machiavelli, as a way of contextualizing the behavior of Barabas that is about to be unleashed upon the audience. The message seems to be that the culturally liminal figure of the Jewish merchant makes him a very effective stage Machiavel, and the interest of the audience becomes focused on his various machinations, some of which require very impressive special effects. As with *Othello* (1603–4), Marlowe's earlier play picks up on the extreme military threat posed by the Ottoman Empire to the Christian powers in the Mediterranean, imbricating Christianity, Islam, and Judaism into a historically precise structural relationship. None of the religions seems to be ethically preferable to any of the others in *The Jew of Malta*, and many of the representatives of each of them are deeply hypocritical and power-hungry. It could be argued that Barabas is perfectly placed to show just how embroiled in the sordid world of war and politics the religions can be, despite each of their claims to be interested ultimately in spirituality. In keeping with the logic of the tragic dilemma, however, it is this powerful position that becomes his undoing.[25] In terms of stage presentation, his sheer vitality and the enjoyment of his role mark him out as an early modern updating of the old *Vice* figure, and his exuberant plotting centers the audience's attention upon him in a quite extraordinary way.[26] Barabas therefore owes as much to popular playgoing expectations and stock character types as he does to early modern conceptions of Judaism, however racially inflected they may be.

RITUAL

Religious rituals are perhaps those most obviously and easily available for use onstage in a cultural so obsessed with religion and factional debate. However, this very fact makes it rather dangerous terrain, since too blatant a use of religious ritual can draw the unwelcome attention of the authorities. Such a sensitive subject needs to be dealt with delicately, which on the face of it seems rather strange. However, a major element of Protestantism, which comes about as a result of the return to purely scriptural authority, is a distrust of the rituals that emerged over the long history of the Catholic church. Given that so many early modern tragedies are set in Catholic countries, this presents the playwrights with something of an opportunity and, at the same time, a quandary: how best to take advantage of the meanings to be generated by Catholic ritual in such circumstances?

A safe way to do this is to allude to the ritual, rather than risk showing it directly, as happens, for example, in *Romeo and Juliet*. A full onstage representation might run the risk of seeming blasphemous, which is not a good idea in a period of intense religious conflict. Accordingly, Shakespeare here takes advantage of a standard early modern staging technique, the representation of offstage events.[27] This permits him handily to shorthand an important plot development without having to show a Catholic wedding onstage—and Protestant London is very sensitive to representations of the Catholic sacraments. This enables the playwright to make use of the meaning of the ritual without going down the dangerous route of showing it as possibly something of value, and in any case the Friar's intervention will ultimately end in disaster.

Marriage as a whole is in fact very amenable to this sort of treatment, because in spite of its enduring status and power as an institution, the definition of what constitutes a legal marriage can be rather imprecise. An equally important marriage moment occurs in *The Duchess of Malfi*, when Webster stages what is effectively a marriage ritual at 1.2.266–399. Alone with Antonio, the Duchess puns on marriage and husbandry with him, then chooses him as her husband in a way that seems more like some forms of English Protestant practice than those of Catholic Italy. The dramatic impact is reinforced by juxtaposition with her brothers' warning, not to think about remarrying without their advice. The Duchess's waiting-woman Cariola is then revealed as having secretly been present all along, thus making her the witness to a binding compact, even without a religious personage officiating.[28] Cariola's comment to the audience when she is briefly left onstage alone immediately afterwards is illuminating:

> Whether the spirit of greatness, or of woman
> Reign most in her, I know not, but it shows
> A fearful madness: I owe her much of pity.
>
> —1.2.417–20

This is a crucial observation. Cariola is well aware of the political implications of lineage; even though the Duchess is entitled to act as she will, the realities of Italian power politics dictate that she should not in fact do so. The implications of the term "Reign" are significant because they load this marriage with overtones of political tragedy. By taking agency for herself, the Duchess places herself in serious jeopardy, and this constitutes the tragedy for her.[29]

The revenge enacted upon the Duchess of Malfi by her brothers the Cardinal and Duke Ferdinand accordingly has a consistent social dynamic. They represent the twin elements of Italian patriarchal power in the state and the church. Although the Duchess makes a personal choice in her marriage to Antonio, the rest of the play goes on to show a society that is constituted in such a way that she cannot be allowed to act like this, and so must be destroyed. This is why Ferdinand in particular wants to makes sure not only that his sister is psychologically tortured and then killed, but that her children by Antonio are also murdered.

The social world constructed by tragedies like Webster's has to be seen to be reasonably coherent to function effectively. However, religious ritual and its ramifications are only two elements from a range of possibilities. The relationship between religion and politics provides more examples of ritual observations, perhaps as a result of the long-standing use of religious ritual in political life—yet another instance of the indivisibility of the two in this period. A major developing issue in England is the fact that, after Henry VIII breaks from Rome, the monarch is the Head of the Church of England as well as being head of state. King Henry famously speaks about "ceremony" in his major set-piece soliloquy the night before Agincourt in Shakespeare's *Henry V* at 4.1.207–61 (1599). Of course, this has to be seen in the context of his having met with some of the common soldiers immediately beforehand, but even so, the speech draws attention to the ritualistic elements of kingship.

As with religious ceremonies and rituals, the downfall of royalty could seem to present the playwrights with some excellent opportunities for tragic writing and stage productions. However, again as with religion, they have to be very careful, because it is not always a good idea in such a politically complex and sensitive society to show the death of a king directly on the stage. This is why Shakespeare is so circumspect in showing the killing of the king in *Richard II*, having him die facing his executioners with a dagger in his hand rather than simply being slaughtered out of hand. Marlowe, however, is far less subtle in his staging of the king's death in *Edward II* at 5.5; it can be quite startling in performance as a red-hot poker is forced through the king's rectum in a horrific parody of the male homosexual act. Another variation has even a usurper like Macbeth being killed offstage. What all of these instances have in common is an unwillingness to dramatize the direct spilling of a monarch's blood.

There may be an underlying reason for the variety of choices made by the playwrights when killing royalty, and that is the residual feeling that a monarch is a semi-sacred personage. Certainly, the rituals associated with the coronation give the highest position in the land something of a sacral or sacramental flavor, and even early modern Protestant rulers of England retain such a semblance due to their insistence on being Head of the Church of England (or, in Elizabeth's case, "Governor" because of her problematic status as a woman). The symbolic power of the coronation ritual is invoked in Shakespeare's *Richard II* (1595) when the king inverts it at (5.6); the fact that Richard is able to stage it in this way demonstrates the residual visual and emblematic effects of the crowning spectacle.

This goes on to cause them some serious problems, including some revolutionary wars, not to mention a bout of regicide, when the faultlines of conflict along political and religious contours become too wide. There is a great deal to be exploited here for purposes of dramatic spectacle, but of course there is much more to it than this, since the social function of tragedy requires a scapegoat figure—and a monarch is an especially useful example of the type.

In *Julius Caesar* (1599), the conspirators (especially Brutus) repeatedly represent their target in sacrificial terms:

> Our course will seem too bloody, Caius Cassius,
> To cut the head off and then hack the limbs—
> Like wrath in death and envy afterwards—
> For Antony is but a limb of Caesar.
> Let's be sacrificers but not butchers, Caius.
>
> —2.1.161–5

As with the later *Duchess of Malfi*, there is a crucial political element to all of this, as evidenced by Cassius' suggestion just prior to this extract from an important speech by Brutus. As an astute operator, Cassius wants Caesar's lieutenant Antony killed as well. Brutus' well-known refusal comes in the midst of a discussion of how best to proceed with the conspiracy, immediately after he has agreed to join it. However, his language of sacrifice—"Let's carve him as a dish fit for the gods" (2.1.1172)—eventually seems rather empty when it comes to the stabbing frenzy that ends Caesar's life. Even here, though, there is a ritualistic element, as the conspirators bathe their hands and arms in the dead man's blood (3.1.105) before parading themselves to the citizenry. This scene operates in several ways at the same time, enacting a complex series of associations of "blooding" from the hunt, together with the symbolic uniting of the conspirators by means of an emblematic badging of their arms with the dead dictator's life force. It also plays upon the almost taboo aspect of showing a dead king's blood on stage as noted previously. Shakespeare's play manages to invoke the horror of doing so while at the same time perhaps suggesting that Caesar was in fact not aiming at the kingship—otherwise his death could not be staged in this way.

Paying attention to the wider implications of these tragic events inevitably leads to a consideration of the social function of tragedy as a form. To some extent this goes against a very long tradition that reads tragedy purely in terms of the individual, especially the so-called "tragic flaw." A broader view would contest the suggestion that tragedy is something inherent to the individual, and in fact has a ritual purpose in its own right. However, as any high school or college English major somehow "knows," Macbeth's downfall stems from his ambition, as does that of Caesar. Othello is destroyed by his jealousy, Hamlet by his inability to act, and Lear by his willful blindness—and this is just to mention a handful of Shakespeare plays. Usually this critical position is ascribed to an Aristotelian understanding of character, but close attention to what Aristotle wrote, as opposed to making some assumptions about his work, shows that he dismisses characterization almost out of hand:

> Dramatic action, therefore, is not with a view to the representation of character: character comes in as subsidiary to the actions. Hence the incidents and the plot are the end of a tragedy; and the end is the chief thing of all. Again, without action there cannot be a tragedy; there may be without character.
>
> —Book VI[30]

Aristotle insists on the primacy of the plot in action; the characters, and this includes the protagonist, are vehicles for the events and are therefore subsidiary. There are two rather startling implications to be drawn from Aristotle here. The first is that tragedy is absolutely not produced by an individual; and the second, logically enough, is that his work has been consistently misunderstood. The problem can be firmly centered in his concept of *hamartia*, which has been used to underpin the meanings assumed to exist in the concept of the tragic flaw—in fact, "tragic flaw" has become synonymous with *hamartia*, almost a translation of it. But if characterization has no primacy, then it is possible to recognize that *hamartia* has a whole range of socially produced meanings, which have been obscured by an insistence on the primacy of the tragic individual.

Accordingly, *Macbeth* is located at the critical fissure of a state structure that requires powerful warriors at the periphery, because the king is weak. *Julius Caesar* dramatizes what happens in the state once the monarchical figure is brutally removed, as a struggle erupts over who will succeed him. Othello is a liminal figure who is needed for war by a state that otherwise sees him as an outsider. Hamlet is caught in a socially constructed double-bind, as the requirement to kill his father's murderer will lead to him committing regicide. And Lear is a king who crucially misunderstands the power structure that underpins royalty; by dividing the kingdom, he inevitably destroys himself, not to mention the wider effects on everyone around him—a king who fails as a king. It is therefore possible to recast *hamartia* as a form of tragic dilemma in the purest sense, and as a form it requires the ritual purgation of these high-status victims so that the state can be remade anew. This is a much richer understanding of the term than one that seeks to reduce it to the purely personal alone.[31]

MYTH

The folklore aspect of myth can be encountered easily in tragedies such as Shakespeare's *King Lear*, which is based on a very imprecise understanding of pre-Roman, Celtic British history. This play constitutes a mythic explanation for the division of Britain into three parts, roughly corresponding to modern Scotland, England, and Wales plus the West

Country.³² Understood as legendary history, this myth of origins is relatively obscure for early modern audiences, so Shakespeare "translates" it into more easily understood contemporary terminology. Hence the use of aristocratic titles that are much more reminiscent of feudalism, such as the appearance of a King of France, a Duke of Burgundy, a Duke of Cornwall, an Earl of Gloucester, and an Earl of Kent. These familiar terms correspond to geographical areas that are more easily digested by English audiences than Gaul, for example, or a plethora of Celtic tribal names, to which the playwright would have had very little access in any case. This procedure also inevitably flavors the tragedy with contemporary anxieties about kingship, lineage, and inheritance, especially given the problems encountered by the Tudors in the female line. The playwright's shorthand therefore serves a doubly familiarizing purpose.³³ Other elements of medieval folklore and myth can be found in plays such as *The Two Noble Kinsmen* (1613) by Fletcher and Shakespeare, a mixed genre play (or tragicomedy) based on Chaucer's *Knight's Tale*. Set in the same mythical milieu as *A Midsummer Night's Dream* (1595), it intersperses the classical with aspects of chivalric romance, as the two knights joust for the love of the same lady. A similar mixed use of chivalric and classical elements occurs in *Troilus and Cressida* (1602), which although set during the Trojan War nevertheless makes use of familiar tropes of heroic combat derived from the medieval romance tradition.

Perhaps the most familiar use of myth in early modern tragedy, however, is in the form of reasonably straightforward allusions to the Western European classical tradition. These often occur as short vignettes within scenes, such as the references to the Trojan War and Ovid's *Metamorphoses* in *Titus Andronicus* 4.1.³⁴ Many playwrights are attracted by the possibilities offered by the Greek and Roman classics to write tragedies that are not so much about a particular story or character from myth as they are concerned with the legendary historical qualities suggested by the topic. The reason for this is the stature of the personages involved. Shakespeare's *Julius Caesar* or *Antony and Cleopatra* and Samuel Daniel's *The Tragedie of Cleopatra* (first version published 1594, and revised thereafter) are at least as much concerned with mythic and legendary matters of state formation as they are about the titular protagonists, especially given their location at the prolonged crisis that saw the final emergence of the Roman Empire out of the civil wars of the Republic. Cleopatra is an exceptionally important figure in all of this, because she functions not just as a historical representation, but as a major *locus classicus* for the concerns of imperial ideology.

The sheer importance of Cleopatra here is nothing new in Western European culture. As David Quint points out, representations of the Ptolemaic Greek queen of Egypt emerge as an absolutely crucial index of ideas and anxieties about women rulers, in effect positioning her as doubly "other" due to her femininity and also her re-inscription as an easternized figure.³⁵ What matters here is that early modern English representations of Cleopatra, regardless of how much they are based on historical texts, are affected at least as much by the mythic overtones of her presence as they are by any historical events.³⁶

Marlowe's *Dido, Queen of Carthage* (c. 1593) produces similar effects. Another tragedy that has its roots in classical antecedents, again in the form of the *Aeneid*, this one plays on the status of the encounter in Virgil's poem between his eponymous hero and the founder of Carthage as an archetypal foundation myth. It also picks up elements of Ovid's *Heroides* 7 (Dido to Aeneas) as it translates and updates the invented encounter between Aeneas and Dido for an early modern theater audience.³⁷ Cleopatra may perhaps be more familiar to modern audiences, but as her mythic predecessor, Dido figures many of the same anxieties over femininity and the easternized "other." Dido's fateful and fatal love affair with the Trojan hero who goes on to found Rome looms large in the Roman mythic consciousness because of the immense historical conflict between Rome and Carthage, as epitomized in the career of the great Carthaginian general, Hannibal Barca. Virgil's poem locates the root of this deadly war in the encounter between two founding figures, producing in effect an extraordinary discourse of destroyed queens as the victims of imperialist Trojan/Roman aggression. In the case of Aeneas and Dido, a divine command to Aeneas to leave and become the progenitor of Rome is responsible for generations of hatred and chaos. Marlowe makes Dido into a great tragic protagonist and Shakespeare goes on to do the same for Cleopatra. Both queens appear in Virgil, and the result is an enfolding of one within the other in a move that has had tremendous and enduring mythical potency for Western classical civilization.

The cultural weight of classical antiquity mostly explains the importance of such figures to tragedians in the period of the Renaissance. However, early modern England is not simply looking backwards, it is also expanding. Wales has formed part of the English polity for several centuries by this point, but one should also bear in mind the extension of a unitary state to other parts of the British Isles. The history of the English (and Scottish) relationship with Ireland needs to be remembered, as does the unification of the crowns of England and Scotland with the accession of James in 1603, to be followed a century later by the unification of the parliaments. These momentous events have massively critical consequences for the emergence of the British Empire, although it is still nascent in the early modern period. Rome in particular serves as the memorial resource *par excellence* for discourses of empire, whether historical or mythic. However, since the situation is still developing, the tragedies of the period play out some moments of myth-making of their own.

The drive to colonization inevitably has a major impact in such circumstances, and has perhaps most famously been fruitfully investigated in relation to *The Tempest* (1610–11).[38] However, it would seem strange for there not to be similar elements in tragedy, and indeed there are some aspects of colonization and discovery to be found. Alsemero in *The Changeling* affords just such an opportunity. His witty conversation with his friend Jasperino at 1.1.13–50 indicates that he was intending to travel to Malta (until he caught a glimpse of Beatrice-Joanna), which has implications of Spanish sea power, along with hints of a crusading impetus. However, a crucial element of the plot hinges on his strange closet, an almost room-sized piece of furniture he carries with him, which Beatrice-Joanna investigates, finding a useful powder that can prove whether or not a woman is a virgin. Alsemero is well placed to own a cabinet of curiosities; as a Spanish grandee, he has access to the wealth and secrets of the New World, and this may well be the root for the manuscript his erstwhile bride finds in the closet, entitled "The Book of Experiment, called *Secrets in Nature*" (4.1.24–5). An alternative explanation could be that he is something of an early chemist, or alchemist to use the correct terminology. Either way, he is as much a forward thinking Renaissance man as scientist or geographer as he is conventionally religious. This discovery leads to Beatrice-Joanna trying out the potion she finds on her servant Diaphanta, and so being able later to counterfeit the effects herself. The ritualistic experiment suggests a mythic relationship with the natural world that refines, enhances, and extends folklore discourses of the Old World as a means of deciphering the encounter with the New. Since the "discoveries" are still in full flow, so too are the terms, metaphors, and symbols being deployed in attempts to make sense of them. Hence the confusion of elements of alchemy, folklore, and magic.

All three aspects of religion, ritual, and myth are accordingly interrelated, although to some extent it is possible to separate out the various strands for the purposes of analysis. The playwrights are in the business of presenting entertaining, if sometimes harrowing, tragic fictions and all three elements are important aspects of their culture. The performative power derived from them, however, comes from the ways in which they all play off against one another. This is why it can be so difficult to tell in the case of Dido or Cleopatra, for example, where history leaves off and the mythic begins. The social function of tragedy in this period allows it to perform multiple functions, and the mixture of religion, ritual, and myth becomes far more dramatically exciting than any single one of them on its own. It seems rather obvious to say that tragic conflict is well served by social contradictions and faultlines. However, this is still well worth reiterating, if only because of a modern propensity to locate the impulse to tragedy within the individual; as if that somehow explains everything. Marlowe, Webster, Middleton, and their contemporaries are simply too sophisticated for their tragedies to be explained away so neatly. The tragic dilemma cannot be reduced to a personality index.

CHAPTER SIX

Politics of City and Nation

Tragic Politics: Drama and the City in Early Modern Europe

IVAN LUPIĆ

I

The history of modern tragedy begins with violent civil conflict. The scene is early fourteenth-century Padua, the author is Albertino Mussato (1261–1329), and the play is *Ecerinis*. Unjustly dismissed as "a false dawn" for Renaissance tragedy, Mussato's neo-Latin drama, probably composed between October 1314 and December 1315, is in fact a powerful, difficult masterpiece that does well what tragedies often do—it interrogates the audience's sense of its own identity, its ethical certainties, and the wisdom of its moral and political actions.[1] The play's immediate success, so unexpected and so implausible in any evolutionary account of the tragic genre, owes a great deal to Mussato's decision to turn to Seneca as his model but to take as his theme the recent political events from his own city and to seek in them significant resonances for the present and the future.[2] While dramatizing the rise and fall of the thirteenth-century Veronese tyrant Ezzelino da Romano (1194–1259), the play has regularly been read as Mussato's warning to the city of Padua against the pretensions of Cangrande della Scala (1291–1329), a Veronese signore and Mussato's contemporary. If the play was indeed designed to constitute such a warning, it did not have a long-lasting effect, for Padua eventually fell into the hands of Cangrande and Mussato died in exile.[3]

That Mussato's tragedy is not quite like any single tragedy by Seneca has caused some critical discomfort.[4] As a result, the first author of a modern tragedy has frequently been described as somewhat too medieval, too wedded to the understanding of tragedy as a species of narrative rather than a species of drama, and too clumsy in his imitation of Senecan dramaturgy. One of the most perceptive recent critics of Senecan tragedy in the early modern period would have us believe that Mussato "misses almost the entire point" and is "prophetic of much that is bad" in later drama.[5] But perhaps we, too, miss the point in wanting Mussato to be what he is not, and perhaps there is much that should be valued in *Ecerinis* as a piece of dramatic and not just narrative art. More to the point, we need to ask what kind of relationship Mussato actually forges between the play and its audience when he chooses to dramatize his city's recent and turbulent history. While it is true that there is a great deal of narration in *Ecerinis*, the narrative element is designed to draw the audience into the world of the play and to intensify rather than diminish the fundamentally theatrical experience the play affords. As Gregory A. Staley points out, it is the *imago facti*, the image of the deed, that in the longer narrative sections of *Ecerinis* characters "envision and in turn re-create for their audience." Tragedy as "image and imitation," where the visualization of human experience is at the center, is "the Senecan version of Aristotelian mimesis" that Mussato recognizes and adheres to in his play.[6]

The tendency of modern criticism to emphasize the narrative elements of *Ecerinis* without stopping to consider their dramatic function is not new. On the contrary, it is disappointingly old. Soon after its composition, Mussato's play was furnished with an extensive commentary penned by Guizzardo of Bologna and Castellano of Bassano, Mussato's learned acquaintances. The commentary on *Ecerinis*, preserved together with one of the many manuscript copies of the play, remains to this day an extraordinary critical document.[7] It shows that the beginning of modern tragedy is at the same time the beginning of modern criticism on tragedy, in the sense of close and extended analysis of a particular dramatic text. In their analysis of *Ecerinis*, Guizzardo and Castellano approach Mussato as if he were Vergil, for whom, after all, they had a significant tradition of medieval commentary upon which to draw. They refer to the play as *tragicus tractatus* (81) and divide it into three parts, which they describe as *libri* (books), just as one would describe the books of an epic poem. According to them, the first book treats of the origin and rise of Ecerinus and his brother Albricus, the second describes the vicious nature of their tyranny, while the third depicts their fall and destruction (88). While the division is neat, it tells us little about the structurally interesting features of *Ecerinis*, about the play's significant dramatic detail, or about its potential impact on the audience.[8]

The play opens with a striking scene of passion that serves at once to introduce the protagonist (or, as we shall see, protagonists) and to set the play in motion.[9] At its center is a traumatic past experience of a female figure who decides to reveal it for the first time and is clearly strongly moved by the recollection. The female figure is a mother, Adelheita, and her addressees are her two adult sons, Ecerinus and Albricus. They both learn from her that they had been violently conceived by the devil, who had approached her in the form of a bull and had, as she graphically describes it, "filled / My belly with his fatal juice" (48). The news is not horrifying; instead, it prompts in Ecerinus, the elder son, the recognition that he is descended from gods. His father, "the lord of retributions" (80), is a god to be venerated and a model to be imitated. Ecerinus feels so empowered by the news that his performance of his newly discovered self is deliberately outrageous: "I have / Denied Christ," he exclaims, "I've always hated Him. / I loathe the hostile name of the Cross" (100–1). The audience is thus prepared to expect tyrannous behavior of truly monstrous proportions. Cities will be destroyed and people will be killed.

Ecerinus' rise to power over the years is summarized by a messenger, from whom we learn that Ecerinus "[h]as with guile and cunning subdued Verona / to his yoke" (216–17) and has also "bought / Control of Padua" (219–20). Although tyranny is a "fierce serpent" (215–16), its success in part depends on the support of others, especially the more powerful social classes.[10] The problem is not simply the tyrant, but also the city: people obey the tyrant and brother kills brother in order to please him (261–2). According to the messenger, the people are not to be trusted because they are unstable (*labans*), a "herd disaster-bent and criminal," quick to follow orders and incapable of judging truly (201–2). The city, in other words, is not entirely innocent, and its faults deserve punishment.[11] Ecerinus' rhetoric is consequently one of vengeance (287). In a scene of counsel, during which a friar attempts to persuade Ecerinus to more virtuous behavior, Ecerinus argues that he is the scourge of God, "born to punish sin / At His command" (380–1). The space of the city is transformed into a stage decorated with dead bodies; the image of absolute political power is the city exposed to the tyrant's sword (328). The image invites a stark contrast between the evil of the tyrant and the innocence of the city, but the messenger's report has already complicated the relationship.

In fact, it is those who had left the city under the assault of the tyrant, the exiles of Padua, that return to repossess it, joined by the Venetians (401–5). And it is those who had been taken out of the city by force that now have to suffer: Ecerinus "[r]eturns to Verona in fury, / He rushes wildly to slaughter / And slays the captive innocents of Padua / With hunger, dark dungeons, and thirst" (446–8). The results of his crimes—11,000 people murdered—constitute a spectacle to be observed. The city, again, is imagined as a stage, while Ecerinus is its privileged if still bloodthirsty spectator.[12] This is one of the few times in the play that Ecerinus's atrocities are explicitly mentioned as committed acts. Earlier in the play dungeons, fires, crosses, torments, death, exile, and famine are listed as his threats (223–4), and the audience was told that he proposes (*censet*) to mutilate infants' genitalia and slice away their mothers' breasts in order "[t]o kill all hope of progeny" (267–9). The act is not described except in its terrible consequence: "Lying in their cradles a chorus of maimed innocents / laments, though they have not yet learned to speak" (270–1).[13]

If the point of *Ecerinis* is to show how tyrants ought to be punished and how cities are to avoid tragedies, it fails spectacularly. Having given up on Padua, Ecerinus directs his attention to Lombardy. Now already "the aged tyrant" (488), he is compared to a wolf surrounded by dogs: "his mouth grows white / With foam; his eyes go spinning 'round" (495). While the image is unflattering, it still accords to Ecerinus a singular role and reduces his opponents to a pack of dogs. Moreover, the furious wolf is not killed; he is merely wounded in his left foot. When they captured Ecerinus, "[s]omeone struck his head and cracked / His skull, no one knows for sure" (514–15), but he is not killed. On the contrary, he is defiant and he chooses to die by refusing food and the doctor's help. Despite the play's overt insistence on Ecerinus' monstrous nature, he is given a dignified death, defined by choice, resistance, and defiance.[14]

This is not the only difficulty with which *Ecerinis* presents its audience. As critics regularly complain, Ecerinus disappears from the play well before its end, and the entire fifth act is devoted to the fall of his brother Albricus. It is, however, more accurate to say that the entire fifth act is devoted to the suffering of Albricus' family, who become the primary object of the people's revenge (see Figure 6.1). Several cities—Treviso, Vicenza, and Padua—join forces to pursue "a proper vengeance" (542). The citizens besiege Albricus' citadel where they will perform the kind of violent revenge that Ecerinus had himself announced after discovering his parentage. The description, delivered at length by a messenger, constitutes the bloodiest part of the tragedy. A baby's skull is smashed against a wall; the scattered brains stain the mother's face (552–5). What the people did not do to Ecerinus, who died out of defiance, they now do to young Ecerinus, Albricus' son and the late Ecerinus' nephew. The child's head is fixed atop a spear, his rolling eyes are described, and, worse, one citizen sinks his teeth into the child's liver. Even the messenger seems appalled by his own description (565–6). The added irony is that the young Ecerinus, only three years old, called one of the citizens "uncle," mistaking him for his actual uncle, the tyrant Ecerinus. From the child's perspective there is no distinction between the violence of the tyrant and the violence of the city.[15]

The chief spectator of these cruel events is supposed to be Albricus, who is forced to watch his children die. His five daughters are burned alive. This is the only actual, named family in the play whose tragedy the audience is invited to observe with the help of the

FIGURE 6.1: "Massacre of Alberico da Romano's family," by Giovanni Demin, 1849–50. Nineteenth century, fresco. Italy, Veneto, Feltre, Berton Palace.

messenger's extended report. However, the people are also forced to observe themselves because the mob, their counterpart, has surrounded the family and is reproaching them for crimes. The figure is again of a wolf surrounded by dogs (580), as it was in the case of Ecerinus, but most of these individuals—children, daughters, mother—are very unlike wolves and nothing like Ecerinus. The false, imperfect analogy is hard to ignore. As they listen to the report and visualize the torture, the people, represented by the chorus, ask for more: "Go and tell us how they died" (583). Their burning at the stake is then described in detail, with Albricus and his wife compelled to watch and the wife finally thrust into the fire herself. Clearly, "Satan's self was there" (590), but what is not clear is whether one is to look for him in the victims or in their punishers.

The play constructs a complex spectating position for the audience, and consequently for the city. The chorus specifically wants Albricus' reaction to the events described even though, because he had been gagged by the citizens, he could not speak: "And Alberic, how did he take his wife's and daughters' / Death? He could not talk, but what were his looks?" (602–3). The messenger provides more than an account; he provides an interpretation: "The savage kept turning his head as though implying / With his nods he cared but little for them" (604–5). A natural human reaction—the inability to watch the slaughter of one's own family—is presented as a savage trait that disqualifies Albricus from humanity and makes both him and his family available for blameless killing. Consequently, the mob dismembers Albricus and feeds his body parts to the dogs (dogs, it will be remembered, were earlier the figure for the people). The chorus concludes the play by noting that "[t]his rule of justice last[s] for ever" (616–17) and that "this stable law" (628–9), which rewards the just and punishes the evil, must be learnt by everyone. This is, apparently, the advice to be taken home by the audience.

The advice to learn this stable law sounds more like a threat not just to those who would consider the career of a tyrant, but also to all those who support the tyrant or are in any way related to him. Merely removing the tyrant is not enough because tyranny resides in the people as a permanent possibility that only fear of the law and retribution can eradicate. It is easy to understand why this play immediately became required Christmas reading for the entire city of Padua.[16] When placed against what had just been described—the monstrous killing of Albricus' children and wife, and Albricus' own dismemberment—the comment of the chorus chills instead of comforting. If anyone in the city has felt sympathy for the victims, the sympathy is misplaced because it conflicts with the law. Mussato spends so much time—the entire fifth act—on describing in detail the atrocities committed upon Albricus and his family that the conclusion the chorus offers is entirely incapable of containing the natural ethical response of the audience and of controlling the direction the play as a whole has taken. The play began with a figure intent on revenge, because his father was a lord of retributions, and it closed with the revenge of the people not upon the tyrant but upon those close to him. Only this latter act of revenge is to be perceived as an expression of the just and stable law.

It is this final section of Mussato's play that, while cast in narrative form, serves to produce a genuinely dramatic response because it draws the audience into the world of the play and forces the citizens of Padua to re-envision the actions of the citizens who came before them. The city leaves the play not so much fearing the tyrant but fearing the institutions that make civic life possible. It is, paradoxically, the fear of the city that will ensure the city's future. The only way to escape this conclusion, and to turn the play into a simple warning against the dangers of tyranny, is to disregard the events that unfold after the death of Ecerinus.[17] Thus, for Carrie E. Beneš "the climax of the play" occurs with the death of Ecerinus, and the speech of the chorus that follows it encapsulates the ideological position of the play, essentially republican in nature. "Mussato contrasts the da Romano's regime's chaos (*rabies*) with a republic's natural peace (*pax*)," she argues, and "the dangers of tyranny with the blessings of peace under communal rule."[18] What the rest of the play communicates, however, is that communal rule is a blessing informed by terror, founded on an act of violence that dismembers, mutilates, and burns. Rather than skewing the moral and dramatic design of the play, the final section of Mussato's tragedy is where the moral climax occurs and where narrative means and dramatic experience coalesce.

In his focus on violence Mussato had an excellent teacher in Seneca, who in *Thyestes*, one of his bloodiest plays, similarly chooses to let the messenger report in detail how Atreus kills his brother's sons, "handles the entrails" that are "still trembling, the veins pulsing and the hearts throbbing in terror."[19] While it is Atreus who prepares the wicked dinner for his brother, it is Thyestes who is "mangling his sons, gnawing his own limbs with entombing teeth" (778–9). Thyestes, however, commits the deed in ignorance and, once he realizes what he has done, is convulsed by moral disgust: "The flesh churns within me, the imprisoned horror struggles with no way out, seeking to escape" (1041–2). Mussato's deliberate echoes of these Senecan scenes in *Ecerinis* are undeniable, but what is striking about them is that the horrific, savage deeds are performed by the avenging people, not the tyrant or his brother, and they are performed in full awareness. There is, in other words, nothing noble about what the people in *Ecerinis* do, and consequently their actions are as unlikely to provoke sympathy as are the actions of the tyrant Atreus, likewise intent on revenge. The Senecan subtext complicates audience response, helping us understand why this first modern encounter between tragedy and the city continues to challenge our expectations. Instead of assuming that Mussato turned to Seneca and, because he was a pioneer, did not know how to imitate him properly, we need to be more willing to consider *Ecerinis* as a deliberate, creative engagement with

Senecan drama that, rather than being a piece of simple propaganda, forges an ethically complex relationship between tragedy and the city.

II

When, some 250 years later, modern tragedy begins to be written in England, it similarly seeks inspiration in Seneca.[20] Again, the imitation is not slavish and the subject matter is taken from national history rather than from mythology. *Gorboduc*, composed by Thomas Sackville and Thomas Norton for the Christmas revels at the Inner Temple in 1561/2, draws on Senecan dramaturgy and rhetoric to tell the story of an ancient British king who decides to retire, dividing his kingdom between his two sons, Ferrex and Porrex. Like *Ecerinis*, *Gorboduc* opens with a mother figure, Videna, and closes with an entire act from which the play's principal characters are absent. The opening lines of Act 5 tell us that "The brother hath bereft the brother's life; / The mother, she hath dyed her cruel hands / In blood of her own son; and now at last / The people, lo, forgetting truth and love, / Contemning quite both law and loyal heart, / Even they have slain their sovereign lord and queen."[21] If this is a tragedy of Gorboduc, as the first printed edition of the play would have it, his disappearance from dramatic action in the interval between the fourth and the fifth acts is surprising; if it is a tragedy of the two brothers, Ferrex and Porrex, as the second edition of the play claims, their tragedy was concluded already in the fourth act, when the audience was given a vivid description of how Videna killed her younger son, Porrex, because he had killed his elder brother and her favorite, Ferrex.[22]

Critical accounts of *Gorboduc* have paid a great deal of attention to the play's engagement with the political issues of its own day. The division of the kingdom and its unfortunate aftermath have suggested allusions to the contested question of succession in the early years of Elizabeth's reign and the importance of having an heir named in unequivocal terms; the prevalence of counselor figures in the play has suggested a concern with the role of the Privy Council, and counsel more generally, in the activities of Elizabethan government; the invocation of parliament in the fifth act as well as the fact that the play was originally performed by law students with definite political aspirations has opened the play up to more capacious political readings, where the question is the degree of participation of different agents—the monarch, the council, the parliament, the educated classes—in the business of government.[23] Interestingly, little can be found in these readings that can help us understand why it is the people who prove to be the greatest force in the political world of the play, for it is the people who slay both the king and the queen, and who seem to stand as guards at the limits of the political nation.

The people are not given a voice in *Gorboduc*, but they actively participate in the play's offstage action and are frequently invoked as the crucial element in the definition of the state. The argument prefacing the tragedy, for example, tells us that the people, once they learn that the queen has killed her younger son, are "moved with the cruelty of the fact" and rebel against what they see as government gone awry.[24] Concerned about the rising tension between Ferrex and Porrex, one of the counselors suspects that it will mean a disaster not just for the two brothers but for everyone: "The prince, the people, the divided land" (2.1.213). It is not clear whether the line is an enumeration of three different constituents of the state or an equation that sees in the people and the land they occupy the ultimate legitimizing force for the prince.[25]

The fifth act of *Gorboduc* introduces nobles who are much less concerned for the people than they are for their own safety and their pre-eminence in the headless kingdom. The people, who inhabit the kingdom, seem to be the kingdom's chief enemy. It is almost amusing to listen to the nobles make their case. Clotyn uses the word tyrant in connection with Videna and her two sons (5.1.1), because their bloody actions are morally inexcusable, but Mandud quickly turns to the "traitorous crime" of the people that cries for quick punishment (5.1.8). The problem is that the people "threaten still / A new bloodshed unto the prince's kin, / To slay them all and to uproot the race / Both of the king and queen" (5.1.10–13). We are clearly witnessing a rebellion that is designed to change the form of government and not simply replace one, immoral ruler with another, more moral one. Mandud presents the facts in such a way that the people's moral improbity is foregrounded, whereas their morally motivated action, the killing of the murdering queen, is presented as an afterthought: "so are they moved / With Porrex' death, wherein they falsely charge / The guiltless king, without desert at all, / And traitorously have murdered him therefor, / And eke the queen" (5.1.13–17). Gwenard, the third duke to speak, similarly conflates the interests of the nobility with the interests of the country, which seems in his account to be populated only by the wives and children of the nobles (5.1.60–4).

It is hard not to notice the inconsistencies and the self-serving nature of these arguments. When the three dukes exit, Fergus, the Duke of Albany, remains on the stage only to tell us that he, too, wants to save the country from itself. In Fergus' speech, Britain is imagined as an empty land ("And Britain land, now desert, left alone / Amid these broils"), available for the taking, despite the fact that battles are fought all over it by the nobility and the people (5.1.137–43). The argument is worthy of a Machiavellian villain, but even this villain forgets by the end of his speech where his argument began. While he will depart to Albany to raise forces, he tells us that "here my secret friends / By secret practice shall solicit still / To seek to win to me the people's hearts" (5.1.168–70). It seems, after all, that there are still people in the empty land of Britain, and that their hearts, the same hearts that moved them to kill their king and queen, continue to matter.

That land actually has people on it is something that Shakespeare's King Lear, who also divides his kingdom, will learn the hard way.[26] The same insight does not seem to have been reached by the end of *Gorboduc*. Instead, the play closes with a lengthy speech delivered by Eubulus, the late king's secretary and apparently the voice of good counsel in the play. The speech is at once a resentful complaint, a prophecy, and an attempt to explain history as a series of identifiable causes and predictable effects. It is also a condemnation of the people. Like the nobles before him, Eubulus envisions Britain as an entity that exists outside of its relation to the people that inhabit it: "Lo, Britain realm is left an open prey, / A present spoil by conquest to ensue" (5.2.191–2). Until the rightful royal line is restored, the civil war, he prophesies, will continue. It is not clear from the speech why the people would continue to fight nor why they would fight among themselves, yet this is precisely the dire picture Eubulus paints: raped wives and maidens, children in tears, kinsmen killing one another, fathers killing sons and sons their fathers, towns desolate and burnt, Britain torn, wasted, and destroyed (5.2.209–14, 227–32). The addressee of the speech is Britain, imagined as an entity defined by its people ("thy native folk shall perish," 211) yet continuing despite its unpeopled cities. According to Eubulus, the only way of avoiding the disaster would have been to appoint "certain heirs" to the crown while the king was still alive, which would have preserved "the title of established right / And in the people plant obedience" (5.2.266–7). The problem in *Gorboduc* was not, however, that the heirs were uncertain, but that they were made certain by the king while he was still alive, and made so in consultation with his advisors. Eubulus glosses over the fact, identifying instead the disobedience of the people as the ultimate cause of Britain's troubles.

Gorboduc is a very monarchical play if for no other reason than because it only gives voice to the king, the nobles, and the counselors. Within its early performance contexts of 1561/2—in the Inner Temple and then at Court, before Elizabeth—the voices of the play were safe. Once it reached print in 1565, however, *Gorboduc* became available to the anonymous mass of people who are not given voice in the play but who could still find themselves invoked, described, and condemned. Perhaps this is why Sackville and Norton never intended to publish it. It reached print, we are told by John Day, the printer of the second edition (1570), thanks to a young man "that lacked a little money and much discretion," from whom a manuscript copy of the play was obtained. Day tells us that the authors were displeased by the fact, and goes on to explain the displeasure in terms of textual corruption. But the strange extended conceit that Day develops—in which the book is identified with a fair maid who, once snatched from the authors' custody, is raped, betrayed, disfigured, "and then thrust . . . out of doors dishonested"—suggests that much more was at stake for the authors than the minor imperfections of the young man's copy.[27]

Whereas this first surviving tragedy from the Inns of Court considered, through its dramatization of ancient British history, the larger national context and the relationship of the people to the land, the second attempt in the genre, emerging from the same intellectual context, is a less original but not necessarily less interesting exploration of similar issues. George Gascoigne's and Francis Kinwelmersh's *Jocasta* (first performed in 1566 and first published in 1573) shows how conversant English literary culture was with what went on in the rest of Europe, particularly Italy, even if this fact is purposefully concealed on the play's title page. Rather than being a direct adaptation of Euripides, as the title page of the play claims, *Jocasta* is an adaptation of Lodovico Dolce's *Giocasta* (1549), which in turn was almost certainly founded on a Latin translation of Euripides, not the Greek original.[28] There is every reason to consider *Gorboduc* and *Jocasta* as plays that are in dialogue. In both, there is an interest in fraternal conflict and the uncertain future of the state.[29] But whereas *Gorboduc*'s landscape is expansive, with the entirety of Britain as a single scene of tragedy, in *Jocasta* it is one unhappy city (1.1.36), Thebes, that rises against itself (1.1.8–9). The conflict between Eteocles and Polynices is used in *Jocasta* as an occasion to explore different ways of belonging to the city and the different claims the city, even when besieged, makes upon its citizens (see Figure 6.2). Further, the play poses the question of who can speak on behalf of the city and truly represent it, just as *Gorboduc*, almost against itself, posed the question of who can speak on behalf of Britain. Eteocles is described by Antigone as a "throthlesse tyrant" (1.2.91) because he did not keep his word, refusing to surrender the crown to his brother after the initial year during which he was entitled to rule the city. But Polynices' rightful claim is compromised by his assembling of a foreign army and his turning against his own city (1.1.255–8). Eteocles' usurpation of the throne suddenly becomes a duty to defend it from foreign invasion.

At the center of Gascoigne's and Kinwelmersh's play is neither Eteocles nor Polynices, nor indeed Jocasta, but the city of Thebes itself.[30] The city is addressed early on by the Theban dames, who sense disaster regardless of which of the two brothers proves victorious: "But whosoeuer gets the victory, / We wretched dames, and thou O noble towne, / Shall feele therof the wofull miserie, / Thy gorgeous pompe, thy glorious high renoume, / Thy stately towers, and all shall fall a downe" (1.2.50–4). There is a special connection here between the city and those who innocently inhabit it. This is the connection that Jocasta herself emphasizes throughout the play. During her interview with Polynices she expresses shock at her son's projected invasion, describing the Theban walls as if they had agency and life in them: "And thou, to warre against the *Theban*e walls, / These walls I say whose gates thy selfe should garde" (2.1.484–5). However, the walls still need a voice, and Jocasta herself lends it to them.

There is great irony in Jocasta's statement because, we learn from Tyresias later in the play, it is Jocasta who is in fact to blame. According to Tyresias, Jocasta's "incest foule, and childbirth monstruous" angers Jove so much that he will overcome the city with "famine, flame, rape, murther, dole and death" (3.1.135–9). Like the Theban dames before him, Tyresias gives us a vision of the city's destruction: "These lustie towres shall haue a headlong fall, / These houses burnde, and all the rest be razde, / And soone be sayde, here whilome *Thebes* stoode" (3.1.140–2). Tragedies may be about representing the fall of a great person, but Jocasta cannot qualify for the role. That is, she cannot speak on behalf of the city, being herself the cause of its potential destruction. Nor can her two sons, both of whom are claiming to defend the city while in fact ensuring its devastation through continued conflict.

It is tempting to argue that, instead, the play finds the human symbol for Thebes in Creon's young son Meneceus. He is marked by Tyresias as the sacrificial victim that can redeem the city and save it from future destruction. Meneceus embraces the mission and in a long dialogue with his father Creon presses the patriotic argument. The marginal gloss found in the early edition of the play agrees with him: "No greater honor than to dye for thy countrey."[31] Creon, however, demurs and advises escape from the city before the prophecy is made public. At first it seems Meneceus will play the obedient son and flee, but the messenger's report delivered later in the play informs the audience of Meneceus' death and describes it in some detail. It is a scene of self-sacrifice staged in front of Eteocles, during which Meneceus wants to be perceived as the true representative of the city: "Renoumed King, neither your victorie, / Ne yet the safetie of this princely Realme / In armour doth consist, but in the death / Of me" (4.2.30–3). Similarly, in his address to the citizens of Thebes he insists on the special, indissoluble bond between him and his city: "Of you I craue, O curteous Citizens, / To shrine my corps in tombe of marble stone: / Whereon graue this: *Meneceus here doth lie, / For countries cause that was content to die*" (4.2.45–8).

The actual consequence of Meneceus' sacrifice is not the salvation of the city. As soon as he hears the news of his son's death, Creon uses it to authorize his own claim to the Theban throne (4.2.55–8), and the tragedy continues with the mutual destruction of the two brothers' armies, both claiming to be doing what is right for Thebes. "The ground was couerde all with carcases" (5.1.192). Jocasta's suicide over the dead bodies of her two sons is a desperate act immediately prompted by maternal grief, but it can also be read as her own belated attempt to save the city through self-sacrifice. All of these claims to act on behalf of the city prove futile. The scene at Thebes is best described by the chorus of Theban women, who sense the disaster early despite Meneceus' self-sacrifice. The stanza has no counterpart in either Euripides or Dolce, nor can one easily find in other plays from the period a description of a ravaged city that is as simple as it is powerful, especially in its striking closing image of soldiers suspended in pain and unable to die: "Me thinke I heare the wailfull weeping cries / Of wretched dames, in euerie coast resound, / Me thinkes I see, how vp to heauenly skies / From battred walls, the thundring clappes

FIGURE 6.2: "Eteocles and Polynices fighting against each other outside Thebes." Verona, fifteenth century. Tempera on wood. Museo d'Arte Antica, Pinacoteca, Milan, Castello Sforzesco.

rebound, / Me thinke I heare, how all things go to ground, / Me thinke I see, how souldiers wounded lye / With gasping breath, and yet they can not dye" (4.2.50–6).

Both *Gorboduc* and *Jocasta* emerge from a very specific performance context, that of the London Inns of Court, and both plays are designed to appeal to select audiences defined by their special rhetorical training, by a general familiarity with the culture of classical antiquity, and by an avid interest in Elizabethan politics. But even when they leave behind their original sites of production, enter the world of print, and become available to successive generations of different kinds of readers, they continue to matter. While both plays insist on their topographical identity—the land of Britain and the city of Thebes—they raise issues that are common to all places, wherever there are people willing to consider the nature of their own relationship to the larger social and political structures. Cities and states are built upon piles of dead human bodies, in Thebes as much as in Britain. Still, what we witness at the end of each play is not total destruction but rather the suggestion that cities and states, like the soldiers gasping for breath in the ruins of Thebes, cannot so easily die. Indeed, both plays at their ends point to future histories, and future tragedies.

III

Before traveling westward from the Italian cities, Renaissance tragedy traveled eastward, to the other shore of the Adriatic Sea. This is especially true of a small but prosperous aristocratic republic called Ragusa, encompassing what is today the Croatian city of

Dubrovnik and its immediate environs. Ragusa was an important trading port as well as a thriving cultural center on the eastern coast of the Adriatic. Because the city authorities did not allow the establishment of a printing press until the eighteenth century and because of the devastating earthquake that occurred in 1667, a great portion of the city's literary heritage, preserved in manuscript form, probably perished, but enough remains to suggest the richness and variety of the vernacular literary production in early modern Ragusa. Sometimes we learn about the theatrical activities in the city from the legislation passed by the government in an attempt either to strictly define acceptable playing spaces or to ban performances of plays altogether. The earliest such records come from the 1550s, but the casual manner in which performances of tragedies are mentioned suggests that they were common and established occurrences rather than recent innovations. A tragedy written by a Ragusan author seems to have been published in Venice as early as 1500 but no copy of it survives, nor do we know its title or subject matter.[32]

One of the tragedies performed in Ragusa that has survived is a 1559 version of *Hecuba* by Euripides, indebted to Lodovico Dolce's Italian adaptation of the play but significantly expanded and furnished with carefully crafted and theatrically spectacular intermedi between the acts. It is, as far as we know, the only vernacular version of *Hecuba* that was performed in early modern Europe.[33] Its author was Marin Držić (1508–67), the best-known Ragusan dramatist of the sixteenth-century, famous especially for his comedies that graced aristocratic weddings or provided entertainment for the city. The critical history of Držić's *Hecuba* is of exceptional interest because the play's meanings, and especially its relationship to the city from which it emerged, have become inextricably linked with the activities of its author, who, late in his life, traveled to Florence with some very interesting political ideas on his mind. Držić's journey, the details of which became public only in the twentieth century, deserves discussion both as a fascinating episode in the history of relations between dramatists and their cities and as an event that continues to provoke significant critical disagreement about the meanings of his only tragedy, *Hecuba*.

Despite the strong presence of the citizen class, particularly the merchant class, throughout its history (1358–1808) the Republic of Ragusa was ruled exclusively by the aristocracy, the members of which, if decimated by outbreaks of the plague or natural disasters, would occasionally admit some citizen families to their ranks. Držić's family, however, underwent a reverse process. In the late Middle Ages, the noble family Držić was demoted to the rank of citizens because its members fled the city during an outbreak of the plague in violation of an order that requested all patricians to remain within the city walls. Another version of the family history has it that Marin Držić came from an illegitimate branch of the Držić family, which was thus non-aristocratic from the beginning. At some point Držić became a priest, probably after he studied in Siena, where he had been elected rector of the University. But for reasons that remain mysterious he commenced his studies—of what, we do not know—at the age of thirty or so, with the help of a grant provided by the government of Ragusa.[34]

This family history is of some interest because when Držić visits the Italian peninsula again, his journey is prompted by a desire to overthrow the aristocratic government of Dubrovnik. In this conspiratorial project he hoped to enlist Cosimo de' Medici himself, and he elaborated his ideas in a series of letters sent to the duke and preserved in the Florentine archives. As the earliest genealogy of the Držić family tells us, Marin was well liked by the Ragusan aristocracy. Both his published and unpublished texts suggest that the feelings were mutual. In dedicatory epistles, in poems, in prologues to plays, Ragusan noblemen are extolled for their virtues and praised for their generosity. When, in 1930, evidence of Držić's conspiracy was unearthed, the fact threatened to upend the established understanding of Držić's relations with his city. It was baffling to think that after an apparently enchanting romance with the aristocracy Držić would turn to a foreign ruler to tell him that Ragusa had all the while been ruled by a bunch of "lunatic monsters." The words are Držić's.

The Florentine episode comes at the very end of Držić's life, in 1566. Držić arrived in Florence in May 1566 and stayed there through August, the date of his last preserved letter. We learn from the first letter, written on July 2, that some kind of description of Ragusa was sent by Držić to the duke earlier, but this document does not survive. The first surviving letter is at the same time the most significant one, since it explains in detail how the conspiracy should be organized and why this would be an excellent idea, prompted, Držić says, by legitimate reasons and not by his own whim. The first reason is the failure of the Ragusan government to understand the importance of foreign affairs and of doing politics with decorum; among other examples, Držić mentions a Ragusan nobleman who was sent on an embassy to the Viceroy of Sicily with a gift "at which His Highness laughed," Držić writes, "and gave it back to the nobleman." It was apparently a very simple thing, a completely unremarkable washbasin.[35]

According to Držić, the Ragusan aristocracy would just like to live by and for themselves, like Gods, shut "in that hole" (Držić's way of describing Ragusa) and preferring that the world not know much about them. This is why, he continues, they send on embassies people who are both slow and slow-witted: they don't want the news to travel. Further, Držić considers the city's fear of annoying the Turks both unnecessary and inappropriate, wishing instead for a more explicit alliance with the Catholic countries of Europe.[36] The strict regulations imposed by the Ragusan government upon the city's ships are seen by Držić as deliberately designed to limit the power of the navy without any regard for its potential usefulness in the Christian Mediterranean. The patricians want the ships to be secure "in that hole" (again, the port of Dubrovnik), while the world meanwhile can perish. The Medici could save Ragusa by taking it over by force and making sure it does not meet the fate recently experienced by the island of Chios, which fell to the Ottomans. The only way out is a change of government since the ruling aristocrats are, Držić repeats, "incapable, worthless, and impotent" (8) and their arrogance can no longer be endured. They think they are wise, he concludes, but they are actually stupid. Not only that, they are also cowards, unlike the people over whom they rule. When the Turk frowns at them, they weep "like frightened women" (9) and are ready to hand over the keys to the city without fighting, or they run to prepare the ships for a speedy escape.

It is not clear what exactly the new political arrangement would have been. The duke would take over the city, but he would help create a new little republic (*una nova republichetta*), which would be bound to prosper. All the young people, Držić claims, would be in favor of the project, and even two-thirds of the aristocracy seem to be unhappy with the current power arrangements. Given that they are ruling the city, it is a rather puzzling statement. One colonel, in the service of the duke, would control the city garrison and protect the freedom of the people. The government would no longer be formed on the Venetian model but on that of Genoa: one-half of the council would consist of noblemen, the other of the people (Držić's *popolani* are, however, probably the members of the upper citizen class, not all the people). Držić would also want the council to be open to foreigners. This would be good, he claims, because the city is what it is because of the different people living in it. The arrangement would also make Ragusa an appealing destination for other potential citizens who fear the Turks and would want to find shelter for themselves and their wealth in a well-governed city in which they could live as fully participating members. This would mean an enlargement and an enrichment of Ragusa.

Držić describes his plan as "a good and holy deed" (19) entirely worthy of the duke, and he proceeds to outline it, calling it very simple indeed. The first thing to do would be to secure the pope's excommunication of the ruling elite. The excommunication does not have to be real; a fictitious one would do the trick just as well. This way, things would be done in the name of God, which the local people would appreciate; they are, after all, good Catholics. This would even help to confirm them in their faith and thus help keep the Lutheran heresy away not just from Ragusa but from Bosnia, Serbia, and Dalmatia as well. After the excommunication, everything would be extremely easy. Only fifty soldiers would be required, with four captains and one colonel. They should be sent to Ragusa, preferably via Venice, in groups of five by different ships and at different times, from September to January, without knowing why they are being sent there. They should be poorly dressed and should appear to be looking for employment. The captains should be given tasks such as buying horses or doing whatever else appears convenient until Držić himself shows them the duke's orders. The colonel should be sent independently from the others and should not know anything about the captains. He should pretend that he is hiding from his enemies and that he is trying to get to Sicily via Ragusa. The group should include a blacksmith who knows how to break down a door or deal with bars. Držić would provide the weapons when the time comes and he would gather local supporters. "The world is conquered with skill" (*con arte si vince il mondo*), Držić comments, and Ragusan rulers, anyway, are like rabbits: they are easily scared (19–20). Another good thing is that Mehmed Paša (the Ottoman Grand Vizier at the time) is Bosnian by descent, knows the Slavic vernacular, and is sure to remain Ragusa's friend.

The second surviving letter, sent a day later, on July 3, is much shorter. Držić urges the duke to pay attention to his earlier letter and instructs him that Fortune is always false when she comes to one with a smile on her face; good Fortune only comes with a frown. If the circumstances are not ideal, that is not necessarily a bad sign. The important thing is to do everything with utmost secrecy. When God is on our side, Držić asks, how can we fail? This letter contains another important afterthought: an enterprise of this magnitude would require some cash, and since everything ought to be kept very secret, the cash should come directly from the duke. Držić promises to return the money once the enterprise is over, whatever the outcome. He also begs forgiveness if, being new to these things, he has erred on any count.

Twenty days later, in late July, Držić writes a letter to the duke's son Francesco, asking him to intercede with his father since, on account of great secrecy and confidentiality of the matter, Držić cannot be seen around the court himself. A month or so later, at the end of August, Držić leaves Florence without achieving his purpose; he writes again to Francesco, describing himself as "a humble foreigner" (45) and telling the duke that he realizes the difficulties are too numerous and that the enterprise should therefore be postponed until a more convenient time. He will be traveling back to Ragusa with two noblemen, he writes, but he will tell them that he was in Florence all this time "just for fun" (*per piacer*). He hopes he has not offended or transgressed in any way. He is just a poor foreigner who came to Florence in the hope of doing some good.

When these letters were discovered in 1930, they proved a huge embarrassment. Here was the favorite national author of the Renaissance offering his homeland—a precious symbol of Croatian liberty and independence—to the mercy of the Medici. Držić, clearly, needed to be rescued. One scholar argued that Držić was obviously a good dramatist, but a terribly naive politician, and that he got a little carried away. While he should be scolded for misrepresenting the government of Ragusa, this argument continued, his naive concern for the people of the city should bring a smile to our face. Rather than proclaiming him a traitor, one should look at him as a dramatist with a lively imagination and with a basically good heart.[37] He could not have been taken seriously; his letters were not likely to have been read by anyone of importance.[38] Another early critical authority was, however, more severe. He held that the letters show a man who became psychologically deranged and badly needed cash, so the best he could come up with was this embarrassing plan.[39] In socialist Yugoslavia, and for partly predictable reasons, the narrative gradually changed. Držić was made out to be an isolated but grand instance of the otherwise silent popular voice directed against the tyranny of the Ragusan aristocracy, a voice that communicated the suffering not of the wealthy merchant class but of sailors, of servants, of the Ragusan proletariat. Not a traitor, not a madman, and not a fun-loving but money-deprived creature, Držić instead appeared as a true and tragic revolutionary figure.[40]

This revolutionary reading, formulated as a more generalized critique of corrupt government, has continued to dominate the scholarly discourse. Inspired by Držić's conspiratorial letters, it has found additional legitimation in his literary work. Attention was drawn, first, to the prologues prefacing his comedies, where the dramatist was understood to be communicating his ideological views in an oblique but still decipherable fashion.[41] Soon, however, it was Držić's only tragedy, *Hecuba*, that underwent a major transformation from being just another adaptation of an ancient play via an Italian intermediary to being a key statement of Držić's political philosophy.[42] This transformation was helped by one of the surviving early manuscripts of the Ragusan *Hecuba*, in which hundreds of lines were marked by gnomic pointing in the margin.[43] Whether or not the marks were originally introduced by Držić himself mattered less than the fact that they sometimes highlighted politically charged sentiments and could therefore be read as Držić's subtly encoded critique of the Ragusan oligarchy. *Hecuba* has thus become Držić's most serious and politically most relevant dramatic work.[44]

It is impossible to establish with certainty whether Držić's letters represent an isolated view of the Ragusan regime or whether they contain opinions that circulated among the people of Ragusa but never found a way into the official historical record, which was, after all, kept and supervised by the aristocracy. While the letters can be read as evidence of one man's failed attempt to do something truly extraordinary, they are also a remarkable, if ambiguous, document in the combined history of early modern drama and politics. Držić's letters allow us to ask if he ever really meant the many compliments he paid to the Ragusan aristocracy in his works, as well as to wonder whether the compliments were a way of keeping secret one's actual convictions, or even a way of publicly saying what one thinks by stating the exact opposite. If so, would there have been an audience for such double-speak? We would have to imagine a culture in which Edmund Spenser, when he praises his virgin queen, actually means to say that she is as mad as she is monstrous. Perhaps Spenser's own conspiratorial letters are waiting to be discovered. At the very least, we are reminded that when we speak of early modern drama's relation to the realm of politics we find ourselves in a world of fundamental uncertainty, where dramatists' true intentions are irrecoverable and where the texts of the plays, riven by rhetorical struggle, are as much a stage for our own tentative interpretations as they are enactments of history.

CHAPTER SEVEN

Society and Family

"The Deed's Creature": Family and Gender in English Renaissance Tragedy

COPPÉLIA KAHN

In *The Changeling* by Thomas Middleton and William Rowley, published in 1622, De Flores presses his claim to sex as a reward for murdering, at her request, Beatrice-Joanna's fiancé. She wants him dead so that she can marry the man she desires. De Flores declares, "Y'are the deed's creature," insisting that she, who instigated the murder, shares guilt with him, who committed it.[1] It could be said that all characters engaged in tragic action are morally transformed, and permanently so, by their deeds. But in Renaissance tragedy, male and female characters act within different parameters, from different gendered positions. Those parameters and positions are constructed within the family, so it is imperative to view these tragedies in terms of family structure.

As Catherine Belsey argues, "The family is the place where we learn to reproduce . . . the norms of gender itself."[2] Family begins with marriage, and as the Reformation proceeded, Protestant England became increasingly concerned with re-defining the terms of marriage in the sermons and domestic conduct books that poured from the presses during the heyday of Renaissance drama, roughly 1576–1642. The clerics and moralists who wrote these books wrestled mainly with three problems. What did it mean for a father to rule over his family? To what extent did women have authority in the family? How was marriage to accommodate sexual desire? These are the fault lines and danger zones of the institution. From them, playwrights draw the tragic deeds of which women and men are the creatures.

William Gouge was one of the most influential clerics to attempt this re-definition of marriage and family, in his comprehensive manual *Of Domesticall Duties* (1622, rpt. 1627, 1634). His axiom, "A family is . . . a little Commonwealth . . . a school wherein the first principles and grounds of government and subjection are learned," sums up the analogy that governed, and troubled, the controversy.[3] The following statement from an equally popular work of the same kind by John Dod and Robert Cleaver makes clear who is subject to whom: "It is impossible for a man to understand how to govern the commonwealth, that doth not know to rule his own house."[4] Thus authority within the family was theoretically aligned with the dominant theory of political authority, patriarchalism, which held that by virtue of their innate physical and mental superiority, men should hold authority over women. Indeed they did hold it, through the law of coverture, "a peculiarly English system" according to which "a woman's legal identity was subsumed under that of her husband," her property becoming his upon marriage.[5] Though there were many legal ways around coverture, still, it also prevented married women from testifying in court or entering into contracts. Conversely, single women "could operate exactly as men did," owning, trading, and making investments.[6] However, especially in the middle and upper classes, women couldn't freely remain single: their male guardians could exert extreme pressure on them, and did.[7]

The primary legal underpinning of the father's authority was primogeniture, according to which the oldest son inherited all or the bulk of his father's estate, his younger brothers being forced to make their own fortunes, while his sisters, with or without dowries, were expected to marry. According to Lawrence Stone, primogeniture "went far to determine the behavior and character of both parents and children, and to govern the relationship between siblings."[8] Indeed, the father's power to bestow favor on his eldest son, and his investment in that son's promise to carry on the family name, lays the ground for tragedy.

In theory, then, the family was a little state ruled by fathers, husbands, or any elder male. In practice, however, as David Underdown has argued, England was in a state of "gender crisis" in the period 1580–1640, as evidenced by persecutions of witches and "scolds" (vociferous, rebellious wives), and various attempts to control single women.[9] In fact, the manuals of domestic conduct quoted above, which were intended to insure patriarchal order within the family, offer ample evidence of its opposite: disagreement and unease regarding the simple hierarchical model of male authority and female subjection that they promoted.

A major sticking point was the extent to which the husband ruled over the wife. Gouge first delivered *Of Domesticall Duties* as a series of sermons, in which his idea of a wife's subjection to a husband's authority had evidently provoked much discussion.[10] Gouge struggles to reconcile the hierarchical model of obedience with the different kinds of relationships in a household. Children clearly owe obedience to their parents, and servants to their masters. But if "the wife is by God's providence appointed a joint governor with the husband of the family," in what sense is she also subject to her husband?[11] As Susan Amussen points out, Gouge and his fellow Puritans believed that before God, men and women were equal, yet "they were trying to define an unequal partnership between them" as husband and wife.[12] Within a single sentence, Thomas Gataker, in his *Marriage Duties Briefly couched together* (1620), allows that where husband and wife "be equal, there may be some question, some difficulty, whither shall have priority," but then condemns "a man-kind woman or a masterly wife [as] a monster in nature."[13]

This fault line in family structure results in what Catherine Belsey calls "a discursive instability in the texts about women" that denies female characters a single position that is theirs, that forces them "to speak with equal conviction from incompatible subject positions."[14] As helpmates to their husbands and mistresses of their households, women were considered rational subjects capable of choices and decisions, subjects who could speak for themselves. Yet they were also enjoined to obedience—silence and submission to their male superiors that kept them from speaking for themselves.[15] In the tragedies that I interpret below, we will often find women caught in their subject positions as unequal partners, forced to live out contradictions not of their own making.

Another danger zone arises from changes in the very idea of marriage. As the Reformation advanced, marriage, rather than celibacy, became the most honored condition. In addition to the traditional functions of marriage, the Church of England added another. According to "An Homily of the State of Matrimony," marriage "is instituted of God to the intent that man and woman should live lawfully in a perpetual friendly fellowship, to bring forth fruit, and to avoid fornication."[16] The homily places this new "companionate" aspect of marriage first, but it by no means crowds out the old notion that it is better to marry than to burn. Rather, as sexual pleasure now enters explicitly and legitimately into marriage, fornication becomes an internal rather than external threat.[17] For example, Dod and Cleaver make it a duty for both wives and husbands to render "due benevolence" to their spouses, a euphemism for sex derived from 1 Cor. 7:3–4. In the divinely decreed state of marriage, this mutual sexual indebtedness "serveth as a strong bridle, to pull back the force and headiness of Carnall, Naturall, and brutish lust," the authors affirm. Yet they caution "married folks" against "lascivious excess" which would be "Fornication."[18] Sex belongs within marriage, and marriage is meant to transform lust into legitimate pleasure. Yet that pleasure, in excess, can itself become a kind of whoredom.

The story of Adam and Eve is not only the foundational narrative of marriage, in which God grants Adam's prayer that he create "an help meet for him." It is also the foundational narrative of sexuality, in that Eve's disobedient desire for the apple manifests her physical and moral weakness, enabling the association of lust per se with the feminine.[19] Men who desired women could blame women for that desire, marking them as "the weaker vessel" (a phrase from 1 Peter 3:7 used five times in the homily quoted above), both the symbol and the cause of a lust all were taught to revile. The fleshly weakness held to be innate to women in turn bolstered the idea that, however friendly the fellowship of husband and wife, woman could never fully be "joint governor" of the family, her place equal to her husband's.

Garrett Sullivan defines early modern tragic subjectivity as "The product of the fraught relationship between a socially defined self and desires that are at odds with it."[20] I would add that desires, too, are socially defined, and limited by gendered positions. Macbeth wants children so that he can project his lineage into the future, the conventional longing of an early modern male aristocrat. The Duchess of Malfi dares to choose her own husband: such motivation lacks the cachet accorded to Macbeth's. In tragedy, it is the women whose desires most often clash with the roles and behaviors deemed proper for them. Tragic heroes, on the other hand, often transgress moral boundaries rather than specifically gendered ones. More is open to them, and they dare more. Consider, for example, Marlowe's tragic heroes Tamburlaine and Doctor Faustus: they perform their tragic deeds completely outside the context of the family. Many tragic heroes, on the other hand, act *as* husbands, fathers, sons, or brothers. In contrast, many tragic heroines act *despite* or *against* their positions as daughters, wives, widows. Their conception of themselves as such determines or crucially influences their actions. In the following pages I will read some well-known tragedies to focus on how they dramatize the scope and nature of tragic action for women and for men, as tragic action is influenced or indeed defined by social constructions of the family. Constraints of space force me to center these interpretations on the protagonists, necessarily ignoring many subplots and minor characters that also engage with gender roles emerging from the family.

HEROINES OF WAYWARD DESIRE

The prevailing categories in which Renaissance women are conceived derive from their marital status: they are seen as either maids, wives, or widows.[21] According to a legal handbook for women, *The Lawes Resolution of Womens Rights*, "All of them are understood either married or to be married and their desires are subject to their husband."²² This triad of categories suggests the order in which I will discuss three tragic heroines: Beatrice-Joanna of *The Changeling*, an unmarried daughter; Alice Arden, a wife; and the Duchess of Malfi, a widow.

The Changeling uses its *mise en scène*, the castle owned by the bride's father, as a metaphor for her essential position in the patriarchal family as marriageable virgin daughter—marriageable only if virgin. The virgin daughter's womb is the hidden, prized treasure of her father, to be guarded from or given to other men as he determines. What Page DuBois calls "thesaurisization," the representation of the female body in Greek culture as vase, oven, and temple—enclosures "for keeping safe, for entreasuring"—was highly visible in the Renaissance through the legend of Tuccia, first recounted by St. Augustine in *The City of God*.²³ This vestal virgin proved her chastity by carrying water from the Tiber in a sieve, a "miraculous inversion of the vessel's ordinary function [that] replicates the prodigy of virginity itself."²⁴ For Shakespeare's England, Tuccia was familiar in portraits of Elizabeth as virgin queen, who was several times portrayed with a sieve in her hand.

It is Vermandero, Beatrice-Joanna's father, who identifies the castle as a container of secrets. "Our castles," he says, "Are placed conspicuous to outward view ... / but within are secrets" (1.1.165–7). When Vermandero's steward De Flores murders Piracquo, to whom his master has already betrothed his daughter, he does the deed within a "narrow ... descent" of the "most spacious and impregnable fort" of the castle (3.1.4, 5–6). At this point, the castle's "secret" virgin treasure becomes sullied by the murder, then hopelessly despoiled when De Flores claims his reward: the defloration of Beatrice-Joanna. When she offers him money, he spurns it. What he specifically wants is her virginity, saying

> Were I not resolved in my belief
> That thy virginity were perfect in thee,
> I should but take my recompense with grudging,
> As if I had but half my hopes I agreed for.
>
> —3.4.116–18

De Flores shares exactly the patriarchal mindset of her father and her husband-to-be. He desires her as a virgin, but at the same time, calls her a whore for having and pursuing her desire for Alsemero despite being betrothed to another:

> Though thou writ'st maid, thou whore in thy affection!
> 'Twas changed from thy first love, and that's a kind
> Of whoredom in thy heart ....
>
> —3.4.142–4

By taking Beatrice-Joanna's virginity, De Flores puts her in a tragic bind, for she is no longer the chaste object that Alsemero loved and sought to marry. Desperate to meet the patriarchal criterion of *virgo intacta* on her wedding night, Beatrice-Joanna arranges for her maid Diaphanta to take her place. More and more enmeshed in deceiving her bridegroom, the heroine also becomes more bound to De Flores when he safeguards her honor by murdering her maid. She even begins to desire *him*, changing her affections once again: "The east is not more beauteous than his service," she exclaims (5.1.74), referring both to his continued role as steward in her father's household and to his sexual "service."

Informed of his bride's "back door" meetings with De Flores, Beatrice-Joanna's husband accuses her of adultery. Clinging to the ruse of the wedding night, she cries,

"Remember I am true unto your bed" (5.3.86). When all is finally discovered, De Flores presents her to her father and her husband as "that broken rib of mankind," an emblem of the lust and duplicity associated with Eve (5.3.155). And she too sees herself as guilty, not merely of the murders in which she is complicit, but more significantly, of losing her virginity to De Flores: "Mine honor fell with him, and now my life. / Alsemero, I am a stranger to your bed" (5.3.167–8).

Beatrice-Joanna is both victim and agent: victim of a social structure in which a daughter's virginity is a non-negotiable requirement, yet also agent of her own desire in daring to override her father's choice of husband for her. Throughout, she is driven both by her sexual desires and by her desire to comply with patriarchal expectations, but she never attempts to justify the former and in the end, condemns herself in terms of the latter—the same terms that her father and her husband use—as a defiled, corrupted woman. When Alsemero pledges "a son's duty" to his father-in-law, the tragedy ends with the reconstruction of an all-male household, purged of its "broken rib."

In contrast to Beatrice-Joanna, the heroine of *Arden of Faversham* proclaims her disdain for the strictures of conventional marriage, plainly and often. Alice Arden struggles to imagine a world in which she can follow her desire unconstrained by vows and contracts, but is repeatedly tripped up by them and falls back on them. Indeed, the entire play, written by an anonymous author between 1588 and 1592, falters on the impossibility of living outside a social system built on land ownership, patronage, class distinctions—and marriage. Alice is the worst nightmare of Gouge and his fellows, a woman of headstrong passion who will submit neither to her husband nor to the rule of law. The play centers on her several attempts to murder her husband Arden, a wealthy, grasping landowner, so that she can live with her lover Mosby, once a tailor, now steward in a noble household. Its action veers unsteadily between comic episodes in which would-be murderers are defeated by doors unexpectedly locked, windows suddenly slamming down, or mists inconveniently rising, and passionate confrontations in which Arden, Mosby, and Alice clash over who will possess her.

While Alice is devious and deceitful, repeatedly feigning love for her husband so as to continue her affair with Mosby, she is also shockingly bold in defying marriage as an institution:

> Sweet Mosby is the man that hath my heart . . .
> Love is a god, and marriage is but words,
> And therefore Mosby's title is the best.
> Tush, whether it be or no, he shall be mine,
> In spite of him [Arden], of Hymen, and of rites.
>
> —1.98, 101–4

Yet neither she nor Mosby can envision a life together that *isn't* a marriage: when Mosby suggests he'll "play the husband's part" during Arden's absence, Alice replies, "Who's master of my heart, / He well may be the master of the house" (1.638–40). As their several plots to murder Arden multiply, Mosby envisions eventual marriage to Alice: "Holy church rites makes us two but one." However, he immediately questions those terms:

> But what for that? I may not trust you, Alice;
> You have supplanted Arden for my sake,
> And will extirpen me to plant another.
>
> —8.38–41

Minutes after Arden is finally murdered, though, Mosby declares "I am thy husband" (14.272), unable to envision any other role for himself.

In engaging various accomplices to murder Arden, Alice and Mosby repeatedly depend on their oaths and compacts:

> **Greene** Will you keep promise with me?
> **Alice** Or count me false and perjured while I live.
>
> —1.1.527–8

"What I have promised I will perform," says Michael, a servant in Arden's household, "So have I sworn to Mosby and my mistress; / So have I promised to the slaughtermen" (3.186, 203–4). Outside established structures such as letters patent "sealed and subscribed" by authority, however, such promises prove to be "but words." In dramatizing interrelations between characters at all levels of the social hierarchy—lords and courtiers, gentlemen, artisans, servants, even outlaws—*Arden* shows that all are enmeshed in land ownership, the basis of wealth and prestige, which is sustained by contracts, deeds, binding documents of many kinds—as is marriage. Alice grasps at a life outside such documents, not only in words but deeds, and fails utterly to attain it.

Arden is no better a husband than Alice is a wife. He follows his friend Franklin's questionable advice not to cross her, leaving her free to dally with Mosby while he goes to London on business. Again and again, he believes her excuses, fabrications, and extravagant expressions of affection. In these episodes, the play seems to suggest that such a spineless, credulous husband is to blame for allowing a "mankind" woman such as Alice to call the shots, implicitly endorsing the patriarchal doctrine that a man should rule his own house. Yet in her challenges to marriage, Alice is fully a subject, thinking and acting, however unethically and ineffectually, for herself, as when she declares to Mosby

> Why should he [Arden] thrust his sickle in our corn?
> Or what hath he to do with thee, my love,
> Or govern me that am to rule myself?
>
> —10.86–8

It is precisely in its ambivalences and contradictions that *Arden of Faversham* challenges the assumption that patriarchal marriage can contain desire within its boundaries. Though Alice is clearly guilty of murder and is punished soundly for her crime, the play dramatizes what Catherine Belsey calls "a contest for the control of sexuality in the period, which throws marriage into crisis."[25]

Beatrice-Joanna as a maid was subject to her father; Alice as a wife, to her husband. Each takes a desperate course to circumvent subjection and follow her own desire. As a wealthy, aristocratic widow, we might think, the Duchess of Malfi, title character of John Webster's 1614 tragedy, is indeed free to choose a second husband. Precisely that freedom, however, made widows "threatening figures," as Dympna Callaghan argues. No longer subject to a husband, widows could buy, sell, and make legal contracts in their own names: they were "virtual men." On the other hand, already sexually initiated but without husbands to satisfy them, they were regarded as creatures of unbounded lust. Thus they embodied a peculiar combination of femininity and power that made them dangerous in male eyes.[26] Though the Duchess isn't legally subject to her two brothers, by using the opprobrium associated with widows they try to scare her into submission to *their* desire that she remain unmarried:

> **Ferdinand** You are a widow;
> You know already what man is. And therefore
> Let not youth, high promotion, eloquence—
> **Cardinal** No, nor anything without the addition, honor,
> Sway your high blood.
> **Ferdinand** Marry? They are most luxurious
> Will wed twice.
>
> —1.1.295–300

Daringly, the Duchess not only determines to marry a man of her choice who is below her in rank: she herself initiates the union. In doing so, she compares her domestic action to the martial deeds that make men heroes:

> . . . as men in some great battles,
> By apprehending danger, have achieved
> Almost impossible actions: I have heard soldiers say so—
> So I, through frights and threat'nings, will assay
> This dangerous venture.
>
> —1.1.345–9

Thus she consciously appropriates male heroism for herself. For her as a woman to suggest marriage to Antonio, her steward, is an act of pure independent will tantamount to any hero's heaven-storming deed—and in the end, she pays a hero's tragic price for it.[27]

"This dangerous venture," given her brothers' opposition, must be conducted in secret. That opposition begins even before the Duchess marries, when Ferdinand hires Bosola to spy on her, and comes out in the open only after she has had three children with Antonio. Ferdinand steals into her chamber to surprise her with his knowledge of her marriage, but she is calm and poised as though she always knew he would come after her:

> 'Tis welcome;
> For know, whether I am doomed to live or die,
> I can do both like a prince.
>
> —3.2.70–2

One might say that the Duchess (who is known only by her title) pulls rank on her brother in that she deems herself a prince equal in rank to him, not to be overmastered because she is a woman. Ferdinand, in contrast, never claims full agency as man or brother. First, he works through Bosola as his "intelligencer." Then, when he confronts his sister, oddly he hands his father's poniard to her, instead of using it himself (3.2.72 S.D.). In a patriarchal family, when a father dies, a son takes his place as head of family and guardian of its women: the poniard signifies that office. Ferdinand, though he viciously rebukes his sister for marrying, is unmanned by the very sight of her, and wants above all never to look her in the eye: "Let me not know thee," he declares; "I would not for ten millions / I had beheld thee. . . . I will never see thee more" (3.2.94, 97–8, 139). In contrast, the Duchess is frank, rational, self-possessed: "I am married. . . . Will you see my husband?. . . . Why might not I marry? / I have not gone about, in this, to create / Any new world or custom" (3.2.83, 88, 111–13). Actually, though, she has.

For a brief period, the Duchess out-plots her brothers, but unwittingly places confidence in Bosola, the very spy who has revealed her marriage to Ferdinand. From that point on, she is in her brothers' power, or rather, the powers that they can command: "the Pope, forehearing of her looseness, / Hath seized into the protection of the church / The dukedom which she held as dowager" (3.4.32–4). She faces not just the enmity of her brothers but also the combined powers of church and state, the patriarchal system as a whole.

At this point, Ferdinand and his brother the Cardinal embark on a program of theatricalized persecution of the Duchess. Ferdinand visits her at night and gives her a dead man's hand to kiss, contrives a show of her husband and children "appearing as if they were dead" (4.1.55 S.D.), then sends a troupe of howling madmen to her chambers. Prior to supervising her murder, Bosola pretends to be a tomb maker, preparing her for death. The purpose of such actions, since the brothers have already separated her from her husband and children, and have made her their prisoner, is unclear. The only explanation we are given comes from Ferdinand, who says he torments her "to bring her to despair" (4.1.118). In that, he fails—for she assumes the stance of a Christian stoic, withdrawing her affections from the living, interpreting the suffering he visits on her as "heaven's scourge stick," adversity divinely decreed to test her virtue (3.5.82). In this light, "the wild consort / Of madmen"—lawyer, astrologer, tailor, gentleman-usher, farmer, broker, each crazed by his worldly pursuits—only plays into her hands by portraying the vanity of earthly life. "Tell my brothers," she says, "That I perceive death, now I am well awake, / Best gift is they can give or I can take" (4.2.220–2).

The Duchess cannot lead an army against her brothers, nor effect a palace coup by enlisting aristocratic allies. The kind of Machiavellian entrapment they practice against her is alien to her personality: she has no interest in power over *them*. All she desires, as Linda Woodbridge argues, is "an ordinary everyday marriage."[28] Stripped of all but her title, what she can do is to pursue resistance by moving to a higher spiritual plane. Like any tragic hero, she loses but she also wins.

FATHERS AND SONS

In a patriarchal system, the superior subject position isn't simply that of a man: it is that of a father. A man begins life subject to his father, and fulfills that father's expectations by becoming a father himself. Given the female role in human reproduction, we might think that a mother's contribution to the making of men might at least be acknowledged. Patriarchy, though, is not a rational concept but an ideology. As Louis Althusser says, "Ideology represents the imaginary relationship of individuals to their real conditions of existence."[29] In tragedies shaped by the patriarchal family, mothers are commonly given only a scant presence, and often entirely eliminated. Yet the power of the mother—occluded, repressed, displaced, figured in language if not in characters—can be crucial in the underlying premises of the tragedy, however overtly powerful the father or the idea of him. To establish the father's significance in tragedy, I will begin by discussing a play that in many respects set the bar for Renaissance tragedy in England: Thomas Kyd's *The Spanish Tragedy* (1587). In contrast, Shakespeare's *King Lear* dramatizes what the other plays avoid: the mother's hidden power.

In *The Spanish Tragedy*, the investments of two fathers in their children drive the plot. One, the childless King of Spain, would marry his niece Bel-Imperia to the Portuguese viceroy's son, Balthazar. As her name suggests, this marriage is purely political, designed to continue the king's line while providing a male ruler to unite Portugal with Spain in *imperium*. His nephew Lorenzo pursues this dynastic goal by murdering Horatio, son of the Spanish king's knight marshal Hieronimo, with whom Bel-Imperia is romantically involved. The scene in which Hieronimo discovers his son hanged in his own garden is the emotional core of this complexly plotted play. The garden setting suggests several dimensions of this grievous offense. First it is represented as a *locus amoenus*, replete with "leafy bowers" and nightingale, a perfect refuge for the secret passion between a princess and a lowly courtier's son. Then, when Hieronimo, "pluck[ed] from [his] naked bed," discovers his son's body hanging "in the arbor," it becomes the emblem of blasted family hopes, of a generation destroyed:

> This place was made for pleasure, not for death.
> *He cuts him down.*
> Those garments that he wears I oft have seen—
> Alas, it is Horatio, my sweet son!
> Oh no, but he that whilom was my son.
> Oh, was it thou that called'st me from my bed?
> Oh, speak if any spark of life remain.
> I am thy father. Who hath slain my son?
>
> —2.5.12–18

In a society in which power passes from father to son, and sons carry on the family name while daughters marry into other families, the simple repetition of "son" carries a particular pathos. Calling Horatio "Sweet lovely rose" and "fair worthy son" (2.5.46, 47), his father vows not to bury his son until he takes revenge. Thus the playwright sets up the tension central to revenge tragedy between sympathy for the hero suffering a grievous offense and moral judgment on the vengeance he takes for it. Kyd immediately reinforces the motif of paternal grief and blasted hope in a subplot in which the Viceroy of Portugal mistakenly believes his son Balthazar, "The only hope of our successive line," to be dead (3.1.14).

In a culture that tried to restrict tears to women as the weaker sex, *The Spanish Tragedy* opens the floodgates for the aggrieved father: "O eies, no eies, but fountains fraught with tears," Hieronimo cries as he takes center stage with a soliloquy that not only intensifies his anguish as a father but also magnifies his grief into a questioning of divine justice:

> O sacred heavens, if this unhallowed deed,
> If this inhuman and barbarous attempt,
> If this incomparable murder thus
> Of mine—but now no more—my son
> Shall unrevealed and unrevenged pass,
> How should we term your dealings to be just,
> If you unjustly deal with those that in your justice trust?
>
> —3.2.1, 5–10

The final question, intensified in a fourteener line, gains poignant irony from the fact that as knight marshal, Hieronimo is a magistrate charged with carrying out justice at the court of Spain. Kyd further exploits such irony when Hieronimo sets up the gallows at the trial of a servant accused of murder, saying "Thus must we toil in other men's extremes, / That know not how to remedy our own" (3.6.1–2).

Kyd augments the pathos of the father's path to justice first by delaying the revelation to Hieronimo of the murderer's identity. Then Hieronimo causes further delay by his attempts, in a court fraught with intrigue, to confirm the revelation. Finally, Hieronimo goes mad from grief and from the frustration of his desire for justice. The king, preoccupied with arranging the dynastic marriage, unaware that Horatio is dead, and manipulated by the nephew who murdered him, doesn't grasp the sense of his loyal marshal's plea "Give me my son" (3.12.70). Yet he remarks on the distraught Hieronimo, "This is the love that fathers bear their sons" (3.12.91). To drive home the exquisite pathos of this father's situation, Kyd contrives an encounter between him and Don Bazulto, an old man seeking justice for *his* murdered son, whom Hieronimo calls "The lively image of my grief" (3.13.162). The more he projects his grief and outrage onto others in his madness, the less effective is his quest for justice, but the more intense the playwright's focus on his paternal love.

Finally, in a clever entwining of plots, Hieronimo is invited by the Portuguese prince Balthazar (who was complicit in Horatio's murder) to contrive an entertainment for the royal wedding. In an ironic line that could still be quoted effectively onstage decades later, he acquiesces: "Why, then, I'll fit you" (4.1.70). In fitting or accommodating the royal request, he at last achieves his revenge, for the tragedy he devises replicates his own, and his enemies act the parts they played in life. Under the guise of its fictions, however, they are murdered for real. Hieronimo caps this shocking conclusion with an even more gruesome spectacle, the corpse of his son, which he has preserved throughout the vicissitudes of his path to revenge:

> *He draws back the curtain and shows his dead son.*
> See here my show. Look on this spectacle!
> Here lay my hope, and here my hope hath end;
> Here lay my heart, and here my heart was slain.
> Here lay my treasure, here my treasure lost;
> Here lay my bliss, and here my bliss bereft;
> But hope, heart, treasure, joy, and bliss
> All fled, failed, died, yea, all decayed with this.
> —4.4.89–95

Kyd focuses his rhetorical fireworks on the father's "hope"—his emotional investment in extending his name into posterity through his son. That investment evokes maximum pathos, as Hieronimo recreates the scene of murder in his garden "Where," he says, "hanging on a tree, I found my son" (4.4.111). Addressing the fathers whose sons have just been murdered in the play, the Portuguese Viceroy and the king's brother, Hieronimo flourishes a final visual reminder of his paternal suffering, the bloody handkerchief that he dipped in Horatio's wounds at the murder scene, and which he has kept close to his heart ever since, "Soliciting remembrance of [his] vow to take revenge" (4.4.127). To cap this moment, he bites out his tongue and stabs the two fathers to death, thus wiping out the royal lines of Spain and Portugal. The enduring popularity of this play in its time is at least partly due to the way it centers on and milks for all it's worth the patriarch's plight when he is unmanned by the loss of the son on whom he has counted to carry on his name.

For all Kyd's blinding focus on the father, he does give the murdered son a mother, Isabella. She shares her husband's grief and outrage in the garden; echoing his madness, she "runs lunatic" in a later scene (3.8.5); finally, she cuts down the arbor to leave it "fruitless forever" in sign of her loss (4.2.14) before killing herself. Thus she merely echoes and punctuates her husband's pain. In contrast, Shakespeare's treatment of the mother in *King Lear* is oblique, yet much more insightful. Lear is sole parent to his daughters, their mother being mentioned only once in passing.[30] Yet in Lear's demands for his daughters' affection and in his madness, we can read the maternal subtext of patriarchy: the imprint on the male psyche of being mothered, and a repressed need for its continuance.[31]

A close look at the tragedy's opening scene hints at this subtext. Lear is not only dividing his kingdom among his daughters: he is also giving away his youngest daughter, Cordelia, in marriage—yet his "darker purpose" is to keep her. When Lear disowns and disinherits her, he thinks he renders her, dowered only with his curse, unfit to marry, thus still under his power and at his disposal. The moment after he curses her for her silence, he confesses, "I lov'd her most, and thought to set my rest on her kind nursery" (1.1.121–2). The word "nursery" echoes the terms in which, a few moments earlier, he announced his intention

> To shake all cares and business from our age,
> Conferring them on younger strengths while we
> Unburdened crawl toward death.
>
> —1.1.37–9

Lear wants to regress, to be babied by his most beloved daughter, to enjoy her unlimited attention and affection as, in effect, a surrogate mother. No sooner does he banish her than he claims the same "nursery" from her sisters, who collude to frustrate his wishes and to humiliate him, first Goneril, then Regan denying him hospitality and respect. In the wake of such rejection, he suffers a storm of feeling that he expresses in a striking image:

> O, how this mother swells upward toward my heart!
> *Histerica passio* down, thou climbing sorrow;
> Thy element's below.
>
> —2.2.225–7

From 1900 BCE to the early twentieth century, hysteria was a woman's disease, associated with *hyster*, the womb.[32] In Shakespeare's time, it was known as the mother, suggesting the cultural connection between the quintessentially female capacity to bear children and the idea that women were temperamentally and morally infirm and skittish. In a patriarchal society, it is not only women who are supposed to stay in their element, subjected to men; the needs for love and nurture, the dependency associated with women in the male psyche are also supposed to be repressed and denied.

"The mother" that Lear suffers assaults him with various emotions: the desire to weep, to mourn the loss of the "nursery" on which he had counted, and the equally strong desire to hold back the tears and, instead, accuse, arraign, convict, punish, and humiliate the daughters who have made him realize his vulnerability and neediness. Thus as Lear enacts a child-like rage, the repressed need for the mother makes its re-entry into the patriarchal world from which she been excluded. It takes the form of images that overturn and confound parent–child and father–daughter relationships,. For example, when he first denies any "propinquity and property of blood" with Cordelia, with scalding irony he assures her

> The barbarous Scythian,
> Or he that makes his generation messes
> To gorge his appetite, shall to my bosom
> Be as well neighbour'd, pitied, and reliev'd,
> As thou my sometime daughter.
>
> —1.1.114–18

When Cordelia refuses to feed him the kind of love he demands, he thinks angrily of eating *her*, his "generation." Lear again voices this complex of ideas about the nurturing mother, the devouring mother, and the child's hostility toward the mother, when he sees Edgar's mutilated body, and remarks:

> Is it the fashion, that discarded fathers
> Should have this little mercy on their flesh?
> Judicious punishment! 'twas this flesh begot
> Those pelican daughters.
>
> —3.4.67–70

Projecting onto Edgar his desire to wound the daughters—his "flesh"—who discarded him, at the same time he envisions Edgar's flesh as his own, wounded by his "pelican daughters." Lear identifies with the legendary pelican whose children strike her; she retaliates, killing them, then wounds herself, her blood bringing them back to life. Lear's rage at not being fed by the daughters whom, pelican-like, he has nurtured, fills the storm scenes.

Regan and Goneril wound Lear by refusing to act as mothers to him, but in another sense they shame him by bringing out the woman in *him*. As the king turns toward the heath, Shakespeare takes us close to the nerve and bone of Lear's shame at being reduced to an impotence he considers womanish:

> You see me here, you gods, a poor old man,
> As full of grief as age, wretched in both.
> If it be you that stirs these daughters' hearts
> Against their father, fool me not so much
> To bear it tamely. Touch me with noble anger,
> And let not women's weapons, water-drops,
> Stain my man's cheeks.
>
> —2.2.438–44

We can read the storm as a metaphor for the tears that Lear fails to hold in. The breaking open of the heavens lets out a flood of rain, an image of Lear's heart cracking, letting out the hungry, mother-identified part of him in a flood of tears. He exhorts the winds to crack their cheeks, and the thunder to crack nature's molds and spill their seeds; he envisions close pent-up guilts riven from "their concealing continents" (3.2.1–9, 56–7).

In his madness, Lear thinks weeping an ignoble surrender of his masculine authority. In contrast, when Cordelia re-enters the play, she conceives her tears as a key to unlock nature's powers to heal her father: "All blest secrets, / All you unpublished virtues of the earth," she says, "Spring with my tears" (4.3.15–17). In tending to her father, in a sense Cordelia becomes the daughter-mother that the father wanted her to be. Yet even before they are reunited, Lear radically changes his understanding of what tears can mean, when he invokes the crying infant as a common denominator of humanity: "When we are born, we cry that we come / To this great stage of fools" (4.5.171–2). Shakespeare carries the imagery to its final stage when, upon waking from his madness, Lear says "I am bound / Upon a wheel of fire, that mine own tears / Do scald like molten lead" (4.6.39–41). These are manly tears of self-knowledge, arising from his realization of the havoc that his original childish demands created.

Over the play's arc, Lear travels a great emotional distance. He begins as the epitome of a patriarch who unquestioningly subjects women to his demands, and ends, in these lines, with a simple recognition of his human limitations:

> I fear I am not in my perfect mind.
> ... Do not laugh at me,
> For as I am a man, I think this lady
> To be my child, Cordelia.
>
> —4.6.56, 61–3

Lear acknowledges his manhood and his daughter's womanhood in the same line and the same breath. He has ceased to imagine her as the maternal woman he yearned for, and accepts her as a "lady," separate from himself. Yet he also calls her his child, re-establishing the bond of paternity that he denied in the first scene, but no longer threatened by her autonomy as a person nor obsessed with the fleshly tie between parent and child.

HORNED MEN: THE HUSBAND'S TRAGEDY

The *OED* defines "cuckold" as "a derisive name for the husband of an unfaithful wife," thought to derive from the cuckoo, the bird that lays its eggs in other birds' nests.[33] The word, however, doesn't denote a male seducer who flits from one marital nest to another, but his victim, the husband who may be the unknowing father of another man's child. Cuckoldry is something that happens only to husbands, not to wives, *because* they are husbands. A man unfaithful to his wife doesn't confer upon her the peculiarly galling identity that the erring wife visits upon her husband when she makes him a cuckold.

Cuckoldry is created from the confluence of three mutually reinforcing phenomena. First, misogyny, in particular the belief that woman are by nature lustful and fickle; second, the double standard, by which a husband's infidelity is tolerable while a wife's is inexcusable; and third, patriarchal marriage, which makes a husband's honor dependent on his wife's chastity. No matter what the circumstances of the wife's infidelity, it only confirms what all men know: *cosi' fan tutte*. According to the double standard, she has become a whore, irrevocably degraded by even a single sexual transgression, and he has incurred everlasting shame, while the cuckolder merely earns disapproval at most.

The single greatest source of this shame is patriarchal marriage, which determines, according to Keith Thomas, "that men have property in women, and that the value of this property is immeasurably diminished if the woman at any time has sexual relations with anyone other than her husband."[34] I take "property" to be a metaphor for the honor that a chaste wife brings to her husband: the reputation of being an upright head of household, worthy of respect. Furthermore, "due benevolence" also figures into cuckoldry, in that a husband is under the obligation to keep his wife sexually satisfied. If she is faithful, in effect she certifies his virility; if she strays, she calls it into question. The loss of a wife's chastity is more than a material loss to a husband, because the dishonor and shame he endures from it are a loss of status in his community of male peers, and a crushing diminution of his sense of self-worth.

The cuckold's stigma is symbolized and imprinted on our visual imaginations by the horns that sprout from his forehead, producing the quibbles, allusions, puns, and jokes that populate English drama from the Renaissance into the eighteenth century. Dictionaries of slang list many idioms implying that the horn is a phallic symbol, "the physical sign of sexual excitement in the male" or "the male member itself."[35] Horned animals such as bulls, stags, and goats are traditionally considered virile, and readily lend themselves to allusions of cuckoldry. Curiously, though, horns are associated not with the lecherous seducer cuckold, but rather with the hapless husband. Horns express a social critique of the husband, mocking his virility by displaying it out of place, on his forehead. They suggest that he has allowed his wife to make him no more than a dumb animal. That part of him that is at once his pride and his vulnerability is exposed as his nemesis. In horns, its power is mocked and its bestiality confirmed.

Shakespeare's *Othello* is the tragedy of cuckoldry *par excellence*, which Iago uses as the prime instrument of the Moor's destruction. Iago first proposes to Roderigo, "If thou canst cuckold him, thou dost thyself a pleasure, me a sport" (1.3.357–8). Then, with seeming casualness, he includes himself in the scene:

> I hate the Moor,
> And it is thought abroad that 'twixt my sheets
> He has done my office. I know not if't be true,
> But I, for mere suspicion in that kind,
> Will do as if for surety.
>
> —1.3.368–72

Finally, he settles on Cassio as the alleged cuckolder of Othello, but intensifies his fantasy that the Moor that "the lusty Moor / Hath leapt into my seat" (2.1.283–4), claiming that

> ... nothing can or shall content my soul
> Till I am evened with him, wife for wife ....
>
> —2.1.285–6

He adds: "For I fear Cassio with my nightcap, too" (2.1.294). Iago imagines his world as a network of cuckoldries, man against man, in which women seem to be the objects but are actually secondary to the ambivalent bonds of rivalry and shared victimhood among men. Once he has made Othello suspect Cassio with *his* nightcap, he moves with smooth facility from jealousy to cuckoldry:

> O, beware, my lord, of jealousy.
> It is the green-eyed monster that doth mock
> The meat it feeds on. That cuckold lives in bliss
> Who, certain of his fate, loves not his wronger.
>
> —3.3.169–72

"Certain of his fate": Othello quickly comes to believe that all women are driven by restless sexual appetite, and that men, especially "great ones" like himself, face the "destiny unshunnable" of becoming cuckolds. "Even then this forked plague is fated to us / When we do quicken," he says, invoking the cuckold's horns (3.3.277–81).

When he tells Desdemona, "I have a pain upon my forehead here," he imagines those horns as his (3.3.288). His demand that Iago "prove my love a whore" offers a defense against such humiliation, for if he is a cuckold, his wife has made herself a whore (3.3.364). By the end of the scene, the two men have knelt to swear revenge, a vow that in effect supplants Othello's wedding vows, and unites them in a virtual wedding ceremony: "Now art thou my lieutenant," says the Moor, and Iago replies, "I am your own forever" (3.3.481–2).

What binds them together as Iago accumulates "proofs" that Desdemona has slept with Cassio is the idea that all married men share the same cuckold's fate—an ironic, perverse foundation of their masculinity. "Good sir, be a man," Iago urges Othello: "Think every bearded fellow that's but yoked / May draw with you" (4.1.63–5). He neatly sutures the yoke as a familiar icon of marriage to the image of the cuckold as a horned beast, an ox bearing a yoke, whose wife has reduced him to that state. This imagery is the stuff of comedies in the period, but here Shakespeare makes it integral to Othello's tragedy as an outsider in sophisticated Venetian society and a man of high ideals swept away by his first passion for a woman. Iago's vision of cuckolded men forming a defensive alliance against lustful, scheming women both bolsters his false proofs of Desdemona's duplicity and offers Othello a bond to counteract the chaos left by his loss of faith in her.

Through the character of Leantio, Thomas Middleton's tragedy *Women Beware Women* (c. 1621) registers a middle-class husband's anxiety about keeping his wife from other men who might make him a cuckold, and his jarring accommodation to that status when she is raped and publicly appropriated as his mistress by the Duke of Florence. In the opening scene, Leantio imagines his beautiful wife Bianca as a valuable possession that he must protect from theft:

> As often as I look upon that treasure
> And know it to be mine—there lies the blessing—
> It joys me that I ever was ordained
> To have a being, and to live 'mongst men . . . .
> And here's my masterpiece: do you now behold her!
> Look on her well, she's mine, look on her better— . . . .
> Who could imagine now a gem were kept
> Of that great value under this plain roof?
>
> —1.1.15–18, 42–3, 173–4

"Look on her well, she's mine": his anxious gloating replays *The Changeling*'s "thesaurization" of the virgin daughter walled up in her father's castle. Leantio is called away from his "plain roof" by business. In his absence, the Duke spies the lovely Bianca framed by the window from which she watches the annual procession that establishes his power and authority. He inveigles Leantio's mother and Bianca to his palace, then entraps and rapes the young wife. In the aftermath, Bianca immediately perceives her honor as "leprous": "I'm made bold now," she reflects: "sin and I'm acquainted" (2.2.427, 442–3). Unlike Beatrice-Joanna, she does see that she is now "the deed's creature," even though she was powerless to resist the Duke's assault.

And for Leantio, marriage is no longer a house that hides his conjugal treasure. Now he sees it as an orchard of "overladen trees" bearing "cares" and "jealousies," "distractions . . . fears . . . doubts," a perpetual harvest of emotional torment, the shame of cuckoldry from which nothing can protect a husband (3.2.190–214). However, Middleton doesn't make Leantio a tragic figure, as Othello is, but rather, a typical one, *l'homme moyen sensuel* who must change when circumstances change. Accepting the captaincy the Duke confers on him to keep him quiet, he calls it "a fine bit / To stay a cuckold's stomach" (3.3.50–1): he must eat to live, and live with his horns.

"THE PRIMAL ELDEST CURSE": PRIMOGENITURE AND BROTHER-RIVALS

Immediately after Richard, Duke of Gloucester, stabs King Henry VI to death, culminating his family's bid for the throne of England, he says:

> I had no father, I am like no father;
> I have no brother, I am like no brother;

> And this word "love," which graybeards call divine,
> Be resident in men like one another
> And not in me—I am myself alone.
>
> —*Richard, Duke of York*, 5.6.80–4

His words hint at the rivalry inherent in brotherly relations in the patriarchal family. Richard does indeed have a father, and brothers, but as a *younger* brother he feels cheated of his deserts, because primogeniture decrees that the eldest son inherit the patrimony. This practice was followed more zealously in England than on the continent, by gentry and lesser landowners as well as by aristocratic families.[36] In royal families, primogeniture meant succession to the throne. While primogeniture enabled families to enlarge and perpetuate their estates, it also set younger brothers apart from their eldest sibling in resentful impoverishment, and sowed the seeds of rivalry between fathers and eldest sons eager to seize their inheritance. In his book of characters, John Earle describes what primogeniture meant for a younger brother:

> His father . . . taskes him to be a Gentleman, and leaves him nothing to maintaine it. . . . His birth and bringing up will not suffer him to descend to the meanes to get wealth; but hee stands at the mercy of the world, and which is worse of his brother. . . . Nature hath furnisht him with a little more wit upon compassion. . . . Hee is commonly discontented, and desperate . . . .[37]

Interpretations of Richard's character usually stress his deformity as the source of his alienation and aggression, but his position as a younger brother counts as well. While it is he who eliminates Henry VI, it is his oldest brother Edward who ascends the throne. Richard's career of murder in *Richard III* is virtually laid out for him by the terms of primogeniture: he must simply cut down the brothers and nephews standing in his way. Again and again Shakespeare dramatizes the travesty of brotherly love resulting from this career path. For instance, after plotting to get his brother Clarence imprisoned, Richard hypocritically commiserates with him, blaming their brother Edward's wife, and lamenting "this deep disgrace in brotherhood" (1.1.112). When Clarence recalls how "our princely father York . . . charged us from his soul to love each other," he is on the point of being murdered by the assassins Richard hired (1.4.223–5). Mercifully, when Edward dies of natural causes, he saves Richard from having to murder him, but Richard, in order to strengthen his claim to the crown, then alleges that his brother is a bastard (3.5.84–92).

It is a younger brother who instigates the tragic action in *Hamlet* when he murders King Hamlet, asleep in his orchard. The Ghost views Claudius as the devil himself when he calls him "The serpent that did sting thy father's life" (1.5.39), and Claudius, racked by guilt, links his crime to its ancient Scriptural precedent, Cain's murder of Abel, when he cries, "It hath the primal eldest curse upon't, / A brother's murder" (3.3.37–8). Fraternal rivalry creeps into the Ghost's narrative when he calls his brother "a wretch whose natural gifts were poor / To those of mine" and compares him to "garbage" (1.4.51–2, 55–7). Yet Claudius makes a plausible ruler, brusquely dispatching diplomatic business in the early scenes and turning Machiavel when he senses Hamlet on his trail: perhaps his "gifts" went unrecognized because he was a younger brother.

In Shakespeare's *King Lear*, the younger brother's anger at being deprived of means merges with the bastard's resentment at being disinherited, in the figure of Edmond, bastard son of Gloucester. He is "twelve or fourteen moonshines lag of a brother" (1.2.5–6), Edgar. Like Richard and Claudius, Edmond has a "disruptive energy," in Michael Neill's words, that results paradoxically from the circumstances of his conception.[38] As Edmond explains it, he was conceived "in the lusty stealth of nature," which gives him "More composition and fierce quality" than his legitimate brother Edgar has. Edmond professes himself bound to the law of nature, giving himself license to flaunt the laws of inheritance and pursue his "natural" ambition to wrest Edgar's land from him: "Well then, / Legitimate Edgar, I must have your land," he crows (1.2.1–2, 15–16). When he fakes a letter written by his older brother in which Edgar seemingly proposes that they rise up against their father's "aged tyranny," offering Edmond "half his [Gloucester's] revenue for ever," he projects his own enmity as a bastard son onto his legitimate brother, and assimilates a generational conflict between father and son into the bastard's sense of injured merit (1.2.45–52). Counterpointing the breakdown of Lear's relations with his daughters, Edmond plots winning a zero-sum game against his father, to get "That which my father loses: no less than all. / The younger rises when the old doth fall" (3.3.21–2).

King Lear as a whole dramatizes the implosion of two patriarchal families under the misguided authorities and unexamined faults of their fathers and brothers, as well as the rampant desires and ineffectual kindnesses of daughters and wives. Cracked open by their tragedies like the heavens on Lear's heath, these families are destroyed, leaving audiences then and now to find what lessons they can for the futures of their own families.

CHAPTER EIGHT

Gender and Sexuality

Undoing the Tragic Subject

GORAN STANIVUKOVIC

The argument to George Gascoigne and Francis Kinwelmarshe's conjoint blank-verse rendering of Euripides' tragedy *Phoenissae*, which they renamed *Iocasta*, does not merely introduce the plot of this play but also puts gender at the heart of the violent destruction of the protagonists. *Iocasta*, the argument says, binds the social roles of men and women with the tragedy's frightening world of wickedness and sexual aggression, and it links, importantly, transgression to fear and tyranny. The audience of *Iocasta* is promised a play that will show how

> To scourage the crime of wicked Laius,
> And wrecke the fonde incest of Oedipus,
> The angry Gods stirred vp their sonnes by strife,
> With blades imbrewed to reane each others life.
> The wife, the mother, and the concubine,
> (Whose fearfull hart foredrad their fatall fine)
> Her sonnes thus dead disdained longer life,
> And slaies hirselfe with self-same bloudie knife:
> The daughter she, surprisde with chiddish dread
> (That durst not die) a loathsome life doth lead.
> Yet rather chose to guide her banish sire,
> Then cruel Creon should haue his desire.
> Creon is king, the tripe of tyrannie,
> And Oedipus mirror of miserie.
>
> —sig. F5r[1]

Incest, banishment, tyranny, and murder dissolve not only the familial world of the tragic protagonists in *Iocasta*, but also show the two forces which reshape that tragic word, gender and sexual passion. Across social, political, and familial levels, *Iocasta* shows that tragedy dramatizes not only "the ambitious life and death" of the great,[2] but also stages the demise of the gendered and sexual subject. The argument about this tragedy reminds the audience of the incestuous nature of the Greek myth of Iocasta, Laius, and Oedipus, calling attention to Iocasta's gendered and sexual roles as "[t]he wife, the mother, and the concubine" (for marrying her own son who is also her husband's murderer); it also refers to Oedipus' tragedy as "the mirror of miserie," because of his erroneous killing of his father and incestuous marriage to his mother.

First performed before an all-male audience of Gascoigne's and Kinwelmarshe's fellow students of law at Gray's Inn in 1556, *Iocasta* heralded what the new early English tragedy would soon become when the genre started to flourish in the London theaters of the 1590s, that is, a rhetorical and dialogic exploration of new spaces for gender.

The early modern tragedy started to ask what the sexual passions of the protagonist make possible for the gendered subject, and what new connections between gender, desire, the body, language, and space are created by this undoing of gender.[3] As plays like *Gorboduc*, *Antony and Cleopatra*, *The Revenger's Tragedy*, *Edward II*, *Hamlet*, and *The Duchess of Malfi* show, the demise of the tragic protagonist is bound with the violence exercised upon their gendered selves, as these features are articulated in "rhetorical and dialogic structures."[4] What I mean by undoing the gender and sexuality of early modern tragedy concerns how the texts and language of the tragedies I explore reveal meanings of gender that socio-historiographic analyses may not address.[5] As A.D. Nuttall maintains,[6] if the suffering and the tragic fall of a protagonist intensify grief, they also show ruptures in the conceptualization of the self, and in the idea of gender and sexual desire in each of the plays.

What is commonly considered to be the first English tragedy, *Gorboduc*, co-authored by Thomas Sackville and Thomas Norton and published in 1561, is not based on the classical model as *Iocasta*, but on English chronicle history. Although a tragedy framed by Tudor political history and based on the national myth of the origins of Britain, *Gorboduc*, like *Iocasta*, turns familial conflict and murder into the subject of both political and gendered tragic history. In *Iocasta*, incest and fratricide unravel tragedy, but in *Gorboduc* light is shed on how early English tragedy conceptualized gender at the heart of the conflict within the state, at the very moment in the social history of England from the late feudal medievalism to the early modernity of the Elizabethan period, when masculinity started increasingly to be associated with independence. At the core of this shift, fraternal conflict over dependence[7] and inherited rule became not only a fact of social history but also a subject of drama, such as *Gorboduc*.

The early scenes in *Gorboduc* dramatize ruling feudal masculinity at the point of ceasing public, political power because of old age, illustrated in the king's, Gorboduc's, division of his kingdom between his two sons, Porrex and Ferrex: "When fatal death shall end my mortal life, / My purpose is to leave unto them twain / The realm divided into two sundry parts. / The one, Ferrex, mine elder son, shall have; / The other shall the younger, Porrex, rule" (1.2.59–62).[8] The issue of the realm's division into two equal parts and "[f]or profit and advancement of [the king's] sons" (1.2.154) is not unproblematic—"I think not good for you, for them, nor us" (1.2.160)—because giving the sons rule of the kingdom while the father is still alive represents, as the king's counselor, Philander, advises, a dangerous move on both political and gendered grounds. The problem of such rule, Philander maintains, is that the elder brother might be inclined to force the younger brother into subordination:

> As an unkind wrong it seems to be
> To throw the brother subject under feet
> Of him whose peer he is by course of kind.
> And nature, that did make this egalness,
> > Oft so repineth at so great a wrong
> That oft she raiseth up a grudging grief,
> Is younger brethren at the elder's state,

> Whereby both towns and kingdoms have been razed
>   And famous stocks of royal blood destroyed.
> The brother, that should be the brother's aid
> And have a wakeful care for his defense,
> Gapes for his death and blames the lingering years
> That draw not forth his end with faster course;
>
> —1.2.183–95

The theory behind this political counsel imagines the gendered basis of primogeniture not as a stabilizing but as a threatening force to the realm. The elder brother acts against this law, which equalized him with his younger brother, and in subjugating the younger the elder brother destabilizes the state. *Gorboduc* dramatizes the social and moral complexity of the social practice of primogeniture as a problem of both succession and masculinity. The play stages essentially the revenge of the younger brother against the social and familial practice of primogeniture, a topic which Shakespeare also explores in the subplot involving Edgar and Edmund in *King Lear*, a play that, like *Gorboduc*, stages a split-up of kingdom. In *Gorboduc*, Porrex is accused of the murder of the elder brother, Ferrex, because of "the mindful malice of his grudging heart" (2.1.62). The social obverse of the political tension between the brothers and the murder of the elder one in the play, however, can be found in the chapter "The state of great younger brethren," included in Thomas Wilson's *The State of England* (1600). Wilson writes that

> [a father] may demise as much as he thinks good to his younger children, but such a fever hectic hath custom brought in an inured amongst fathers, and such fond desire they have to leave a great shew of the stock of their house, though the branches be withered, that they will not do it, but my elder brother forsooth must be my master. He must have all, and all the rest, that which the cat left on the malt heap, perhaps some small annuity during his life or what please our elder brother's worship to bestow upon us if we please him, and my mistress his wife.[9]

In social history, the younger brother, excluded from inheritance and left at the mercy of his brother and his sister-in-law, at best may have been taken care of by his elder brother. This was the case unless he left the paternal home in search of education and military service. But this is not the case in *Gorboduc*, and, so, denied of his share in the divided land, the younger brother enacts his dramatic revenge. If, as Wilson's text suggests, in social history the younger brother is unmoored from the established political stability and safety in his father's kingdom, in a stage tragedy he becomes an agent of the rebellious masculine order within the state. In a tragedy rooted in discourses about land, succession, and royal rule within a feudal kingdom, the younger brother assumes his own political and gendered autonomy, against nature and despite the gods (2.1.81). *Gorboduc* is a tragedy, as Hermon says, in which masculinity defines "nature" as a property germane to filial bonds:

> If nature and the gods had pinched so
> Their flowing bounty and their noble gifts
> Of princely qualities from you, my lord
> And poured them all at one in wasteful wise
> Upon your father's youngest son alone,
> Perhaps there be that in your prejudice
> Would say that birth should yield to worthiness.
>
> —2.181–7

The younger brother's daring in shattering such natural bonds of social and familiar cohesion represents not only a deviation from his father's illusionary idea of tranquil co-existence of two brothers, but, and more importantly, of a new gendered and social role that the younger brother has assumed. By treating his given status as a source of power and dominance, the younger brother redesigns the idea of governance. By asserting his effective, if violent, agency against nature which relegated him to the subordinate position in relation to the first-born son, the younger brother, Ferrex, violates the social rule that marriage was a major route towards social and political advancement, by breaking the order and law of the state. From a subordinate position vis-à-vis his elder brother, by the end of the play Porrex, ruled by his belief that "Mischief for mischief is a due reward" (2.1.54), embodies heroic masculinity, rebelling against the familial order in the household and the state.

Gorboduc undoes kinship as the locus of political and familial stability and exposes the fracture in the long-established practice of primogeniture. As Ralph Houlbrooke reminds us, writing about the changes in the family and kinship in early modern England, "[k]inship was not in our period the mainspring of English politics or the individual's most important source of security,"[10] *Gorboduc* tragically reveals this at both private and social levels. The only woman in this homosocial world is the brothers' mother, Videna. At the end of the play, the discourse shifts register from the masculine public rhetoric to the language of reproduction, motherhood, and privacy, at the point when Videna addresses fratricide. "Shall I still think," asks Videna of Ferrex, "that from this wound thou sprung?/That I thee bare? Or take thee for my son?" (4.1.63–4). Her speech turns to the language of woman's reproductive body—"O wretch, this womb conceived thee" (4.1.67), shifting the focus in this tragedy from a play about male power to one of motherhood. The vindictive feminine fury embodied in Videna, and the connection between woman's reproductive body and tragedy, counter the tragic demise of the sons whose conflict over rule threatens the kingdom's stability both now and in the future.

Like other tragedies performed at the London schools of law, *Gorboduc* was written by men and for men. They were performed before a male audience, and many of them combined personal histories of the tragic protagonist with the national history. As one of those plays, *Gorboduc* casts a long shadow over the tragedies written for popular theater, in which state politics, history, and gender representations are closely related to power relations between sexes.

Like *Gorboduc*, *Hamlet* is a tragedy in which the themes of sovereignty and kinship intersect with those of gender and sex. The amount and diversity of language about gender and sex in *Hamlet* at times takes over the revenge plot so much that we can argue that *Hamlet* is in fact a tragedy in which the demise of a young hero of noble birth also brings about the collapse of most gendered unions. Margreta de Grazia has observed that, "[t]he focus of the play moved inward, and expressed itself not by the action primary to ancient drama, but by the withdrawal from action into the depths and intersections of character."[11] The psychological turn in the criticism of Hamlet (and of *Hamlet*) has also meant recently that explorations of gender and sex have been revised and that criticism of gender and sex have been balanced by a recent fresh analysis of the play through the lens of political knowledge and humanist learning that informs Hamlet's thinking and speaking.[12] Yet gender remains the locus of political agency and the understanding of character in *Hamlet*. King Claudius believes that persistent expression of sympathy ("obstinate condolement," 1.2.94) emasculates because it causes "unmanly grief" (1.2.95).[13] Grief not only emasculates, but it also softens and skews perception and understanding, as Claudius infers, because such emasculating state of emotions also "shows a will most incorrect to heaven,/A heart unfortified, a mind impatient,/An understanding simple and unschooled" (1.2.95–7). Engulfing grief, Claudius maintains, is "a fault to heaven" and "a fault against the dead" as well as "a fault to nature" and a threat to a reasonable (natural?) acceptance of the death of father (1.2.101–3). The tragic subject that the text imagines at this point is opposite of what Claudius states is natural, that is, heroic, masculine, and coherent—much like himself in his first appearance in the play in Act 1, Scene 1 in which he dazzles the listeners with his ability to set out to work on the business of the state. Such transgression is, in the words of Jonathan Dollimore, "constituted" by "the pre-existing structures of language and ideology."[14] The idea that Hamlet is emasculated by grief makes him a tragic subject and a gendered subject, separated from the militant symbolic order which demarcated masculinity of his father, or Fortinbras, his young heroic opponent. As Horatio says:

> our last king,
> Whose image even by now appeared to us,
> Was, as you know, by Fortinbrass of Norway
> Thereto pricked on by a most emulate pride,
> Dared to the combat: to which our valiant Hamlet—
> For so this side of our known world esteemed him—
> Did slay Fortinbras, who by a sealed compact,
> Well ratified by law and heraldry,
> Did forfeit, with his life, all those his lands
> Which he stood sealed on to the conqueror.
>
> —1.1.80–9

This speech is as much about kinship and heroic valor as foundations of the state as it is about the image of masculinity belonging to the old, late feudal order of the state, an order that falls with the murder of Hamlet and with the Fortinbras' march towards Elsinore. At the end, *Hamlet* brings on Horatio's philosophical, almost epicurean acceptance of the tragic consequences of drama that has just ended, which gives him a "cause to speak" (5.2.343). It also brings on Hamlet's humanistic hubris, which left him his "dying voice" (5.2.309), at once controlling the story of his tragic fall, but also entrusting its telling to Horatio, the most loyal man in his dramatic life. Yet in those last moments of the tragic action, the play dramatizes the masculinity of three young men (Hamlet, Horatio, and young Fortinbras), which has been held up to scrutiny throughout the play. If the bond of loyalty between Horatio and Hamlet in the play characterizes the affective and intellectual bond of friendship of the kind recognized in the complex culture of early modern friendship, or *amicitia*, Fortinbras' militant purpose sharply contrasts the humanist basis of friendship as a loving, passionate, and intellectual bond between socially equal men. Alone on the political stage of *Hamlet*, Fortinbras embodies heroic masculinity in action. He is a young man without a friend but is a leader of an army of men. In playing this heroic part, Fortinbras' militant masculinity is the obverse of Hamlet's masculinity defined by grace, aesthetic affiliation with the role and work of theater, and cerebral introspection.

Young Fortinbras, set on a political gain and military victory, belongs to the same worldview with which the play characterizes Claudius, a man of action and political resoluteness, a kind of "painted tyrant" (2.2.471), as Pyrrhus described in the First Player's synopsis of the plot of the play-within-the-play about to be performed before the court audience at Elsinore. But Fortinbras' age reminds us of other young men whose masculinity is barely asserted, like Rosencranz and Guilderstern, who are parodies of humanist friends. Other young men, like Laertes, reproduce protective yet stifling, and oppressive roles, men played culturally as the guardians of women's chastity within the household. If war and victory define Fortinbras' masculinity, what are the young men on the margin of *Hamlet*, Rosencranz, Guilderstern, and Laertes, defined by? Their confused, sycophantic, literal, even dumb perspective on the reality in which they are presented as Hamlet's false and failed friends, appear opposite to Horatio. What to make of Laertes' nervousness at Elsinore, his persistent desire to leave the household of an oppressive father, Polonius? He is a man who nervously yet persistently wishes to leave for France, a place of freedom from the paternal power in suffocating Elsinore. It is hard, when one hears Laertes speaking of Hamlet

> For Hamlet, and the trifling of his favour,
> Hold it a fashion and a toy in blood,
> A violet in the youth of primy nature,
> Forwarded not permanent, sweet not lasting,
> The perfume and suppliance of a minute,
> No more.
>
> —1.3.3–8

to not be conscious that this is as much a portrait of Hamlet as a Renaissance youth as a reflection of Laertes' perceptive ability to estimate another man in sensory terms and quality. The affective quality of Laertes' idea of another man in play makes *Hamlet* also a tragedy of Laertes, not just of Hamlet. For Laertes speaks and feels like a friend without the other; he is characterized as a sensitive, emotional, and poetical youth, one perceptive about interiority. Like Hamlet and Fortinbras, Laertes has also lost a father and is bent on revenge. His individuality, even loneliness, or aloneness, makes his masculinity, his secretive adoration as well as open warning to Ophelia of Hamlet, his elusive sexuality, and his flight from the patriarchal head, Polonius, of the household to which he belongs, a young man of interior motivation and place in the world of this tragedy.

One way of thinking about how Shakespeare understands gender, how he reveals gender's multiple and conflicting expressions and representations in *Hamlet*, and how he paces the tragic action in its rush towards the resolution, is to consider the relationship between Hamlet, Gertrude, and Ophelia.[15] Gertrude strikes us as a key character in this tragedy only if we think of her in terms of psychoanalytic criticism which explores the fraught relationship between her and her son. Otherwise, she does not have a central presence in the play, nor does she speak much. We might wish to ask why a character that often comes to mind instantly upon a mention of this play is, in fact, a marginalized dramatic part? Why are the woman and mother in her relegated to the outer edges of the plot? Her relationship with Hamlet is complicated by his grievance against her second marriage to his uncle Claudius following the murder of Hamlet's father. "Mother, you have my father much offended" (3.4.11), Hamlet tells her, bursting into her bedroom. "Come, come, you answer with an idle tongue" (3.4.12); her reply tempers the blame. But the seriousness of Hamlet's blame has to do with the fact of inheritance (again, we are hearing the echo of *Gorboduc* in this tragedy), as he says to Horatio at the very end of the play, when outlining Claudius' crimes:

> He that hath killed my king and whored my mother,
> Popped in between th'election and my hopes,

> Thrown out his angle for my proper life,
> And with such cozenage—is't no perfect conscience
> To quit him with this arm?
>
> —5.2.65–9

Hamlet first accuses Claudius of murder, and then of whoring his mother, and finally of theft (which is how C.T. Onions glosses "cozenage"[16]), for Claudius has taken what is rightfully Hamlet's in terms of inheritance. To Hamlet, Gertrude's incest may not matter nearly as much as Claudius' theft. As Lisa Jardine has argued persuasively in her discussion of Gertrude's marriage, in historical terms, the second marriage was problematic primarily from the perspective of "the complexity of kind and inheritance obligations."[17] It was less problematic when it involved incest, for such marriages did take place sometimes. A marriage like Gertrude's would have been considered incestuous in the Elizabethan period, but only because a woman was marrying her late husband's kin. In other words, such marriages were regarded as marriages taking place within her own family, but not within her own bloodline. Therefore, the culture was ready to turn a blind eye to such marriages.[18] Hamlet's concern is as much economic as it is moral, which is where his problem with his mother's marriage is individualized. He worries that his mother's second marriage would take him out of inheritance. Therefore, her "offense" is a cause for Hamlet's private grievance but not a crucial motivating factor for Hamlet's own tragic demise.

The way Shakespeare erases Gertrude from the play when she is dying by drinking from the poisoned cup intended for her son reinforces Gertrude's insignificance in the tragic action of the play. This can be illustrated down to the cause included in the text on the scene of Gertrude's death. Simon Palfrey and Tiffany Stern have examined such repeated cues in detail and have demonstrated how they shape the meaning of this tragic scene in *Hamlet*.[19] Repeated cues reveal the relationship between the text and the tragic action. Gertrude's cue, "the drink, the drink" (5.2.264), repeated four times (twice in line 265 as well), remains unheard in the commotion and the shouts "treason, treason" (5.2.276) by all the courtiers present. She dies unheard. Palfrey and Stern insightfully comment on the moment of Gertrude's death, helping us see how Shakespeare manages tragedy down to such verbal detail. They say:

> The Gertrude-actor might well have recognized a tantalizing, almost cruelly denied temptation to seize the stage and die like a true queen. And this fastidious refusal of repeated cues is an emphatic sign that we, like the Gertrude-actor's fellow players, are not ultimately to be allowed "in" to her dying, as we weren't into her life. She dies alone, and remains as impenetrably opaque as ever.[20]

Forgotten, unheard, opaque when dying, Gertrude's fate is a reminder not only of the relationship between theater as a shaping force of tragedy but also of gender as a source of tragic meaning. Gertrude's dying on the edge of, and in the background of, the tragic unraveling is a reminder of how limited her agency was in the composition of the tragic plot in its entirety.

Gertrude neither dies nor lives as a dramatic character memorably. In contrast, regal Cleopatra dominates the space of tragedy physically in her almost constant presence on stage in *Antony and Cleopatra* (written *c.* 1606–7), and linguistically in a palette of extravagant hyperboles which mark her mode of speaking. She also dies the most unforgettable death of all Shakespeare's female tragic protagonists. *Antony and Cleopatra* is a tragedy which, perhaps more than any other tragedies of Shakespeare, shows that gender and sex are constructs of language. The play makes a point of presenting Cleopatra's gender in terms of race, which brings out anxieties among the Romans over racial difference at their door. "Cleopatra's darkness," writes Kim Hall, "makes her the embodiment of an absolute correspondence between fears and racial and gender difference and the threat they pose to imperialism."[21] The opening lines of the tragedy register these fears and anxieties. When one of Anthony's soldiers, Philo, reflects on the infatuation of his general with the Egyptian:

> Nay, but this dotage of our General's
> O'erflows the measure: those his goodly eyes,
> That o'er the files and musters of the war
> Have glowed like plated Mars, now bend, now turn
> The office and devolution of their view
> Upon a tawny front; his captain's heart,
> Which in the scuffles of great fights hath burst
> The buckles on his breast, reneges all temper,
> And is become the bellows and the fan
> To cool a gypsy's lust.
>   Look where they come:
> Take but a good note, and you shall see in him,
> The triple pillar of the world transformed
> Into strumpet's fool. Behold and see.
>
> —1.1.1–14[22]

we hear the extent to which the physical presence of Antony and Cleopatra—lovers hardly ever alone on the stage throughout the play—ends up being (for those who observe it, whether Romans or spectators) a parody of a sexual affair, because such an affair distorts the militant values of Rome. The buckle which secures Antony's breastplate to the other parts of his torso armor had "burst" in the past, "in the scuffles of great fights," because his heart was beating so fiercely. Now, the beating has become "the bellows and the fan / To cool a gypsy's lust." Antony's heroic masculinity has been emasculated by his erotic unrestraint. Such unrestraint, rather than cooling the fire of desire and love within his bosom, has become the source that rekindles and incites such love, as bellows do. In the last few words of his speech, "Behold and see," which come after the entry on the stage of Antony and Cleopatra and her retinue of ladies and eunuchs, Philo invites spectators to watch the gendered spectacle of this entry, as Rome is showing those spectators an exotic pageant as if Egypt were an oriental show of sound, color, and flesh on display. Philo's speech has a choric function. But it is a Roman chorus that is inviting the spectators to see Cleopatra through Roman eyes. The strangeness of this erotic display is only part of other kinds of strangeness which are associated with Cleopatra's gender, as Romans are always ready to associate Cleopatra with witchcraft. Pompey, speaking of Cleopatra, says: "Let witchcraft join with beauty, lust with both, / Tie up the libertine in a field of feasts, / Keep his brain fuming!" (2.1.22–4). This denigration of Cleopatra on both racial and gender lines is one of the persistent preoccupations of the Romans in this tragedy. This is most impressively conveyed in Enobarbus' account to Agrippa and Maecaenas, Caesar's lieutenants, about feasting in Egypt and of Cleopatra, always an object of Roman men's curiosity at the same time as their denigration of her. Enobarbus' story of watching Cleopatra's barge sailing down the river Cydnus "like a burnished throne" (2.2.198) is told in a mini allegory, and gives an aestheticized image of Cleopatra as an idea of glamorous body on display for Roman's sensuous satisfaction.

> For her own person,
> It beggared all description: she did lie
> In her pavilion—cloth-of-gold of tissue—
> O'er picturing that Venus where we see
> The fancy out-work nature; on each side her
> Stood pretty, dimpled boys, like smiling Cupids,
> With diverse-coloured fans, whose wind did seem
> To glow the delicate cheeks which they did cool,
> And what they did undid.
>
> —2.2.194–212

The bombast with which the exoticism of Cleopatra's passage is described shows not only how Shakespeare takes liberty with his source in Plutarch, elevating Enobarbus from a minor character in the source to a major one in the tragedy, but also how this scene, by creating this image in which the Renaissance aesthetic of love and desire is mixed with Enobarbus' oriental fiction of Cleopatra, creates a memorable image of a woman as an eroticized and sexualized distant idea. Other women in this play—most of whom are bit parts or only referred to—are integrated in the immediate environment in which they live, either Rome (Octavia) or Egypt (Cleopatra's female attendants), but Cleopatra "made a gap in Nature" (2.2.224). This is the culmination of Enobarbus' satirical commentary on Cleopatra's greatness. Cleopatra's association with water, with mobility, invoked in Antony's lines, "Let Rome in Tiber melt, and the wide arch / Of the ranged empire fall!" (1.1.15–16) shows that place does not matter when it comes to imagining Cleopatra.

That the east, the pagan world beyond Christianity, was considered a space in which vice flourished is well-known in literary and cultural histories of this region. In some early formulations of the east, vice and sexual transgression were linked to tragedy because they helped explain the fall of an ambitious life. This is the case in a dramatic fragment of a tragedy, extant in manuscript from around 1590, from the Folger Shakespeare Library. The writer announces "[a] stately Tragedy containing the ambitious Life and death of the great Cham the enchantments of Bagous the Brachman wth the straunge fortunes of Roxen the Captiuity release and death of his brother Manzor the Turchestan King and happy Fortunes of the Sophy of Persia with the loke of Bargandell his sonne."[23] This tragedy set in the east isolates the fate of the tragic protagonist, the great Cham, through enchantment and magic, from the historical and political theme. But, as the text of the fragment of this play shows, this tragedy also connects witchcraft with incest and the work of Venus, the goddess of love and sexual desire. "Venus puttinge on hir Ceston cranes," the author of this tragedy goes on,

> That I crosse Incest and recite same loue
> Which she will Hymeneus ratefyed.
> Then Hecate with frightful visions
> Coniueres me to declare heer in the most
> The workes of her east Indian Ministers
> And how euen with Tobacco now well knowne.
>
> —fol. 1

The background of this tragedy, as in *Gorboduc*, is incest and witchcraft which bewitches man to perform such transgressive act. For tragedy to perform its work as a kind of drama rooted in excess, which fascinates by its strangeness and forbiddenness, by its tilting towards drastic and "self-aggrandizement in grief,"[24] it must drive its gendered subjects towards catastrophe and resolution by shocking, violent forces and the working of the supernatural. Only in contrast to such energies can the vision and circumstances which shape gender be meaningfully perceived.

As a tragedy built on rhetorical exaggeration and a visual imagination rooted in images of excess, *Antony and Cleopatra* is the most distinct of Shakespeare's tragedies of self-aggrandizement. Moments like the one when Enobarbus ambiguously represents Cleopatra as an object of sarcasm and admiration show that despite the way Jacobean Shakespeare approaches sex and desire from an ironic distance, *Antony and Cleopatra* captures some key tragic elements, like the death scenes, as moments to undo gender from some of its normative representations. Antony's botched suicide, for example, parodies both the idea of Roman heroic suicide and tragedy as a type of play in which death scenes are moments that lead to the resolution of tragic complications and move the audience to the cleansing of emotions. "How? Not dead?" (4.15.103), asks Antony as he falls on his sword, after which tragedy turns into melodrama, when he reflects on the death scene gone wrong: "I have done my work ill, friends / O make an end of what I have begun" (4.15.105–6). The instability of gender roles in *Antony and Cleopatra*, often marked by the appropriation of the signifiers of the other gender, as in Antony's first appearance onstage dressed in Cleopatra's mantles, acts as a powerful signifier of the emasculation of his heroic Roman prowess and represents a way in which political roles and norms have been blurred, if not completely destabilized, in this tragedy. As he admits at the end of the play, Antony is no longer the Antony of Roman imperial power. He says,

> I, that with my sword
> Quartered the world, and o'er greet Neptune's back
> With ships made cities, condemn myself to lack
> The courage of a woman.
>
> —4.1.557–60

Rendered unheroic because of his pursuit of Cleopatra, Antony is presented as an emasculated parody of a triumvir of imperial and militant Rome. Cleopatra's frequent outbursts of aggression and anger at the height of passion of frustration in Antony's absence appropriated traits of masculine behavior, according to the early modern cultural semiotics of masculinity. As Patricia Simons has demonstrated, in north-western Europe, socio-cultural behaviors suggested that "[o]nly men were . . . roguish, assertive, insistent and heated in character."[25] Both the historical Cleopatra, who was Macedonian, and the Egyptian Cleopatra of Shakespeare's tragedy, belong to the non-Christian world of the eastern Mediterranean, to the Levantine ethnic milieu, and their actions do not conform to the north-western European cultural system of gendered behavior that Simons describes. But Shakespeare's tragedy is a play for the English audience, and by bringing Cleopatra's roguish, masculine behavior to the stage in London, Shakespeare's tragedy troubles the representational codes of the gendered system prevailing in his own world. Cleopatra's ironic concern how her role will be played later—"I shall see / Some squeaking Cleopatra boy my greatness / I'th'posture of a whore" (5.2.219–21)—reveals how theater was perceived to undo gender that the play has strived, and struggled, to portray in dazzling terms.

Antony and Cleopatra features a female protagonist that is elaborated, in her words and in the accounts of others, in a way that always exceed her actions. There is a moment in Shakespeare's other major Mediterranean tragedy, *Othello* (written 1604), featuring the conflict between race, ethnicity, and gender at the heart of tragedy. The tragic demise of Othello and Desdemona has been treated in criticism as the outcome of a relationship that the world in which they came together could not tolerate and accommodate. Kiernan Ryan has put this point well when he says that

> The destruction of Othello and Desdemona lays bare the barbarity of a culture whose preconception about race and gender cannot allow a love like theirs to survive and flourish. The modern significance and value of the play are rooted in this revelation. In loving and marrying each other, Othello and Desdemona instinctively act according to principles of racial equality and sexual freedom which are far from generally accepted and practised in our own day, let alone in Shakespeare's. As a result they find unleashed on them, through Iago, the fury of a society whose foundations are rocked by the mere fact of their relationship.[26]

Ryan makes a strong claim about external social obstacles to the survival of this cross-ethnic, -religious, and -racial marriage, and about the fragility of such bonds even across time. Desdemona and Othello's marriage cannot survive in a world that seems to be set up to erode their marital felicity. In that world, Iago, who says that he "do[es] know the state" (1.1.146)[27], and Brabantio, who cannot believe that his daughter Desdemona fell in love with Othello, unless Othello's supernatural power—"thou hast enchanted her"—bound Desdemona "in chains of magic" (1.2.63, 65), are the two agents that subvert this marriage from the start. The temporality of this doomed marriage, according to Ryan, lies not in the familiar conflict central to gender roles as such, but in the worldview which produces conflict before the opposites meet. Yet there is a moment in the play, easily passed over, which, if it does not challenge the view Ryan and others have eloquently voiced, at least demonstrates Desdemona's own agency in possibly resisting the tragedy of race and gender by a thought whose source is what was "generally accepted and practised" when it came to choosing a mate. In moments like this, gender is undone in the sense that something hitherto hidden, maybe even repressed, has surfaced to shake up the discourse that the tragic plot and narrative (and the play's critics) have forwarded thus far.

As the play nears the catastrophe of the tragic fall of Othello and Desdemona, at the end of a scene in which almost all major dramatic parts in this play are on stage at one time or another, the audience hears what I believe is an important exchange between Lodovico and Iago. Desdemona has just sought Lodovico's help in resolving the conflict between Othello and Cassio, caused by Othello's belief in Desdemona's infidelity. Shocked at hearing reports of Othello's treatment of his wife ("What? Strikes his wife? . . . Is it his use?", 4.2.264, 267), Lodovico, a cultured Venetian endowed with physical beauty and also graced with temperance and emotional restraint, two key elements of masculine virtue in the Renaissance aetiology of masculinity, now crops up as the subject of conversation between Desdemona and Emilia in 4.3, the scene to which, in the 1623 Folio text, the willow song was added. In this private scene, Desdemona remembers a mourning song of love and death that she first heard from her mother's maid, Barbary, evoking Barbary Moors and the Barbary coast. This invocation of the east, love, and death is then suddenly interrupted by a far less meditative thought, at the point at which she changes garments and Emilia helps her put on a nightgown. "This Lodovico is a proper man," states Desdemona (4.3.34), and continues to inquire about him for a few more lines, prompted by Emilia's praise of the young Venetian. "I know a lady in Venice would have walked barefoot to Palestine for a touch of his nether lip" (4.3.34–5), prods Emilia, at which point Desdemona bursts into a song: "The poor soul sat sighing by a sycamore tree, / Sing all a green willow" (4.3.36–7). What is the audience to make of this reference of Lodovico at this private, intimate moment? Emilia's prompt promotes him as a most desirable Venetian, just as she starts singing a song that ends with the following lines: "I called my love 'false love', but what said he then? / . . .If I court more women, you'll couch with more men." (4.3.50, 2). This enquiry of Lodovico from a distance provides a hint of a distant romantic interest, something which Emilia quickly picks up on and butters up. The song is about the fidelity of men and women in general terms, but the relative cause and effect of fidelity concerning men and women—"If I court more women, you'll couch with more men"—leaves the audience pondering whether Othello may not be the only man on her mind, and whether the alternative is not Cassio, over whose role the plot thickens, but another, unsuspected, Venetian, Lodovico. At this moment, it is theater and the speech action on the stage that give Desdemona affective agency. The audience is asked to comprehend where the limits and lineaments are of Desdemona's attraction and attachment to Othello until the end of the tragedy.

If this is a moment at which Desdemona's transgression is that of her private thought, transgression played out on the larger and more open field of politics unfolds more complexly and explicitly in Christopher Marlowe's *Edward the Second* (1592), in which sexuality drives politics of the state to its final catastrophe more than any other tragedy of the English Renaissance. Much criticism addresses the erotic and sexual bond between King Edward and his minion, Gaveston, as sodomitical, that is, subversive of procreative sexual activity and thus of heterosexual normativity more broadly, viewing this male–male relationship as embodying non-normative sexual desire and the non-procreative eroticism that it brings, as the period understood such close affective relationships that stood outside the realm of male friendship (*amicitia*). Likewise, critics have amply used *Edward II* as an instance of queer early modern drama, producing arguments about sodomy as a socially and politically disruptive force in the play. Recently, Mario DiGangi has summarized and commented on these arguments in his detailed discussion of sexual types in English Renaissance drama and represented across the culture that produces that drama.[28] Yet, as Alan Sinfield has cautioned, some of that criticism fails to address the way in which "Marlowe's play is distinctive in presenting same-gender partners not as in some sense women."[29] Queer in *Edward II*, then, poses a challenge to both male and female desire, and in a tragedy in which "heroism and gender take on"[30] variations on both genders, the kind of claim made by Sinfield, asks us to consider a woman as an agent in, even shaping, the queer discourse in the play involving men only. Sinfield's point calls on consideration of both genders as equally active in the play's language and representation of transgression. In that sense, Marlowe's play is distinctive in making the male same-gender desire a constituent part of an erotic triangle that includes a woman, Queen Isabella, too. She is subject to male aggression ("Fawn not on me, French strumpet; get thee gone" [1.4.145], says Edward[31]), and she is humiliated by Gaveston's insults and sexual transgressions—"Is 't not enough that thou corrupts my lord, / And art a bawd to his affections, / But thou must call mine honour thus in question?" (1.4.148–50)—but the boundless love which she expresses for Edward make her a tragic figure. Her social status of a future queen does not permit her, it seems, to unmoor herself from the male–male relationship between Gaveston and Edward that she is all too aware of even before she married Edward. She says: "rather will I die a thousand deaths. / And yet I love in vain"

(1.4.196–7). In an early appearance on the stage, when she acknowledges her awareness of the sexual liaison of Gaveston and Edward ("For never doted Jove on Ganymede / So much as he on cursed Gaveston," 1.4.180–1; "[thou] are a bawd to his affections" [4.4.151]), Isabella's own choice of erotic desire, not her status as a future queen, is troubled and violated by Edward's rejection of her (he says to Gaveston: "Speak not unto her; let her droop and pine" [4.4.162]). It is in this split between the erotic and the political, a split shared between two differently-gendered subjects, Gaveston and Isabella, that the subversive, queer nature of this play resides. If in *Edward II* tragic fall comes as the consequence of the conflict between Edward and the "proud, overdaring peers" (4.4.47) and "headstrong barons" (6.7.259) of his kingdom, who are concerned more for stability of the state than for the monarch's sexual proclivity, we ignore the extent to which the play uses Isabella's role in that relationship as also a consequence leading to her tragic collapse. The play alternates between the theme of sexual transgression that threatens the state, the representation of Isabella's love for Edward, and her relationship with Mortimer Senior. Love of and for a woman is a feeling always at risk in Marlowe's plays; in this one, Isabella's for Edward is thwarted by the plot of Gaveston and her turning to Mortimer, an icon of militant masculinity in the play, for physical satisfaction.

In *Edward II*, love can only be salvaged, ironically, by more transgression. Isabella's love for Mortimer ("Heavens can witness, I love none but you" [8.8.15]), sharply contrasts Edward's hyperbolic claim about Gaveston's love for him ("he loves me more than all the world" [4.4.77]). Edward's love for Isabella ("witness heaven how dear thou [Isabella] art to me" [4.4.167]) and Isabella's commitment to Edward through marriage ("On whom but on my husband should I fawn" [4.4.146]) show how objects of love and desire shift and change in this tragedy. Isabella's promiscuity is a form of feminine transgression, but it is also a sign of powerful liberation from men's hostility and abuse, which she has suffered from both Edward and Gaveston. Isabella's resilient quest for amorous fulfilment suggests her quest also for settling into what would then and now be perceived a normative heterosexual union. Her promiscuity defies the notion of companionate marriage as an affective union, and woman's dependence on man's agency to help establish it. The issue Isabella's promiscuity raises, however, is that the freedom that promiscuity gives her in abandoning one lover and choosing another, renders her sexually rapacious and thus morally repellent in a culture that valorizes female chastity, virtue, and marital fidelity. Marlowe's is a misogynistic construction of Isabella's agency, a way of keeping her in the domain of the male discourse of women as sexually unbridled and changeable. It may be a rumor in which Baldock and Spencer Junior are happy to indulge. Yet, Gaveston, whose manipulation of sexual desire causes the political and personal tragic falls in the play, seems to shift objects of sexual satisfaction, when he is implied to be the lover of Margaret de Clare, daughter of the dead Earl of Gloucester. "I had thought," says Baldock, "the match had been broken off / And that his banishment had changed her mind" (5.5.25–6). But the match between Gaveston, her "first love" and Margaret "is not wavering," the audience is told, and therefore, say Spencer Junior, "she will have Gaveston" (5.5.27, 28). Whether this reading of the tragic subjectivity of Isabella and the instability of her transgressive sexual agency is enough to expose what Valerie Traub has called "the conceptual terms available to signify sexual knowledge,"[32] reveals the full scope and the deep layers of shifting sexual meanings in this tragedy. What signifies sexual knowledge in *Edward II* depends less on the chosen object of desire than on how the dramatic narrative and plot unfold the story of sexual bonds to the end of this play. Transgressions in the ways in which gender is imagined, and in which sexual passions are staged, represent one of the key forces that drive early modern tragedies.

The Revenger's Tragedy (published 1608), now attributed to Thomas Middleton,[33] heralds the genre of "horror tragedies"[34] on the early modern stage. It is also a forerunner of plays in which sexual perversion is the main discourse via which social and personal decline is dramatized. "Duke: royal lecher" (1.1.1), the first three words of the play not only make for a remarkably dramatic opening but also frame the entire play of moral, gendered, and sexual degradation and transgressions at the level of sex, desire, and the agency of gender. How does transgression, which overarches this play, reformulate gender and sex in this play? In an assessment of the relationship between subjectivity, sexuality, and transgression in Jacobean drama, Jonathan Dollimore has argued that

> Issues of transgression are inextricably bound up with those of subjectivity, and if poststructuralism enables us better to understand transgression in the Renaissance, this is perhaps because its conceptions of subjectivity are actually closer to those found in the Renaissance than is commonly reckoned.[35]

Dollimore wrote this before queer early modern studies started to flourish as a critical method that not only elucidates the depth and extent of the kinds of transgression that give energy to early modern drama, but also shows the extent to which early modern and modern subjectivities are in fact historically specific and not easily translatable across time. *The Revenger's Tragedy* demonstrates the extent to which transgression in terms of sex determines gendered roles, not identities, in the world of decaying power in the sick state that is the place where the revenge and horror take place in Middleton's tragedy.

Thus, there is something perverse, elusive, and queer about the syntax of Vindice's aside, musing about women while speaking to his mother, Gratiana:

> I e'en quake to proceed, my spirit turn edge,
> I fear me she's unmothered, yet I'll venture—
> "That woman is all male whom none can enter!"
>
> —2.1.109–11

The impossibility of entering sexually becomes a way of speaking about the prohibition of entering a man, sodomitically. It is as if Vindice, a revenging lover, thinks about erotic pleasure for a woman in terms of sexual submission with another man. Throughout the play, the spurned lover Vindice has now curiously detached from the thought of a woman. In this dramatically, ideologically, and erotically difficult play, brimming with some of the most splendid dramatic syntax of any revenge drama, moments like this rewrite the idea of normativity and the normal at all levels of gender and sex. In a play notorious for its references to sadistic eroticism and misogynistic violence, men take pleasure in coming up with plots for a violent ruination of women and family, as Vindice does when he plots ways of using women as bait for men, especially Lussurioso. Masculinity in this profoundly misogynistic tragedy is abjected and threatening, because the younger generation of men is excluded from the oligarchy of rule dominated by lecherous hegemonists. The men in *The Revenger's Tragedy* inhabit margins of a decayed society, ruled by the syphilis-stricken Duke. These men are young and educated, savvy but socially underused and therefore marginalized, as Vindice tells the audience:

> Duke: royal lecher: go, grey haired Adultery,
> And thou his son, as impious steeped as he:

> And thou his bastard true-begot in evil:
> And though his duchess that will do with devil:
> Four ex'lent characters!—Oh that marrowless age
> Would stuff the hollow bones with damned desires,
> And 'stead of heat kindle infernal fires
> Within the spendthrift veins of a dry duke,
> A parched and juiceless luxur.
>
> —1.1.1–9

Such a corrupted, decadent, powerless and emasculated, infertile world inhabited by men who are either impotent or threatening to women's sexuality, is also a world of false appearances and hypocrisy, and gender is the locus of such modes of being, as Vindice knows all too well: "The old duke, / Thinking my outward shape and inward heart / Are cut out of one piece / Hires me by price" (3.5.8–11). It is against the background of this corruption of social harmony, that sexual perversion and transgression twist gender and erotic desire to the point that some of the most distorted sexual thoughts begin to sound like chilling comedy or tragicomedy.

Vindice, "melancholy, passionate and embittered,"[36] is one of the young men for whom women and pleasure, like employment and social status, are denied in the world of "dislocated energy"[37] of the sick Duke's state. Excluded from a social role and the world of women, Vindice, Lussurioso, and the bastard Young Son turn to one another for help with cunning and plotting, for understanding and affect. Vindice's uncontrolled sexual desire and unbridled erotic imagination conjure up man's relationship with women in terms of violence and hyperbolic misogyny: "I would. . . / Take coach upon her lip, and all the parts, / Should keep men after men and I would ride / In pleasure upon pleasure" (2.1.95, 97–9). Vindice's ideal of unlimited pleasure is articulated in the context of woman's shameful humiliation. The connection of "ride" with a repeated gang-rape style of sexual intercourse turns into specific acts of sexual fantasy the motto of Vindice's agency, "'Tis no shame to be bad, because 'tis common" (2.1.33), or Piero's ironic comment, "Delay the doom for rape?" (1.4.53), in which hyperbole contains the truth about men in this play who act as sexual predators.

The sexual intentions and actions of the unattached, unloved, and unloving men of shared class against women in *The Revenger's Tragedy* put pressure on the early modern idea of instrumental friendship intended to entrench male alliances and define masculinity as "the workings of network of influence" leading to inverting and stretching the notion of "the passionate investment possible in instrumental bonds."[38] In *The Revenger's Tragedy* friendship is invoked not only as an alternative to marriage by those who have been excluded from courting women, but also as an emotionally fulfilling bond between men, as Lussurioso says:

> I'm one of that number can defend
> Marriage is good; yet rather keep a friend.
> Give me my bed by stealth—there's true delight;
> What breeds a loathing in't but night by night?
>
> —1.3.105–8

However, friendship, so desired exists only as an idea, not an ideal sought in society, because Lussurioso, clear though he is on the topic of friendship, is asking the "well experienced" (1.2.111) Vindice to make his sister, Castizia, available to Lussurioso.

Friendship based on parity collapses at this point. It is compromised by making it hinge on the ruination of female virtue and family, as Vindice coaches Lussurioso to have sex with the mother first: "Venture upon the mother, and with gifts / begin with her" (1.3.149–50). Vindice twists the idea of friendship, based on affective bonds between men, and on emotional and intellectual closeness of men, by proclaiming that "[w]e are made strange fellows, brothers, innocent villains" (1.3.70), proving that opportunistic male bonds masquerade as instrumental friendship; it is not status and power but women and sex, that he has been procuring for his villainous friends. And when Gratiana attempts to explain to Vindice women's motivation in responding to man's desire, Vindice's reply, "Oh suffering heaven with thy invisible finger / Even at this instant turn the precious side / Of both mine eyeballs inward, not to see myself" (2.1.127–9). This misogyny of this response, of Vindice's turning his ears away from knowing womanhood, reveals the extent to which *The Revenger's Tragedy* is a play about the distortion of the social idea of man's temperance and virtue. The sexually rapacious and transgressive masculinity of *The Revenger's Tragedy* warps heterosexuality as a social organization of masculinity in this tragedy in which men inhabiting the margins of society act as diabolical plotters of sexual perversion in a diseased society of dislocated male agency. As subjects whose dramatic lives exist outside the normative narratives of family, political rule, and social power, these men are open to inscription of other kinds of desire. They are denied a procreative relationship with a woman in a state in which women's options are "bleak"[39] because their fate lies not in marriage but in the protection of their chastity and virtue from men in a diseased society. If the "tragic revenger uses violence to articulate rage,"[40] that rage in *The Revenger's Tragedy* is ignited by their social and sexual marginalization; hence their destruction of the lecherous Duke's life and his household; hence Vindice's ruin of his sister Castizia; hence the thwarted, frustrated sexual desire for men who cannot be penetrated: "That woman is all male whom none can enter."

This homophobic outburst prompts thinking about what this homophobic queer moment means. That the aggressive homosocial milieu in the play offers an opportunity to push the text's meaning toward the homoerotic has been tested in a highly popular production of the play, directed by Melly Still at the National Theatre in London in 2008. This production exploded with sexual romp and titillating camp, with Rory Kinnear playing Vindice as a mildly neurotic, campy homosexual, highlighting his outsider status, and with Lussurioso dressed for a night out in a gay dance club, casually but persistently working on Vindice as a potential sexual prey. The rest of the men in this production—Ambitioso, Supervacuo, and the Younger Son—are all presented as queer. They are willing to reciprocate Lussurioso's queer performance with casual homoerotic dalliance. Only hyper-virile but silly Spurio remains alone in his hypermasculinity on the margin of the rest of the queer spectacle. Queer is neither an easy nor a single concept of mobility and sexual mutability. Traub has described in terms that are useful for exploring "what is normal for the early modern period" to determine what is "a crucial modifier of sexuality and the meanings of queer" in gender.[41] Queer is one way in which gender is deconstructed and undone in revenge tragedies; it is one way in which gendered plots of tragedies shock their audiences into seeing the potential of tragedy to reimagine the self in the process of formation on stage.

Sexual desire and bodily corruption provide a framework for the stories and plots of seduction and intrigue which, together with strange stage effects that put odd twists to such stories, make revenge tragedies some of the most compelling dramas about gender in seventeenth-century theater. *The Revenger's Tragedy* has shown how political distortion in a state leads to devastating ends for both men and women. John Webster's *The Duchess of Malfi* (written *c.* 1612–13) contrives a plot in which consequences of perverted desire, including incest involving a brother and a sister, are played out in a claustrophobic environment of a noble household in which the Duchess attempts but tragically fails to assert her rule as both a political figure and an individual. Her desire and downfall have been the subject of a substantial body of feminist criticism, which started by asserting that "[t]he text [of the play] valorizes women's equality to the point where the Duchess woos Antonio [her steward], repudiating the hierarchy of birth in favour of individual virtue."[42] Feminist criticism has teased out many nuances of the Duchess's complex character, the power of her language, wit, and independence in defending her status and her gendered agency,[43] and has considered the Duchess's integrity as basis for arguments about her as "an insidiously subversive force to be reckoned with."[44]

The play, however, dramatizes female forcefulness and resourcefulness only in a limited way within the plot. In a dramatic move that reveals the masculinist twist of Webster's feminist dramaturgy, the playwright returns the plot to masculine concerns, putting a male-gendered twist onto a woman-driven plot. To begin, the death of the Duchess in Act 4 is not the end of drama. Act 5 begins following the stage direction *Exit [carrying the body]*, referring to Bosola's taking the body of the dead Duchess offstage. The homosociality of Act 5 makes the Duchess only a memory, displaced by Antonio's conversation in the last scene of the play: "What think you of my hope of reconcilement / To the Aragonian brethren?" (5.1.1–2).[45] From this moment on, Delio, Antonio, and Pescara talk—about land, friendship, and plot against the Cardinal—in a manner that reconstitutes male power and loyalty. To Delio's "I'll second you in all danger: and howe'er, / My life keeps rank with yours" (5.2.74–5), Antonio replies: "You are still my lov'd and best friend" (5.2.76). At this point, we might wish to ask to what extent is the resilient integrity of the Duchess and the insidiously subversive force of her independence and care for her children the theme that the play promotes. The play's structure, the last masculine act specifically, challenges the notion of such female power and autonomy, as the play reverts to where it opened: the world of male moral and libidinal decline. This makes *The Duchess of Malfi* a peculiar tragedy, for its end is not about staging a scene that cleanses emotions, that features a revelation which opens out a vision into a new, bettered world. Instead, the play about a woman's strife for public and private freedom ends up being a tragedy about men competing for possession of a woman and for their own place in the world of transgression which they engender. A woman who is alive at the end of the play, Julia, Castruchio's wife and the Cardinal's mistress, is alive because she plays the role men want to her to occupy: sexually available and loose. "The nice modesty in ladies," says Julia, "Is but a troublesome familiar / That haunts them" (5.2.166–8);

> We that are the great women of pleasure, use to cut off
> These uncertain wishes and unquiet longings,
> And in an instant join the sweet delight
> And the pretty excuse together: had you been i'the street,
> Under my chamber window, even there
> I should have courted you.
>
> —5.2.189–94

The woman who has some of the last words is not the powerful Duchess, not even the Echo of her ghost, which appears in this act briefly to haunt the men, but the sexually loose Julia, a woman ready for agency in return for sexual pleasure, a counter-lover in the sense that she sees herself as one who courts, not who is courted, in the courtly tradition that circumscribed the culture of love. The tragic end is that of the fall of men, the tragedy of civic and religious masculinity, stylized in the poetry that invokes the theme of the fall of princes. Antonio says:

> I would not now
> Wish my wounds balm'd, not heal'd: for I have no use
> To put my life to. In all our quest of greatness,
> Like wanton boys, whose pastime is their care,
> We follow after bubbles, blown in th'air.
>
> —5.5.61–5

In this vision of man's glory and status, life's greatness is not bigger than frivolous pastime, and man's purpose is about as solid as a bubble. The fall of princes theme, which dominates the remainder of this act, culminates in Bosola's image of the Cardinal's diminished significance, expressed in the image of a pyramid's "little point, a kind of nothing" (5.5.78). The suffocating, dangerous and menacing world of *The Duchess of Malfi* is full of poison, mental disturbance (lycanthropy), and deathly tricks, a world that destroys and diminishes characters, where the men die, one by one, in an almost tragi-comical manner. Horror is piled up on horror so quickly that it becomes unbelievable, a reminder that the play is about the collapse of all the institutions of male power—in governing, in friendship, in politics, in love, and in marriage—that society gave them. Men in *The Duchess of Malfi* not only brought death to the female protagonist, but they brought it upon themselves in the final act of disorderly patriarchy which undoes itself. The ending of *The Duchess of Malfi* is almost a theatrical anticlimax to the tragedy of the Duchess as a woman, because in the process masculinity has been created in ways that dominate other concerns and that remind us of the tragic battle between genders, and of the weight one gender carries as a burden of victory in such a tragedy of gender and sex.

NOTES

Introduction

1. I want to thank Rebecca Bushnell, series editor, and Mark Dudgeon at Bloomsbury for inviting me to edit this volume, and for their patience in allowing me the time needed to complete it. I also want to thank Gina Balestracci, Jonathan Greenberg, Tanya Pollard, and Gloria Waldman for persistent encouragement and for treasured friendship. Dean Rob Friedman of the College of Humanities and Social Science at Montclair State University provided material support for which I am very grateful. Constance Humphrey, my amazing, tireless, and perpetually cheerful graduate assistant, brought technological expertise that pulled me back from the edge more times than I can count. Most of all, I thank the eight superb scholars whose essays make up this book: I asked you all for something special, and you delivered.
2. The basic outlines of the parable and its recognizable lessons about perception, open-mindedness, and tolerance vary and persist well into the modern age: Tolstoy tucked a truncated version of it into his *Fables for Children*. Count Lev Tolstoy, *Fables for Children; Stories for Children; Natural Science Stories; Popular Education; Decembrists; Moral Tales*, trans. and ed. Leo Weiner (London: J.M. Dent 1904), 28.
3. G.W.F. Hegel, "Tragedy as a Dramatic Art," in *Hegel on Tragedy*, ed. Anne and Henry Paolucci (New York and London: Harper Torchbooks, 1975); Friedrich Nietzsche, *The Birth of Tragedy and The Case of Wagner*, trans. and ed. Walter Kaufmann (New York: Random House, 1967); Lucien Goldmann, *The Hidden God: A Study of Tragic Vision in the Pensées of Pascal and the Tragedies of Racine*, trans. Philip Thody (London: Routledge and Kegan Paul, 1976); Walter Benjamin, "Trauerspiel and Tragedy," in *The Origin of German Tragic Drama*, trans. John Osborne (London: Verso, 1985); Carl Schmitt, *Hamlet or Hecuba: The Intrusion of the Time into the Play*, trans. David Pan and Jennifer Rust, intro. Jennifer R. Rust and Julia Reinhard Lupton (Candor, NY: Telos Press, 2009). See also, among others, Jane O. Newman, "Tragedy and *Trauerspiel* for the (Post)Westphalian Age," *Renaissance Drama* 40 (2012): 197–208, and Richard Wilson, "Murdered Majesty: The Stuarts in Tragedy and *Trauerspiel*" (this volume).
4. See Helene P. Foley and Jean E. Howard, "The Urgency of Tragedy Now," *PMLA* 129:4 (October 2014): 617–33.
5. Blair Hoxby, *What was Tragedy: Theory and the Early Modern Canon* (Oxford: Oxford University Press, 2015).
6. Gerald F. Else, Introduction to *Aristotle Poetics*, trans. and intro. Gerald F. Else (Ann Arbor: University of Michigan Press, 1967), 4.
7. Stephen Halliwell, *The Poetics of Aristotle: Translation and Commentary* (Chapel Hill: University of North Carolina Press, 1987), 4.
8. *OED*, *c*. 1450.
9. *Hamlet*, ed. Ann Thompson and Neil Taylor (London: Arden Shakespeare, 2006). Citations to the play follow this edition.
10. See Rebecca Bushnell, "Forms and Media" (in this volume), for elaboration on this hybridity.

11. *Poetics*, Ch. 9 (Else 25).
12. Stephen Booth, *King Lear, Macbeth, Indefinition, and Tragedy* (New Haven: Yale University Press, 1983), 81.
13. Robert S. Miola, "Early Modern Antigones: Receptions, Refractions, Replays," *Classical Receptions Journal* 6 (2014): 224.
14. Hoxby, 8.
15. http://www.oed.com.ezproxy.montclair.edu:2048/view/Entry/204352?redirectedFrom=tragedy#eid
16. I follow the dates and lineation given in F.N. Robinson's edition of Chaucer's *Complete Works* (xxix). Robinson comments in his introduction to the *Boece*: "In England, long before the time of any ... Continental versions, Boethius' treatise was selected by King Alfred as one of the four great works which he translated, or had translated, for the education of his people. And centuries later, after the Renaissance had enlarged men's knowledge of classical literature, the Consolation still held so important a place that another sovereign, Queen Elizabeth, undertook its 'Englishing.' Throughout all the generations from Alfred to Elizabeth, it exerted a steady influence on poets and philosophers." *The Works of Geoffrey Chaucer*, 2nd edn. (Boston: Houghton Mifflin, 1957), 319. Editor's note: for ease of reading, I have regularized the spellings of most of the Middle English words quoted.
17. *OED, tragedy* def. 2.
18. *OED, tragedy* def. 1a.
19. For a thorough discussion of English tragedies in these early modern centuries, looking before and after (as it were and with a nod to a cautionary line in *Hamlet*) to their development, and their major critical assessments in our own time, see Rebecca Bushnell, "The Fall of Princes: The Classical and Medieval Roots of English Renaissance Tragedy," in *A Companion to Tragedy* (New York: Blackwell, 2005), 289–306.
20. *The tragedies, gathered by Ihon Bochas, of all such princes as fell from theyr estates throughe the mutability of fortune since the creacion of Adam, vntil his time wherin may be seen what vices bring menne to destruccion, wyth notable warninges howe the like may be auoyded. Translated into Englysh by Iohn Lidgate, monke of Burye*. Imprinted at London: By Iohn Wayland, at the signe of the Sunne oueragainst the Conduite in Flete-strete. Cum priuilegio per septennium, [1554?]. EEBO-TCP Phase 1, Ann Arbor, MI; Oxford (UK), 2005–10.
21. *OED, tragedy* def. 1a.
22. Else, 38–9.
23. Halliwell, 44–5.
24. Kenneth A. Telford, *Aristotle's Poetics: Translation and Analysis* (Chicago: Henry Regnery, 1961), 23.
25. Telford, 23n60. Paul Innes' chapter in this volume also takes up this point.
26. Telford, 15. See also Else: "it is the imitation of an action and imitates the persons primarily for the sake of their action" (*Aristotle Poetics*, 28).
27. *Macbeth*, ed. Kenneth Muir, The Arden Shakespeare (London: Methuen, 1962), xlix.
28. Halliwell, 47–8.
29. Bernard M.W. Knox, *The Heroic Temper: Studies in Sophoclean Tragedy* (Berkeley: University of California Press and Cambridge: Cambridge University Press, 1964), 1.
30. See *Seneca His Tenne Tragedies Translated into English*, ed. Thomas Newton, *anno* 1581, with an Introduction by T.S. Eliot (1927) (Bloomington and London: Indiana University Press, 1964). But cf. Tanya Pollard's compelling argument that Greek tragedies were known

in early modern England to a much wider extent than has been previously acknowledged: "Greek playbooks and dramatic forms in early modern England," in *Formal Matters: Reading the Materials of English Renaissance Literature*, ed. Allison Deutermann and András Kiséry (Manchester: Manchester University Press, 2013), 99–123.

31. Leslie Fiedler, *No! In Thunder: Essays on Myth and Literature* (New York: Stein and Day, 1960), 7.
32. Gordon Braden identifies this isolation as the legacy of stoic protagonists even before—but culminating in—Seneca's tragic heroes, who, he argues, "go much further [than Greek tragic figures] in their isolation . . . because their drive encounters no such network of social nuance and interconnection." *Renaissance Tragedy and the Senecan Tradition: Anger's Privilege* (New Haven and London; Yale University Press, 1985), 35.
33. Without meaning to trivialize any of these points, it might help to remember the immortal line spoken by cartoon *femme fatale* Jessica Rabbit in Robert Zemeckis' 1988 film, *Who Framed Roger Rabbit:* "I'm not bad," she says; "I'm just drawn that way."
34. Braden, 34.
35. On the idea of community in Shakespearean tragedy, see Naomi Conn Liebler, *Shakespeare's Festive Tragedy: The Ritual Foundations of Genre* (London and New York: Routledge, 1995). Although it is beyond the scope of this essay, I believe a fuller study of the idea of collective *hamartía* in tragedy (early modern or indeed modern) remains to be done.
36. Hoxby, 8.
37. For a comprehensive list of Greek and Roman plays known to have been read at Cambridge and Oxford, at lower schools, and in private libraries, see Tanya Pollard, "Greek Playbooks and Dramatic Forms in Early Modern England", and in even greater detail, Bruce R. Smith's capacious *Ancient Scripts and Modern Experience on the English Stage, 1500–1700* (Princeton: Princeton University Press, 1988).
38. Charles Read Baskervill, Introduction to *Gorboduc* in *Elizabethan and Stuart Plays* (New York: Holt, Rinehart, and Winston, 1934), 77.
39. I omit reference to the peerless Wakefield *Noah* and *Second Shepherds' Play* only because their structures and story lines participate squarely in the comic mode and in those biblical stories that narrate moments of joyous salvation. They do not participate in the tragic.
40. Michel Foucault, "Two Lectures," in *Power/Knowledge: Selected Interviews and Other Writings,* edited and translated by Colin Gordon (New York: Pantheon, 1980), 82–3.
41. Joseph Quincy Adams, *Chief Pre-Shakespearean Dramas: A Selection of Plays Illustrating the History of the English Drama from its Origin Down to Shakespeare*. Boston: Houghton Mifflin, 1924.
42. Adams omits the Crucifixion play; I quote here from the modernized edition by John Gassner, *Medieval and Tudor Drama* (New York: Applause Theatre and Cinema Books, 1963), 160.
43. For an extended discussion of the *Mactatio Abel's* legacy made visible in Shakespeare's *Richard II*, see Liebler, "The Mockery King of Snow: *Richard II* and the Sacrifice of Ritual," in *Shakespeare's Festive Tragedy*, 57–85, esp. 77ff.
44. Fredson Bowers, *Elizabethan Revenge Tragedy* (Princeton: Princeton University Press, 1940), 39.
45. Irving Ribner, *Jacobean Tragedy: The Quest for Moral Order* (London: Methuen, 1962), 5.
46. Ribner, 5.
47. Antonin Artaud, *The Theater and its Double*, trans. Mary Caroline Richards (New York: Grove Press, 1958), 30, 79.

Chapter One

1. Introduction to *Doctor Faustus*, in David Bevington, Lars Engle, Katharine Eisaman Maus, and Eric Rasmussen, eds., *English Renaissance Tragedy: A Norton Anthology* (New York: W.W. Norton, 2002), 245.
2. David Bevington and Eric Rasmussen argue that it was performed earlier at the Belsavage playhouse in 1588, while other scholars believe that it was composed in the short interlude between the 1592 publication of the "Faust Book" and Marlowe's own lurid death in 1593: David Bevington and Eric Rasmussen, eds., *Doctor Faustus: A- and B-texts (1604, 1616): Christopher Marlowe and his Collaborators and Revisers* (Manchester: Manchester University Press, 1993), 49.
3. Actors also appear to have brought the drama to the continent: according to David Bevington and Eric Rasmussen, "A company of English players acted some version of *Doctor Faustus* in Graz, Austria in January 1608. English 'comedians' performed *'eine tragoedia von Dr. Faustus'* in Dresden on 7 July 1626"; ibid., 49–50. Scholars also speculate that a puppet-play version of the story that originated in England also migrated to Germany in the seventeenth century: see Wilhelm von Hamm, T.C.H. Hedderwick, Gotthold Ephraim Lessing, and Guido Bonneschky, *The Old German Puppet Play of Doctor Faustus* (London: K. Paul Trench, 1887).
4. It was included in the nineteenth-century Roxburghe collection of ballads and has been tentatively dated to1640. Bevington and Rasmussen, *Doctor Faustus*, 2, think they are essentially the same, citing Mac D.P Jackson, "Three old ballads and the date of *Doctor Faustus*," *Journal of the Australasian Universities, Language and Literature Association* 36 (1971): 187–200.
5. British Library—The Roxburghe Ballads, accessed in Patricia Fumerton, ed., *The English Broadside Ballad Archive* (EBBA), ID# 30993. https://ebba.english.ucsb.edu/ballad/30993/image
6. Samuel Pepys records having seen a performance in London in 1662, "wretchedly and poorly done" (Bevington and Rasmussen, *Doctor Faustus*, 51).
7. Henry Jenkins, *Convergence Culture: Where Old and New Media Collide* (New York: New York University Press, 2006), 95. See also Linda Hutcheon, with Siobhan O' Flynn, *A Theory of Adaptation*, second edn (London: Routledge, 2006), citing Henry Jenkins' 2011 blog on transmedia, defining it as "a process where integral elements of a fiction get dispersed systematically across multiple delivery channels for the purpose of creating a unified and coordinated entertainment experience. Ideally, each medium makes in own unique contribution to the unfolding of the story" [location 335–6 in Kindle text].
8. Jenkins, *Convergence Culture*, 13.
9. Jay David Bolter and Richard Grusin, *Remediation: Understanding New Media* (Cambridge: MIT Press, 1999), 45.
10. Ibid., 66.
11. For a general overview, see Timothy Reiss, "Renaissance Theater and Theories of Tragedy," in *The Cambridge History of Literary Criticism: Vol 3: The Renaissance*, ed. Glynn P. Norton (Cambridge: Cambridge University Press, 1999), 229–47.
12. Cited in J.V. Cunningham, *Woe or Wonder: The Emotional Effect of Shakespearean Tragedy* (Denver: University of Denver Press, 1951; rpt. Chicago: Swallow Press, 1964), 44.
13. Julius Caesar Scaliger, *Poetices*, 3. 96, translated by F.M. Padelford, *Select Translations from Scaliger's Poetics* (New York, 1905), 57.
14. Thomas Puttfarkan, *Titian and Tragic Painting: Aristotle's "Poetics" and the Rise of the Modern Artist* (New Haven: Yale University Press, 2005), 115. See also Luba Freedman,

Classical Myths in Italian Renaissance Painting (Cambridge: Cambridge University Press, 2011), which focuses on the depiction of classical myths in painting in the style *all'antica*, where the new painting projected "a contemporary vision of classical myths as stories full of dramatic expressions of human emotion, and expression of the humanistic desire for rearticulating the human subject" (214).

15. Robert C. Ketterer, "Opera," in Anthony Grafton, Glenn W. Most, and Salvatore Settis, eds., *The Classical Tradition* (Harvard: Harvard University Press, 2010), 656. In their *A History of Opera: Updated Edition* (New York: W.W. Norton, 2012), Carolyn Abbate and Roger Parker revise the narrative that "Opera was invented in or around Florence and the first operas date from somewhere between 1598 and 1600; and high-minded ideas about Greek theatre play a significant role" (38) arguing instead that there was "a huge, centuries-old series of experiments devoted to combining drama, dance, song and instrumental music" (39). See also Piero Weiss, "Opera and Neoclassical Dramatic Criticism in the Seventeenth Century," *Studies in the History of Music* 2 (1988): 1–30.

16. Tanya Pollard, "Greek Playbooks and Dramatic Forms in Early Modern England," in *Formal Matters: Reading the Materials of English Renaissance Literature*, ed. Allison Deutermann and Andras Kisery (Manchester: Manchester University Press, 2013), 99–123; 100.

17. This account is partially adapted from Rebecca Bushnell, "Tragedy," in Grafton, Most, and Settis, *Classical Tradition*, 942–7. See also Betine von Zyl Smit, ed., *A Handbook to the Reception of Greek Drama* (London: Wiley-Blackwell, 2006), chaps. 7–9.

18. See Reiss, "Renaissance theater." For more on Aristotle's *Poetics* and Renaissance commentary, see Daniel Javitch, "The Assimilation of Aristotle's Poetics in Sixteenth-Century Italy," in Norton, *Cambridge History of Literary Criticism*, 53–65.

19. See Micha Lazarus, "Aristotelian Criticism in Sixteenth-Century England," *Oxford Handbooks Online*. http://www.oxfordhandbooks.com/view/10.1093/oxfordhb/9780199935338.001.0001/oxfordhb-9780199935338-e-148 (accessed May 29, 2017).

20. Tessa Watt, *Cheap Print and Popular Piety 1550–1640* (Cambridge: Cambridge University Press, 1991), 5. See also Roger Chartier, *The Cultural Uses of Print in Early Modern France*, trans. Lydia G. Cochrane (Princeton: Princeton University Press, 1988).

21. Chartier, *Cultural Uses of Print*, 4.

22. Cited by Cunningham, *Woe or Wonder*, 46.

23. Giovanni Boccaccio, *The Fates of Illustrious Men*, trans. Louis Brewer Hall (New York: Frederick Ungar, 1965), 1–2, cited in Paul Budra, *A Mirror for Magistrates and the de casibus Tradition* (Toronto: University of Toronto Press, 1999), 16.

24. Ibid., 16.

25. Willard Farnham, *The Medieval Heritage of Elizabethan Tragedy* (Berkeley: University of California Press, 1936), 171. See also Nigel Mortimer, *John Lydgate's Fall of Princes: Narrative Tragedy in its Literary and Political Contexts* (Oxford: Oxford University Press, 2005).

26. Lily B. Campbell, ed., *The Mirror for Magistrates* (Cambridge: Cambridge University Press, 1938), 68. *A Mirror for Magistrates* was first edited by William Baldwin and printed in 1559 then reprinted and expanded in numerous editions for four different editors up through 1610.

27. Farnham, *Medieval Heritage*, 290–1.

28. *The Mirror*, 65.

29. Ibid., 153.

30. Ibid., 154. See Paul Budra, "A miserable time full of piteous tragedies," in *A Mirror for Magistrates in Context: Literature, History, and Politics in Early Modern England*, ed. Harriet

Archer and Andrew Hatfield (Cambridge: Cambridge University Press, 2016), on whether there is a "meaningful pattern" in the representation of the stories as tragic; he notes, "if Baldwin and his collaborators were making a statement about the nature of tragedy and history, critics have not be able to agree on what it was, but then critics have not be able to agree on the argument of the *Mirror* as a whole" (37).

31. *The Mirror*, 64. The text was first printed by Thomas Marshe in 1559 after an earlier lost edition was apparently suppressed.
32. Ibid., 69.
33. Wolfgang Clemen, *English Tragedy before Shakespeare: The Development of Dramatic Speech* (London: Methuen, 1961; rpt. 1980), 212. For a more recent treatment of the relationship between complaint poetry and Shakespearean tragedy in particular, see Emily Shortslef, *Weeping, Wailing, Sighing, Railing: Shakespeare and the Drama of Complaint*, Ph.D. dissertation, Columbia University, 2015.
34. See Jennifer Richards, "Reading and listening to William Baldwin," in Archer and Hadfield, *A Mirror for Magistrates in Context*, 71–85. It certainly was unprecedented in print; Budra, *Mirror and the de casibus Tradition*, notes the example of the manuscript of George Cavendish's *Metrical Vision*s (*c*. 1552–4), which not only drew on the stories of "near contemporaries" but also had the stories of a fall narrated in the first person (7).
35. See Richards, "Reading and listening to William Baldwin," on "the effect of writing when it is enlivened by the speaking voice" (74).
36. Budra, "A miserable time," 41: here he focuses more on emotional rhetoric in the Senecan tradition.
37. *The Mirror*, 111–12.
38. Ibid., 119.
39. See Mike Pincombe, "Tragic and untragic bodies in the *Mirror for Magistrates*," in Archer and Hadfield, *A Mirror for Magistrates in Context*, 53–70; see 65–6, on this scene.
40. *The Mirror*, 181.
41. Ibid, 63. Budra also sees this grotesqueness as ultimately undermining the tragic effect.
42. Thomas Preston, *Cambyses, King of Persia*, in *Drama of the English Renaissance Vol 1: The Tudor Period*, ed. Russell A. Fraser and Norman Rabkin (New York: Macmillan, 1976), 79.
43. See Clemen, *English Tragedy before Shakespeare*, 212: "For our present purposes, however, it will be sufficient to accept the premise that practically all the 'lament-topi' referred to in the following pages in connexion with the pre-Shakespearean dramatic lament have their roots in the past, whether in medieval Latin poetry, or in patristic literature, or in the medieval vernacular drama and epic, from which their ancestry can in most cases be traced back to ancient times."
44. Shortslef, *Weeping, Wailing, Sighing, Railing*, abstract.
45. Farnham, *Medieval Heritage*, cites a long list of examples of what he calls the "progeny of *A Mirror*" (Chap. 8). For a substantial discussion of the tradition of female complaint or lament from the Middle Ages to the Restoration, see John Kerrigan, ed., *The Motives of Woe: Shakespeare and Female Complaint: A Critical Anthology* (Oxford: Oxford University Press, 1991). See also Katherine Goodland, *Female Mourning and Tragedy in Medieval and Renaissance English Drama* (Aldershot: Ashgate, 2005).
46. See Jessica Winston, "Rethinking Absolutism: English *de casibus* Tragedy in the 1560s," in Asher and Hadfield, *Mirror for Magistrates in Context*, 199–215.
47. Farnham, 315 (Churchyard was a contributor to *A Mirror*).
48. Peter Lake, "Deeds Against Nature: Cheap Print, Protestantism and Murder in Early Seventeenth Century England," in *Culture and Politics in Early Stuart England*, ed. Kevin Sharpe and Peter Lake, 257–384 (Stanford: Stanford University Press, 1993), 276–7.

49. See Charles Dale Cannon, ed., *A Warning for Fair Women: A Critical Edition* (The Hague: Mouton, 1975), 63.
50. There are variant spelling of Faversham/Feversham; for the most part, unless reproducing an historical title, I will use Faversham. Another contemporary domestic tragedy, Thomas Heywood's *A Woman Killed with Kindness*, was not derived from a true crime story (as far as we know). In the past *A Yorkshire Tragedy* and *Arden of Faversham* have been attributed to Shakespeare, but that is no longer the case. In the introduction to his edition of *A Warning for Fair Women* (London: 1893), A.F. Hopkinson lists other potentially similar plays now lost: *Page of Plymouth, The Bristol Tragedy, Black Batman of the North, The Stepmother's Tragedy*, and *The Tragedy of John Cox of Collumpton* (ii).
51. Peter Holbrook, *Literature and Degree in Renaissance England: Nashe, Bourgeois Tragedy, Shakespeare* (Newark: University of Delaware Press, 1994), 86.
52. Cannon, ed., *A Warning for Fair Women*, 97–100.
53. Scholars speculatively date the play earlier to "near 1590": see Cannon, introduction to *A Warning for Fair Women*, 43–8.
54. It was published anonymously, but has now been attributed to Golding.
55. Cannon, 64–75 on the source. Text of *a Brief Discourse* is reproduced in Cannon, 216–36.
56. Farnham cites an anonymous pamphlet issued by Thomas Hacket in 1584, called *A most rare and wonderful Tragedy for all other in our age most admirable, of the life and death of a miserable usurer of Fraunce, who hanged himself in Hell streete*: it was "a tragedie for the rarenesse there of no leses pleasaunte than for the terror Tragicall" (318).
57. Thomas Kyd, *The trueth of the most wicked and secret murthering of John Brewen, Goldsmith of London, committed by his owne wife though the provocation of one John Parker whom she loved* (London: 1592), 6.
58. See Tom Cheesman, *The Shocking Ballad Picture Show: German Popular Literature and Cultural History* (Oxford: Berg, 1994), on the culture of "shocking" ballads in early modern Germany: Cheesman also provides a bibliography of works on ballad culture in Holland, Italy, Flanders, and France (1).
59. See Eric Nebeker, "The heyday of the broadside ballad," at the Early English Ballads Archive, http://ebba.english.ucsb.edu/page/heyday-of-the-broadside-ballad
60. See Frances E. Dolan, *Dangerous Familiars: Representations of Domestic Crime in England, 1550–1700* (Ithaca: Cornell University Press, 1994) on ballads as the most accessible form of domestic crime news (7). She comments on the ballads "in the voices of aggrieved women" (50).
61. Tiffany Stern, Lecture delivered at the workshop series of "The History of the Material Text," University of Pennsylvania, April 3, 2017.
62. I would just note the irony that this is the same William Mountfort who composed the farce based on *Doctor Faustus*; Mountfort was murdered as part of a famous love triangle, commemorated in *The Player's Tragedy: Fatal Love* (1693).
63. Kerrigan, *Motives of Woe*, 14.
64. Stern has counted more than 50 ballads all with tune of "Fortune my foe."
65. *The Yorkshire Tragedy* also appeared in chapbook and ballad form.
66. Richard Helgerson, "Murder in Faversham: Holinshed's impertinent history," in *The Historical Imagination in Early Modern Britain: History, Rhetoric and Fiction, 1500–1800*, ed. Donald R. Kelley and David Harris Sacks, 133–58 (Cambridge: Cambridge University Press, 1997), 136–7.
67. See Patricia Hyde, *Thomas Arden in Faversham: The Man Behind the Myth* (The Faversham Society: 1996), 14. The story was also related in John Stow's *Chronicles* and *Annals* and Thomas Heywood's *Troia Britannica* (see Helgerson, "Murder in Faversham," 134).

68. Raphael Holinshed, *Chronicles of England, Scotland, and Ireland* (1587), Vol. 3, 1062–6.
69. Helgerson, "Murder in Faversham," notes that, outside of political assassinations, "Holinshed's 1587 index lists some twenty-three murders"; the Arden account is unusually long at "nearly five thousand words" (133).
70. See Hyde, *Thomas Arden*, 14.
71. Lena Cowen Orlin, *Private Matters and Public Culture in Post-Reformation England* (Ithaca: Cornell University Press, 1994). Orlin sees the play's references to Arden's property crimes as part of the configuration of his abandonment of his patriarchal responsibilities.
72. Orlin, *Private Matters and Public Culture*, 68.
73. On the play in the context of contemporary discourse of tragedy, see Orlin, *Private Matters and Public Culture*, 75–6.
74. Tom Lockwood, introduction to *Arden of Faversham*, play text ed. Martin White (London: Bloomsbury, 2007): Franklin is a "dramatized voice within the play world who can pass judgement during and after it in ways akin to those judgements passed by other early modern commentators on Arden's murder" (xxviii).
75. *Arden of Faversham*, 112.
76. Lockwood, introduction to *Arden of Faversham*, suggests that "in its old-fashioned black-letter type" the broadside accessed "a more popular and financially less well-off audience than the modern-looking, roman-set playbook; but as is so often the case with *Arden of Faversham*, the connections created by the shared woodcut serve to complicate any such easy distinction" (xxvii).
77. British Library—Roxburghe 3.1567, EBBA ID # 30458 https://ebba.english.ucsb.edu/ballad/30458/image

Chapter Two

1. I am grateful to the volume editor, Naomi Liebler, for giving me the opportunity to revisit the subject of my first book, *Ancient Scripts and Modern Experience on the English Stage 1500-1700* (Princeton: Princeton University Press, 1988; rpt. 2014) and to update and extend that subject in terms of the interests of two more recent books, *Phenomenal Shakespeare* (Oxford: Wiley-Blackwell, 2010) and *Shakespeare | Cut: Rethinking Cutwork in an Age of Distraction* (Oxford: Oxford University Press, 2016). I also want to thank Carla Della Gatta, Thomas Habinek, and Anna Rosensweig for their advice and Pavel Drábek and Jennifer Richards for sharing work with me in advance of its publication.
2. Ingrid D. Rowland, "High Culture," in *A Companion to the Worlds of the Renaissance*, ed. Guido Ruggiero (Oxford: Blackwell, 2002), Blackwell Reference Online, http://www.blackwellreference.com/subscriber/tocnode.html?id=g9780631215240_chunk_g978063121524020 (accessed June 6, 2017). "Repertorium Pompanianum," a complete biographical dictionary of Pomponio's associates, is to be found at www.repertoriumpomponianum.it
3. Giovanni Sulpizio da Veroli, "Raphaeli Riario, Cardinali, Sanctaeque Romanae Ecclesiae Camerario, Jo[hannes] Sulpitius Feolicitatem," in Marcus Pollio Vitruvius, *De architecturâ*, ed. Sulpizio [Rome: Eucharius Silber, *c*. 1468], rpt. in Beriah Botfield, ed., *Prefaces to the First Editions of the Greek and Roman Classics and of the Sacred Scriptures* (London, 1861), 177–9, my translation. A facsimile of Sulpizio's full text is available at https://archive.org/stream/prefacestofirste00botfuoft#page/176/mode/2up
4. Neither Sulpizio nor Erasmus names the Campo de' Fiori explicitly. Sulpizio says that the first performance took place *in foro*: by that he almost certainly did not mean the ancient

Roman Forum, which was still unexcavated in the fifteenth century, but a piazza. Erasmus locates the performance *in area, quae est ante Palatium* Cardinalis Raphaelis Georgiani ("in the piazza in front of the palace of Cardinal Raffaele Riario San Giorgio"), adding "So I was told by the cardinal himself" (Disderius Erasmus, *The Correspondence of Erasmus: Letters 1252 to 1523*, trans. R.A.B. Mynors, annotated James M. Estes [Toronto: University of Toronto Press, 1989], 421). The palace in question must not have been the Florentine-inspired Palazzo della Cancellaria that still anchors the north-west corner of the Campo de' Fiori, since construction was not started until 1489, three years after the date of Sulpizio's letter, but it is likely that the cardinal already resided in the vicinity, if not on the actual site, since he held the entitlement to the minor basilica of San Lorenzo in Damaso, which was incorporated into the new palace.

5. Wilhelm Creizenach, *Geschichte des Neueren Dramas*, 3 vols (Halle: M. Niemeyer, 1918), 2:347, my translation.
6. Oxford English Dictionary Online, "meme, *n.*," etymology, citation from Richard Dawkins, *The Selfish Gene* (Oxford: Oxford University Press, 1976). http://www.oed.com (accessed April 29, 2017).
7. Louise George Clubb, "Theatregrams," in *Comparative Critical Approaches to Renaissance Comedy*, ed. Donald A. Beecher and Massimo Ciavolella (Ottawa: Dovehouse, 1986), 15–33, and "Looking Back on Shakespeare and Italian Theater," *Renaissance Drama* n.s. 36/37 (2010): 3–19. To Clubb's list of play materials—character types, actions, speeches, thematic designs—I would add theater buildings, staging arrangements, critical ideas about tragedy, expectations about audiences, and attitudes toward performance.
8. Oxford English Dictionary Online, "ethos," etymology, http://www.oed.com (accessed February 4, 2017).
9. Maria Ruvoldt, "Sacred to Secular, East to West: The Renaissance Studiolo and Strategies of Display," *Renaissance Studies* 20 (2006): 640–57.
10. John Florio, *A Worlde of Words, or Most Copious, and Exact Dictionary in Italian and English* (London: Arnold Hatfield for Edw[ard] Blount, 1598), sig. Ll 4v. In this and other quotations from texts in early modern English spelling has been modernized but original punctuation retained.
11. See images of Isabella d'Este's study at https://www.brooklynmuseum.org/eascfa/dinner_party/place_settings/isabella_d_este
12. Jennifer Richards, *Voices and Books in the English Renaissance: A New History of Reading* (Oxford: Oxford University Press, forthcoming).
13. Charles Fernyhough, *The Voices Within: The History and Science of How We Talk to Ourselves* (New York: Basic Books, 2016), 75–90.
14. Philip Horne, *The Tragedies of Giambattista Cinthio Giraldi* (Oxford: Oxford University Press, 1962), 5.
15. Jonas Barish, "The Problem of Closet Drama in the Italian Renaissance," *Italica* 71.1 (1994): 4–30, and Marta Straznicky, "Closet Drama," in *A Companion to Renaissance Drama*, ed. Arthur Kinney (Oxford: Blackwell, 2002), 416–30.
16. The Database of Italian Academies, available through the British Library (http://www.bl.uk/catalogues/ItalianAcademies/Default.aspx), catalogues all books published by the academies; the website The Italian Academies 1525–1700 (http://italianacademies.org/) offers access to books, articles, and conferences.
17. Aristotle, *Poetics*, trans. Gerald F. Else (Ann Arbor: University of Michigan Press, 1967), 27–9.
18. Sulpizio da Veroli, 177.

19. On rhetoric as the basis of Renaissance educational practices see Lynn Enterline, *Shakespeare's Schoolroom: Rhetoric, Discipline, Emotion* (Philadelphia: University of Pennsylvania Press, 2016) and Christy Desmet, *Reading Shakespeare's Characters: Rhetoric, Ethics, and Identity* (Amherst: University of Massachusetts Press, 1992).
20. Desiderus Erasmus, *De ratione studii ac legendi interpretandique auctores*, trans. Brian McGregor, in *Collected Works*, ed. Craig R. Thompson, vol. 2 (Toronto: University of Toronto Press, 1978), 687.
21. Robert S. Knapp, "The Academic Drama," in Kinney 257–65.
22. Michel de Montaigne, *Essays Written in French by Michael Lord of Montaigne*, trans. John Florio (London: Melch[ior] Bradwood for Edward Blount and William Barret, 1613), sig. I1v.
23. Stagings of other extant plays by Buchanan, *Jephthes sive Votum* and a Latin translation of Euripides' *Alcestis*, are not documented during Montaigne's time at the college. The tragedy by Marc-Antoine Muret (a.k.a. Muretus, 1526–85) was almost certainly his *Julius Caesar*, in high Senecan style. Plays by the elusive Guérente have not survived, according to Michel de Montaigne, *The Complete Essays*, trans. M.A. Screech (London: Allen Lane, 1991), 198, n.105.
24. "Beza, Theodore," *Encyclopædia Britannica. Encyclopædia Britannica Online*. Encyclopædia Britannica, Inc., 2017. Accessed May 12, 2017. Charles Mazouer, *Le Théâtre Français de la Renaissance* (Paris: Champion, 2002), 252–7.
25. Théodore de Bèze, *A tragedie of Abrahams sacrifice*, trans. Arthur Golding (London: Thomas Vautroullier, 1577), sig. A4. See John D. Lyons, "*Abraham sacrifiant* and the End of Ethics," in *French Renaissance and Baroque Drama: Text, Performance, and Theory*, ed. Michael Meere (Newark: University of Delaware Press, 2015), 21–37.
26. *The Jesuit Ratio Studiorum of 1599*, trans. Allan P. Farrell, S.J. (Washington, DC: Conference of Major Superiors, 1970), "Rules of the Teacher of Rhetoric" sec. 7, "Rules of the Rector" sec. 13, with footnote by Farrell explaining that "rarely" was usually interpreted to mean three or four times a year (121–2): http://www.bc.edu/sites/libraries/ratio/ratio1599.pdf (accessed May 12, 2017).
27. Helen Watanabe-O'Kelly, "The Early Modern Period (1450-1720)," in *The Cambridge History of German Literature*, ed. Helen Watanabe-O'Kelly, 92–146 (Cambridge: Cambridge University Press, 1997), 107; Christopher J. Wild, "Jesuit Theater and the Blindness of Self-Knowledge," in *A New History of German Literature*, ed. David E. Wellbery and Judith Ryan (Cambridge, MA: Harvard University Press, 2004), 270–5.
28. Quoted from Étienne Pasquier, *Recherches de la France* (1560), in Mazouer, *Le Theatre Francais de la Renaissance*, 257.
29. Bruce R. Smith, *Ancient Scripts and Modern Experience on the English Stage, 1500–1700* (Princeton: Princeton University Press, 1988; rpt. 2014), 111–12.
30. Robert Weimann, *Shakespeare and the Popular Tradition in the Theater: Studies in the Social Dimension of Dramatic Form and Function* (Baltimore: Johns Hopkins University Press, 1978), 73–85.
31. Gary R. Grund, *Humanist Tragedies* (Cambridge, MA: Harvard University Press, 2011), xxi.
32. Marvin T. Herrick, *Italian Tragedy in the Renaissance* (Urbana: University of Illinois Press, 1965), 4–6; Salvatore Di Maria, *The Italian Tragedy in the Renaissance: Cultural Realities and Theatrical Innovations* (Lewisburg, PA: Bucknell University Press, 2002), 18.
33. The translated text is available in *Humanist Tragedies*, trans. Gary R. Grund (Cambridge: Harvard University Press, 2011), 2–47.
34. David Mann, "The Roman Mime and Medieval Theatre," *Theatre Notebook: A Journal of the History and Technique of the British Theatre* 46.3 (1992): 136–44.

NOTES 157

35. Mazouer, 48.
36. Thomas Coryate, *Coryat's Crudities: Hastily Gobbled Up in Five Months' Travels* (London: Printed for the author, sig. G8.
37. J. Enrique Duarte, "Spanish Sacramental Plays: A Study of Their Evolution," in *A Companion to Early Modern Hispanic Theater*, ed. Hilaire Kallendorf (Leiden: Brill, 2014), 59–74.
38. Melveena McKendrick, *Theatre in Spain, 1490–1700* (Cambridge: Cambridge University Press, 1989), 16–17.
39. McKendrick, 34–5.
40. McKendrick, 140–69; Edward M. Wilson and Duncan Moir, *A Literary History of Spain: The Golden Age Drama 1492–1700* (London: Benn, 1971), 99–119.
41. For a general survey of the phenomenon see Pavel Drábek and M.A. Katritzky, "Shakespearean Players in Early Modern Europe," in *The Cambridge Guide to the Worlds of Shakespeare*, gen. ed. Bruce R. Smith, 2 vols. (Cambridge: Cambridge University Press, 2016), 2:1527–33, and and their edited volume *Transnational Connections in Early Modern Theatre* (Manchester University Press, forthcoming at the time of this publication).
42. McKendrick, 42; Wilson and Moir, 22–3, with quotation of Cervantes' reminiscences.
43. Wilson and Moir, 24–5, 45.
44. Mazouer, 22.
45. Sybile Chevallier-Micki, "Stage Designs of Cruelty: Theater in Rouen at the Turn of the Seventeenth Century," in *French Renaissance and Baroque Drama: Text, Performance, Theory*, ed. Michael Meere (Newark: University of Delaware Press, 2015), 213–31.
46. Information in this paragraph comes from Drábek and Katritzky 2:1527–33 and Drábek, "The English Comedy," in *Transnational Connections in Early Modern Theatre* (Manchester University Press, forthcoming).
47. Quotations from *Hamlet* come from William Shakespeare, *Hamlet*, rev. edn, ed. Ann Thompson and Neil Taylor, The Arden Shakespeare, third series (London: Bloomsbury, 2016).
48. Drábek and Katritzky, 2:1530.
49. Drábek, "The English Comedy."
50. Watanabe-O'Kelly, 105.
51. Pierre Bourdieu and Jean-Claude Passeron, *Reproduction in Education, Society, and Culture*, trans. Richard Nice (Ann Arbor: University of Michigan Press, 1977) and John Guillory, *Cultural Capital: The Problem of Literary Canon Formation* (Chicago: University of Chicago Press, 1993).
52. Di Maria, 38.
53. Herrick, 55; Mazouer, 194.
54. McKendrick, 10–15; Wilson and Moir, 1–6.
55. Horne, 10, 12.
56. Franklin J. Hildy, "European Theater Scene," in *The Cambridge Guide to the Worlds of Shakespeare*, gen. ed. Bruce R. Smith, 2 vols (Cambridge: Cambridge University Press, 2016), 1:79.
57. Nikolas Pevsner, *A History of Building Types* (London: Thames and Hudson, 1976), 66. On the cultural history of Ferrara in the sixteenth century see Louise George Clubb, "Staging Ferrara: State Theater from Borso to Alfonso II," in *Phaethon's Children: The Este Court and Its Culture in Early Modern Ferrara*, ed. Dennis Looney and Deanna Shemek (Tempe, AZ: Arizona Center for Medieval and Renaissance Studies, 2005), 345–62, and Horne, 4–10.
58. Horne, 58–9.
59. Horne, 39.

60. Sulpizio da Veroli, 177. According to Rowland, "The production made use of the local buildings as well; dressed as Queen Phaedra, the 16-year-old prodigy Tommaso Inghirami emoted in Latin from a real tower, and then descended to the stage itself to meet one of the occupational hazards of amateur theater: a piece of the scenery collapsed. As the students hauled the fallen set back into place, Tommaso Inghirami held forth undaunted in extemporized Latin, and stole the show" (Rowland, no pagination).
61. Richard Beadle, "Rightwise, John (c.1490–1533)," in *Oxford Dictionary of National Biography*, ed. H.C.G. Matthew and Brian Harrison (Oxford: Oxford University Press, 2004); online edn, ed. David Cannadine, January 2008, http://www.oxforddnb.com.libproxy1.usc.edu/view/article/23649 (accessed May 22, 2017).
62. Sybil M. Jack, "Wolsey, Thomas (1470/71–1530)," in *Oxford Dictionary of National Biography*, ed. H.C.G. Matthew and Brian Harrison (Oxford: Oxford University Press, 2004); online edn, ed. David Cannadine, January 2012, http://www.oxforddnb.com.libproxy1.usc.edu/view/article/29854 (accessed May 22, 2017).
63. Alfred Harbage, *Annals of English drama, 975–1700*, 3rd edn, rev. S. Schoenbaum and Sylvia Stoler Wagonheim (London: Routledge, 1989); Carter Anderson Daniel, "Patterns and Traditions of the Elizabethan Court Play to 1590," diss., University of Virginia, 1966.
64. Charles Nicholl, "Marlowe, Christopher (*bap.* 1564, *d.* 1593)," in *Oxford Dictionary of National Biography*, ed. H.C.G. Matthew and Brian Harrison (Oxford: OUP, 2004); online edn, ed. David Cannadine, January 2008, http://www.oxforddnb.com.libproxy1.usc.edu/view/article/18079 (accessed May 22, 2017). On the boys' acting for paying customers see Michael Shapiro, "Boy Companies and Private Theaters," in Kinney, 314–25.
65. Andrew Gurr, *The Shakespearian Playing Companies* (Oxford: Clarendon Press, 1996), 167–95.
66. Andrew Gurr, *The Shakespeare Company 1594–1642* (Cambridge: Cambridge University Press, 2004), 167–8.
67. Watanabe-O'Kelly, 108.
68. William N. West, "The Idea of a Theater: Humanist Ideology and the Imaginary Stage in Early Modern Europe," *Renaissance Drama*, n.s. 28 (1997), 246.
69. A complete census, with maps and pictures, is available at http://www.theatrum.de/ and https://en.wikipedia.org/wiki/List_of_Roman_theatres
70. Hildy, 1:77–83.
71. Pevsner, 66.
72. Giambattista Giraldi Cinthio, *Orbecche Tragedia* (Venice: Aldine Press, 1543), sig. A2v; Horne, 16–18; Herrick, 93ff. The argument about perspective scenery as having been introduced by Pellegrino da Udine is made in Fabio Finotti, "Perspective and Stage Design, Fiction and Reality in the Italian Renaissance Theater of the Fifteenth Century," *Renaissance Drama* n.s. 36/37 (2010): 28–9.
73. Quoted in Finotti, 30.
74. Herrick, 44.
75. Finotti, 21–42.
76. Weimann, 73–85.
77. Bert O. States, *Great Reckonings in Little Rooms: On the Phenomenology of Theater* (Berkeley: University of California Press, 1987), 157–206.
78. Smith, 12–58.
79. Mazouer, 175–94; Simon Tidworth, *Theatres: An Illustrated History* (London: Pall Mall Press, 1973), 59–60.
80. Mazouer, 194; Alan Howe, *Le Théâtre professionnel à Paris, 1600–1649* (Paris: Archives nationales, 2000).

NOTES 159

81. Buffequin's designs are incorporated in a manuscript memoire written by Laurent Mahelot, now in the Bibliothéque nationale (http://gallica.bnf.fr/ark:/12148/btv1b90631697/f110.image.r=24330). The designs are studied in Marc Bayard, "Pour une archéologie de l'objet théâtral: Le décor comme objet dans l'esthétique théâtrale irrégulière du XVIIe siècle," http://agon.ens-lyon.fr/index.php?id=2024 (accessed January 3, 2017).
82. Howe, *Le Théâtre professionnel à Paris*. For a case study centered on Rouen see Chevallier-Micki, 213–31.
83. McKendrick, 178–208; Hildy, 1:81–2.
84. Jonathan Thacker, *A Companion to Golden Age Theatre* (Woodbridge, Suffolk: Boydell and Brewer, 2007), 123–42; McKendrick, 178–208.
85. Wilson and Moir, 14–15.
86. Frederick A. de Armas, "The *Comedia* and the Classics," in *Early Modern Hispanic Theater*, ed. Kallendorf, 34.
87. Miguel de Cervantes, *The History of the Valorous and Witty-Knight-Errant, Don-Quixote, of the Mancha*, trans. Thomas Shelton (London: R. Hodgkinsonne for Andrew Crooke, 1652), sigs. Ii2v-Ii3.
88. Miguel de Cervantes, *Numantia: A Tragedy*, trans. James Y. Gibson (London: Kegan Paul, Trench, 1885), 56–7.
89. Adrienne L. Martin, "Onstage/Backstage: Animals in the Golden Age *Comedia*," in Kallendorf, 127–44.
90. Gurr, *Shakespeare Company*, 169–72.
91. Peter H. Greenfield, "'The Actors are Come Hither': Traveling Companies," in *A Companion to Renaissance Drama*, ed. Arthur F. Kinney (Oxford: Blackwell, 2002), 212–22; Andrew Gurr, *The Shakespearean Playing Companies* 36–54; Jerzy Limon, "Players and the Playing Business," in *The Cambridge Guide to the Worlds of Shakespeare*, gen. ed. Bruce R. Smith, 2 vols (Cambridge: Cambridge University Press, 2016), 1:83–8; Herbert Berry, "Playhouses," in *A Companion to Renaissance Drama* 147–62; Gabriel Egan, "Playhouses," in *The Cambridge Guide to the Worlds of Shakespeare* 1:89–95.
92. Berry, 148; Egan, 1:89.
93. J.R. Mulryne, "Kyd, Thomas (*bap.* 1558, *d.* 1594)," in *Oxford Dictionary of National Biography*, online ed., ed. David Cannadine. Oxford: OUP, 2004. http://www.oxforddnb.com.libproxy1.usc.edu/view/article/15816 (accessed June 4, 2017).
94. Daniel, 160–2.
95. Robert Garnier, *Cornelia*, trans. Thomas Kyd (London: James Roberts, for N[icholas] L[ing] and Iohn Busbie, 1594), sig. aiii. I find no evidence in either the first or the second edition of Kyd's translation that he also dedicated the translation to Mary Sidney, Countess of Pembroke, as claimed by Mulryne, via Lukas Erne, "Beyond *The Spanish Tragedy*: A Study of the Works of Thomas Kyd," diss., University of Oxford, 1998.
96. Gurr, *Playing Companies*, 174–7.
97. Thomas Kyd, *The Spanish Tragedy*, ed. Michael Neill (New York: Norton, 2014), 4.1.76–8, 99–103. Further quotations are taken from this edition and are cited in the text by act, scene, and line numbers.
98. I make these speculations on the basis of Allen C. Dessen and Leslie Thomson, *A Dictionary of Stage Directions in English Drama, 1580–1642* (Cambridge: Cambridge University Press, 1999), 1 ("above") and 19–20 ("banquet").
99. W.M.H. Hummelen, "Jacob van Campen Bouwt de Amsderdamse Schouwburg," in *Een Theatergeschiedenis der Nederlanden*, ed. R.L. Erenstein (Amsterdam: Amsterdam University Press, 1996), 192–203

100. M.B. Smits-Veldt, "Opening van de Amsterdamse Schouwburg met Vondels *Gysbreght van Aemstel*," in Erenstein, *Een Theatergeschiedenis*, 204–11.
101. Andrea Frisch, "French Tragedy and the Civil Wars," *MLQ* 67.3 (2006): 287–312.
102. Montaigne, trans. Florio, sig. I2.

Chapter Three

1. I wish to thank Naomi Liebler, our editor, as well as Ivan Lupić for their detailed comments and suggestions, and Ann Delehanty, Miles Grier, and James Helgeson for their helpful advice. My essay is informed and inspired by the collaborative project *Europe: a literary history, 1559–1648*, organized and directed by Warren Boutcher.
2. Hans Robert Jauss, *Ästhetische Erfahrung und literarische Hermeneutik* (Frankfurt am Main: Suhrkamp, 1982), 704–52; George Steiner, *Antigones* (Oxford: Clarendon Press, 1984); Christian Biet, *Oedipe en monarchie: Tragédie et théorie juridique à l'âge classique* (Paris: Klincksieck, 1994); Pascale Aebischer, "The Properties of Whiteness: Renaissance Cleopatras from Jodelle to Shakespeare," *Shakespeare Survey* 65 (2012): 221–38; Ivan Lupić, "The Mobile Queen: Observing Hecuba in Renaissance Europe," *Renaissance Drama* 46 (2018): 25–56.
3. For serviceable summaries of the Sophonisba plays, see A. Andrae, *Sophonisbe in der französischen Tragödie mit Berücksichtigung der Sophonisbe-Bearbeitungen in anderen Litteraturen* (Oppeln und Leipzig: Eugen Franck's Buchhandlung, 1891), A. José Axelrad, *Le thème de Sophonisbe dans les principales tragédies de la littérature occidentale* (Lille: Bibliothèque Universitaire, 1956), and Charles Ricci, *Sophonisbe dans la tragédie classique Italienne et Française* (Grenoble: Allier Frères, 1904).
4. Anston Bosman, "Mobility," in *Early Modern Theatricality*, ed. Henry S. Turner (Oxford: Oxford University Press, 2013), 493–515.
5. Warren Boutcher, "Intertraffic: Transnational Literatures and Languages in Late Renaissance England and Europe," in *International Exchange in the Early Modern Book World*, ed. Matthew McLean and Sara Barker, (Leiden and Boston: Brill, 2016), 343–73.
6. Pierre Corneille, *Théâtre complet*, volume 3/2, ed. Alain Niderst (Rouen: Université de Rouen, 1986), 239–41.
7. Corneille, *Théâtre*, 239.
8. Alain Niderst, *Pierre Corneille* (Paris: Fayard, 2006), 251–69; François Hédelin, abbé d'Aubignac, *Dissertations contre Corneille*, ed. Nicholas Hammond and Michael Hawcroft (Exeter: University of Exeter Press, 1995); Bernard Bourque, ed., *Jean Donneau de Visé et la querelle de "Sophonisbe": écrits contre l'abbé d'Aubignac* (Tübingen: Narr, 2014).
9. Corneille, *Théâtre*, 239–40.
10. Max Vernet, "Naissance du critique," in *Le champ littéraire*, ed. P. Citti and M. Détrie (Paris: J. Vrin, 1992), 29–37.
11. Jean-Marc Civardi, ed. *La querelle du Cid (1637–1638): édition critique intégrale* (Paris: Honoré Champion, 2004); W.D. Howarth, ed. *French Theatre in the Neo-Classical Era, 1550–1791* (Cambridge: Cambridge University Press), 253–8.
12. Alain Viala, "Corneille et les institutions littéraires de son temps," in *Pierre Corneille: Actes du colloque*, ed. Alain Niderst (Paris: Presses Universitaires de France, 1985), 197–204; Alain Viala, "Corneille, premier auteur moderne?" in *Pratiques de Corneille*, ed. Myriam Dufour-Maitre (Mont-Saint-Aignan: Publications des Universités de Rouen et du Havre, 2012), 29–40.
13. Civardi, *La querelle du Cid*, 557, 649.

14. Thomas Dekker, "The Gull's Horn Book (1609)," in *Shakespeare's Theater: A Sourcebook*, ed. Tanya Pollard (Malden: Blackwell, 2004), 207–13; Bruscambille, *Oeuvres complètes*, ed. Hugh Roberts and Annette Tomarken (Paris: Honoré Champion, 2012), 206–8, 276–9.
15. Michael Gavin, *The Invention of English Criticism 1650–1760* (Cambridge: Cambridge University Press, 2015).
16. Michael West, "Were There Playgoers During the 1580s?" *Shakespeare Studies* 45 (2017).
17. Charles Whitney, *Early Responses to Renaissance Drama* (Cambridge; New York: Cambridge University Press, 2006); John Lough, *Seventeenth-Century French Drama: The Background* (Oxford: Clarendon Press, 1979), 76–98.
18. Stephen Orgel, *The Illusion of Power: Political Theater in the English Renaissance* (Berkeley: University of California Press, 1975).
19. Musa Gurnis, *Mixed Faith and Shared Feeling: Theater in Post-Reformation London* (Philadelphia: University of Pennsylvania Press, 2018); Peter Lake, *How Shakespeare Put Politics on the Stage: Power and Succession in the History Plays* (New Haven: Yale University Press, 2016).
20. Ralf Haekel, *Die englischen Komödianten in Deutschland: eine Einführung in die Ursprünge des deutschen Berufsschauspiels* (Heidelberg: Winter, 2004).
21. Bernard Weinberg, *A history of literary criticism in the Italian Renaissance* (Chicago: University of Chicago Press, 1961), 912–53.
22. Holger Schott Syme, "The Meaning of Success: 1594 and Its Aftermath," *Shakespeare Quarterly* 61 (2010), 524.
23. Zachary Lesser, "Walter Burre's *The Knight of the Burning Pestle*," *English Literary Renaissance* 29 (1999): 23–5.
24. Alan B. Farmer and Zachary Lesser, "Canons and Classics: Publishing Drama in Caroline England," in *Localizing Caroline Drama: Politics and Economics of the Early Modern English Stage, 1625–1642*, ed. Adam Zucker and Alan B. Farmer (New York: Palgrave, 2006).
25. Emma Depledge, ed. *Canonising Shakespeare: Stationers and the Book Trade, 1640–1740* (Cambridge: Cambridge University Press, 2017).
26. Alan Howe, "L'entrée au Parnasse d'un dramaturge professionel: le cas d'Alexandre Hardy," in *Le Parnasse du théâtre: les recueils d'oeuvres complètes de théâtre au XVIIe siècle*, ed. Georges Forestier, Edric Caldicott, and Claude Bourqui (Paris: PUPS, 2007), 227–44.
27. Ágnes Ritoók-Szalai, "'Enarrat Electram Sophoclis'," in *Dona Melanchthoniana: Festgabe für Heinz Scheible zum 70. Geburtstag*, ed. Johanna Loehr (Stuttgart: Frommann-Holzboog, 2001), 325–37.
28. Günter Frank and Martin Treu, eds., *Melanchthon und Europa, 1. Teilband: Skandinavien und Mittelosteuropa* (Stuttgart: Jan Thorbecke Verlag, 2001).
29. István Borzsák, "Sophocles, Melanchthon und die ungarische Literatur," in *Antike Rezeption und nationale Identität in der Renaissance: Insbesondere in Deutschland und in Ungarn*, ed. Tibor Klaniczay, Katalin S. Németh and Paul Gerhard Schmidt (Budapest: Balassi, 1993), 7–17; Ritoók-Szalai, "'Enarrat Electram Sophoclis.'"
30. Szabolcs Oláh, "A mítosz átértelmezése a keresztény humanista színpadon," in Péter Bornemisza, *Tragédia magyar nyelven a Szophoklész Élektrájából, M.D.LVIII* (Budapest: Balassi Kiadó, 2009), 5–52.
31. Gedeon Borsa, "Euripidész magyar fordításának 16. századi kiadása," *Magyar Könyvszemle* 114 (1998): 44–8; Géza Szentmártoni Szabó, "Euripidész magyar fordítása a 16. század második feléből," *Irodalomtörténeti közlemények* 102 (1998): 225–39.
32. János Heltai, "Balassi és Buchanan Iephtese," *Irodalomtörténeti közlemények* 101 (1997): 541–9.
33. Blair Hoxby, *What Was Tragedy? Theory and the Early Modern Canon* (Oxford: Oxford University Press, 2015).

34. Naomi Conn Liebler, "Introduction: Wonder Woman, or the Female Tragic Hero," in *The Female Tragic Hero in English Renaissance Drama*, ed. Naomi Conn Liebler (New York: Palgrave, 2002), 21–4; Salvatore Di Maria, *The Italian Tragedy in the Renaissance: Cultural Realities and Theatrical Innovations* (Lewisburg: Bucknell University Press, 2002), 101–25.
35. Pamela Allen Brown, "The Traveling Diva and Generic Innovation," *Renaissance Drama* 44 (2016): 251, 260.
36. S.P. Cerasano, "Edward Alleyn, the New Model Actor, and the Rise of the Celebrity in the 1590s," *Medieval & Renaissance Drama in England* 18 (2005): 47–58.
37. David Kathman, "Players, Livery Companies, and Apprentices," in *The Oxford Handbook of Early Modern Theatre*, ed. Richard Dutton (Oxford: Oxford University Press, 2011).
38. Tanya Pollard, *Greek Tragic Women on Shakespearean Stages* (Oxford: Oxford University Press, 2017): 117–42.
39. Rolf Lohse, *Renaissancedrama und humanistische Poetik in Italien* (Paderborn: Wilhelm Fink, 2015), 289–92.
40. Lohse, *Renaissancedrama*, 24–59, 69–249.
41. Felix Gilbert, "Bernardo Rucellai and the Orti Oricellari: A Study on the Origin of Modern Political Thought," *Journal of the Warburg and Courtauld Institutes* 12 (1949): 101–31; Kristin Phillips-Court, "Performing Anachronism: A New Aetiology of Italian Renaissance Tragedy," *Renaissance Drama* 36/37 (2010): 48.
42. Kristin Phillips-Court, *The Perfect Genre: Drama and Painting in Renaissance Italy* (Burlington, VT: Ashgate, 2011), 58–9.
43. Ronald L. Martinez, "Tragic Machiavelli," in *The Comedy and Tragedy of Niccolò Machiavelli: Essays on the Literary Works*, ed. Vickie B. Sullivan (New Haven: Yale University Press, 2000).
44. Bruno Migliorini, *The Italian Language*, transl., abridged, recast and revised by T. Gwynfor Griffith, rev. ed. (London and Boston: Faber and Faber, 1984): 214–31; Robert C. Melzi, "The two Bembos: a fresh look at the Italian *questione della lingua*," *Rivista di Studi Italiani* 1:1 (1983): 31–50.
45. Andreas Michel, "Italian Orthography in Early Modern Times," in *Orthographies in Early Modern Europe*, ed. Susan Baddeley and Anja Voeste (Berlin and New York: Walter de Gruyter, 2012), 79–81.
46. We know of 23 editions of *Sofonisba* before 1620, and 17 editions over the sixteenth century, as compared to 10 of *Orbecche* and six of *Canace*, see Richard Andrews, "Theatre," in *The Cambridge history of Italian Literature*, ed. Peter Brand and Lino Pertile (Cambridge: Cambridge University Press, 1997), 288 and Johannes Hösle, *Das italienische Theater von der Renaissance bis zur Gegenreformation* (Darmstadt: Wissenschaftliche Buchgesellschaft, 1984), 61.
47. Giovanbattista Giraldi Cinthio, *Orbecche* (Venice, Gabriel Giolito de Ferrari e fratelli, 1551), sig. F3.
48. Di Maria, *The Italian Tragedy*, 41.
49. Eugene J. Johnson, *Inventing the Opera House: Theater Architecture in Renaissance and Baroque Italy* (Cambridge: Cambridge University Press, 2018), 122–51.
50. Raymond Lebègue, "La Représentation d'une Tragédie à la Cour des Valois," *Comptes rendus des séances de l'Académie des Inscriptions et Belles-Lettres* 90/1 (1946): 138–44.
51. Luigia Zilli, "Mellin de Saint-Gelais, Jacques Amyot e un manoscritto della tragedia Sophonisba," *Studi di Letteratura Francese* 17 (1991): 19.
52. Howarth, *French Theatre*, 81.
53. Louise Frappier, "Spectacle Tragique et Conception de l'Histoire dans la Seconde Moitié du XVIe siècle en France," in *Les Arts du Spectacle au Théâtre (1550–1700)*, ed. Marie-France Wagner and Claire Le Brun-Gouanvic (Paris: Honoré Champion, 2001), 38–40.

54. Mellin de Saint-Gelais, *Sophonisba. Tragedie tresexcellente, tant pour l'argument, que pour le poly langage et graves sentences dont elle est ornée: représentée & prononcée devant le Roy, en sa ville de Bloys* (Paris: De l'Imprimerie de Philippe Danfrie, et Richard Breton, 1559).
55. Ludwig Fries, ed., *Montchrestien's Sophonisbe: Paralleldruck der drei davon erschienenen Bearbeitungen* (Marburg: N.G. Elwert, 1889), 43.
56. Louis Petit de Julleville, ed., *Les tragédies de Montchrestien* (Paris: E. Plon, Nourrit et cie, 1891), x.
57. Alan Howe, "La place de la tragédie dans le répertoire des comédiens français à la fin du XVIe siècle et au debut du XVIIe siècle," *Bibliothèque d'Humanisme et Renaissance* 59, no. 2 (1997).
58. Sybile Chevallier-Micki, "Panorama de l'édition théâtrale et de la composition dramatique à Rouen (fin XVIe siècle-début XVIIe siècle)," in *Pratiques de Corneille*, ed. Myriam Dufour-Maître (Mont-Saint-Aignan: Publications des Universités de Rouen et du Havre, 2012), 52–4.
59. Déborah Blocker, "Une 'muse de province' négocie sa centralité: Corneille et ses lieux," *Les Dossiers du Grihl* 2008/01 (2008), https://journals.openedition.org/dossiersgrihl/2133 (accessed April 14, 2018).
60. Frances A. Yates, "Some New Light on *L'écossaise* of Antoine de Montchrétien," *The Modern Language Review* 22, no. 3 (1927): 287.
61. Walter Devereux, *Lives and Letters of the Devereux Earls of Essex*, 2 vols (London: John Murray, 1853), 2: 99.
62. Norbert Elias, *The Civilizing Process: Sociogenetic and Psychogenetic Investigations*, ed. Eric Dunning, Johan Goudsblom, and Stephen Mennell, trans. Edmund Jephcott (Oxford and Cambridge, MA: Blackwell, 2000).
63. Bettina Boecker, *Imagining Shakespeare's Original Audience, 1660-2000: Groundlings, Gallants, Grocers* (Houndmills: Palgrave Macmillan, 2015).
64. Natasha Korda, "Women in the Theater," in *The Oxford Handbook of Early Modern Theatre*, ed. Richard Dutton (Oxford: Oxford University Press, 2011).
65. Allison K. Deutermann, *Listening for Theatrical Form in Early Modern England* (Edinburgh: Edinburgh University Press, 2016).
66. Richard Dutton, *Shakespeare, Court Dramatist* (Oxford: Oxford University Press, 2016).
67. Barbara Palmer, "Playing in the Provinces: Front or Back Door?" *Medieval & Renaissance Drama in England* 22 (2009): 81–127.
68. Wilfrid R. Prest, *The Inns of Court under Elizabeth I and the Early Stuarts, 1590–1640* (Totowa, N.J.: Rowman and Littlefield, 1972); Jessica Winston, *Lawyers at Play: Literature, Law, and Politics at the Early Modern Inns of Court, 1558–1581* (Oxford: Oxford University Press, 2016).
69. Philip J. Finkelpearl, *John Marston of the Middle Temple: An Elizabethan Dramatist in His Social Setting* (Cambridge: Harvard University Press, 1969).
70. Jeremy Lopez, *Theatrical Convention and Audience Response in Early Modern Drama* (Cambridge: Cambridge University Press, 2003), 147–58, and esp. 148n7.
71. Lucy Munro, *Children of the Queen's Revels: A Jacobean Theatre Repertory* (Cambridge: Cambridge University Press, 2005), 134–63.
72. Jacqueline Chauchaix, "Un personnage et ses origines: Le Gelosso de la Sophonisbe de Marston," *Confluents* 5/1 (1979): 19–26.
73. Phillip John Usher, "Courtroom Drama During the Wars of Religion: Robert Garnier and the Paris *Parlement*," in *French Renaissance and Baroque Drama: Text, Performance, and Theory*, ed. Michael Meere (Newark: University of Delaware Press, 2015), 143.
74. Viala, "Corneille, premier auteur moderne?"

75. Alberto Martino, *Daniel Casper von Lohenstein: Geschichte seiner Rezeption, Band I. 1661–1800*, trans. Heribert Streicher (Tübingen: Max Niemeyer Verlag, 1978), 176–77.
76. Pierre Béhar, "Lohenstein oder der verhinderte Dichter. Zur Deutung des Trauerspiels Sophonisbe," *Wolfenbütteler Barock-Nachrichten* 37 (2010): 5–14.
77. Joyce Green MacDonald, *Women and Race in Early Modern Texts* (Cambridge: Cambridge University Press, 2002), 7–9.
78. Jane O. Newman, *The Intervention of Philology: Gender, Learning, and Power in Lohenstein's Roman Plays* (Chapel Hill, NC: University of North Carolina Press, 2000), 37–72.
79. Pierre Béhar, *Silesia Tragica: Épanouissement et fin de l'école dramatique Silésienne dans l'oeuvre tragique de Daniel Casper von Lohenstein (1635–1683)*, 2 vols, (Wiesbaden: Otto Harrassowitz, 1988), 32–8; Martino, *Lohenstein*, 166–71.
80. Bärbel Rudin, "Deutsches Theater nach dem westfälischen Frieden—zwanzig Jahre des Aufbaus," in *Die Welt des Daniel Casper von Lohenstein*, ed. Peter Kleinschmidt, Gerhard Spellerberg, and Hanns-Dietrich Schmidt (Köln: Wienand Verlag, 1978), 51–3.
81. Martino, *Lohenstein*, 176–7.
82. Jerzy Limon, *Gentlemen of a Company: English Players in Central and Eastern Europe, 1590–1660* (Cambridge: Cambridge University Press, 1985), 37–62; Bosman, "Mobility," 504–15.

Chapter Four

All quotations of Shakespeare are from the Norton edition, based on the Oxford text, edited by Stephen Greenblatt, Walter Cohen, Jean Howard, and Katharine Eisaman Maus (New York: Norton, 2007).

1. "supreme moment of tragedy": John Staines, *The Tragic Histories of Mary Queen of Scots* (London: Routledge, 2009), 89.
2. Antonia Fraser, *Mary Queen of Scots* (London: Weidenfeld & Nicolson, 2015), 644, 647, 649, 676.
3. Stephen Greenblatt, *Shakespearean Negotiations: The Circulation of Social Energy in Renaissance England* (Oxford: Clarendon Press, 1988), 64. The authoritative genealogy of the dual concept of sovereignty remains Ernst Kantorowicz, *The King's Two Bodies: A Study in Medieval Political Theology* (repr. Princeton: Princeton University Press, 1997). For the salience of the idea in current philosophical thinking, see Robert Esposito, *Two: The Machine of Political Theology and the Place of Thought (Commonalities)*, trans. Zakiya Hanafi (New York: Fordham University Press, 2015).
4. Stephen Orgel, "Making Greatness Familiar," *Genre*, 15 (1982), 41–8, at 45. See also Andreas Höfele, *Stage, Stake, and Scaffold: Humans and Animals in Shakespeare's Theatre* (Oxford: Oxford University Press, 2011), 72–3.
5. Andrew Marvell, "A Horatian Ode upon Cromwell's Return from Ireland": ll. 53–6, in *The Poems of Andrew Marvell*, ed. Nigel Smith (London: Pearson Longman, 2007), 276.
6. Robert Wyngfield, *An Account of the Execution of Mary, the Late Queen of Scots* (London, 1587), and Anon., *King Charles His Speech Made Upon the Scaffold at Whitehall Gate* (London, 1649), quoted in Jayne Elizabeth Lewis, *Mary Queen of Scots: Romance and Nation* (London: Routledge, 1998), 13 and 75.
7. "beautiful theatre": Staines, 181; "lamentable tragedy": Clarendon, *History of the Rebellion and Civil Wars in England* (Oxford: Clarendon Press, 1888, repr. 1992), XI, 238; "same unconcernedness": Sir Philip Warwick, *Memoires of the Reign of King Charles I* (London, 1701), 309.

8. Franco Moretti, "The Great Eclipse: Tragic Form as the Deconsecration of Sovereignty," in *Signs Taken For Wonders: On the Sociology of Literary Forms* (London: Verso, 1983), 42–82, at 42; cf. David Scott Kastan, "Proud Majesty Made a Subject: Representing Authority on the Early Modern English Stage," in *Shakespeare After Theory* (New York: Routledge, 1999), 109–27.
9. Michel Foucault, *Psychiatric Power: Lectures at the Collège de France: 1973-1974*, ed. Jacques Lagrange, trans. Graham Burchell (London: Palgrave Macmillan, 2006), 19–37, at 20.
10. See Nancy Klein Maguire, "The Theatrical Mask / Masque of Politics: The Case of Charles I," *Journal of British Studies*, 28 (1989): 1–22.
11. For the postfiguration of the Christian savior image onto a historical person in Baroque theatre, see Eric Auerbach, "Figura," *Archivivium Romanicum*, 22 (1938): 436–89.
12. Marvell, ll. 58, 65, 71–2.
13. Blair Hoxby, *What Was Tragedy? Theory and the Early Modern Canon* (Oxford: Oxford University Press, 2015), 10.
14. Julian Young, *The Philosophy of Tragedy: From Plato to Žižek* (Cambridge: Cambridge University Press, 2013), 34, 39–40; Aristotle, *Poetics*, 1452b 31–1453a 10.
15. Robert Buch, *The Pathos of the Real: On the Aesthetics of Violence in the Twentieth Century* (Baltimore: Johns Hopkins University Press, 2010), 20.
16. James Emerson Phillips, *Images of a Queen: Mary Stuart in Sixteenth-Century Literature* (Berkeley: University of California Press, 1964), 191–2; Jean de Bordes, *Maria Stuarta Tragoedia*, unpub. mss., Morgan Library, New York.
17. Phillips, 191.
18. Ibid., 193–4; *Adriana Roulerii Insulani Stuarta Tragoedia*, ed. Roman Woerner (Berlin, 1906).
19. "daughter of debate": Elizabeth I, "The Doubt of Future Foes," in *Collected Works of Queen Elizabeth I*, ed. Leah Marcus, Janel Mueller, and Mary Beth Rose (Chicago: Chicago University Press, 2000), 134.
20. Staines, 91.
21. James VI quoted in Phillips, 202.
22. Michel de Montaigne, *The Complete Essays*, trans. M.A. Screech (London: Allen Lane, 1991), 86, 1040. For Mary and the philosopher's turn away from Stoicism, see Staines, 148–9.
23. Ibid., 151.
24. Joost van den Vondel, *Mary Stuart, or Tortured Majesty*, trans. and ed. Kristiaan P. Aercke (Ottawa: Dovehouse, 1996), 64.
25. James Parente Jr. and Jan Bloemendal, "The Humanist Tradition: *Mary Stuart*," in *Joost van den Vondel (1587-1679): Dutch Playwright in the Golden Age*, ed. Jan Bloemendal and Frans-Willem Korsten (Leiden: Brill, 2012), 341–58, at 353.
26. Vondel quoted ibid., 352.
27. See Nigel Smith, "Exile in Europe During the English Revolution and its Literary Impact," in *Literatures of Exile in the English Revolution and its Aftermath, 1640–1690*, Philip Major (Farnham: Ashgate, 2010), 105–18, at 112.
28. Jacob Zevecotius, *Maria Stuarta*, unpub. mss., trans. and quoted in Parente and Bloemendal, 350.
29. Ibid.
30. Howard Eiland and Michael Jennings, *Walter Benjamin: A Critical Life* (Cambridge, MA: Belknap Press, 2014), 227.
31. Walter Benjamin, *The Origin of German Tragic Drama*, trans. John Osborne (London: Verso, 2009). All quotations are referred to parenthetically.

32. "Winter Fruit": see Dale Randall, *Winter Fruit: English Drama 1642-1660* (University Press of Kentucky, 1995), 95–105; "not quite dead": Thomas Laqueur, *The Work of the Dead: A Cultural History of Human Remains* (Princeton: Princeton University Press, 2015), 17.

33. Sigmund Freud, "Mourning and Melancholia," in *The Complete Psychological Works of Sigmund Freud*, trans. James Strachey (24 vols.; London: Hogarth Press, 1956–74), 14: 243–58. See Sarah Ley Roff, "Benjamin and Psychoanalysis," in *The Cambridge Companion to Walter Benjamin* (Cambridge: Cambridge University Press, 2004), 121–2.

34. Arthur Marotti, "Shakespeare and Catholicism," in Richard Dutton, Alison Findlay, and Richard Wilson, *Theatre and Religion: Lancastrian Shakespeare* (Manchester: Manchester University Press, 2003), 218–41, at 228. See also Stephen Greenblatt, *Hamlet in Purgatory* (Princeton: Princeton University Press, 2001).

35. For the doctrine of *cuius regio, eius religio*—"whose realm, his is the religion"—declared at the Peace of Augsburg in 1555, see Diarmaid MacCulloch, *Reformation: Europe's House Divided, 1490-1700* (London: Allen Lane, 2003), 164, 274–5, 356.

36. Benjamin, 197; Howard Caygill, *Walter Benjamin: The colour of experience* (London: Routledge, 1997), 60.

37. Friedrich Nietzsche, *The Birth of Tragedy*, trans. Douglas Smith (Oxford: Oxford University Press, 2000), 46.

38. Julia Lupton, "The *Hamlet* Elections," in *Thinking with Shakespeare: Essays on Politics and Life* (Chicago: University of Chicago Press, 2011), 89. See also Rebecca Comay, *Mourning Sickness: Hegel and the French Revolution* (Stanford: Stanford University Press, 2011), 146.

39. Carl Schmitt, *Political Theology: Four Chapters on the Concept of Sovereignty*, trans. George Schwab ([1922] Chicago: University of Chicago Press, 2005), 5, 36.

40. See Samuel Weber, "Taking Exception to Decision: Walter Benjamin and Carl Schmitt," in *Benjamin's –abilities* (Cambridge, MA: Harvard University Press, 2008), 176–94, at 186; and Ilit Ferber, *Philosophy and Melancholy Benjamin's Early Reflections on Theater and Language* (Stanford: Stanford University Press, 2013), 94–5.

41. For Gryphius' reaction against Vondel's Stuart hagiography, see James Parente Jr., *Religious Drama and the Humanist Tradition: Christian Theater in Germany and the Netherlands, 1500-1680* (Leiden: Brill, 1987), 156–9, 168.

42. See Andrew Lacey, *The Cult of King Charles the Martyr* (Woodbridge: Boydell, 2003), 61–5. For the analogy between "remembering" sovereign body parts and organ transplants, see Philip Lorenz, *The Tears of Sovereignty: Perspectives of Power in Renaissance Drama* (New York: Fordham University Press, 2013), 23–4, 63–4.

43. Frances Yates, *The Rosicrucian Enlightenment* (London: Routledge & Kegan Paul, 1972), 47, 50–1. For the English players in Prague in 1618–19, see E.K. Chambers, *The Elizabethan Stage* (4 vols., Oxford: Clarendon Press, 1924), vol. 2, 285.

44. See Willem Schrickx, "English Actors at the Courts of Wolfenbüttel, Brussels and Graz During the Lifetime of Shakespeare," *Shakespeare Survey*, 33 (1980), 153–68, at 155.

45. Sir William Davenant, "To Him Who Prophecy'd," l. 72, in *The Shorter Poems, and Songs from the Plays and Masques*, ed. A.M. Gibbs (Oxford: Oxford University Press, 1972), 123; Hugh Powell, "Introduction," in *Andreas Gryphius: "Cardenio und Celinde"* (Leicester: Leicester University Press, 1967), xx–xxiv, at xxiv.

46. René Descartes to Elizabeth, February 22, 1649, *Oeuvres philosophiques*, ed. Fernand Alquié (3 vols, Paris: Garnier, 1963–73), 3: 899, trans. and repr. Timothy Reiss, "Descartes, the Palatinate, and the Thirty Years War: Political Theory and Political Practice," *Yale French Studies: 80: Baroque Topographies* (New Haven: Yale University Press, 1991), 108–45, at 115.

47. Andreas Gryphius quoted in Philip Freund, *Laughter and Grandeur: Theatre in the Age of the Baroque* (London: Peter Owen, 2006), 276.
48. Giorgio Agamben, *State of Exception*, trans. Kevin Attell (Chicago: University of Chicago Press, 2005), 55–7.
49. "Hitler's Crown Jurist": Waldemar Gurian, "Carl Schmitt: der Kronjurist des III Reichs," quoted in Reinhard Mehring, *Carl Schmitt: A Biography*, trans. Daniel Steuer (Cambridge: Polity, 2014), 329.
50. Michael Dobson, "Short Cuts," *London Review of Books*, August 6, 2009, 22.
51. Carl Schmitt, *Hamlet or Hecuba: The Intrusion of the Time into the Play*, trans. David Pan and Jennifer Rust ([1956] New York: Telos, 2009), 25–6. Further quotations are referred to parenthetically. Peter Thomson, *Shakespeare's Professional Career* (Cambridge: Cambridge University Press, 1992), 169.
52. Lupton, 72.
53. Dobson, 22.
54. Noël O'Sullivan, *Fascism* (London: Dent, 1983), 153–4.
55. Walter Benjamin, "Critique of Violence," in *Walter Benjamin: selected writings*, ed. Marcus Bullock and Michael Jennings (3 vols., Cambridge MA: Belknap Press, 1996), 1: 236–5.
56. *Historic Manuscripts Commission: Salisbury Papers*, vol. 3, 310–11, quoted in Alan Stewart, *The Cradle King: A Life of James VI and I* (London: Chatto & Windus, 2003), 86.
57. Carl Schmitt, "Foreword to the German Edition of Lilian Winstanley's *Hamlet and the Scottish Succession*," *Telos*, 153 ([1952] Winter 2010), 164–77: 172.
58. David Howarth, *Images of Rule: Art and Politics in the English Renaissance, 1485-1649* (Basingstoke: Macmillan, 1997), 166.
59. "jump beyond the limits": Schmitt, "National State of Emergency," lecture to the Association for Research in State Theory, Weimar, March 27, 1933, quoted Mehring, 278; John McCormick, *Carl Schmitt's Critique of Liberalism* (Cambridge: Cambridge University Press, 1997), 175.
60. Jan-Werner Müller, *A Dangerous Mind: Carl Schmitt in Post-War European Thought* (New Haven: Yale University Press, 2003), 58.
61. Christopher Marlowe, *Doctor Faustus*, 13.90, in *Christopher Marlowe: The Complete Plays*, ed. Frank Romany and Robert Lindsey (London: Penguin, 2003), 390.
62. Richard Marienstras, *Shakespeare au XXIe Siècle: Petite introduction aux tragedies* (Paris: Minuit, 2000), 22–3, 96. Written for the *Pléiade* translation, Marienstras' introduction to the Tragedies was suppressed by the edition's publishers.
63. James Joyce, *Ulysses*, ed. Richard Ellmann (Harmondsworth: Penguin, 1968), 187.
64. See R.S. White, *Innocent Victims Poetic Injustice in Shakespearean Tragedy* (London: Athlone, 1986).
65. Schmitt, "Foreword to the German Edition," 171–2.
66. "direct democracy": Carl Schmitt, *The Crisis of Parliamentary Democracy*, trans. Ellen Kennedy ([1923] Cambridge, MA: MIT Press, 1986), 16–17; "gruesomely comic": Schmitt, *Political Theology*, 53. See O'Sullivan, 157–8: "The election of 1933, he explained, was not an election in the old liberal-democratic sense at all . . . It was, rather, an occasion which had given the German people the chance to recognize its destiny by acclaiming its leader."
67. Esposito, 47.
68. Eric Santner, *The Royal Remains: The People's Two Bodies and the Endgames of Sovereignty* (Chicago: University of Chicago Press, 2011), 92.
69. Ibid., 158.
70. Ibid., 50.

71. Giorgio Agamben, *Homo Sacer: Sovereign Power and Power and Bare Life*, trans. Daniel Heller-Roazen (Stanford: Stanford University Press, 1998), 168–9.
72. Michel Foucault, *Society Must Be Defended: Lectures at the Collège de France, 1975-1976*, trans. David Macey (London: Allen Lane, 2003), 176; *Security, Territory, Population: Lectures at the Collège de France, 1977–1978*, trans. Graham Burchell (Basingstoke: Macmilllan, 2007), 266.
73. See Richard Halpern, "The King's Two Buckets: Kantorowicz, *Richard II*, and Fiscal *Trauerspiel*," *Representations*, 106 (2009): 67–76; Victoria Kahn, "Political Theology in *The King's Two Bodies*," *Representations*, 106 (2009): 77–101.
74. See David Norbrook, "The Emperor's New Body? *Richard II*, Ernst Kantorowicz, and the Politics of Shakespeare Criticism," *Textual Practice*, 10 (1996): 329–57; and Deborah Shuger, *Political Theologies in Shakespeare's England: The Sacred and the State in "Measure for Measure"* (Basingstoke: Macmillan, 2001), 36. For a critique of this reading, see Lorna Hutson, "Imagining Justice: Kantorowicz and Shakespeare," *Representations*, 106 (2009): 118–42, at 120–1.
75. Alain Boureau, *Kantorowicz: Stories of a Historian*, trans. Stephen Nichols and Gabrielle Spiegel (Baltimore: Johns Hopkins University Press, 2001), 106.
76. Kantorowicz, 312–13; Carl Schmitt, *Dictatorship*, translated by Michael Hoezl and Graham Ward ([1921] (Cambridge: Polity Press, 2014), 65.
77. "Speech to Parliament, 21 March 1610," in John Sommerville, *King James VI and I: Political Writings* (Cambridge: Cambridge University Press, 1994), 179.
78. Kantorowicz, 312–13, 387.
79. Ibid., 20–3, 39–41.
80. Ernst Kantorowicz to Stefan George, July 10, 1933, repr. in Robert Lerner, *Ernst Kantorowicz: A Life* (Princeton: Princeton University Press, 2017), 165.
81. Ernst Kantorowicz to Edith Landman, quoted in Andreas Höfele, *No Hamlets: German Shakespeare from Nietzsche to Carl Schmitt* (Oxford: Oxford University Press, 2016), 102.
82. Benjamin, *The Origin*, 69; Carl Schmitt, *The Leviathan in the State Theory of Thomas Hobbes: Meaning and Failure of a Political Symbol*, trans. George Schwab and Erna Hilfstein (Chicago: University of Chicago, 2008), 34.
83. Kantorowicz, 32–3, 39–41.
84. Höfele, *No Hamlets*, 116.
85. John Dover Wilson, "Introduction," William Shakespeare, *Richard II* (Cambridge: Cambridge University Press, 1939), xii.

Chapter Five

1. The single most impressive historical overview of the religious crises in early modern Europe is Diarmaid McCullough, *Reformation: Europe's House Divided, 1490–1700* (London: Penguin Books, 2004). See especially 382–93 for the so-called "Elizabethan Settlement."
2. For the social position of the protagonist, see Terry Eagleton, *Sweet Violence: The Idea of the Tragic* (Oxford: Blackwell, 2003), 85.
3. A full discussion of the play's effects on subsequent events can be found in Margot Heinemann, *Puritanism & Theatre: Thomas Middleton and Opposition Drama under the Early Stuarts* (Cambridge: Cambridge University Press, 2007), 151–71.
4. The malcontent figure is related to an overall context of religion and power in Jonathan Dollimore, *Radical Tragedy: Religion, Ideology and Power in the Drama of Shakespeare and*

His Contemporaries, 2nd edition (Hertfordshire: Harvester Wheatsheaf, 1989), 49–50. For Machiavellism on stage, see Alison Findlay, *Illegitimate Power: Bastards in Renaissance Drama* (Manchester: Manchester University Press, 1994), 81–3.

5. For a very full discussion, especially of the doctrinal differences between diverse forms of Protestantism, see Adrian Streete, *Protestantism and Drama in Early Modern England* (Cambridge: Cambridge University Press, 2009).
6. The associations and functions of the stage trapdoor are discussed in Andrew Gurr and Mariko Ichikawa, *Staging in Shakespeare's Theatres* (Oxford: Oxford University Press, 2000), 60.
7. A recent edition has a foreword by Stephen Greenblatt: C.L. Barber, *Shakespeare's Festive Comedy: A Study of Dramatic Form and its Relation to Social Custom* (New Jersey and Oxford: Princeton University Press, 2012).
8. See the Introduction to F.H. Sandbach, *Ancient Culture and Society: The Comic Theatre of Greece and Rome* (London: Chatto & Windus, 1977), 9–13.
9. A more recent edition is René Girard, *Violence and the Sacred* (London: Bloomsbury Academic, 2013).
10. A successor volume to Girard is Francois Laroque, *Shakespeare's Festive World: Elizabethan Seasonal Entertainment and the Professional Stage* (Cambridge: Cambridge University Press, 1993). Phrases such as "anthropological turn" are more commonly applied to the influence of Clifford Geertz on the first wave of early American New Historicists, but in fact the relationship between the two disciplines has been close on several other occasions. In his well-known book chapter entitled "Invisible Bullets," Stephen Greenblatt makes a typical reference to Geertz. Stephen Greenblatt, *Shakespearean Negotiations* (Oxford: Oxford University Press, 1992), 65. In the UK, the work of Mary Douglas has had similar effect. The most accessible recent edition of her best-known work on symbolic culture is *Purity and Danger: An Analysis of Concepts of Pollution and Taboo* (London: Routledge, 2002). She theorises the boundaries between civilization and its "others."
11. The work of Michael D. Bristol has been important here, following on from his reading of the Russian theorist Mikhail Bakhtin. See, for example, Michael D. Bristol, *Carnival and Theatre: Plebeian Culture and the Structure of Authority in Renaissance Britain* (London: Routledge, 1985), which fully engages with M.M. Bakhtin, *Rabelais and His World* (Bloomington, IN: Indiana University Press, 1984). Together with Girard, these have in turn been succeeded specifically in the study of tragedy by Naomi Conn Liebler, *Shakespeare's Festive Tragedy: The Ritual Foundations of Genre* (London and New York: Routledge, 1995).
12. Liebler, *Shakespeare's Festive Tragedy,* discusses the figure of the scapegoat and the concept of the sacrifice throughout. See also Eagleton, *Sweet Violence*.
13. For a discussion of the Weird Sisters as figures of cultural translation, see Paul Innes, "Harming *Macbeth*: A British Translation," in *Shakespeare and the Translation of Identity in Early Modern England*, ed. Liz Oakley-Brown (London and New York: Continuum, 2011), 103–30.
14. For example, see Northrop Frye, *A Natural Perspective: The Development of Shakespearean Comedy and Romance*, 2nd edition (New York and London: Columbia University Press, 1995) and Northrop Frye, *The Myth of Deliverance: Reflections on Shakespeare's Problem Comedies* (Toronto, Buffalo and London: University of Toronto Press, 1983).
15. Jan Kott, *Shakespeare Our Contemporary*, trans. Boleslaw Taborski, reprinted (London and New York: Routledge, 1994). This edition has a foreword by Peter Brook, whose aesthetic was so heavily influenced by Kott's work, most famously his stage production of *A Midsummer Night's Dream* (1970) and his film of *King Lear* with Paul Scofield (1971).

16. For a very full discussion of Shakespeare's classical learning, see Colin Burrow, *Shakespeare & Classical Antiquity* (Oxford: Oxford University Press, 2013). Many of his observations could be extended to other early modern playwrights. For an example of a very precise analysis of the ways in which a play refers to classical mythology, see Liz Oakley-Brown, "*Titus Andronicus* and the Cultural Politics of Translation in Early Modern England," *Renaissance Studies* 19, no. 3 (2005): 325–47.
17. A full discussion of tragedy and Shakespeare's Roman plays can be found in Paul Innes, *Shakespeare's Roman Plays* (London: Palgrave Macmillan, 2015).
18. Streete, *Protestantism and Drama*, examines this play's relationship with Calvinism at 140–61; see also Dollimore, *Radical Tragedy*, 109–19.
19. The "B-Text" of the play inserts a whole series of comic interludes to underline the importance of the inability of the characters fully to comprehend the powers at their disposal. There is a detailed analysis of the relationships between the two versions of the text and their implications in Leah S. Marcus, *Unediting the Renaissance: Shakespeare, Marlowe, Milton* (London: Routledge, 1996), 38–67.
20. This is a different scenario from that in *The Duchess of Malfi*, where the tragedy is also driven by the desire of the Duchess of the play's title. In her case, however, she does nothing she is not entitled to do given her status as a widow. Technically, she is free to marry, but the weight of Italian patriarchal power in the form of her brothers the Cardinal and Duke Ferdinand ensures that she has to marry secretly, especially because the husband she chooses is of much lower social class, no matter how worthy. For more details, see Linda Woodbridge, "Queen of Apricots: The Duchess of Malfi, Hero of Desire," in *The Female Tragic Hero in English Renaissance Drama*, ed. Naomi Conn Liebler (London and New York: Palgrave Macmillan, 2002), 161–84.
21. Zeffirelli's 1968 film of the play takes advantage of its medium to show this happening; another friar carrying the letters to Romeo moves off the main path, presumably to have his lunch, and then moments later Romeo thunders past on horseback from the opposite direction. It is almost as if Zeffirelli feels the need to explain how this event takes place in the play for a modern audience unused to filling in gaps in the plot for themselves, in a manner that is unnecessary for Elizabethan theatregoers.
22. The classic essay on these subjects and more is a chapter entitled "'And wash the Ethiop white': Femininity and the Monstrous in Othello," in Karen Newman, *Fashioning Femininity and English Renaissance Drama* (Chicago: University of Chicago Press, 1991), 71–94.
23. The use of anachronism in early modern drama is discussed in Innes, *Shakespeare's Roman Plays*, 108–10, following on from Brian Walsh's useful theorising of the "historical consciousness" that seems to have been prevalent in the theatre-going culture of the time. See Brian Walsh, *Shakespeare, the Queen's Men and the Elizabethan Performance of History* (Cambridge: Cambridge University Press, 2009), 29.
24. Perhaps the single most famous is the Jewish physician to Queen Elizabeth I, Rodrigo Lopez, whose death in a cloudy suspicion of treason and conspiracy seems to have been unwarranted. Some useful contextual information about the Jewish presence in Elizabethan England is provided in a chapter on the Lopez conspiracy by Alan Haynes, *Invisible Power: The Elizabethan Secret Services 1570-1603* (Stroud: Alan Sutton Publishing, 1992), 111–20.
25. James Shapiro discusses *The Jew of Malta* at many points, mostly in terms of its influence on Shylock. James Shapiro, *Shakespeare and the Jews* (New York: Columbia University Press, 1996).
26. On the character type of the *Vice* as derived from the medieval popular dramatic tradition, see Robert Weimann, *Shakespeare and the Popular Tradition in the Theater: Studies in the*

Social Dimension of Dramatic Form and Function ed. Robert Schwartz (Baltimore and London: Johns Hopkins University Press, 1978), 112–60.

27. See Paul Innes, "Some of the Most Important Events in Shakespeare do not Happen," *English* 64, no. 247 (2015): 254–67.
28. Anne Laurence provides a useful overview of these issues in the form of a chapter on marriage. Anne Laurence, *Women in England 1500-1760: A Social History* (London: Weidenfeld and Nicolson, 1995), 41–60. She spends quite a bit of space initially defining the various elements of marriage, and then proceeds to note just how often the exact legal status of a marriage could be challenged. This brings to mind the various political machinations of monarchs such as Henry VIII over pre-contracts, betrothals, and annulments.
29. On agency in *The Duchess of Malfi* and other plays, see Dympna Callaghan, *Woman and Gender in Renaissance Tragedy: A Study of King Lear, Othello, The Duchess of Malfi and The White Devil* (Hertfordshire: Harvester Wheatsheaf, 1989), 66–8.
30. The most easily accessible edition is part of the Penguin Classics series: *Aristotle: Poetics* (Harmondsworth, 1996).
31. There is discussion of *hamartia* at various places in Liebler, *Shakespeare's Festive Tragedy*, especially at 20–2, 37–9, and 41–4. She notes that the word looks (to Greekless readers) like a noun. However, it is in fact a verb clause, "he missed the mark," which makes it an action and thus not dependent on nor reflective of character. An early modern play that condenses all of these issues, almost as a kind of set text, is Elizabeth Cary's *The Tragedy of Mariam* (published 1613). This so-called "closet" play (because it was not originally intended for publication and performance) reads almost like a set-piece analysis of tragedy in the period. It also has the added advantage of being a drama that includes very positive Jewish figures, as well as the figure of Herod the Great. Mariam in particular is a good example of the role of the protagonist, since she would be on the stage for very little actual performance time. In accordance with Aristotelian dictates, she functions as a plot device as opposed to some form of fully realised character with presumed psychological inwardness.
32. The legendary story of Leir (in its alternative spelling) comes from Geoffrey of Monmouth, *The History of the Kings of Britain*, ed. Michael D. Reeve, trans. Neil Wright (Woodbridge: The Boydell Press, 2009).
33. This is an entirely different technique from the kinds of uses of almost medieval folklore that can be found in some of Shakespeare's comedies, such as the woods in *A Midsummer Night's Dream, As You Like It*, or even *The Two Gentlemen of Verona*, all of which echo the Robin Hood figure. The tragic division of the country in *King Lear* is structurally reliant on British myth in a much more fundamental manner. As noted near the outset of this current chapter, comedy and tragedy have many aspects in common; they just process them differently because they serve different ritual functions.
34. Sir Arthur Golding's 1567 translation of the *Metamorphoses* was widely influential in early modern England, and indeed is still reprinted today. Ovid (Publius Ovidius Naso), *Metamorphoses*, trans. Arthur Golding, ed. Madeleine Forey (London: Penguin Books, 2002). References and allusions can be found in writing throughout the period, up to and including Eve admiring herself in *Paradise Lost* 4.460–5, in an echo of the myth of Narcissus. A fine example of another type of classical reference in a comedy occurs in Ben Jonson's *Volpone* 1.2, when his carnivalesque entourage entertains the old fox with a performance of the various incarnations of Pythagoras.
35. David Quint locates the origin of this powerful imperialist discourse in Virgil's description of the centrepiece of the shield of Aeneas, the Battle of Actium. David Quint, *Epic and Empire: Politics and Generic Form from Virgil to Milton* (New Jersey: Princeton University Press,

1993), 24–8 as discussed in Innes, "Some of the Most Important Events," 86–9. The proleptic prophecy of the triumph of Augustus over the Orientalized Egyptian Queen and her feminized Roman partner Marcus Antonius is an effacement of the very real political struggle for dominance between Romans. In effect, it becomes almost impossible to separate history from myth-making because the effects of this discourse are so far-reaching.

36. A book that goes into detail about the implications of these issues and more is Lisa Hopkins, *The Cultural Uses of the Caesars on the English Renaissance Stage* (Hampshire and Burlington: Ashgate, 1988).
37. A very useful modern edition is *Ovid's Heroides: A New Translation and Critical Essays*, ed. Paul Murgatroyd et al. (London: Routledge, 2017).
38. Two of the best known essays were first published in close proximity: Paul Brown, "'This Thing of Darkness I Acknowledge Mine': *The Tempest* and the Discourse of Colonialism," in *Political Shakespeare: Essays in Cultural Materialism*, ed. Jonathan Dollimore and Alan Sinfield, 48–71, 2nd edition (New York: Cornell University Press, 1985); Francis Barker and Peter Hulme, "Nymphs and Reapers heavily vanish: the discursive con-texts of *The Tempest*," in *Alternative Shakespeares*, ed. John Drakakis, 2nd edition (London: Routledge, 2002), 194–208.

Chapter Six

1. On *Ecerinis* as "a false dawn," see G. Braden, *Renaissance Tragedy and the Senecan Tradition: Anger's Privilege* (New Haven and London: Yale University Press, 1985), 101. On the play's date, see H. Müller, *Früher Humanismus in Oberitalien: Albertino Mussato*, Ecerinis (Frankfurt am Main: Peter Lang, 1987), 57, drawing on A. Mussato, *Ecerinide*, ed. Luigi Padrin (Bologna: Nicola Zanichelli Padrin, 1900), X. S. Locati, *La rinascita del genere tragico nel medioevo: L'Ecerinis di Albertino Mussato* (Firenze: Franco Cesati, 2006), 104, mentions, but then dismisses, the possibility that *Ecerinis* was Mussato's youthful work.
2. Because of *Ecerinis* Mussato was crowned poet laureate in December 1315. This was the first crowning of a poet in the West since antiquity. For details of the event as well as its significance, see J.-F. Chevalier, "Le couronnement d'Albertino Musat ou le renaissance d'une célébration," *Bulletin de l'Association Guillaume Budé* 2 (2004): 42–55.
3. There is no explicit allusion to Cangrande della Scala in Mussato's play nor are there any contemporary documents that make the connection. Locati, *La rinascita*, 108–15, lists moments in *Ecerinis* that might make one think of Cangrande, but is forced to admit (104) that the connection is never made explicit.
4. The many Senecan allusions and borrowings are recorded in the commentary provided by Müller, *Früher Humanismus*. See also A. Mussato, *Ecérinide*, ed. J.-F. Chevalier (Paris: Belles lettres, 2000). R.G. Witt, *In the Footsteps of the Ancients: The Origins of Humanism from Lovato to Bruni* (Leiden and Boston: Brill, 2000), 127, sees *Thyestes* as the main stylistic model, while Locati, *La rinascita*, 148–56, considers *Octavia*, accepted as Seneca's play at the time, an important precedent because it is the only play in the Senecan corpus that dramatizes events from the dramatist's time rather than from mythology. According to this view, Ezzelino is to be understood as a version of Nero, the archetypal tyrant.
5. Braden, *Renaissance Tragedy*, 102–3.
6. G. Staley, *Seneca and the Idea of Tragedy* (Oxford: Oxford University Press, 2010), 54.
7. The commentary, completed in 1317, is printed in Mussato, *Ecerinide*, ed. Padrin; my parenthetical references are to this edition.
8. Guizzardo and Castellano are also the first to mention that the title of *Ecerinis* (after Ecerinus, the Latin form for Ezzelino) is similar in its grammatical form to titles such as *Aeneis*

and *Thebais*, which are epic poems rather than plays (80). This connection is made by Mussato himself, who in one of his epistles invokes *Thebais* as a parallel to *Ecerinis*, but observes that *Thebais* was staged: "Carmine sic laetam non fecit Statius Urbem, / Thebais in scenis cum recitata fuit, / ne minus haec tragico fregit subsellia versu / grata suis meritis sic ECERINIS erat" (Müller, *Früher Humanismus*, 46; see also Mussato, *Ecerinide*, ed. Padrin, 276–7).

9. References will be to *Mussato's* Ecerinis *and Loschi's* Achilles, tr. J.R. Berrigan (München: Wilhelm Fink Verlag, 1975); the line numbers refer to the Latin text, which Berrigan, like all the modern translations, takes from Padrin's edition. I have also consulted the English translations in *Humanist Tragedies*, trans. Gary R. Grund (Cambridge, MA, and London: The I Tatti Renaissance Library, Harvard University Press, 2011), and in A. Mussato, *The Tragedy of Ecerinis*, trans. Robert W. Carrubba et al. (University Park, PA: Department of Classics, the Pennsylvania State University, 1972), which I mention when their solutions seem to me superior to Berrigan's or when they widely differ.

10. "The nobles, in justice, are the first to suffer. / Those who sold out, atone now for their crimes" (226–7).

11. While Mussato at times distinguishes between *plebs* (the common people) and *populus* (something like the middle class), as in lines 252–3 ("Plebe cum tota populus subegit / colla"), their behavior is identical and several lines later they are all described as citizens (*cives*, 256). This tendency toward inclusiveness is evident elsewhere in the text ("Gentes e requie trahit, / Cives otia deserunt," 153–4). The chorus at one point explicitly refers to itself as *plebs*: "O quam multa potentium / Nos et scandala cordibus / Plebs vilissima iungimus!" (133–5). Ecerinus maintains the distinction between the nobles and the common people only in order to reduce them all to the same level, that of annihilation: "Cum plebe pereat omne nobilium genus" (329).

12. "Spectator queritur iudicii parum, / dum restat Patavum quod reparet genus" (457–8).

13. This translation is taken from *Humanist Tragedies*, trans. Grund.

14. And this despite the fact that, as Carruba points out, Mussato "passes over reports that Ezzelino not only refused medical aid and food but also refused to speak and tore off the bandages applied to his wounds" (V).

15. It is worth noting that the translations by Grund and by Carruba et al. call the unnamed citizens "soldiers," thus making the identification between the tyrant Ecerinus and "a soldier" more palatable. But Mussato only speaks of unnamed individuals, not soldiers (using words such as *hic*, *ille*, or third-person verb forms without specifying the subject).

16. Müller, *Früher Humanismus*, 57; Chevalier, "Le couronnement," 44.

17. Locati, *La rinascita*, 115: "Con il quarto atto la tragedia è di per sé conclusa." Commenting on the fate of Albricus and his family, Braden, *Renaissance Tragedy*, 103, observes: "None of Ecerinus' own crimes is described with comparable force or detail; the retributive murdering of his hapless relations caps the play's mounting rhetoric of outrage but skews its moral and dramatic design. Mussato learns playwriting from a bad teacher [i.e., Seneca] and does not learn very well." Grund, on the other hand, draws a parallel between "the shocking scene of the immolation of Alberico's wife and five daughters" and the fires of hell in *sacre rappresentazioni*, but does not explain why the wife and the daughters deserve to burn in hell; *Humanist Tragedies*, xxii.

18. C.E. Beneš, *Urban Legend: Civic Identity and the Classical Past in Northern Italy, 1250–1350* (University Park, PA: Pennsylvania State University Press, 2011), 54.

19. Seneca, *Tragedies*, trans. J.G. Fitch, vol. 2 (Cambridge, MA: Harvard University Press, 2004), *Thyestes*, 755–8.

20. For the context of the early uses of Seneca in England, see J. Winston, *Lawyers at Play: Literature, Law, and Politics at the Early Modern Inns of Court, 1558-1581* (Oxford: Oxford University Press, 2016), esp. Chapter 6.
21. T. Sackville and T. Norton, *Gorboduc, or Ferrex and Porrex*, ed. I.B. Cauthen, Jr. (Lincoln: University of Nebraska Press, 1970), 5.1.2–7.
22. The first edition was printed in 1565, the second in 1570. The relationship between them is discussed by I.B. Cauthen, Jr., "*Gorboduc, Ferrex and Porrex*: The First Two Quartos," *Studies in Bibliography* 15 (1962): 231–3. The format is actually octavo.
23. See D. Bevington, *Tudor Drama and Politics: A Critical Approach to Topical Meaning* (Cambridge, MA: Harvard University Press, 1968), 141–55; M. Axton, *The Queen's Two Bodies: Drama and the Elizabethan Succession* (London: Royal Historical Society, 1977), 38–60; G. Walker, *The Politics of Performance in Early Renaissance Drama* (Cambridge: Cambridge University Press, 1998), Chapter 6; K. Dunn, "Representing Counsel: *Gorboduc* and the Elizabethan Privy Council," *English Literary Renaissance* 33.3 (2003): 279–308; D. Cavanagh, *Language and Politics in the Sixteenth-Century History Play* (New York: Palgrave Macmillan, 2003), Chapter 2; Winston, *Lawyers at Play*, Chapter 7. My own contribution to this lively scholarly conversation will be found in *Subjects of Advice: Drama and Counsel from More to Shakespeare* (Philadelphia: University of Pennsylvania Press, 2019), Chapter 3.
24. Sackville and Norton, *Gorboduc*, ed. Cauthen, 3.
25. On the native land in relation to issues of sovereignty in the play, see J. Vanhoutte, "Community, Authority, and the Motherland in Sackville and Norton's *Gorboduc*," *Studies in English Literature* 40.2 (2000): 227–39.
26. On the connections between the two plays, see B.H.C. de Mendonça, "The Influence of *Gorboduc* on *King Lear*," *Shakespeare Survey* 13 (1960): 41–8.
27. Sackville and Norton, *Gorboduc*, ed. Cauthen, 4. The second edition was in fact set from a corrected copy of the first. Interestingly, while the first, unauthorized edition announces Sackville and Norton as the authors of the play on its title page, the second edition, apparently authorized, suppresses the fact. It also suppresses eight lines (5.1.42–9) in which Eubulus mentions the possibility of rebellion only to dismiss it as unacceptable regardless of circumstances.
28. The indebtedness to the 1541 Latin translation of Euripides evident in both Dolce and Gascoigne and Kinwelmersh is established by J.W. Cunliffe in his edition of *Early English Classical Tragedies* (Oxford: Clarendon Press, 1912), xxxvi–xxxvii, 312, and further developed in S. Dewar-Watson, "*Jocasta*: 'A Tragedie Written in Greeke,'" *International Journal of the Classical Tradition* 17.1 (2010): 22–32. My quotations from *Jocasta* are taken from Cunliffe's edition.
29. Winston, *Lawyers at Play*, 173–4.
30. On Jocasta as the central figure, see A.E. Ward, *Women and Tudor Tragedy: Feminizing Counsel and Representing Gender* (Madison: Fairleigh Dickinson University Press, 2013), 62–71. Winston, *Lawyers at Play*, 205–8, lays emphasis on Oedipus as the unifying figure in the play.
31. *Early English Classical Tragedies*, ed. Cunliffe, 119.
32. I. Bratičević and I. Lupić, "Držićeva *Hekuba* između izvedbe i knjige," *Colloquia Maruliana* 22 (2013): 77–116, 85.
33. I. Lupić, "The Mobile Queen: Observing *Hecuba* in Renaissance Europe," *Renaissance Drama* 46.1 (2018): 25–56.
34. The most comprehensive guide to Držić's life and works is *Leksikon Marina Držića*, ed. M. Tatarin et al. (Zagreb: Leksikografski zavod Miroslav Krleža, 2009).
35. M. Držić, *The Conspiracy Letters to Cosimo I de' Medici*, trans. N. Milas, T. L. Jockims, and P. Brailo (Dubrovnik: Dom Marina Držića, 2008), 6. The original letters were first published

in M. Držić, *Djela*, ed. M. Rešetar (Zagreb: JAZU, 1930), and have been reprinted several times since.
36. On Ragusa's position as a tributary state of the Ottoman Empire, see L. Kunčević, "Janus-Faced Sovereignty: The International Status of the Ragusan Republic in the Early Modern Period," in *The European Tributary States of the Ottoman Empire in the Sixteenth and Seventeenth Centuries*, ed. G. Kármán and L. Kunčević (Leiden and Boston: Brill, 2013), 91–121.
37. This was the view of M. Rešetar, the first editor of the letters; see M. Držić, *Djela*, ed. Rešetar, LXXII.
38. In 2007, however, yet another letter by Držić came to light in the Medici archives. Written in late July, a month before Držić's departure from Florence, the letter shows not only that Držić's letters were read but that they were followed up by very specific questions. The letter is addressed to Cosimo, the ailing duke, and it makes clear the chain of communication: it was the duke's son Francesco's secretary, Bartolomeo Concino, who communicated with a certain Francesco Vinta, who in turn was linked with Držić. On behalf of Francesco, to whom the matter seems to have been assigned by his father, Concino asked, first, whether Držić was sent by the people, by one part of the people only or by someone else; second, how would it be possible to overthrow a government that is not weak at all and that has a very high opinion of its own strength; third, if a new government were successfully instituted, how would one make sure that the deposed aristocrats do not get support from either the Turks or the Venetians? In response to the first question, Držić argues that secrecy forbids him from saying much, but that he should be trusted; in response to the second question, he observes that it is precisely the confidence of the ruling aristocracy that will ensure the success of the undertaking since they do not suspect the extent of discontent among the people; finally, all Ragusans, regardless of status, hate both Turks and Venetians, so that is not a real concern. Further evidence from Concino's memoranda shows that the duke was skeptical but willing to hear the whole story. The conclusion the Medici reached was that the Ragusan priest presented them with spectacular fireworks that feature lots of fire but produce no lasting effect. We do not know whether this conclusion was in any way communicated to Držić. See L. Kunčević, "'Ipak nije na odmet sve čuti': medičejski pogled na urotničke namjere Marina Držića," *Anali Dubrovnik* 45 (2007): 9–46.
39. J. Tadić, *Dubrovački portreti* (Beograd: Srpska književna zadruga, 1948), 124–5.
40. A call to arms was sounded in Ž. Jeličić, *Marin Držić, pjesnik dubrovačke sirotinje* (Zagreb: Novo pokoljenje, 1950). The title of his book translates as *Marin Držić, the Poet of the Ragusan Poor*.
41. The central document here is the elaborate and highly opaque prologue delivered by a character called Long Nose, a necromancer from the Great Indies, in Držić's *Dundo Maroje*.
42. See F. Čale, "Što je Držiću Hekuba," *Forum* 6 (1967): 797–822; F. Čale, "O šibenskom rukopisu *Hekube*," *Forum* 16 (1977): 25–42. The approach is taken to its extreme in S.P. Novak, *Planeta Držić: Držić i rukopis vlasti* (Zagreb: CEKADE, 1984).
43. Archives of the Croatian Academy of Sciences and Arts, Zagreb, MS VII. 33.
44. For the problems this reading encounters in the context of Renaissance culture of commonplacing, see Bratičević and Lupić, "Držićeva *Hekuba* između izvedbe i knjige."

Chapter Seven

1. Unless otherwise noted, all quotations from non-Shakespearean plays will be taken from *English Renaissance Drama: A Norton Anthology*, gen. ed. David Bevington (New York: W.W. Norton and Co., 2002).

2. Catherine Belsey, *Shakespeare and the Loss of Eden* (New Brunswick, NJ: Rutgers UP, 1999), 21.
3. William Gouge, *Eight Treatises of Domesticall Duties*, 3rd edn (London, 1634), 17.
4. John Dod and Robert Cleaver, *A Godly Forme of Household Governance: for the ordering of private families, according to the direction of God's Word* (London, 1612), f. A8v.
5. Laura Gowing, *Gender Relations in Early Modern England* (Harlow, UK: Pearson Education Ltd.), 45.
6. Gowing, 6.
7. See Lynda E. Boose, "The Father's House and the Daughter in It," in *Daughters and Fathers*, ed. Lynda E. Boose and Betty S. Flowers (Baltimore: Johns Hopkins University Press, 1989), 17–24, for a compelling analysis of the father's cultural and legal power over his daughter.
8. Lawrence Stone, *The Family, Sex and Marriage in England, 1500-1800* (New York: Harper and Row, 1977), 87–8.
9. David Underdown, "The Taming of the Scold: The Enforcement of Patriarchal Authority in Early Modern England," in *Order and Disorder in Early Modern England*, ed. Anthony Fletcher and John Stevenson, (Cambridge: Cambridge UP, 1985).
10. Gouge, *Of Domesticall Duties*, 3–4.
11. Gouge, *Of Domesticall Duties*, 3–4.
12. Susan Amussen, *An Ordered Society: Gender and Class in Early Modern England* (Oxford: Basil Blackwell, 1988), 46.
13. Thomas Gataker, *Marriage Duties Briefely couched together* (London, 1620), 8, 9–10.
14. Catherine Belsey, *The Subject of Tragedy: Identity and Difference in Renaissance Drama* (London and New York: Methuen, 1985), 149.
15. For a searching inquiry into the male position in this controversy over authority and subjection, see Mark Breitenberg, *Anxious Masculinity in Early Modern England* (Cambridge: Cambridge University Press, 1996).
16. *The Second Tome of Homilies* (1563), rpt. in *Daughters Wives & Widows: Writings by Men about Women and Marriage in England, 1500–1640*, ed. Joan Larsen Klein (Urbana and Chicago: University of Illinois Press, 1992), 11–27. The homilies were distributed to parish churches, which were commanded by the crown to have them read from the pulpit successively each Sunday.
17. For a more detailed elaboration of this argument, see Coppélia Kahn, "Whores and Wives in Jacobean Drama," in *In Another Country: Feminist Perspectives on Renaissance Drama*, ed. Dorothea Kehler and Susan Baker (Metuchen, NJ and London: Scarecrow Press, 1991), 246–60.
18. Dod and Cleaver, rpt. in *Conduct Literature for Women*, ed. William St. Clair and Irmgard Maassen, 6 vols. (London: Pickering and Chatto, 2000), vol. 3, 25–412, 209.
19. See Valerie Traub's masterful explication of the nexus of associations between women, sex, and duplicity in the figure of Eve, in her *Thinking Sex With the Early Moderns* (Philadelphia: University of Pennsylvania Press, 2016), 21–2.
20. Garrett Sullivan, Jr., "Tragic Subjectivities," in *The Cambridge Companion to English Renaissance Tragedy*, ed. Garrett Sullivan, Jr. and Emma Smith (Cambridge: CUP, 2010), 73–85.
21. See Carol Thomas Neely, *Broken Nuptials in Shakespeare's Plays* (New Haven: Yale University Press, 1985), especially 2.
22. T.E., *The Lawes Resolution of Womens Rights; or the Lawes Provision for Women. A Methodicall Collection of such Statutes and Customes, with the Cases, Opinions, Arguments and points of Learning in the Law, as do properly concerne Women* (London: John Grove, 1632), 6.

23. Page DuBois, *Sowing the Body: Psychoanalysis and Ancient Representations of Women* (Chicago: University of Chicago Press, 1988), 97, 103. This conception of the virgin daughter as her father's treasure is adapted from my book, *Roman Shakespeare: Warriors, Wounds and Women* (London: Routledge, 1997), 50–1.
24. Marina Warner, *Monuments and Maidens: The Allegory of the Female Form* (New York: Pantheon, 1985), 242.
25. Belsey, *Subject of Tragedy*, 138.
26. Dympna Callaghan, "*The Duchess of Malfi* and Early Modern Widows," in *Early Modern English Drama: A Critical Companion*, ed. Garrett Sullivan, Patrick Cheney, and Andrew Hadfield (Oxford: Oxford UP, 2006), 272–86.
27. On forms of female heroism in drama of this period, see Naomi Conn Liebler, ed., *The Female Tragic Hero in English Renaissance Drama* (London, New York, Shanghai: Palgrave-Macmillan, 2002).
28. Linda Woodbridge, "Queen of Apricots: The Duchess of Malfi, Hero of Desire," in *The Female Tragic Hero in English Renaissance Drama*, ed. Naomi Conn Liebler (New York and Houndmills, Basingstoke, UK: Palgrave, 2002), 178.
29. Louis Althusser, "Ideology and Ideological State Apparatuses," in *Lenin and Philosophy and other essays*, trans. Ben Brewster (New York: Monthly Review Press, 1971), 162.
30. See *King Lear*, 2.2.294–6. This and all other quotations from Shakespeare's plays are taken from *The Norton Shakespeare*, gen. ed. Stephen Greenblatt (New York: W.W. Norton, 1997). I quote from the First Folio text of *King Lear*.
31. The following interpretation of this maternal subtext is adapted and revised from Coppélia Kahn, "The Absent Mother in *King Lear*," in *Rewriting the Renaissance: The Discourses of Sexual Difference in Early Modern Europe*, ed. Margaret W. Ferguson, Maureen Quilligan, and Nancy J. Vickers (Chicago: University of Chicago Press, 1986), 33–49.
32. Its symptoms included feelings of choking and suffocation, paralysis, convulsions, aphasia, numbness, and lethargy, all thought to be caused by the womb wandering in the female body. See Edward Jordan, *A Briefe Discourse of a Disease Called the Suffocation of the Mother* (London, 1603); Ilza Veith, *Hysteria: The History of a Disease* (Chicago: University of Chicago Press, 1965); Hilda Smith, "Gynecology and Ideology in Seventeenth Century England," in *Liberating Women's History*, ed. Berenice Carroll (Urbana: Illinois University Press, 1976), 97–114.
33. The following discussion of cuckoldry is adapted and revised from Coppélia Kahn, *Man's Estate: Masculine Identity in Shakespeare* (Berkeley and Los Angeles: University of California Press, 1981), 120–2.
34. Keith Thomas, "The Double Standard," *Journal of the History of Ideas* 20 (1959): 195–216; see especially 203–4.
35. Eric Partridge, *A Dictionary of Slang and Unconventional English* (New York: Macmillan, 1937); John S. Farmer and W.E. Henley, eds, *Slang and Its Analogues Past and Present*, 7 vols. (London: Routledge, 1891–1904).
36. Louis Adrian Montrose, "'The place of a brother' in *As You Like It*: Social Process and Comic Form," in *Materialist Shakespeare: A History*, ed. Ivo Kamps (London/New York: Verso, 1995), 39–70.
37. John Earle, *Micro-Cosmographie* (1628), ed. Edward Arber (1869; rpt. New York: AMS Press, 1966), 29–30.
38. Michael Neill, "'In everything illegitimate': Imagining the Bastard in English Renaissance Drama," in *Putting History to the Question: Power, Politics, and Society in English Renaissance Drama* (New York: Columbia University Press, 2000), 127–47.

Chapter Eight

1. *Iocasta. A Tragedy written in Greek by Euripides, Translated, and digested into acte, by George Gascoigne and Francis Kinwelmarshe of Greies Inne, and there by them presented, Anno 1556*, in *The pleasauntest works of George Gascoigne Esquyre newlye compiled into one volume, that is to say: his flowers, hearbes, weedes, the fruites of warre, the comedie called Supposes, the tragedies of Iocasta, the Steele glasse, the complaint of Phylomene, the strorie of Ferdinando Ieronimi, and the pleasure at Kenelworth Castle*. (London: Abell Ieffes [for R. Smith]), 1587. Folger MS X.d.259
2. Ibid., fol. 1.
3. In drawing on the rhetoric of the gender's tragic demise, I am aided by Judith Butler's notion of "undoing gender" as a multi-faceted approach to interpreting the multiple ways in which the body is represented and interpreted socially and in the context of cultural semiotics, proposed in *Undoing Gender* (New York and London: Routledge, 2004).
4. Helene P. Foley and Jean E. Howard, "The Urgency of Tragedy Now," *PMLA* 129:4 (October 2014): 617–33, 624.
5. I have adopted the phrase "undoing gender" from Judith Butler, but I use it to explore genders and desires within a different historical contingency, different from Butler's elaboration of the idea of undoing gender figures in her analysis of gender and sexuality "understood as modes of being disposed" within a contemporary cultural sphere in which "a relational view of the self over an autonomous one" is at the core of her analysis of gender and sexuality. Butler, *Undoing Gender*, 19.
6. A.D. Nuttall, *Why Does Tragedy Give Pleasure?* (Oxford: Clarendon Press, 2001), 86.
7. The social background of this shift towards independence as an aspect of the formation of masculinity in Elizabethan England is discussed by Susan Staves, "Resentment or resignation?: Dividing the spoils among daughters and younger sons," in *Early Modern Conceptions of Property*, ed. John Brewer and Susan Staves (London and New York: Routledge, 1995), 194–218, esp. 196.
8. Thomas Sackville and Thomas Norton, *Gorboduc or Ferrex and Porrex*, ed. Irby B. Cauthen, Jr. (Lincoln, NE: University of Nebraska Press, 1970). All quotations are from this edition.
9. Thomas Wilson, *The State of England* (1600), ed. F.J. Fisher, Camden Society, 3rd Series, LII (1936), original pagination, 16–25; reprinted in *Seventeenth-Century Economic Documents*, ed. Joan Thirsk and J.P. Cooper (Oxford: Clarendon Press, 1972), 756.
10. Ralph A. Houlbrooke, *The English Family, 1450–1700* (London and New York: Longman, 1984), 45.
11. Margreta de Grazia, Hamlet *Without Hamlet* (Cambridge: Cambridge University Press, 2007), 18–19.
12. András Kiséry, *Hamlet's Moment: Drama and Political Knowledge in Early Modern England* (Oxford: Oxford University Press, 2016) and Rhodri Lewis, *Hamlet and the Vision of Darkness* (Princeton and Oxford: Princeton University Press, 2017).
13. William Shakespeare, *Hamlet*, ed. G.R. Hibbard (Oxford: Oxford University Press, 1994). All quotations are from this edition.
14. Jonathan Dollimore, "Subjectivity, Sexuality, and Transgression: The Jacobean Connection," *Renaissance Drama*, n.s. 17 (1986): 54.
15. This part of my argument is an expanded and adapted version of my discussion in Goran Stanivukovic and John H. Cameron, *Tragedies of the English Renaissance: An Introduction* (Edinburgh: University of Edinburgh Press, 2008).
16. C.T. Onions, *A Shakespeare Glossary* (Oxford: Clarendon Press, 1986), 62.

17. Lisa Jardine, *Reading Shakespeare Historically* (London and New York: Routledge, 1996), 46.
18. Jardine, *Reading*, 45.
19. Simon Palfrey and Tiffany Stern, *Shakespeare in Parts* (Oxford: Oxford University Press, 2007), 219–24.
20. Palfrey and Stern, *Shakespeare*, 222.
21. Kim F. Hall, *Things of Darkness: Economies of Race and Gender in Early Modern England* (Ithaca and London: Cornell University Press, 1995), 153–4.
22. William Shakespeare, *Antony and Cleopatra*, ed. Michael Neill (Oxford: Oxford University Press, 1994). All subsequent quotations are from this text of the play.
23. Folger MS X.d.259, fol. 1.
24. George Steiner, "Tragedy, Pure and Simple," in *Tragedy and the Tragic: Greek Theatre and Beyond*, ed. M.S. Silk (Oxford: Clarendon Press, 1996), 534.
25. Patricia Simons, *The Sex of Men in Premodern Europe: A Cultural History* (Cambridge: Cambridge University Press, 2011), 36.
26. Kiernan Ryan, *Shakespeare* (New York: Palgrave, 2002), 83–4.
27. William Shakespeare, *Othello, the Moor of Venice*, ed. Michael Neill (Oxford: Oxford University Press, 2006). All citations are to this edition of the play.
28. Mario DiGangi, *Sexual Types: Embodiment, Agency, and Dramatic Character from Shakespeare to Shirley* (Philadelphia: University of Pennsylvania Press, 2011), 25–6.
29. Alan Sinfield, *Shakespeare, Authority, Sexuality: Unfinished Business in Cultural Materialism* (London and New York: Routledge, 2006), 108.
30. Sinfield, *Shakespeare*, 108.
31. Christopher Marlowe, *Edward the Second*, ed. Martin Wiggins and Robert Lindsey (London: A & C Black and New York: W.W. Norton, 1997). All quotations from the play are from this text.
32. Valerie Traub, *Thinking Sex with the Early Moderns* (Philadelphia: University of Pennsylvania Press, 2016), 10.
33. MacDonald P. Jackson, ed., *The Revenger's Tragedy*, in *Thomas Middleton and Early Modern Textual Culture: A Companion to the Collected Works*, ed. Gary Taylor and John Lavagnino (Oxford: Oxford University Press, 2007), 548–51.
34. *The Revenger's Tragedy*, ed. Brian Gibbons (London: A & C Black and New York: W.W. Norton, 1991), x. All quotation from this play are from this text.
35. Dollimore, "Subjectivity," 53.
36. J.W. Lever, *The Tragedy of State: A Study of Jacobean Drama* (London and New York: Methuen, 1987), 29.
37. Jonathan Dollimore, *Radical Tragedy: Religion, Ideology and Power in Drama of Shakespeare and His Contemporaries* (New York and London: Harvester Wheatsheaf, 1989), 148.
38. Cedric C. Brown, *Friendship and Its Discourses in the Seventeenth Century* (Oxford: Oxford University Press, 2016), 9.
39. Celia R. Daileader, "Middleton's Vindication of Women," in *The Revenger's Tragedy by Thomas Middleton*, Theatre Program (London: The National Theatre, 2008), 17.
40. John Kerrigan, *Revenge Tragedy: Aeschylus to Armageddon* (Oxford: Clarendon Press, 2001), 294.
41. Traub, *Thinking*, 17.
42. Catherine Belsey, *The Subject of Tragedy: Identity and Difference in Renaissance Drama* (London: Methuen, 1985), 197–8.
43. Kathleen McLuskie, *Renaissance Dramatists* (Atlantic Heights, NJ: Humanities Press International, 1989); Katherine Rowe, *Dead Hands: Fictions of Agency, Renaissance to*

Modern (Stanford, CA: Stanford University Press, 1999); and Christina Luckyj, *A Winter's Snake: Dramatic Form in the Tragedies of John Webster* (Athens, GA: University of Georgia Press, 1989).
44. Lisa Jardine, *Still Harping on Daughters: Women and Drama in the Age of Shakespeare* (New York and London: Harvester Wheatsheaf, 1983), 98.
45. John Webster, *The Duchess of Malfi*, ed. John Brennan (London: A&C Black and New York: W.W. Norton, 1996).

BIBLIOGRAPHY

Abbate, Carolyn and Roger Parker. *A History of Opera: Updated Edition.* New York: W.W. Norton, 2012.
Adams, Joseph Quincy. *Chief Pre-Shakespearean Dramas: A Selection of Plays Illustrating the History of the English Drama from its Origin Down to Shakespeare.* Boston: Houghton Mifflin, 1924.
Aebischer, Pascale. "The Properties of Whiteness: Renaissance Cleopatras from Jodelle to Shakespeare," *Shakespeare Survey* 65 (2012): 221–38
Agamben, Giorgio. *Homo Sacer: Sovereign Power and Power and Bare Life.* Translated by Daniel Heller-Roazen. Stanford: Stanford University Press, 1998.
Agamben, Giorgio. *State of Exception.* Translated by Kevin Attell. Chicago: University of Chicago Press, 2005.
Akhimie, Patricia. "Strange Episodes: Race in Stage History." *Shakespeare Bulletin* 27 (2009): 363–76.
Althusser, Louis. "Ideology and Ideological State Apparatuses." In *Lenin and Philosophy and Other Essays,* trans. Ben Brewster. New York: Monthly Review Press, 1971.
Amussen, Susan. *An Ordered Society: Gender and Class in Early Modern England.* Oxford: Basil Blackwell, 1988.
Anderson Daniel, Carter. "Patterns and Traditions of the Elizabethan Court Play to 1590." PhD diss., University of Virginia, 1966.
Andrae, A. *Sophonisbe in der französischen Tragödie mit Berücksichtigung der Sophonisbebearbeitungen in anderen Litteraturen.* Oppeln und Leipzig: Eugen Franck's Buchhandlung, 1891.
Andrews, Richard. "Scripted Theatre and the *Commedia dell'Arte.*" In *Theatre of the English and Italian Renaissance,* edited by J.R. Mulryne and Margaret Shewring, 21–54. New York: St. Martin's Press, 1991.
Andrews, Richard. "Theatre." In *The Cambridge history of Italian Literature,* ed. Peter Brand and Lino Pertile, 288. Cambridge: Cambridge University Press, 1997.
Anon. *A Warning for Fair Women: A Critical Edition.* Edited by Charles Dale Cannon. The Hague: Mouton, 1975.
Anon. *A Warning for Fair Women.* Edited by A.F. Hopkinson. London: 1893.
Anon. *Arden of Faversham.* Edited by Martin White. London: Bloomsbury, 2007.
Anon. *The Second Tome of Homilies* (1563). Rpt. in *Daughters, Wives and Widows: Writings by Men about Women and Marriage in England, 1500–1640,* edited by Joan Larsen Klein. Urbana and Chicago: University of Illinois Press.
Archives of the Croatian Academy of Sciences and Arts, Zagreb, MS VII. 33.
Aristotle. *Poetics.* Translated by Gerald F. Else. Ann Arbor: University of Michigan Press, 1967.
Aristotle. *Poetics.* Translated by S.H. Butcher. http://classics.mit.edu/Aristotle/poetics.1.1.html (accessed May 27, 2017).
Artaud, Antonin. *The Theater and its Double.* Translated by Mary Caroline Richards. New York: Grove Press, 1958.

Auerbach, Eric. "Figura." *Archivivium Romanicum* 22 (1938): 436–89.

Auerbach, Erich. *Scenes from the Drama of European Literature*. Minneapolis: University of Minnesota Press, 1984.

Axelrad, A. José. *Le thème de Sophonisbe dans les principales tragédies de la littérature occidentale*. Lille: Bibliothèque Universitaire, 1956.

Axton, M. *The Queen's Two Bodies: Drama and the Elizabethan Succession*. London: Royal Historical Society, 1977.

Bakhtin, M.M. *Rabelais and His World*. Bloomington, Indiana: Indiana University Press, 1984.

Barber, C.L. *Shakespeare's Festive Comedy: A Study of Dramatic Form and its Relation to Social Custom*. Princeton: Princeton University Press, 2012.

Barish, Jonas. "The Problem of Closet Drama in the Italian Renaissance." *Italica* 71 (1994): 4–30.

Baskervill, Charles Read. Introduction to *Gorboduc* in *Elizabethan and Stuart Plays*. New York: Holt, Rinehart, and Winston, 1934.

Bayard, Marc. "Pour une archéologie de l'objet théâtral: Le décor comme objet dans l'esthétique théâtrale irrégulière du XVIIe siècle," http://agon.ens-lyon.fr/index.php?id=2024 (accessed January 3, 2017).

Beadle, Richard. "Rightwise, John (c.1490–1533)." In *Oxford Dictionary of National Biography*. Oxford University Press, 2004; online edn, 2008. http://www.oxforddnb.com.libproxy1.usc.edu/view/article/23649

Béhar, Pierre. "Lohenstein oder der verhinderte Dichter. Zur Deutung des Trauerspiels Sophonisbe." *Wolfenbütteler Barock-Nachrichten* 37 (2010): 5–14.

Béhar, Pierre. *Silesia Tragica: Épanouissement et Fin de l'École Dramatique Silésienne dans l'Oeuvre Tragique de Daniel Casper von Lohenstein (1635–1683)*. 2 vols, Wolfenbütteler Arbeiten zur Barockforschung. Wiesbaden: Otto Harrassowitz, 1988.

Belsey, Catherine. *Shakespeare and the Loss of Eden*. New Brunswick, NJ: Rutgers University Press, 1999.

Belsey, Catherine. *The Subject of Tragedy: Identity and Difference in Renaissance Drama*. London: Methuen, 1985.

Beneš, C.E. *Urban Legend: Civic Identity and the Classical Past in Northern Italy, 1250–1350*. University Park, PA: Pennsylvania State University Press, 2011.

Benjamin, Walter. "Critique of Violence." [1921] In *Walter Benjamin: selected writings*, edited by Marcus Bullock and Michael Jennings, 236–52. Vol. 1. Reprint, Cambridge MA: Belknap Press, 1996.

Benjamin, Walter. "Trauerspiel and Tragedy." In *The Origin of German Tragic Drama*, translated by John Osborne. London: Verso, 1985.

Benjamin, Walter. *The Origin of German Tragic Drama*. Translated by John Osborne. 1925. Reprint, London: Verso, 2009.

Berry, Herbert. "Playhouses." In *A Companion to Renaissance Drama*, edited by Arthur F. Kinney, 147–62. Oxford: Blackwell, 2002.

Bevington, David, and Eric Rasmussen, eds. *Doctor Faustus: A- and B-texts (1604, 1616): Christopher Marlowe and his Collaborators and Revisers*. Manchester: Manchester University Press, 1993.

Bevington, David, Lars Engle, Katharine Eisaman Maus, and Eric Rasmussen, eds. *English Renaissance Tragedy: A Norton Anthology*. New York: W.W. Norton, 2002.

Bevington, David. *Tudor Drama and Politics: A Critical Approach to Topical Meaning*. Cambridge, MA: Harvard University Press, 1968.

Biet, Christian. *Oedipe en Monarchie: Tragédie et Théorie Juridique à l'Âge Classique*. Paris: Klincksieck, 1994.

Blocker, Déborah "Une 'muse de province' négocie sa centralité: Corneille et ses lieux," *Les Dossiers du Grihl* 2008/01 (2008): https://journals.openedition.org/dossiersgrihl/2133 (accessed April 14, 2018).

Bloemendal, Jan, and Frans-Willem Korsten, eds. *Joost van den Vondel (1587–1679): Dutch Playwright in the Golden Age*. Leiden: Brill, 2012.

Boccaccio, Giovanni. *The tragedies, gathered by Ihon Bochas, of all such princes as fell from theyr estates throughe the mutability of fortune since the creacion of Adam, vntil his time wherin may be seen what vices bring menne to destruccion, wyth notable warninges howe the like may be auoyded. Translated into Englysh by Iohn Lidgate, monke of Burye.* Imprinted at London: By Iohn Wayland, at the signe of the Sunne oueragainst the Conduite in Flete-strete. Cum priuilegio per septennium, [1554?]. EEBO-TCP Phase 1, Ann Arbor, MI; Oxford (UK), 2005–10.

Boccaccio, Giovanni. *The Fates of Illustrious Men*. Translated by Louis Brewer Hall. New York: Frederick Ungar, 1965.

Boecker, Bettina. *Imagining Shakespeare's Original Audience, 1660–2000: Groundlings, Gallants, Grocers*. Houndmills: Palgrave Macmillan, 2015.

Bolter, Jay David and Richard Grusin. *Remediation: Understanding New Media*. Cambridge: MIT Press, 1999.

Boose, Lynda E. "The Father's House and the Daughter in It." In *Daughters and Fathers*, edited by Lynda E. Boose and Betty S. Flowers, 17–24. Baltimore: Johns Hopkins, University Press, 1989.

Booth, Stephen. *King Lear, Macbeth, Indefinition, and Tragedy*. New Haven: Yale University Press, 1983.

Borsa, Gedeon. "Euripidész magyar fordításának 16. századi kiadása." *Magyar Könyvszemle* 114 (1998): 44–8.

Borzsák, István. "Sophocles, Melanchthon und die ungarische Literatur." In *Antike Rezeption und nationale Identität in der Renaissance: Insbesondere in Deutschland und in Ungarn*, ed. Tibor Klaniczay, Katalin S. Németh, and Paul Gerhard Schmidt, 7–17. Budapest: Balassi, 1993.

Bosman, Anston. "Mobility." In *Early Modern Theatricality*, ed. Henry S. Turner, 493–515. Oxford: Oxford University Press, 2013.

Bourdieu, Pierre and Jean-Claude Passeron. *Reproduction in Education, Society, and Culture*. Translated by Richard Nice. Ann Arbor: University of Michigan Press, 1977.

Boureau, Alain. *Kantorowicz: Stories of a Historian*. Translated by Stephen Nichols and Gabrielle Spiegel. Baltimore: Johns Hopkins University Press, 2001.

Bourque, Bernard, ed. *Jean Donneau de Visé et la querelle de "Sophonisbe": écrits contre l'abbé d'Aubignac*. Tübingen: Narr, 2014.

Boutcher, Warren. "Intertraffic: Transnational Literatures and Languages in Late Renaissance England and Europe." In *International Exchange in the Early Modern Book World*, ed. Matthew McLean and Sara Barker, 343–73. Leiden and Boston: Brill, 2016.

Bowers, Fredson. *Elizabethan Revenge Tragedy*. Princeton: Princeton University Press, 1940.

Braden, Gordon. *Renaissance Tragedy and the Senecan Tradition: Anger's Privilege*. New Haven and London: Yale University Press, 1985.

Bratičević, Irena, and Ivan Lupić. "Držićeva *Hekuba* između Izvedbe i Knjige." *Colloquia Maruliana* 22 (2013): 77–116.

Breitenberg, Mark. *Anxious Masculinity in Early Modern England*. Cambridge: Cambridge University Press, 1996.

Bristol, Michael D. *Carnival and Theatre: Plebeian Culture and the Structure of Authority in Renaissance Britain*. London: Routledge, 1985.

Brown, Cedric. *Friendship and Its Discourses in the Seventeenth Century*. Oxford: Oxford University Press, 2016.

Brown, Pamela Allen. "The Traveling Diva and Generic Innovation." *Renaissance Drama* 44, no. 2 (2016): 249–67.

Brown, Paul. "'This Thing of Darkness I Acknowledge Mine': *The Tempest* and the Discourse of Colonialism." In *Politicial Shakespeare: Essays in Cultural Materialism*, edited by Jonathan Dollimore and Alan Sinfield, 48–71. 2nd edition. New York: Cornell University Press, 1985.

Bruscambille. *Oeuvres complètes*. Edited by Hugh Roberts and Annette Tomarken. Paris: Honoré Champion, 2012.

Buch, Robert. *The Pathos of the Real: On the Aesthetics of Violence in the Twentieth Century*. Baltimore: Johns Hopkins University Press, 2010.

Buci-Glucksmann, Christine. *Baroque Reason: The Aesthetics of Modernity*. Translated by Patrick Camiller. London: Sage, 1994.

Budra, Paul. "A miserable time full of piteous tragedies." In *A Mirror for Magistrates in Context: Literature, History, and Politics in Early Modern England*, edited by Harriet Archer and Andrew Hatfield. Cambridge: Cambridge University Press, 2016.

Budra, Paul. *A Mirror for Magistrates and the de casibus Tradition*. Toronto: University of Toronto Press, 1999.

Burrow, Colin. *Shakespeare & Classical Antiquity*. Oxford, Oxford University Press, 2013.

Bushnell, Rebecca. "The Fall of Princes: The Classical and Medieval Roots of English Renaissance Tragedy." In *A Companion to Tragedy*, edited by Rebecca Bushnell, 289–306. London and Oxford: Blackwell, 2005.

Bushnell, Rebecca. "Tragedy." In *The Classical Tradition*, edited by Anthony Grafton, Glenn W. Most, and Salvatore Settis. Harvard: Harvard University Press, 2010.

Butler, Judith. *Undoing Gender*. New York and London: Routledge, 2004.

Čale, F. "O šibenskom rukopisu *Hekube*." *Forum* 16 (1977): 25–42.

Čale, F. "Što je Držiću Hekuba." *Forum* 6 (1967): 797–822.

Callaghan, Dympna. "*The Duchess of Malfi* and Early Modern Widows." In *Early Modern English Drama: A Critical Companion*, edited by Garrett Sullivan, Patrick Cheney, and Andrew Hadfield, 272–86. Oxford: Oxford University Press, 2006.

Callaghan, Dympna. *Woman and Gender in Renaissance Tragedy: A Study of King Lear, Othello, The Duchess of Malfi and The White Devil*. Hertfordshire: Harvester Wheatsheaf, 1989.

Campbell, Lily B. ed. *The Mirror for Magistrates*. Cambridge: Cambridge University Press, 1938.

Cauthen, Jr., I.B. "*Gorboduc, Ferrex and Porrex*: The First Two Quartos." *Studies in Bibliography* 15 (1962): 231–3.

Cavanagh, Dermot. *Language and Politics in the Sixteenth-Century History Play*. New York: Palgrave Macmillan, 2003.

Caygill, Howard. *Walter Benjamin: The Colour of Experience*. London: Routledge, 1997.

Cerasano, S.P. "Edward Alleyn, the New Model Actor, and the Rise of the Celebrity in the 1590s." *Medieval & Renaissance Drama in England* 18 (2005): 47–58.

Chambers, E.K. *The Elizabethan Stage*. Vol. 2. Oxford: Clarendon Press, 1924.

Chartier, Roger. *The Cultural Uses of Print in Early Modern France*. Translated by Lydia G. Cochrane. Princeton: Princeton University Press, 1988.

Chauchaix, Jacqueline. "Un personnage et ses origines: Le Gelosso de la Sophonisbe de Marston." *Confluents* 5/1 (1979): 19–26.

Cheesman, Tom. *The Shocking Ballad Picture Show: German Popular Literature and Cultural History*. Oxford: Berg, 1994.

Chevalier, J.-F. "Le couronnement d'Albertino Musat ou le renaissance d'une célébration." *Bulletin de l'Association Guillaume Budé* 2 (2004): 42–55.

Chevallier-Micki, Sybile. "Panorama de l'édition théâtrale et de la composition dramatique à Rouen (fin XVIe siècle-début XVIIe siècle)." In *Pratiques de Corneille*, ed. Myriam Dufour-Maître, 52–4. Mont-Saint-Aignan: Publications des Universités de Rouen et du Havre, 2012.

Chevallier-Micki, Sybile. "Stage Designs of Cruelty: Theater in Rouen at the Turn of the Seventeenth Century." In *French Renaissance and Baroque Drama: Text, Performance, Theory*, edited by Michael Meere, 213–31. Newark: University of Delaware Press, 2015.

Chovanec, Kevin. "*Faust mit Springen*: On the English Players Returning *Faustus* to the German-Speaking Lands." *Renaissance Drama* 44 (2016): 125–56.

Cinthio, Giambattista Giraldi. *Orbecche Tragedia*. Venice: Aldine Press, 1543.

Civardi, Jean-Marc, ed. *La querelle du Cid (1637–1638): édition critique intégrale*. Paris: Honoré Champion, 2004.

Clarendon, Edward Hyde, Earl of. *History of the Rebellion and Civil Wars in England*. Oxford: Clarendon Press, 1888. Reprint, Oxford: Clarendon Press, 1992.

Clemen, Wolfgang. *English Tragedy before Shakespeare: The Development of Dramatic Speech*. London: Methuen, 1961; rpt. 1980.

Clubb, Louise George. "Looking Back on Shakespeare and Italian Theater." *Renaissance Drama* 36 (2010): 3–19

Clubb, Louise George. "Theatregrams." In *Comparative Critical Approaches to Renaissance Comedy*, edited by Donald A. Beecher and Massimo Ciavolella, 15–33. Ottawa: Dovehouse, 1986.

Clubb, Louise, George. "Staging Ferrara: State Theater from Borso to Alfonso II." In *Phaethon's Children: The Este Court and Its Culture in Early Modern Ferrara*, edited by Dennis Looney and Deanna Shemek, 345–62. Tempe, AZ: Arizona Center for Medieval and Renaissance Studies, 2005.

Comay, Rebecca. *Mourning Sickness: Hegel and the French Revolution*. Stanford: Stanford University Press, 2011.

Corneille, Pierre. *Théâtre complet*. Volume 3/2, ed. Alain Niderst. Rouen: Université de Rouen, 1986.

Coryate, Thomas. *Coryat's Crudities: Hastily Gobbled Up in Five Months' Travels*. London:1611.

Creizenach, Wilhelm. *Geschichte des Neueren Dramas*. 3 vols. Halle: M. Niemeyer, 1918.

Critchley, Simon, and Jamieson Webster. *The Hamlet Doctrine: Knowing too much, doing Nothing*. London: Verso, 2013.

Cunliffe, J.W. *Early English Classical Tragedies*. Oxford: Clarendon Press, 1912.

Cunningham, J.V. *Woe or Wonder: The Emotional Effect of Shakespearean Tragedy*. Denver: University of Denver Press, 1951; rpt. Chicago: Swallow Press, 1964.

da Veroli, Giovanni Sulpizio. "Raphaeli Riario, Cardinali, Sanctaeque Romanae Ecclesiae Camerario, Jo[hannes] Sulpitius Feolicitatem." In Marcus Pollio Vitruvius, *De architecturâ*, ed. Sulpizio [Rome: Eucharius Silber, *c*. 1468], rpt. in Beriah Botfield, ed., *Prefaces to the*

First Editions of the Greek and Roman Classics and of the Sacred Scriptures, 177–9. London, 1861.

Daileader, Celia R. "Middleton's Vindication of Women." In *The Revenger's Tragedy by Thomas Middleton*, Theatre Program. London: The National Theatre, 2008.

Davenant, Sir William. *The Shorter Poems, and Songs from the Plays and Masques*. Edited by A.M. Gibbs. Oxford: Oxford University Press, 1972.

de Armas, Frederick A. "The *Comedia* and the Classics." In *A Companion to Early Modern Hispanic Theater*, edited by Hillaire Kallendorf, 33–58. Brill: Leiden, 2014.

de Bèze, Théodore. *A tragedie of Abrahams sacrifice*. Translated by Arthur Golding. London: Thomas Vautroullier, 1577.

de Bordes, Jean. *Maria Stuarta Tragoedia*, unpub. mss., Morgan Library, New York.

de Cervantes, Miguel. *Numantia: A Tragedy*. Translated by James Y. Gibson. London: Kegan Paul, Trench, 1885.

de Cervantes, Miguel. *The History of the Valorous and Witty-Knight-Errant, Don-Quixote, of the Mancha*. Translated by Thomas Shelton. London: R. Hodgkinsonne for Andrew Crooke, 1652.

Dekker, Thomas. "The Gull's Horn Book (1609)." In *Shakespeare's theater: a sourcebook*, ed. Tanya Pollard, 207–13. Malden: Blackwell, 2004.

de Madariaga, Salvador. *On Hamlet*. London: Hollis & Carter, 1948.

de Mendonça, Barbara Heliodora Carneiro. "The Influence of *Gorboduc* on *King Lear*." *Shakespeare Survey* 13 (1960): 41–8.

de Montaigne, Michel. *Essays Written in French by Michael Lord of Montaigne*. Translated by John Florio. London: Melch[ior] Bradwood for Edward Blount and William Barret, 1613.

de Montaigne, Michel. *The Complete Essays*. Translated by M.A Screech. London: Allen Lane, 1991.

de Grazia, Margreta. *Hamlet Without Hamlet*. Cambridge: Cambridge University Press, 2007.

Depledge, Emma, ed. *Canonising Shakespeare: Stationers and the Book Trade, 1640–1740*. Cambridge: Cambridge University Press, 2017.

Descartes, René. *Oeuvres philosophiques*. Edited by Fernand Alquié. Vol. 3. Paris: Garnier, 1963–73.

Desmet, Christy. *Reading Shakespeare's Characters: Rhetoric, Ethics, and Identity*. Amherst: University of Massachusetts Press, 1992.

Dessen, Allen C. and Leslie Thomson. *A Dictionary of Stage Directions in English Drama, 1580–1642*. Cambridge: Cambridge University Press, 1999.

Deutermann, Allison K. *Listening for Theatrical Form in Early Modern England*. Edinburgh: Edinburgh University Press, 2016.

Dewar-Watson, S. "*Jocasta*: 'A Tragedie Written in Greeke.'" *International Journal of the Classical Tradition* 17 (2010): 22–32.

Di Maria, Salvatore. *The Italian Tragedy in the Renaissance: Cultural Realities and Theatrical Innovations*. Lewisburg: Bucknell University Press, 2002.

DiGangi, Mario. *Sexual Types: Embodiment, Agency, and Dramatic Character from Shakespeare to Shirley*. Philadelphia: University of Pennsylvania Press, 2011.

Dobson, Michael. "Short Cuts: Deutschland ist Hamlet." *London Review of Books* 31, no. 15 (August 6, 2009): 22.

Dod, John and Robert Cleaver, *A Godly Forme of Household Governance: for the ordering of private families, according to the direction of God's Word*. Rpt. in *Conduct Literature for Women*, ed. William St. Clair and Irmgard Maassen. 6 vols. London: Pickering and Chatto, 2000.

Dolan, Frances E. *Dangerous Familiars: Representation of Domestic Crime in England, 1550–1700*. Ithaca: Cornell University Press, 1994.
Dollimore, Jonathan. "Subjectivity, Sexuality, and Transgression: The Jacobean Connection." *Renaissance Drama* 17 (1986): 53–81.
Dollimore, Jonathan. *Radical Tragedy: Religion, Ideology and Power in Drama of Shakespeare and His Contemporaries*. New York and London: Harvester Wheatsheaf, 1989.
Dollimore, Jonathan and Alan Sinfield, eds. *Political Shakespeare: Essays in Cultural Materialism*, 2nd edition. Manchester: Manchester University Press, 1996, 48–71.
Douglas, Mary. *Purity and Danger: An Analysis of Concepts of Pollution and Taboo*. London: Routledge, 2002.
Drábek, Pavel and M.A. Katritzky. "Shakespearean Players in Early Modern Europe." In *The Cambridge Guide to the Worlds of Shakespeare*, gen. edited by Bruce R. Smith, 1527–33. Vol. 2. Cambridge: Cambridge University Press, 2016.
Drábek, Pavel. "'Why, sir, are there other heauens in other countries?': The English Comedy within a Transnational Network." Forthcoming.
Drakakis, John, ed. *Alternative Shakespeares*, 2nd edition. London: Routledge, 2002.
Držić, M. *Djela*, ed. M. Rešetar. Zagreb: JAZU, 1930.
Držić, M. *The Conspiracy Letters to Cosimo I de' Medici*. Translated by N. Milas, T.L. Jockims, and P. Brailo. Dubrovnik: Dom Marina Držića, 2008.
Držića, Leksikon Marina. Edited by M. Tatarin et al. Zagreb: Leksikografski zavod Miroslav Krleža, 2009.
Duarte, J. Enrique. "Spanish Sacramental Plays: A Study of Their Evolution." In *A Companion to Early Modern Hispanic Theater*, edited by Hilaire Kallendorf, 59–74. Leiden: Brill, 2014.
DuBois, Page. *Sowing the Body: Psychoanalysis and Ancient Representations of Women*. Chicago: University of Chicago Press, 1988.
Dunn, K. "Representing Counsel: *Gorboduc* and the Elizabethan Privy Council." *English Literary Renaissance* 33 (2003): 279–308.
Dutton, Richard. *Shakespeare, Court Dramatist*. Oxford: Oxford University Press, 2016.
Eagleton, Terry. *Sweet Violence: The Idea of the Tragic*. Oxford: Blackwell, 2003.
Earle, John. *Micro-Cosmographie* (1628). Edited by Edward Arber. New York: AMS Press, 1966.
Eiland, Howard, and Michael Jennings. *Walter Benjamin: A Critical Life*. Cambridge, MA: Belknap Press, 2014.
Elias, Norbert. *The Civilizing Process: Sociogenetic and Psychogenetic Investigations*. Edited by Eric Dunning, Johan Goudsblom, and Stephen Mennell, translated by Edmund Jephcott. Oxford and Cambridge, MA: Blackwell, 2000.
Elizabeth I. *Collected Works of Queen Elizabeth I*. Edited by Leah Marcus, Janel Mueller, and Mary Beth Rose. Chicago: Chicago University Press, 2000.
Else, Gerald F. Introduction to *Aristotle Poetics*. Translated by Gerald F. Else. Ann Arbor: University of Michigan Press, 1967, 1–14.
Enterline, Lynn. *Shakespeare's Schoolroom: Rhetoric, Discipline, Emotion*. Philadelphia: University of Pennsylvania Press, 2016.
Erasmus, Desiderius. *De ratione studii ac legendi interpretandique auctores*. In *Collected Works*, edited by Craig R. Thompson. Translated by Brian McGregor, Vol. 2. Toronto: University of Toronto Press, 1978.
Erasmus, Desiderius. *The Correspondence of Erasmus: Letters 1252 to 1523*. Translated by R.A. B. Mynors. Annotated by James M. Estes. Toronto: University of Toronto Press, 1989.

Erne, Lukas. "Beyond *The Spanish Tragedy*: A Study of the Works of Thomas Kyd." Ph.D. diss., University of Oxford, 1998.

Esposito, Roberto. *Two: The Machine of Political Theology and the Place of Thought (Commonalities)*. Translated by Zakiya Hanafi. New York: Fordham University Press, 2015.

Farmer, Alan B. and Zachary Lesser. "Canons and Classics: Publishing Drama in Caroline England." In *Localizing Caroline Drama: Politics and Economics of the Early Modern English Stage, 1625–1642*, edited by Adam Zucker and Alan B. Farmer, 17–41. Palgrave: New York, 2006.

Farmer, John S. and W.E. Henley, eds. *Slang and Its Analogues Past and Present*. 7 vols. London: Routledge, 1891–1904.

Farnham, Willard. *The Medieval Heritage of Elizabethan Tragedy*. Berkeley: University of California Press, 1936.

Farrell, Allan P.S.J. trans. *The Jesuit Ratio Studiorum of 1599*. Washington, DC: Conference of Major Superiors, 1970, http://www.bc.edu/sites/libraries/ratio/ratio1599.pdf (accessed May 12, 2017).

Ferber, Ilit. *Philosophy and Melancholy Benjamin's Early Reflections on Theater and Language*. Stanford: Stanford University Press, 2013.

Fernyhough, Charles. *The Voices Within: The History and Science of How We Talk to Ourselves*. New York: Basic Books, 2016.

Fiedler, Leslie. *No! In Thunder: Essays on Myth and Literature*. New York: Stein and Day, 1960.

Findlay, Alison. *Illegitimate Power: Bastards in Renaissance Drama*. Manchester: Manchester University Press, 1994.

Finkelde, Dominik. "The Presence of the Baroque: Benjamin's *Ursprung des deutschen Trauerspiels* in Contemporary Contexts." In *A Companion to the Works of Walter Benjamin*, edited by Rolf Goebel, 46–79. Rochester, NY: Camden House, 2009.

Finkelpearl, Philip J. *John Marston of the Middle Temple: An Elizabethan Dramatist in His Social Setting*. Cambridge: Harvard University Press, 1969.

Finotti, Fabio. "Perspective and Stage Design, Fiction and Reality in the Italian Renaissance Theater of the Fifteenth Century." *Renaissance Drama* 36 (2010): 21–42.

Florio, John. *A Worlde of Words, or Most Copious, and Exact Dictionary in Italian and English*. London: Arnold Hatfield for Edw[ard] Blount, 1598.

Foley, Helene P. and Jean E. Howard. "The Urgency of Tragedy." *PMLA* 129 (2014): 617–33.

Foucault, Michel, *Psychiatric Power: Lectures at the Collège de France: 1973–1974*. Edited by Jacques Lagrange. Translated by Graham Burchell. London: Palgrave Macmillan, 2006.

Foucault, Michel. "Two Lectures." In *Power/Knowledge: Selected Interviews and Other Writings*, edited by Colin Gordon, 78–108. New York: Pantheon, 1980.

Foucault, Michel. *Security, Territory, Population: Lectures at the Collège de France, 1977–1978*. Translated by Graham Burchell. Basingstoke: Macmilllan, 2007.

Foucault, Michel. *Society Must Be Defended: Lectures at the Collège de France, 1975–1976*. Translated by David Macey. London: Allen Lane, 2003.

Frank, Günter and Martin Treu, eds. *Melanchthon und Europa, 1. Teilband: Skandinavien und Mittelosteuropa*. Stuttgart: Jan Thorbecke Verlag, 2001.

Frappier, Louise. "Spectacle Tragique et Conception de l'Histoire dans la Seconde Moitié du XVIe siècle en France." In *Les Arts du Spectacle au Théâtre (1550–1700)*, edited by Marie-France Wagner and Claire Le Brun-Gouanvic, 35–50. Paris: Honoré Champion, 2001.

Fraser, Antonia. *Mary Queen of Scots*. London: Weidenfeld & Nicolson, 2015.

Freedman, Luba. *Classical Myths in Italian Renaissance Painting*. Cambridge: Cambridge University Press, 2011.
Freud, Sigmund. "Mourning and Melancholia." In *The Complete Psychological Works of Sigmund Freud*, 243–58. Vol. 14. Translated by James Strachey. London: Hogarth Press, 1956–74.
Freund, Philip, *Laughter and Grandeur: Theatre in the Age of the Baroque*. London: Peter Owen, 2006.
Frisch, Andrea. "French Tragedy and the Civil Wars." *MLQ* 67 (2006): 287–312.
Frye, Northrop. *A Natural Perspective: The Development of Shakespearean Comedy and Romance*. Second edition. New York and London: Columbia University Press, 1995.
Frye, Northrop. *The Myth of Deliverance: Reflections on Shakespeare's Problem Comedies*. Toronto, Buffalo and London: University of Toronto Press, 1983.
Fumerton, Patricia, ed. *The English Broadside Ballad Archive* (EBBA). https://ebba.english.ucsb.edu/ballad/30993/image
Garnier, Robert. *Cornelia*. Translated by Thomas Kyd. London: James Roberts, for N[icholas] L[ing] and Iohn Busbie, 1594.
Gascoigne, George. *Iocasta. A Tragedy written in Greek by Euripides, Translated, and digested into acts, by George Gascoigne and Francis Kinwelmarshe of Greies Inne, and there by them presented, Anno 1556. The plesasauntest works of George Gascoigne Esquyre newlye compiled into one volume, that is to say: his flowers, hearbes, weedes, the fruites of warre, the comedie called Supposes, the tragedies of Iocasta, the Steele glasse, the complain of Phylomene, the storie of Ferdinando Ieronimi, and the pleasure at Kenelorth Castle*. London: Abell Jeffes [for R. Smith], 1587.
Gassner, John, ed. *Medieval and Tudor Drama*. New York: Applause Theatre and Cinema Books, 1963.
Gataker, Thomas. *Marriage Duties Briefely couched together*. London, 1620.
Gavin, Michael. *The Invention of English Criticism 1650–1760*. Cambridge: Cambridge University Press, 2015.
Gilbert, Felix. "Bernardo Rucellai and the Orti Oricellari: A Study on the Origin of Modern Political Thought." *Journal of the Warburg and Courtauld Institutes* 12 (1949): 101–31.
Girard, René. *Violence and the Sacred*. London: Bloomsbury Academic, 2013.
Goldmann, Lucien. *The Hidden God: A Study of Tragic Vision in the Pensées of Pascal and the Tragedies of Racine*. Translated by Philip Thody. London: Routledge and Kegan Paul, 1976.
Goodland, Katherine. *Female Mourning and Tragedy in Medieval and Renaissance English Drama*. Aldershot: Ashgate, 2005.
Gouge, William. *Eight Treatises of Domesticall Duties*. Third edn. London, 1634.
Gowing, Laura. *Gender Relations in Early Modern England*. Harlow, UK: Pearson Education Ltd., 2012.
Greenblatt, Stephen. *Hamlet in Purgatory*. Princeton: Princeton University Press, 2001.
Greenblatt, Stephen. *Shakespearean Negotiations: The Circulation of Social Energy in Renaissance England*. Oxford: Clarendon Press, 1988; rpt. 1992.
Greenfield, Peter H. "'The Actors are Come Hither': Traveling Companies." In *A Companion to Renaissance Drama*, edited by Arthur F. Kinney, 212–22. Oxford: Blackwell, 2002.
Grund, Gary R. trans. *Humanist Tragedies*. Cambridge, MA: Harvard University Press, 2011.
Gryphius, Andreas. *Cardenio und Celinde*. Edited by Hugh Powell. Leicester: Leicester University Press, 1967.
Guillory, John. *Cultural Capital: The Problem of Literary Canon Formation*. Chicago: University of Chicago Press, 1993.

Gurnis, Musa. *Mixed Faith and Shared Feeling: Theater in Post-Reformation London.* Philadelphia: University of Pennsylvania Press, 2018.

Gurr, Andrew and Mariko Ichikawa. *Staging in Shakespeare's Theatres.* Oxford: Oxford University Press, 2000.

Gurr, Andrew. *Playgoing in Shakespeare's London.* Third edn. Cambridge: Cambridge University Press, 2004.

Gurr, Andrew. *The Shakespeare Company 1594–1642.* Cambridge: Cambridge University Press, 2004.

Gurr, Andrew. *The Shakespearian Playing Companies.* Oxford: Clarendon Press, 1996.

Haekel, Ralf. *Die englischen Komödianten in Deutschland: eine Einführung in die Ursprünge des deutschen Berufsschauspiels.* Heidelberg: Winter, 2004.

Hall, Kim F. *Things of Darkness: Economies of Race and Gender in Early Modern England.* Ithaca and London: Cornell University Press, 1995.

Halliwell, Stephen. *The Poetics of Aristotle: Translation and Commentary.* Chapel Hill: University of North Carolina Press, 1987.

Halpern, Richard. "The King's Two Buckets: Kantorowicz, *Richard II*, and Fiscal *Trauerspie*." *Representations* 106 (2009): 67–76.

Hamm, Wilhelm von, T.C.H. Hedderwick, Gotthold Ephraim Lessing, and Guido Bonneschky, *The Old German Puppet Play of Doctor Faustus.* London: K. Paul Trench, 1887.

Harbage, Alfred. *Annals of English drama, 975–1700.* Third edn. Revised by S. Schoenbaum and Sylvia Stoler Wagonheim. London: Routledge, 1989.

Haynes, Alan. *Invisible Power: The Elizabeth Secret Services 1570–1603.* Stroud: Alan Sutton Publishing, 1992.

Hédelin, François, abbé d'Aubignac. *Dissertations contre Corneille.* Ed. Nicholas Hammond and Michael Hawcroft. Exeter: University of Exeter Press, 1995.

Hegel, G.W.F. "Tragedy as a Dramatic Art." In *Hegel on Tragedy*, edited by Anne and Henry Paolucci. New York: Harper Torchbooks, 1975.

Heinemann, Margot. *Puritanism & Theatre: Thomas Middleton and Opposition Drama under the Early Stuarts.* Cambridge: Cambridge University Press, 2007.

Helgerson, Richard. "Murder in Faversham: Holinshed's impertinent history." In *The Historical Imagination in Early Modern Britain: History, Rhetoric and Fiction, 1500–1800*, edited by Donald R. Kelley and David Harris Sacks, 133–58. Cambridge: Cambridge University Press, 1997.

Heltai, János. "Balassi és Buchanan Iephtese." *Irodalomtörténeti közlemények* 101 (1997): 541–9.

Herrick, Marvin T. *Italian Tragedy in the Renaissance.* Urbana: University of Illinois Press, 1965.

Hildy, Franklin J. "European Theater Scene." In *The Cambridge Guide to the Worlds of Shakespeare*, gen. edited by Bruce R. Smith, 77–83. Vol. 1. Cambridge: Cambridge University Press, 2016.

Höfele, Andreas. *Stage, Stake, and Scaffold: Humans and Animals in Shakespeare's Theatre.* Oxford: Oxford University Press, 2011.

Höfele, Andreas. *No Hamlets: German Shakespeare from Nietzsche to Carl Schmitt.* Oxford: Oxford University Press, 2016.

Holbrook, Peter. *Literature and Degree in Renaissance England: Nashe, Bourgeois Tragedy, Shakespeare.* Newark: University of Delaware Press, 1994.

Holinshed, Raphael. *Chronicles of England, Scotland, and Ireland.* London: 1587.

Hopkins, Lisa. *The Cultural Uses of the Caesars on the English Renaissance Stage.* Hampshire and Burlington: Ashgate, 1988.

Horne, Philip. *The Tragedies of Giambattista Cinthio Giraldi*. Oxford: Oxford University Press, 1962.
Hösle, Johannes. *Das italienische Theater von der Renaissance bis zur Gegenreformation*. Darmstadt: Wissenschaftliche Buchgesellschaft, 1984.
Houlbrooke, Ralph A. *The English Family, 1450–1700*. London: Longman, 1984.
Howarth, David. *Images of Rule: Art and Politics in the English Renaissance, 1485–1649*. Basingstoke: Macmillan, 1997.
Howarth, W. D., ed. *French Theatre in the Neo-Classical Era, 1550–1791*. Cambridge: Cambridge University Press, 1997.
Howe, Alan. "L'entrée au Parnasse d'un dramaturge professionel: le cas d'Alexandre Hardy." In *Le Parnasse du théâtre: les recueils d'oeuvres complètes de théâtre au XVIIe siècle*, ed. Georges Forestier, Edric Caldicott, and Claude Bourqui, 227–44. Paris: PUPS, 2007.
Howe, Alan. "La Place de la Tragédie dans le Répertoire des Comédiens Français à la Fin du XVIe Siècle et au Debut du XVIIe Siècle." *Bibliothèque d'Humanisme et Renaissance* 59, no. 2 (1997): 283–303.
Howe, Alan. *Le Théâtre professionnel à Paris, 1600–49*. Paris: Archives nationales, 2000.
Hoxby, Blair. *What Was Tragedy? Theory and the Early Modern Canon*. Oxford: Oxford University Press, 2015.
Hummelen, W.M.H. "Jacob van Campen Bouwt de Amsderdamse Schouwburg." In *Een Theatergeschiedenis der Nederlanden*, edited by R.L. Erenstein, 192–203. Amsterdam: Amsterdam University Press, 1996.
Hunter, G.K. "The Marking of *Sententiae* in Elizabethan Printed Plays, Poems, and Romances." *The Library* 5th ser. 6 (1951): 171–88.
Hutcheon, Linda and Siobhan O' Flynn. *A Theory of Adaptation*. Second edition. London: Routledge, 2006.
Hutson, Lorna. "Imagining Justice: Kantorowicz and Shakespeare." *Representations* 106 (2009): 118–42.
Hyde, Patricia. *Thomas Arden in Faversham: The Man Behind the Myth*. The Faversham Society: 1996.
Innes, Paul. "Harming *Macbeth*: A British Translation." In *Shakespeare and the Translation of Identity in Early Modern England*, edited by Liz Oakley-Brown, 103–30. London: Continuum, 2011.
Innes, Paul. "Some of the Most Important Events in Shakespeare do not Happen." *English* 64, no. 247 (2015): 254–67.
Innes, Paul. *Shakespeare's Roman Plays*. London: Palgrave Macmillan, 2015.
Jack, Sybil M. "Wolsey, Thomas (1470/71–1530)." In *Oxford Dictionary of National Biography*. Oxford University Press, 2004; online edn, 2012, http://www.oxforddnb.com.libproxy1.usc.edu/view/article/29854 (accessed May 22, 2017).
Jackson, MacD.P. "Three old ballads and the date of *Doctor Faustus*." *Journal of the Australasian Universities, Language and Literature Association* 36 (1971): 187–200.
Jardine, Lisa. *Reading Shakespeare Historically*. London and New York: Routledge, 1996.
Jardine, Lisa. *Still Harping on Daughters Women and Drama in the Age of Shakespeare*. New York: Harvester Wheatsheaf, 1983.
Jauss, Hans Robert. *Ästhetische Erfahrung und literarische Hermeneutik*. Frankfurt am Main: Suhrkamp, 1982.
Javitch, Daniel. "The Assimilation of Aristotle's Poetics in Sixteenth-Century Italy." In *The Cambridge History of Literary Criticism: Vol 3: The Renaissance*, edited by Glynn P. Norton, 53–65. Cambridge: Cambridge University Press, 1999.

Jeličić, Ž. *Marin Držić, pjesnik dubrovačke sirotinje.* Zagreb: Novo pokoljenje, 1950.

Jenkins, Henry. *Convergence Culture: Where Old and New Media Collide.* New York: New York University Press, 2006.

Johnson, Eugene J. *Inventing the Opera House: Theater Architecture in Renaissance and Baroque Italy.* Cambridge: Cambridge University Press, 2018.

Jordan, Edward. *A Briefe Discourse of a Disease called the Suffocation of the Mother.* London, 1603.

Joyce, James. *Ulysses.* Edited by Richard Ellmann. Harmondsworth: Penguin, 1968.

Kahn, Coppélia. "The Absent Mother in *King Lear.*" In *Rewriting the Renaissance: The Discourses of Sexual Difference in Early Modern Europe*, edited by Margaret W. Ferguson, Maureen Quilligan, and Nancy J. Vickers, 239–262. Chicago: University of Chicago Press, 1986.

Kahn, Coppélia. "Whores and Wives in Jacobean Drama." In *In Another Country: Feminist Perspectives on Renaissance Drama*, edited by Dorothea Kehler and Susan Baker, 246–60. Metuchen, NJ: Scarecrow Press, 1991.

Kahn, Coppélia. *Roman Shakespeare: Warriors, Wounds and Women.* London: Routledge, 1997.

Kahn, Coppélia. *Man's Estate: Masculine Identity in Shakespeare.* Berkeley and Los Angeles, 1981.

Kahn, Victoria. "Political Theology in *The King's Two Bodies.*" *Representations* 106 (2009): 67–76.

Kantorowicz, Ernst. *The King's Two Bodies: A Study in Medieval Political Theology.* Reprint, Princeton: Princeton University Press, 1997.

Kastan, David Scott. *Shakespeare After Theory.* New York: Routledge, 1999.

Kathman, David. "Players, Livery Companies, and Apprentices." In *The Oxford Handbook of Early Modern Theatre*, edited by Richard Dutton, 413–28. Oxford: Oxford University Press, 2011.

Kerrigan, John, ed. *The Motives of Woe: Shakespeare and Female Complaint: A Critical Anthology.* Oxford: Oxford University Press, 1991.

Kerrigan, John. *Revenge Tragedy: Aeschylus to Armageddon.* Oxford: Clarendon Press, 2001.

Ketterer, Robert C. "Opera." In *The Classical Tradition*, edited by Anthony Grafton, Glenn W. Most, and Salvatore Settis. Harvard: Harvard University Press, 2010.

Kiséry, András. *Hamlet's Moment: Drama and Political Knowledge in Early Modern England.* Oxford: Oxford University Press, 2016.

Klein, Joan Larsen, ed. *Daughters Wives & Widows: Writings by Men about Women and Marriage in England, 1500–1640.* Urbana and Chicago: University of Illinois Press, 1992.

Kliman, Bernice W. "At Sea About Hamlet at Sea: A Detective Story." *Shakespeare Quarterly* 62 (2011): 180–204.

Knapp, Éva. *"Judit képit én viseltem": kora újkori színház- és drámatörténeti tanulmányok.* Budapest: Argumentum, 2007.

Knapp, Robert S. "The Academic Drama." In *A Companion to Renaissance Drama*, edited by Arthur Kinney, 257–65. Oxford: Blackwell, 2002.

Knox, Bernard M.W. *The Heroic Temper: Studies in Sophoclean Tragedy.* Berkeley: University of California Press and Cambridge: Cambridge University Press, 1964.

Korda, Natasha. "Women in the Theater." In *The Oxford Handbook of Early Modern Theatre*, edited by Richard Dutton, 456–74. Oxford: Oxford University Press, 2011.

Kott, Jan. *Shakespeare Our Contemporary.* Translated by Boleslaw Taborski. Reprint, London and New York: Routledge, 1994.

Kottman, Paul. "Why think about Shakespearean tragedy today." In *The Cambridge Companion to Shakespearean Tragedy*, edited by Claire McEachern, 240–61. Cambridge: Cambridge University Press, 2013.

Kunčević, L. "'Ipak nije na odmet sve čuti': medičejski pogled na urotničke namjere Držića." *Anali Dubrovnik* 45 (2007): 9–46.

Kunčević, L. "Janus-Faced Sovereignty: The International Status of the Ragusan Republic in the Early Modern Period." In *The European Tributary States of the Ottoman Empire in the Sixteenth and Seventeenth Centuries*, edited by G. Kármán and L. Kunčević, 91–121. Boston: Brill, 2013.

Kyd, Thomas. *The Spanish Tragedy*. Edited by Michael Neill. New York: Norton, 2014.

Kyd, Thomas. *The trueth of the most wicked and secret murthering of John Brewen, Goldsmith of London, committed by his owne wife though the provocation of one John Parker whom she loved.* London: 1592.

Lacey, Andrew. *The Cult of King Charles the Martyr*. Woodbridge: Boydell, 2003.

Lake, Peter. "Deeds Against Nature: Cheap Print, Protestantism and Murder in Early Seventeenth Century England." In *Culture and Politics in Early Stuart England*, edited by Kevin Sharpe and Peter Lake, 257–384. Stanford: Stanford University Press, 1993.

Lake, Peter. *How Shakespeare Put Politics on the Stage: Power and Succession in the History Plays*. New Haven: Yale University Press, 2016.

Laqueur, Thomas. *The Work of the Dead: A Cultural History of Human Remains*. Princeton: Princeton University Press, 2015.

Laroque, François. *Shakespeare's Festive World: Elizabethan Seasonal Entertainment and the Professional Stage*. Cambridge: Cambridge University Press, 1993.

Laurence, Anne. *Women in England 1500–1760: A Social History*. London: Weidenfeld and Nicolson, 1995.

Lazarus, Micha. "Aristotelian Criticism in Sixteenth-Century England." In *Oxford Handbooks Online*, http://www.oxfordhandbooks.com/view/10.1093/oxfordhb/9780199935338.001.0001/oxfordhb-9780199935338-e-148 (accessed May 29, 2017).

Lebègue, Raymond. "La Représentation d'une Tragédie à la Cour des Valois." *Comptes rendus des séances de l'Académie des Inscriptions et Belles-Lettres* 90 (1946): 138–44.

Lerner, Robert. *Ernst Kantorowicz: A Life*. Princeton: Princeton University Press, 2017.

Lesser, Zachary and Peter Stallybrass. "The First Literary *Hamlet* and the Commonplacing of Professional Plays." *Shakespeare Quarterly* 59 (2008): 371–420.

Lesser, Zachary. "Walter Burre's *The Knight of the Burning Pestle*." *English Literary Renaissance* 29 (1999): 21–43.

Lever, J.W. *The Tragedy of State: A Study of Jacobean Drama*. London and New York: Methuen, 1987.

Lewis, Jayne Elizabeth. *Mary Queen of Scots: Romance and Nation*. London: Routledge, 1998.

Lewis, Rhodri. *Hamlet and The Vision of Darkness*. Princeton: Princeton University Press, 2017.

Liebler, Naomi Conn, ed. *The Female Tragic Hero in English Renaissance Drama*. London, New York, Shanghai: Palgrave-Macmillan, 2002.

Liebler, Naomi Conn. *Shakespeare's Festive Tragedy: The Ritual Foundations of Genre*. London and New York: Routledge, 1995.

Limon, Jerzy. "Players and the Playing Business." In *The Cambridge Guide to the Worlds of Shakespeare*, gen. edited by Bruce R. Smith, 83–8. Vol. 1. Cambridge: Cambridge University Press, 2016.

Limon, Jerzy. *Gentlemen of a Company: English Players in Central and Eastern Europe, 1590–1660.* Cambridge: Cambridge University Press, 1985.

Locati, X.S. *La rinascita del genere tragico nel medioevo: L'Ecerinis di Albertino Mussato.* Firenze: Franco Cesati, 2006.

Lohse, Rolf. *Renaissancedrama und humanistische Poetik in Italien.* Paderborn: Wilhelm Fink, 2015.

Lopez, Jeremy. *Theatrical Convention and Audience Response in Early Modern Drama.* Cambridge: Cambridge University Press, 2003.

Lorenz, Philip. *The Tears of Sovereignty: Perspectives of Power in Renaissance Drama.* New York: Fordham University Press, 2013.

Lough, John. *Seventeenth-Century French Drama: The Background.* Oxford: Clarendon Press, 1979.

Luckyj, Christina. *A Winter's Snake: Dramatic Form in the Tragedies of John Webster.* Athens, GA: University of Georgia Press, 1989.

Lupić, Ivan. *Subjects of Advice: Drama and Counsel from More to Shakespeare.* Philadelphia: University of Pennsylvania Press, 2019.

Lupić, Ivan. "The Mobile Queen: Observing Hecuba in Renaissance Europe." *Renaissance Drama* 46.1 (2018): 25–56.

Lupton, Julia. *Thinking with Shakespeare: Essays on Politics and Life.* Chicago: University of Chicago Press, 2011.

Lyons, John D. "*Abraham sacrifiant* and the End of Ethics." In *French Renaissance and Baroque Drama: Text, Performance, and Theory*, edited by Michael Meere, 21–37. Newark: University of Delaware Press, 2015.

MacDonald, Joyce Green. *Women and Race in Early Modern Texts.* Cambridge: Cambridge University Press, 2002.

Maguire, Nancy Klein. "The Theatrical Mask / Masque of Politics: The Case of Charles I." *Journal of British Studies* 28 (1989): 1–22.

Mann, David. "The Roman Mime and Medieval Theatre." *Theatre Notebook: A Journal of the History and Technique of the British Theatre* 46 (1992): 136–44.

Marcus, Leah S. *Unediting the Renaissance: Shakespeare, Marlowe, Milton.* London: Routledge, 1996.

Marienstras, Richard. *Shakespeare au XXIe Siècle: Petite introduction aux tragédies.* Paris: Minuit, 2000.

Marlowe, Christopher. *Dr. Faustus: The A- and B- Texts (1604, 1616).* Edited by David Bevington. Manchester: Manchester University Press, 2013.

Marlowe, Christopher. *Edward the Second.* Edited by Martin Wiggins and Robert Lindsey. London: A&C Black and New York: W.W. Norton, 1997.

Marlowe, Christopher. *The Complete Plays.* Edited by Frank Romany and Robert Lindsey. London: Penguin, 2003.

Marlowe, Christopher. *The Complete Works of Christopher Marlowe.* Edited by Fredson Bowers. Second edn. Cambridge: Cambridge University Press, 2009.

Marotti, Arthur. "Shakespeare and Catholicism." In *Theatre and Religion: Lancastrian Shakespeare*, edited by Richard Dutton, Alison Findlay, and Richard Wilson, 218–41. Manchester: Manchester University Press, 2003.

Martin, Adrienne L. "Onstage/Backstage: Animals in the Golden Age *Comedia*." In *A Companion to Early Modern Hispanic Theater*, edited by Hilaire Kallendorf, 127–44. Leiden: Brill, 2014.

Martinez, Ronald L. "Tragic Machiavelli." In *The Comedy and Tragedy of Niccolò Machiavelli: Essays on the Literary Works*, edited by Vickie B. Sullivan, 102–19. New Haven: Yale University Press, 2000.

Martino, Alberto. *Daniel Casper von Lohenstein: Geschichte seiner Rezeption, Band I. 1661–1800*. Translated by Heribert Streicher. Tübingen: Max Niemeyer Verlag, 1978.

Marvell, Andrew. *The Poems of Andrew Marvell*. Edited by Nigel Smith. London: Pearson Longman, 2007.

Mayer, Jean-Christophe. "The Saint-Omer First Folio: Perspectives on a New Shakespearean Discovery." *Cahiers Elisabéthains* 87 (2015): 7–20.

Mazouer, Charles. *Le Théâtre Français de la Renaissance*. Paris: Champion, 2002.

McCormick, John. *Carl Schmitt's Critique of Liberalism*. Cambridge: Cambridge University Press, 1997.

McCullough, Diarmaid. *Reformation: Europe's House Divided, 1490–1700*. London: Penguin Books, 2004.

McKendrick, Melveena. *Theatre in Spain, 1490–1700*. Cambridge: Cambridge University Press, 1989.

McLuskie, Kathleen. *Renaissance Dramatists*. Atlantic Heights, NJ: Humanities Press International, 1989.

Mehring, Reinhard. *Carl Schmitt: A Biography*. Translated by Daniel Steuer. Cambridge: Polity, 2014.

Melzi, Robert C. "The two Bembos: a fresh look at the Italian *questione della lingua*." *Rivista di Studi Italiani* 1:1 (1983): 31–50.

Michel, Andreas. "Italian Orthography in Early Modern Times." In *Orthographies in Early Modern Europe*, edited by Susan Baddeley and Anja Voeste, 63–96. Berlin and New York: Walter de Gruyter, 2012.

Middleton, Thomas. *The Revenger's Tragedy*. Edited by Brian Gibbons. London: A&C Black and New York: W.W. Norton, 1991.

Middleton, Thomas. *The Revenger's Tragedy*. Edited by P. Jackson MacDonald. In *Thomas Middleton and Early Modern Textual Culture: A Companion to the Collected Works*, edited by Gary Taylor and John Lavagnino. Oxford: Oxford University Press, 2007.

Middleton, Thomas. *Thomas Middleton: The Collected Works*. Edited by Gary Taylor and John Lavagnino. Oxford: Oxford University Press, 2010.

Migliorini, Bruno. *The Italian language*. Translated, abridged, recast and revised by T. Gwynfor Griffith, rev. edn. London and Boston: Faber and Faber, 1984.

Miola, Robert S. "Jesuit Drama in Early Modern England." In *Theatre and Religion: Lancastrian Shakespeare*, edited by Richard Dutton, Alison Findlay, and Richard Wilson, 71–86. Manchester: Manchester University Press, 2003.

Miola, Robert S. "Early Modern Antigones: Receptions, Refractions, Replays." *Classical Receptions Journal* 6 (2014): 221–44.

Montrose, Louis Adrian. "'The place of a brother' in *As You Like It*: Social Process and Comic Form." In *Materialist Shakespeare: A History*, edited by Ivo Kamps. London: Verso, 1995.

Moretti, Franco. *Signs Taken for Wonders: On the Sociology of Literary Forms*. London: Verso, 1983.

Mortimer, Nigel. *John Lydgate's Fall of Princes: Narrative Tragedy in its Literary and Political Contexts*. Oxford: Oxford University Press, 2005.

Muir, Kenneth. Introduction. *Macbeth*. The Arden Shakespeare. London: Methuen, 1962.

Müller, H. *Früher Humanismus in Oberitalien: Albertino Mussato*, Ecerinis. Frankfurt am Main: Peter Lang, 1987.

Müller, Jan-Werner. *A Dangerous Mind: Carl Schmitt in Post-War European Thought*. New Haven: Yale University Press, 2003.

Mulryne, J.R. "Kyd, Thomas (*bap.* 1558, *d.* 1594)." In *Oxford Dictionary of National Biography*. Oxford University Press, 2004; online edn, 2008, http://www.oxforddnb.com.libproxy1.usc.edu/view/article/15816 (accessed June 4, 2017).

Munro, Lucy. *Children of the Queen's Revels: A Jacobean Theatre Repertory*. Cambridge: Cambridge University Press, 2005.

Mussato, A. *Ecérinide*. Edited by J.-F. Chevalier. Paris: Belles lettres, 2000.

Mussato, A. *Ecerinide*. Edited by Luigi Padrin. Bologna: Nicola Zanichelli Padrin, 1900.

Mussato, A. *The Tragedy of Ecerinis*. Translated by Robert W. Carrubba et al. University Park, PA: Department of Classics, the Pennsylvania State University, 1972.

Mussato's Ecerinis *and Loschi's* Achilles. Translated by J.R. Berrigan. München: Wilhelm Fink Verlag, 1975.

Nebeker, Eric. "The heyday of the broadside ballad." *The Early English Ballads Archive*, http://ebba.english.ucsb.edu/page/heyday-of-the-broadside-ballad

Neely, Carol Thomas. *Broken Nuptials in Shakespeare's Plays*. New Haven: Yale University Press, 1985.

Neill, Michael. "'In everything illegitimate': Imagining the Bastard in English Renaissance Drama." In *Putting History to the Question: Power, Politics, and Society in English Renaissance Drama*, 127–48. New York: Columbia University Press, 2000.

Newman, Jane O. *The Intervention of Philology: Gender, Learning, and Power in Lohenstein's Roman Plays*. Chapel Hill, NC: University of North Carolina Press, 2000.

Newman, Jane O. "Tragedy and *Trauerspiel* for the (Post)Westphalian Age." *Renaissance Drama* 40 (2012): 197–208.

Newman, Karen. *Fashioning Femininity and English Renaissance Drama*. Chicago: University of Chicago Press, 1991.

Nicholl, Charles. "Marlowe, Christopher (*bap.* 1564, *d.* 1593)." In *Oxford Dictionary of National Biography*. Oxford University Press, 2004; online edn, 2008, http://www.oxforddnb.com.libproxy1.usc.edu/view/article/18079 (accessed May 22, 2017).

Niderst, Alain. *Pierre Corneille*. Paris: Fayard, 2006.

Nietzsche, Friedrich. *The Birth of Tragedy and The Case of Wagner*. Translated and edited by Walter Kaufmann. New York: Random House, 1967.

Nietzsche, Friedrich. *The Birth of Tragedy*. Translated by Douglas Smith. Oxford: Oxford University Press, 2000.

Norbrook, David. "The Emperor's New Body? *Richard II*, Ernst Kantorowicz, and the Politics of Shakespeare Criticism." *Textual Practice* 10 (1996): 329–57.

Norland, Howard B. "Neo-Latin Drama in Britain." In *Neo-Latin Drama and Theatre in Early Modern Europe*, edited by Jan Bloemendal and Howard B. Norland, 471–544. Leiden and Boston: Brill, 2013.

Novak, S.P. *Planeta Držić: Držić i rukopis vlasti*. Zagreb: CEKADE, 1984.

Nuttall, A.D. *Why Does Tragedy Give Pleasure?* Oxford: Clarendon Press, 2001.

O'Sullivan, Noël. *Fascism*. London: Dent, 1983.

Oakley-Brown, Liz. "*Titus Andronicus* and the Cultural Politics of Translation in Early Modern England." *Renaissance Studies* 19, no. 3 (2005): 325–47.

Oláh, Szabolcs "A mítosz átértelmezése a keresztény humanista színpadon." In Péter Bornemisza, *Tragédia magyar nyelven a Szophoklész Élektrájából, M.D.LVIII*, 5–52. Budapest: Balassi Kiadó, 2009.

Onions, C.T. *A Shakespeare Glossary*. Oxford: Clarendon Press, 1986.

Orgel, Stephen. *The Illusion of Power: Political Theater in the English Renaissance*. Berkeley: University of California Press, 1975.

Orgel, Stephen. "Making Greatness Familiar." *Genre* 15 (1982): 41–8.

Orlin, Lena Cowen. *Private Matters and Public Culture in Post-Reformation England*. Ithaca: Cornell University Press, 1994.

Palfrey, Simon and Tiffany Stern. *Shakespeare in Parts*. Oxford: Oxford University Press, 2007.

Palmer, Barbara. "Playing in the Provinces: Front or Back Door?" *Medieval & Renaissance Drama in England* 22 (2009): 81–127.

Parente, James Jr. *Religious Drama and the Humanist Tradition: Christian Theater in Germany and the Netherlands, 1500–1680*. Leiden: Brill, 1987.

Parente, James Jr. and Jan Bloemendal. "The Humanist Tradition: *Mary Stuart*." In *Joost van den Vondel (1587–1679): Dutch Playwright in the Golden Age*, edited by Jan Bloemendal and Frans-Willem Korsten, 341–58. Leiden: Brill, 2012.

Partridge, Eric. *A Dictionary of Slang and Unconventional English*. New York: Macmillan, 1937.

Pevsner, Nikolas. *A History of Building Types*. London: Thames and Hudson, 1976.

Phillips-Court, Kristin. "Performing Anachronism: A New Aetiology of Italian Renaissance Tragedy." *Renaissance Drama* 36/37 (2010): 43–67.

Phillips-Court, Kristin. *The Perfect Genre: Drama and Painting in Renaissance Italy*. Burlington, VT: Ashgate, 2011.

Phillips, James Emerson. *Images of a Queen: Mary Stuart in Sixteenth-Century Literature*. Berkeley: University of California Press, 1964.

Pincombe, Mike. "Tragic and untragic bodies in the *Mirror for Magistrates*." In *A Mirror for Magistrates in Context: Literature, History, and Politics in Early Modern England*, edited by Harriet Archer and Andrew Hadfield, 53–70. Cambridge: Cambridge University Press, 2016.

Pollard, Tanya. "Greek Playbooks and Dramatic Forms in Early Modern England." In *Formal Matters: Reading the Materials of English Renaissance Literature*, edited by Allison Deutermann and András Kiséry, 99–123. Manchester: Manchester University Press, 2013.

Pollard, Tanya. *Greek Tragic Women on Shakespearean Stages*. Oxford: Oxford University Press, 2017.

Powell, Hugh. Introduction to *Cardenio und Celinde* by Andreas Gryphius. Leicester: Leicester University Press, 1967.

Prest, Wilfrid R. *The Inns of Court under Elizabeth I and the Early Stuarts, 1590–1640*. Totowa, NJ: Rowman and Littlefield, 1972.

Preston, Thomas. *Cambyses, King of Persia*. In *Drama of the English Renaissance Vol 1: The Tudor Period*, edited by Russell A. Fraser and Norman Rabkin. New York: Macmillan, 1976.

Puttfarkan, Thomas. *Titian and Tragic Painting: Aristotle's "Poetics" and the Rise of the Modern Artist*. New Haven: Yale University Press, 2005.

Rädle, Fidel. "Jesuit Theatre in Germany, Austria, and Switzerland." In *Neo-Latin Drama and Theatre in Early Modern Europe*, edited by Jan Bloemendal and Howard B. Norland, 185–292. Leiden and Boston: Brill, 2013.

Randall, Dale. *Winter Fruit: English Drama 1642–1660*. Lexington: University Press of Kentucky, 1995.

Reiss, Timothy. "Descartes, the Palatinate, and the Thirty Years War: Political Theory and Political Practice." *Yale French Studies* 80 (1991): 108–45.

Reiss, Timothy. "Renaissance Theater and Theories of Tragedy." In *The Cambridge History of Literary Criticism: Vol 3: The Renaissance*, edited by Glynn P. Norton. Cambridge: Cambridge University Press, 1999.

Ribner, Irving. *Jacobean Tragedy: The Quest for Moral Order*. London: Methuen, 1962.

Ricci, C. *Sophonisbe dans la tragédie classique Italienne et Française*. Grenoble: Allier Frères, 1904.

Richards, Jennifer. "Reading and listening to William Baldwin." In *A Mirror for Magistrates in Context: Literature, History, and Politics in Early Modern England*, edited by Harriet Archer and Andrew Hadfield, 71–85. Cambridge: Cambridge University Press, 2016.

Richards, Jennifer. *Voices and Books in the English Renaissance: A New History of Reading*. Oxford: Oxford University Press, forthcoming.

Ritoók-Szalai, Ágnes. "'Enarrat Electram Sophoclis.'" In *Dona Melanchthoniana: Festgabe für Heinz Scheible zum 70. Geburtstag*, ed. Johanna Loehr, 325–37. Stuttgart: Frommann-Holzboog, 2001.

Ritoókné Szalay, Ágnes. *Kutak: tanulmányok a XV–XVI. századi magyarországi művelődés köréből*. Budapest: Balassi Kiadó, 2012.

Robinson, F.N. *The Works of Geoffrey Chaucer*. Second edn. Boston: Houghton Mifflin, 1957.

Roff, Sarah Ley. "Benjamin and Psychoanalysis." In *The Cambridge Companion to Walter Benjamin*, edited by David Ferris, 115–33. Cambridge: Cambridge University Press, 2004.

Rowe, Katherine. *Dead Hands: Fictions of Agency, Renaissance to Modern*. Stanford, CA: Stanford University Press, 1999.

Rowland, Ingrid D. "High Culture." In *A Companion to the Worlds of the Renaissance*, edited by Guido Ruggiero, 316–32. Oxford: Blackwell, 2002, Blackwell Reference Online, http://www.blackwellreference.com/subscriber/tocnode.html?id=g9780631215240_chunk_g978063121524020 (accessed June 6, 2017).

Rudin, Bärbel. "Deutsches Theater nach dem westfälischen Frieden—zwanzig Jahre des Aufbaus." In *Die Welt des Daniel Casper von Lohenstein*, edited by Peter Kleinschmidt, Gerhard Spellerberg, and Hanns-Dietrich Schmidt, 50–7. Köln: Wienand Verlag, 1978.

Ruvoldt, Maria. "Sacred to Secular, East to West: The Renaissance Studiolo and Strategies of Display." *Renaissance Studies* 20 (2006): 640–57.

Ryan, Kiernan. *Shakespeare*. New York: Palgrave, 2002.

Sackville, Thomas and Thomas Norton. *Gorboduc, or Ferrex and Porrex*. Edited by Irby B. Cauthen Jr. Lincoln: University of Nebraska Press, 1970.

Sandbach, F.H. *Ancient Culture and Society: The Comic Theatre of Greece and Rome*. London: Chatto & Windus, 1977.

Santner, Eric. *The Royal Remains: The People's Two Bodies and the Endgames of Sovereignty*. Chicago: University of Chicago Press, 2011.

Scaliger Julius Caesar. *Poetices*. Translated by F.M. Padelford. *Select Translations from Scaliger's Poetics*. New York, 1905.

Schmitt, Carl. "Foreword to the German Edition of Lilian Winstanley's *Hamlet and the Scottish Succession*." *Telos* 153 ([1952] Winter 2010): 164–77.

Schmitt, Carl. *Der Schatten Gottes. Introspektionem, Tagebücher und Briefe: 1921–1924*. Edited by Gerd Geisler, Ernst Hüsmert, and Wolfgang Spindler. Berlin: Duncker & Humblot, 2014.

Schmitt, Carl. *Dictatorship*. Translated by Michael Hoezl and Graham Ward. [1921] Cambridge: Polity Press, 2014.

Schmitt, Carl. *Hamlet or Hecuba: The Intrusion of the Time into the Play.* Translated by David Pan and Jennifer Rust. 1956. Candor, New York: Telos, 2009.
Schmitt, Carl. *Political Theology: Four Chapters on the Concept of Sovereignty.* Translated by George Schwab. 1922. Chicago: University of Chicago Press, 2005.
Schmitt, Carl. *Roman Catholicism and Political Form.* Translated by G.L. Ulmen. 1923. Westport: Greenwood Press, 1996.
Schmitt, Carl. *The Concept of the Political.* Translated by George Schwab. 1932. Chicago: University of Chicago Press, 1996.
Schmitt, Carl. *The Crisis of Parliamentary Democracy.* Translated by Ellen Kennedy. 1923. Cambridge, MA: MIT Press, 1986.
Schmitt, Carl. *The Leviathan in the State Theory of Thomas Hobbes: Meaning and Failure of a Political Symbol.* Translated by George Schwab and Erna Hilfstein. 1938. Chicago: University of Chicago, 2008.
Schrickx, Willem. "English Actors at the Courts of Wolfensbüttel, Brussels and Graz During the Lifetime of Shakespeare." *Shakespeare Survey* 33 (1980): 153–68.
Seneca. *Seneca His Tenne Tragedies Translated into English.* Edited by Thomas Newton. Bloomington and London: Indiana University Press, 1964.
Seneca. *Tragedies.* Translated by J.G. Fitch. vol. 2. Cambridge, MA: Harvard University Press, 2004.
Shakespeare, William. *Anthony and Cleopatra.* Edited by Michael Neill. Oxford: Oxford University Press, 1994.
Shakespeare, William. *Hamlet.* Edited by Ann Thompson and Neil Taylor. The Arden Shakespeare. Third series. London: Bloomsbury, 2016.
Shakespeare, William. *Hamlet.* Edited by Ann Thompson and Neil Taylor. Third series. London: Arden Shakespeare, 2006.
Shakespeare, William. *Hamlet.* Edited by G. R. Hibbard. Oxford: Oxford University Press, 1994.
Shakespeare, William. *Macbeth.* Edited by Kenneth Muir. The Arden Shakespeare. London: Methuen, 1962.
Shakespeare, William. *The Norton Shakespeare.* Edited by Stephen Greenblatt, Walter Cohen, Jean Howard, and Katharine Eisaman Maus. New York: W.W. Norton and Co., 1997. Rpt. 2007; 2016.
Shakespeare, William. *Othello, the Moor of Venice.* Edited by Michael Neill. Oxford: Oxford University Press, 2006.
Shapiro, James. *Shakespeare and the Jews.* New York: Columbia University Press, 1996.
Shapiro, Michael. "Boy Companies and Private Theaters." In *A Companion to Renaissance Drama,* edited by Arthur Kinney, 314–25. Oxford: Blackwell, 2002.
Shortslef, Emily. *Weeping, Wailing, Sighing, Railing: Shakespeare and the Drama of Complaint.* Dissertation, Ph.D., Columbia University, 2015.
Shuger, Deborah. *Political Theologies in Shakespeare's England: The Sacred and the State in "Measure for Measure."* Basingstoke: Macmillan, 2001.
Simons, Patricia. *The Sex of Men in Premodern Europe: A Cultural History.* Cambridge: Cambridge University Press, 2011.
Sinfield, Alan. *Shakespeare, Authority, Sexuality: Unfinished Business in Cultural Materialism.* London and New York: Routledge, 2006.
Smit, Betine von Zyl ed. *A Handbook to the Reception of Greek Drama.* London: Wiley-Blackwell, 2006.

Smith, Bruce R. *Ancient Scripts and Modern Experience on the English Stage, 1500–1700*. Princeton: Princeton University Press, 1988; rpt. 2014.

Smith, Hilda, "Gynecology and Ideology in Seventeenth Century England." In *Liberating Women's History*, edited by Berenice Carroll, 907–114. Urbana, IL: Illinois University Press, 1976.

Smith, Nigel. "Exile in Europe During the English Revolution and its Literary Impact." In *Literatures of Exile in the English Revolution and its Aftermath, 1640–1690*, edited by Philip Major, 105–18. Farnham: Ashgate, 2010.

Smits-Veldt, M.B. "Opening van de Amsterdamse Schouwburg met Vondels *Gysbreght van Aemstel*." In *Een Theatergeschiedenis der Nederlanden*, edited by R.L. Erenstein, 204–11. Amsterdam: Amsterdam University Press, 1996.

Sommerville, John, ed. *King James VI and I: Political Writings*. Cambridge: Cambridge University Press, 1994.

Spenser, Edmund. *The Faerie Queene*. Edited by Thomas P. Roche Jr. and C. Patrick O'Donnell Jr. London: Penguin Classics, 2003.

Staines, John. *The Tragic Histories of Mary Queen of Scots*. London: Routledge, 2009.

Staley, G. *Seneca and the Idea of Tragedy*. Oxford: Oxford University Press, 2010.

Stanivukovic, Goran and John H. Cameron. *Tragedies of the English Renaissance: An Introduction*. Edinburgh: University of Edinburgh Press, 2008.

States, Bert O. *Great Reckonings in Little Rooms: On the Phenomenology of Theater*. Berkeley: University of California Press, 1987.

Staves, Susan. "Resentment or resignation?: Dividing the spoils among daughters and younger sons." In *Early Modern Conceptions of Property*, edited by John Brewer and Susan Staves, 194–218. London and New York: Routledge, 1995.

Steiner, George. "Tragedy, Pure and Simple." In *Tragedy and the Tragic: Greek Theatre and Beyond*, edited by M.S. Silk, 534–46. Oxford: Clarendon Press, 1996.

Steiner, George. *Antigones*. Oxford: Clarendon Press, 1984.

Stern, Tiffany. Lecture delivered at the workshop series of "The History of the Material Text," University of Pennsylvania, April 3, 2017.

Stewart, Alan. *The Cradle King: A Life of James VI and I*. London: Chatto & Windus, 2003.

Stone, Lawrence. *The Family, Sex and Marriage in England, 1500–1800*. New York: Harper and Row, 1977.

Straznicky, Marta. "Closet Drama." In *A Companion to Renaissance Drama*, edited by Arthur Kinney, 416–30. Oxford: Blackwell, 2002.

Streete, Adrian. *Protestantism and Drama in Early Modern England*. Cambridge: Cambridge University Press, 2009.

Sullivan, Garrett, Jr. "Tragic Subjectivities." In *The Cambridge Companion to English Renaissance Tragedy*, edited by Garrett Sullivan, Jr. and Emma Smith. Cambridge: Cambridge University Press, 2010.

Syme, Holger Schott. "The Meaning of Success: 1594 and Its Aftermath." *Shakespeare Quarterly* 61 (2010): 490–525.

Szabó, Géza Szentmártoni. "Euripidész magyar fordítása a 16. század második feléből," *Irodalomtörténeti közlemények* 102 (1998): 225–39.

Szondi, Peter. *An Essay on the Tragic*. Translated by Paul Fleming. Stanford: Stanford University Press, 2002.

T.E. *The Lawes Resolution of Women's Rights; or the Lawes Provision for Women. A Methodicall Collection of Such Statutes and Customes, with the Cases, Opinions, Arguments and points of Learning in the Law, as do properly concerne Women.* London: John Grove, 1632.

Tadić, J. *Dubrovački portreti.* Beograd: Srpska književna zadruga, 1948.

Taubes, Jacob. *To Carl Schmitt: Letters and Reflections.* Translated by Keith Tribe. New York: Columbia University Press, 2013.

Taylor, Gary. "*Hamlet* in Africa, 1607." In *Travel Knowledge: European "Discoveries" in the Early Modern Period*, edited by Ivo Kamps and Jyotsna G. Singh, 223–48. New York: Palgrave, 2001.

Telford, Kenneth A. *Aristotle's Poetics: Translation and Analysis.* Chicago: Henry Regnery, 1961.

Thacker, Jonathan. *A Companion to Golden Age Theatre.* Woodbridge, Suffolk: Boydell and Brewer, 2007.

Thomas, Keith. "The Double Standard." *Journal of the History of Ideas* 20 (1959): 195–216.

Thomson, Peter. *Shakespeare's Professional Career.* Cambridge: Cambridge University Press, 1992.

Tidworth, Simon. *Theatres: An Illustrated History.* London: Pall Mall Press, 1973.

Tolstoy, Lev. *Fables for Children; Stories for Children; Natural Science Stories; Popular Education; Decembrists; Moral Tales.* Translated and edited by Leo Weiner. London: J.M. Dent, 1904.

Tourneur, Cyril. *The Plays of Cyril Tourneur: The Revenger's Tragedy, The Atheist's Tragedy.* Edited by George Parfitt. Cambridge: Cambridge University Press, 1978.

Traub, Valerie. *Thinking Sex with the Early Moderns.* Philadelphia: University of Pennsylvania Press, 2016.

Underdown, David. "The Taming of the Scold: The Enforcement of Patriarchal Authority in Early Modern England." In *Order and Disorder in Early Modern England*, edited by Anthony Fletcher and John Stevenson, 116–36. Cambridge: Cambridge University Press, 1985.

Usher, Phillip John. "Courtroom Drama During the Wars of Religion: Robert Garnier and the Paris *Parlement*." In *French Renaissance and Baroque Drama: Text, Performance, and Theory*, edited by Michael Meere, 139–52. Newark: University of Delaware Press, 2015.

Vanhoutte, Jacqueline. "Community, Authority, and the Motherland in Sackville and Norton's *Gorboduc*." *Studies in English Literature* 40 (2000): 227–39.

Veith, Ilza. *Hysteria: History of a Disease.* Chicago: University of Chicago Press, 1965.

Vernet, Max. "Naissance du Critique." In *Le Champ Littéraire*, edited by P. Citti and M. Détrie, 29–37. Paris: J. Vrin, 1992.

Viala, Alain, ed. *Le Théâtre en France des Origines à nos Jours.* Paris: Presses Universitaires de France, 1997.

Viala, Alain. "Corneille et les Institutions Littéraires de son Temps." In *Pierre Corneille: Actes Du Colloque*, edited by Alain Niderst, 197–204. Paris: Presses Universitaires de France, 1985.

Viala, Alain. *Naissance de l'Écrivain: Sociologie de la Litterature a l'Âge Classique.* Paris: Editions de Minuit, 1985.

Viala, Alain. "Corneille, premier auteur moderne?" In *Pratiques de Corneille*, ed. Myriam Dufour-Maitre, 29–40. Mont-Saint-Aignan: Publications des Universités de Rouen et du Havre, 2012.

Vočadlo, Otakar. "The Problem of the Silesian Quarto of Hamlet: An Essay in Suggestive Hypothesis." *Acta Universitatis Carolinae Philologica* 3 (1969): 59–75.

Vondel, Joost van den. *Mary Stuart, or Tortured Majesty.* Translated and edited by Kristiaan P. Aercke. Ottawa: Dovehouse, 1996.

von Hamm, Wilhelm, T.C.H. Hedderwick, Gotthold Ephraim Lessing, and Guido Bonneschky. *The Old German Puppet Play of Doctor Faustus*. London: K. Paul Trench, 1887.
Walker, G. *The Politics of Performance in Early Renaissance Drama*. Cambridge: Cambridge University Press, 1998.
Walsh, Brian. *Shakespeare, the Queen's Men and the Elizabethan Performance of History*. Cambridge: Cambridge University Press, 2009.
Ward, A.E. *Women and Tudor Tragedy: Feminizing Counsel and Representing Gender*. Madison: Fairleigh Dickinson University Press, 2013.
Warner, Marina. *Monuments and Maidens: The Allegory of the Female Form*. New York: Pantheon, 1985.
Warwick, Sir Philip. *Memoires of the Reign of King Charles I*. London: 1701.
Watanabe-O'Kelly, Helen. "The Early Modern Period (1450–1720)." In *The Cambridge History of German Literature*, edited by Helen Watanabe-O'Kelly, 92–146. Cambridge: Cambridge University Press, 1997.
Watt, Tessa. *Cheap Print and Popular Piety 1550–1640*. Cambridge: Cambridge University Press, 1991.
Weber, Samuel. *Benjamin's–abilities*. Cambridge, MA.: Harvard University Press, 2008.
Webster, John. *The Duchess of Malfi*. Edited by John Brennan. London: A&C Black and New York: W. W. Norton, 1996.
Webster, John. *The Duchess of Malfi*. Edited by Michael Neill. New York: W.W. Norton & Company, 2015.
Webster, John. *The White Devil*. Edited by Christina Luckyj. London: Methuen, 2008.
Weimann, Robert. *Shakespeare and the Popular Tradition in the Theater: Studies in the Social Dimension of Dramatic Form and Function*. Edited by Robert Schwartz. Baltimore: Johns Hopkins University Press, 1978.
Weinberg, Bernard. *A history of literary criticism in the Italian Renaissance*. Chicago: University of Chicago Press, 1961.
Weiss, Piero. "Opera and Neoclassical Dramatic Criticism in the Seventeenth Century." *Studies in the History of Music* 2 (1988): 1–30.
West, Michael. "Were There Playgoers During the 1580s?" *Shakespeare Studies* 45 (2017): 68–76.
West, William N. "The Idea of a Theater: Humanist Ideology and the Imaginary Stage in Early Modern Europe." *Renaissance Drama* 28 (1997): 245–87.
White, R.S. *Innocent Victims Poetic Injustice in Shakespearean Tragedy*. London: Athlone, 1986.
Whitney, Charles. *Early Responses to Renaissance Drama*. Cambridge; New York: Cambridge University Press, 2006.
Wild, Christopher J. "Jesuit Theater and the Blindness of Self-Knowledge." In *A New History of German Literature*, edited by David E. Wellbery and Judith Ryan, 270–5. Cambridge, MA: Harvard University Press, 2004.
Wilson, Edward M. and Duncan Moir. *A Literary History of Spain: The Golden Age Drama 1492–1700*. London: Ernest Benn, 1971.
Wilson, John Dover. Introduction to *Richard II*, by William Shakespeare, vii–lxxvi. Cambridge: Cambridge University Press, 1939.
Wilson, Thomas. *The State of England*. Edited by F.J. Fisher. Camden Society, Third Series, LII. [1600] 1936. Reprinted in *Seventeenth-Century Economic Documents*, edited by Joan Thirsk and J.P. Cooper, 756–65. Oxford: Clarendon Press, 1972.
Winston, J. *Lawyers at Play: Literature, Law, and Politics at the Early Modern Inns of Court, 1558–1581*. Oxford: Oxford University Press, 2016.

Winston, Jessica. "Rethinking Absolutism: English *de casibus* Tragedy in the 1560s." In *A Mirror for Magistrates in Context: Literature, History, and Politics in Early Modern England*, edited by Harriet Archer and Andrew Hatfield, 199–215. Cambridge: Cambridge University Press, 2016.

Witt, R.G. *In the Footsteps of the Ancients: The Origins of Humanism from Lovato to Bruni*. Leiden and Boston: Brill, 2000.

Woerner, Roman, ed. *Adriana Roulerii Insulani Stuarta Tragoedia*. Berlin, 1906.

Woodbridge, Linda. "Queen of Apricots: The Duchess of Malfi, Hero of Desire." In *The Female Tragic Hero in English Renaissance Drama*, edited by Naomi Conn Liebler, 161–84. London: Palgrave Macmillan, 2002.

Yates, Frances A. "Some New Light on *L'Écossaise* of Antoine de Montchrétien." *The Modern Language Review* 22: (1927): 285–97.

Yates, Frances. *The Rosicrucian Enlightenment*. London: Routledge & Kegan Paul, 1972.

Young, Julian. *The Philosophy of Tragedy: From Plato to Žižek*. Cambridge: Cambridge University Press, 2013.

Zemeckis, Robert, dir. *Who Framed Roger Rabbit* [film]. United States: Buena Vista Pictures, 1988.

Zilli, Luigia. "Mellin de Saint-Gelais, Jacques Amyot e un Manoscritto della Tragedia Sophonisba." *Studi di Letteratura Francese* 17 (1991): 7–29.

INDEX

academia, transnational 60–1
academies 35
Accademia degl' Intronati
   Gl'ingannati 35
Accademia Olimpia 64
Accademia Romana 32, 41
actes des apôtres, Les (*The Acts of the Apostles*) 39
acting companies 44, 50 (*see also* touring companies)
   Sussex's Men 51
actors 62, 64, 70
Adam and Eve, story of 113
Agamben, Giorgio 81
Alamanni, Luigi
   Antigone 63
Alberti, Leon Battista 45
Aleotti, Giovanni Battista 45
Alleyn, Edward 62
Amyot, Jacques 64
anachronism 88
ancient Rome 39, 84, 85, 88
Anthoine, Jehan 40
Arden of Faversham 24, 27–8, 115–16
Ariosto, Ludovico
   Cassaria 45
   Suppositi, I 42
Aristotle 2, 3, 72
   characterization 92
   plot 92
   Poetics 2, 3–4, 19, 35
   tragic action 4, 6–7
Artaud, Antonin 13
Athenian culture 2
Atreus, House of 78
d'Aubignac, abbé (François Hédelin) 56
   Remarques 57
audiences 56
   codes of conduct 66
   critical debate 57–8, 68
   English 66
   politics 64, 65–6
   Renaissance communities before 1663 58–62

Baïf, Jean-Antoine de 64
Balassi, Bálint 61
   Beautiful Hungarian Comedy 61
Baldwin, William
   Mirror for Magistrates, A 19, 20–3
ballads 26–7, 28–30
Barber, C.L. 84
Beaumont, Francis 68
Beaumont, Francis and John Fletcher
   Maid's Tragedy 12
Beneš, Carrie E. 101
Benjamin, Walter 74, 76–7
   "Critique of Violence" 77
   Origin of German Tragic Drama, The 74–5, 77
bestrafte Brudermord, Der 77
Bèze, Théodore de (Theodore Beza) 36
   Abraham sacrifiant 36, 39
biblical stories 39 (*see also* mystery plays)
Bidermann, Jakob
   Belisarius 37
   Cenodoxus 36–7
   Cosmarchia 37
   Josephus 37
   Macarius Romanus 37
   Philemon Martyr 37
black characters 69
black-letter broadside ballads 28
Boccaccio, Giovanni 20
   De casibus virorum et feminarum illustrium (*The Falls of Famous Men and Women*) 20
   De casibus virorum illustrium (*Concerning the falls of famous men*) 5–6
Boethius
   Consolation of Philosophy 5, 148 n. 16
Bolter, Jay David 17
Bordez, Jean de
   Maria Stuarta Tragoedia 72
Bornemisza, Péter 60–1
Bowers, Fredson 11–12
Braden, Gordon 8
Breslau 69–70

INDEX

Britain (*see also* England)
  legendary history 92–3, 102–4
  unification 94
broadside ballads 26–7, 28–30
brothers 125–7, 130–2
Browne, Robert 76
Buch, Robert
  Pathos of the Real, The 72
Buchanan, George 36
  Baptistes sive Calumnia 36
  Jephthes 61
Buffequin, Georges 47
Burbage, Richard 62
Burghley, Lord *see* Cecil, William

Calderón de la Barca, Pedro 39–40, 48
  Cabellos de Absalon, Los (*Absalom's Hair*) 39–40
Camerarius, Joachim
  Commentarii 3
Camerata of Florence 35
Campanella, Tommaso
  Tragedia della Regina di Scozia 72
Campen, Jacob van 52
Campo de' Fiori, Rome 38
Carretto, Galeotto del
  Sophonisba 62–3
Carval, Miguel de 39
  Tragedia Llamada Josefina (*Tragedy called Joseph*) 39
Cary, Lady Elizabeth
  Tragedy of Mariam, The 61, 171 n. 31
Castellano of Bassano 98
Castelletti, Cristoforo
  Amarilli 61
Castelvetro, Lodovico
  Poetica d'Aristotele vulgarizzata e sposita 19
catharsis 84
Catholic Counter Reformation 36
Catholicism 77–8, 83–4, 86, 87–8, 89–90 (*see also* religion)
  Jesuit schools 36–7, 70
  Ragusa 109
Cecil, William (Lord Burghley) 79
Cervantes, Miguel de 40, 48
  Don Quixote 48
  Numantia 48–50
Cesarini, Giovn Giorgio 45
Chapman, George
  Bussy d'Amboys 68
  Conspiracy of Biron, The 68
  Revenge of Bussy d'Amboys, The 68
  Tragedy of Biron 68
characterization 92
Charles I (King of England) 71–2, 75–6, 82
Chaucer, Geoffrey 18
  Boece 4
  Canterbury Tales 4
  Troilus & Criseyde 4
children's theater companies 67
Christianity 72, 77–8 (*see also* religion)
Church of England 90, 91
  "Homily of the State of Matrimony, An" 112–13
Churchyard, Thomas
  General Rehearsall of Warres, A (or *Churchyard's Choice*) 23
circulation 32
city, the 97, 98–110
civil conflict 97, 98–110
classical myths 85, 93–4
classical tragedies 18, 60–1, 62–3 (*see also* Greek tragedies)
  myth 93–4
  reviving 41–2
  translations 19, 60–1
  women 61–2
Cleopatra (Queen of Egypt) 93, 94
Clermont-Tallard, Louise de 64
closet drama 34
collège de Guyenne 35–6
colonization 94
comedy 84, 85
commedia dell' arte 41
commedia erudite 45
commercial production 57, 58, 60–1
  children's theater companies 67
  England 59, 62
  royal courts 66–7
communal rule 101
communities 8, 55–6
  audiences as 66
  criticism 58
  Renaissance communities before 1663 58–62
companionate reading 34, 35
"complaint and lamentation of Mistresse Arden of [Fev]ersham in Kent, who for the love of one Mosbie, hired certaine Ruffians [a]nd Villaines most cruelly to murder her Husband; with the fatall end of her and her Associates. To the tune of, Fortune my Foe, the" 28–30
complaint poetry 19, 23, 26

Confrérie de la Passion 40
Corneille, Pierre 55–7, 65, 68
    Cid 56, 57, 62
    Horace 56
    Pompée 62
    Sophonisbe 55–7, 68
coronation ceremony 91
corrales theaters 48–9
Coryate, Thomas 39
coverture, law of 111–12
craft plays 10–11 (*see also* mystery plays)
critical debate 56–8, 59, 68, 98
Crucifixion (Wakefield mystery play) 10, 11
cuckoldry 123–5
cultural differences 4, 6
cultural capital 42, 43, 44
cultural history 9

Daniel, Samuel
    Philotas 67–8
    Tragedie of Cleopatra, The 93
Danzig (Gdańsk) 70
Day, John 104
definitions 3, 4–5
    Aristotle 72
    Chaucer, Geoffrey 18
    Lydgate, John 20
    memes 32
    Schmitt, Carl 78–9
    tragic falls 20
Denmark, performance sites in 41
DiGangi, Mario 140
divine right of kings 80–2, 91
Dolce, Ludovico 63, 107
    Giocasta 37, 104
    Gismond of Salerne 37, 44
    Marianna 63
Dollimore, Jonathan 142
Donneau de Visé, Jean 56–7
    Nouvelles nouvelles 56
Držić, Marin 107–10
    Hecuba 107, 110
Dubrovnik 106–10
Duchess of Malfi, The (Webster, John) 12–13, 113, 116–18, 145–6, 170 n. 20
    conflict 83
    marriage 90
    religion 88

Elizabeth I (Queen of England) 44, 91, 102
Elizabeth Stuart (Electress of the Palatine and Queen of Bohemia) 76

Else, Gerald 2
    hamartía 6
Encina, Juan del 42
    Égloga de Fileno, Zambardo y Cardonio 42
Enders, Jody, Theresa Coletti, John T. Sebastian, and Carol Symes
    Cultural History of Tragedy in the Middle Ages, A 18, 20
England (*see also* Britain)
    children's theater companies 67
    commercial production 59, 62
    continental influence 68
    critical debate 58
    legendary history 92–3
    Master of the Revels 66
    performance 37, 43–4, 59–60
    performance sites in 37, 43–4
    provincial venues 67
    royal court 66–7
    theaters 50–2, 66
    translations 61–2
Englische Comedien und Tragedien Sampt dem Pickelhering (*English Comedies and Tragedies with Pickelherring*) 41
English Comedians 40–1, 44
Erasmus, Desiderius 31, 36
    De ratione studii 35
Ercole I d'Este (Duke of Ferrara) 42
Ercole II d'Este (Duke of Ferrara) 42–3
error 6
Esposito, Roberto 80
Essex, Earl of (Robert Devereaux) 65
ethoi 32
Euripides 104
    Hecuba 107
    Iphigeneia in Aulis 61
    Medea 35
    Phoenician Women 37
Eusebius
    Ecclesiastical History 39
Eve and Adam, story of 113
execution 71–2, 79, 81, 82, 84, 91
Ezzelino da Romano 39

family 111, 132
    authority within 111–13
    brothers 125–7, 130–2
    cuckoldry 123–5
    fathers 118–23, 130–1
    heroines 113–18
    mothers 118, 120–2, 132

primogeniture 112, 125–7, 130–2
    sons 118–23
    women 111–18
Famous Tragedy of King Charles, The 74, 76
fascism 80
fathers 118–23, 130–1
Federico III da Montefeltro 33
female heroes 12–13
feminism 145
Fernández, Lucas
    Auto de la Pasión (*Play of the Passion*) 39
Fernyhough, Charles
    Voices Within, The 34
fidelity 123, 140
Florio, John 33
folklore 85, 92–3
Ford, John
    Broken Heart 12
    'Tis Pity She's a Whore 13
fortune 20–1
Foucault, Michel 81
France 57
    critical debate 56–8
    drama 56–7, 68
    literary sphere 56–8, 62
    Normandy 65
    performance 60, 64, 65
    performance sites in 35–6, 37, 39, 40
    theaters 46–8, 65
    Trissino's *Sophonisba, La* 64
Friedrich V and I (Elector Palatine of the Rhine and King of Bohemia) 76
friendship 133–4, 140, 143–4
Frye, Northrop 85

Garnier Robert 47, 68
    Antony 61
    Bradamante 47
    Cornélie 47, 51
    Hippolyte 40, 47
    Juives, Les 40
    Porcie 47, 51
    Troade, Le 40
Gascoigne, George and Francis Kinwelmershe
    Jocasta 37, 44, 104–6, 129–30
Gataker, Thomas
    Marriage Duties Briefly couched together 112
gender 112, 129–30 (*see also* men; women)
    actors 62, 70
    Antony and Cleopatra 135–7, 138–9
    Duchess of Malfi, The 145–6
    Edward II 140–2
    Gorboduc 130–2
    Hamlet 132–5
    Iocasta 129–30
    Othello 139–40
    queer 144
    Revenger's Tragedy, the 142–5
    "stately Tragedy containing the ambitious Life and death of the great Cham" 137–8
genre 1–2
    tragic complaint, the 22
Germany 68, 77
    performance sites in 36–7, 41, 44
    schools 69–70
    Weimar Republic 75, 77, 79
Giraldi Cinthio, Giambattista 42–3, 51, 63
    Altile 43
    Discorso ovvero lettera intorno al comporre delle commedie 43
    Ecatommiti, Gli (*The Hundred Tales*) 43
    Orbecche 19, 43, 63
Girard, René
    Violence and the Sacred 84
Giustiniano, Orsato
    Edipo tiranno 45
Golding, Arthur
    Brief discourse of the late murther of master George Saunders of London, A 25
Gouge, William 111
    Of Domesticall Duties 111, 112
Gouveia, André (Andreas Goveanus) 35–6
Greek tragedies 3, 7, 148 n. 30
    Braden, Gordon 8
    in print 18–19
    opera 18
Grusin, Richard 18
Gryphius, Andreas 76
    Carolus Stuardus 76
    Murdered Majesty: Charles Stuart 75–6
Guizzardo of Bologna 98

Halliwell, Stephen 2
    hamartía 6
hamartía 6–7, 92
Hamlet (Shakespeare, William) 12, 41, 62, 67

Benjamin, Walter 76–7, 74–5, 82
brothers 126
Browne, Robert 76
gender 132–5
hamartia 92
heroes 3, 7
James VI and I 79, 80
Schmitt, Carl 77–8, 79–80
understage locations 84
Hamlet einen Printzen in Dennemark 41
Hardy, Alexandre 60
Haugwitz, August Adolf von
   Guilty Innocence: Mary Stuart 76
Hecuba 62
Hédelin, François (abbé d'Aubignac) 56
Henry VIII (King of England) 44, 90
Herbert, Lady Mary Sidney 61
Hermann the German 9
heroes 3, 7, 133, 138
   female 12–13
heroines 12–13, 113–18
Historia von D. Johann Fausten, dem weitbeschreiten Zauberer und Schwartkünstler (The History of Dr. Johann Faust, the Famous Wizard and Black Magician) 15
History of the Damnable Life and Deserved Death of Doctor John Faustus, The (Faust Book) 15
Höfele, Andreas
   No Hamlets 82
Holinshed, Ralph
   Arden of Faversham story 27–8
   Chronicles of England, Scotland, and Ireland 23, 25, 27
Holocaust 80
homophobia 144
homosexuality 140–1, 142, 144
horror tragedies 142
hôtel de Bourgogne 46–7, 65
Hughes, Thomas
   Misfortunes of Arthur, The 37
human 3
hysteria 121

ideal, the 2–3, 7
incest 135, 137–8, 145
Inghirami, Tommaso 31, 43
inheritance 130, 134–5 (*see also* primogeniture)
Isidore of Seville
   Etymologiae 39

Islam 88, 89 (*see also* religion)
Italy 62–3 (*see also* ancient Rome)
   academies 32, 35, 41, 64
   actresses 62
   critical debate 58
   literary language 63
   Padua 97–101
   performance sites in 31–5, 38, 39, 42, 43
   theaters 44–6
Itchō, Hanabusa
   Blind monks examining an elephant 1

James VI and I (King of Scotland and of England) 50, 72, 73, 76
   Basilkdon Doron 71
   Burghley, Lord 79
Jenkins, Henry 16–17
Jesuit schools 36–7, 70
Jodelle, Étienne
   Cléopâtre captive 37, 47
Jones, Inigo 51–2
Judaism 88–9 (*see also* religion)
"judgement of God shewed upon John Faustus, Doctor of Divinitye, The" 15, 17

Kantorowicz, Ernst 81–2
   Kings Two Bodies, The 82
kingship 80–2
   death 90–1, 103 (*see also* execution)
   lineage 93, 102, 103–4
   primogeniture 125–7, 130–2
Kinnear, Rory 144
Knox, Bernard 7
Kott, Jan
   Shakespeare Our Contemporary 85
Kyd, Thomas 50–1
   Spanish Tragedy, The 50, 51, 83, 118–20
   Trueth of the most wicked and secret murthering of John Brewen, Goldsmith of London, committed by his owne wife through the provocation of one John Parker whom she loved, The 25–6

Laetus, Julius Pomponius. *See* Leto, Giulio Pomponio
language 63
legal background 68
Leto, Giulio Pomponio (Julius Pomponius Laetus) 31, 32, 35, 38, 39, 41
"Life and Deathe of Doctur Faustus the Great Cunngerer, the" 15
Lily, William 35, 43

Lohenstein, Daniel Casper von 68–70
  Ibrahim Bassa 70
  Sophonisbe 68–70
Lope de Vega 48
Lopez, Rodrigo 89
love 141 (*see also* sexual desire)
Lumley, Lady Jane 61
Lydgate, John 4–5, 6, 20
  Fall of Princes, The 20
  Minor Poems 4
  Troy Book 20, 21
  Troyes Boke 4

Mactatio Abel (Wakefield mystery play) 10, 11
Magdalena Gymnasium, Breslau 69–70
Mairet, Jean
  Sophonisbe 56, 57
Marienstras, Richard 80
Marlowe, Christopher 12, 86
  Dido, Queen of Carthage 93–4
  Dr. Faustus 12, 15–17, 84, 85–6, 113
  Edward II 91, 140–2
  Jew of Malta, The 89
  Massacre at Paris, The 86
  Tamburlaine 12, 113
Marlowe, Christopher and Thomas Nashe
  Tragedy of Dido Queen of Carthage, The 44
marriage 111, 112–14, 135
  Arden of Faversham 115–16
  ceremony 90
  fidelity 123–5
  Othello 139
  patriarchy 123
Marston, John 67, 68
  Sophonisba 67, 68
  Wonder of Women: Or The Tragedie of Sophonisba, The 67
Martelli, Ludovico
  Tullia 63
Marvell, Andrew 71, 72
Mary, Queen of Scots 64, 65, 71, 72, 73–4, 76, 79
masculinity 130, 131–4, 136, 138, 139, 142, 144
Master of the Revels 66
Matthieu, Pierre 68
Médicis, Catherine de (Queen of France) 64
medieval myth 85
Melanchthon, Philipp 60–1
  Cohortatio ad legendas tragoedias et comoedias 60

melos 35
memes 32, 36–7, 40, 41, 42, 43, 51
men (*see also* gender)
  cuckoldry 123–5
  Duchess of Malfi, The 146
  fathers 118–23
  fidelity 123, 140
  heroes 3, 7
  masculinity 130, 131–4, 136, 138, 139, 142, 144
  Revenger's Tragedy, The 142–4
  sons 118–23
  virility 123–4
Middleton, Thomas
  Game At Chess, A 83
  Women Beware Women 83, 125
Middleton, Thomas and Rowley, William
  Changeling, The 83, 87, 94, 111, 114–15
Middleton, Thomas and Tourneur, Cyril
  Revenger's Tragedy, The 83, 142–5
mime 39
Mirror for Magistrates, A 19, 20–3
misogyny 123, 142–4
mobility 56
Montaigne, Michel de 35–6
  "Of the Institution and Education of Children" 35, 52–3
Montchrestian, Antoine de 68
  L'Ecossaise 65
  Escossoise, ou le Deastre Tragedie 73
  Sophonisbe 64–5
Montreux, Nicolas de
  Sophonisbe 68
morality 25
  Arden of Faversham 28
morality plays 10–11 (*see also* mystery plays)
Moritz, Landgarve 44
Mosti, Agostino 34
mothers 118, 120–2
Mountfort, William 26
  Life and Death of Dr. Faustus: with the humours of Harlequin and Scaramouche, The 16
Muir, Kenneth 7
Munday, Anthony
  view of sundry examples, Reporting many straunge murthers, sundry persons perjured, signes and tokens of Gods anger towards us. What straunge and monstrous children have of late been borne: and all memorable murthers since the murther of Maister Saunders

by George Browne, to this present and bloody murther of Abell Bourne Hosyer, who dwelled in Newgate Market, A 25
Mussato, Albertino 97
  Ecerinis 39, 97–101
mystery plays 10–11, 39
myth 83, 84–5, 92–5

national identity 58–9
Native Tradition 10
Netherlands 52
Normandy 65
Norton, Thomas and Thomas Sackville 68
  Gorboduc 9–10, 24, 37, 44, 59, 102–4, 106, 130–2

opera 18, 35
Orlin, Lena 27
Orti Oricellari gardens, Firenze 63
Ovid 35
  Metamorphoses 93

Padua 97–101
Painter, William
  Palace of Pleasure, A 23
painting 18
palaces 41–4
Palazzo del Corte, Ferrara 42
Palfrey, Simon 135
Palladio, Andrea 45, 46
pamphlets 23–4, 25–6
parable of the blind men 1
patriarchy 87, 90, 111–12, 118, 123
  Arden of Faversham 116
  Changeling, The 114–15
  Duchess of Malfi, The 117–18
  King Lear 121
patronage 42–4, 50, 51, 61, 65
Paulsen, Carl Andreas 70
Pazzi, Alessandro de' 19, 63
  Didone 63
pedagogy 35–6
Pellegrino da Udine 45
Pepys, Samuel 26
performance 9, 18, 31–2 (*see also* performance sites)
  ballads 26
  companionate reading 34
  France 60, 64, 65
  Italy 64
  perspective scenery 45, 46
  Phaedra 31–2

  stage design 45–6, 47, 84
  staging 40, 48–9, 51
performance sites (*see also* theaters)
  Denmark 41
  England 37, 43–4, 59–60
  France 35–6, 37, 39, 40
  Germany 36–7, 41, 44
  Italy 31–5, 38, 39, 42, 43
  palaces 41–4
  public spaces 38–41
  schools 35–7, 44
  Spain 39, 40
  studies 32–8
Peri, Jacopo 35
perspective scenery 45, 46
Phillips, Katherine 62
Plautus
  Menaechmi 42
plots
  Aristotle 92
  classical tragedies 60–1
  reusing 56–7, 62–70 (*see also* transmedia storytelling)
poets 2
political history plays 39
politics 65–6, 67, 69, 83 (*see also* civic conflict)
  Julius Caesar 91
  religious ritual 90
  transgression 140–1
Premierfait, Laurent de
  Du cas des nobles hommes et femmes (*The Falls of Famous Men and Women*) 20
Preston, Thomas (attrib.)
  Lamentable tragedy mixed ful of pleasant mirth, conteyning the life of Cambises, King of Persia 9, 23, 44
primogeniture 112, 125–7, 130–2
print 18–19, 23, 30, 104 (*see also* publishing)
productions. *See* performance
promiscuity 141
protagonists 7–8, 83, 93
Protestantism 6 (*see also* religion)
  Dr Faustus 86
  marriage 90, 111, 112–13
  ritual 89–91, 111
  school drama 69–70
  Zevecotius, Jacob 74
public criticism 56–7
public spaces 38–41
public sphere 57, 66
publishing 19, 57 (*see also* print)
  England 23, 59–60, 66

Puttfarkan, Thomas 18
Pynson, Richard 5

queer studies 140, 142, 144
Quint, David 93

race 69, 88, 136–7, 139
Ragusa 106–10
Ratio atque Institutio Studorium Societatis Iesu 36
reading 33–4, 35, 59
real-life stories 24–7
recitare 39
Reformation 6, 36, 74, 111, 112
regicide 90–1, 103 (*see also* execution)
religion 72–5, 77–8, 83–9, 95 (*see also* Catholicism *and* Protestantism)
   Islam 88, 89
   Judaism 88–9
   Reformation 6, 36, 74, 111, 112
   ritual 83–5, 89–92
remediation 17–18, 19
Renaissance communities before 1663 58–62
Revenge tragedies 11–12, 13, 51, 72
rhetoric 35, 70
Riario, Raffaele (cardinal) 31, 32, 41, 43
   palace of 32, 44
Ribner, Irving 12
Richards, Jennifer
   Voices and Books in the English Renaissance: A New History of Reading 34
Rightwise, Dionysia 43
Rightwise, John
   Dido 43
Rinuccini, Ottavio 35
ritual 83–5, 89–92, 95
Robortello, Francesco
   Explicationes 19
Romano, Alberico da 100–1
Romano, Ezzelimo da 97–100
Rouen 65
Roulers, Adrien
   Stuarta Tragoedia 72–3
royal courts (*see also* kingship)
   England 66–7, 71–4, 75–82
   France 64
Rucellai, Giovanni 63
   Rosamunda 63
Rueda, Lope de 40
   Comedia Llamada Eufemia, La 40
Rutland, Earl of (Edmund Plantagenet) 22–3

Ryan, Kiernan 139
Ryer, Pierre du
   Clitophon 47

Sachs, Hans 41
Sackville, Thomas 10, 68
Sackville, Thomas and Thomas Norton 68
   Gorboduc 9–10, 24, 37, 44, 59, 102–4, 130–2
Saint-Gelais, Mellin de 64
   Sophonisbe 64
St. Paul's School 35, 43–4
Salisbury, Earl of (Thomas Montagu) 21
Sam Wanamaker Theatre, London 52
Santer, Eric
   Royal Remains, The 80–1
Savery, Salomon 52
Scala, Cangrande della 97
Scaliger, Julius Caesar
   Poetices 18, 19
Scamozzi, Vincenzo 45, 46
scandal 65–6
Schmitt, Carl 77–8, 79–80, 82
   Dictatorship 77
   Hamlet or Hecuba 77–80
   Nazi Party 77, 80
   Political Theology 75
school performances 44, 69–70
schools 70
Schouwburg, Amsterdam 52
Segni, Bernardo 19
Seneca 8, 18–19, 97
   Phaedra 31–2, 35, 38, 43, 44
   portrait 33, 34
   protagonists 8
   Thebais 8
   Thyestes 101
   Troas 8
sermons 6
sex. *See* gender
sexual desire 123–4, 136–8
   Antony and Cleopatra 136–7
   Arden of Faversham 115–16
   Changeling, The 115
   Duchess of Malfi, The 145–6
   Edward II 140, 141
   incest 135, 137–8, 145
   Iocasta 129–30
   Othello 124, 139–40
   religion 113
   Revenger's Tragedy, The 142–3
   widows 116

sexual perversion 142–4
Shakespeare, William 8, 71–2
   actors 60
   Antony and Cleopatra 85, 93, 94, 135–7, 138–9
   classical learning 170 n. 16
   comedies 84, 85
   Coriolanus 85
   folklore 85
   Foucault, Michel 81
   gender 134–7, 138–9
   Hamlet. See *Hamlet*
   heroes' downfall 92
   Julius Caesar 91, 93
   King Henry V 90
   King Henry VI Part 2 50
   King Henry VI Part 3 50, 125–6
   King Henry VIII (All is True) 86
   King Lear 92–3, 120–3, 126–7, 131
   King Richard II 50, 82, 91
   King Richard III 50, 126
   kingship 81–2
   Kott, Jan 85
   Macbeth 7, 81–2, 85, 92, 113
   Merchant of Venice, The 88
   original play titles 50
   Othello 88, 92, 124–5, 139–40
   religion 86
   Richard, Duke of York 50, 125–6
   Romeo and Juliet 50, 87–8, 89
   Santner, Eric 80–1
   Tempest, The 94
   Titus Andronicus 50, 51, 84, 88, 93
   Troilus and Cressida 93
   Twelfth Night 35
Shakespeare, William and John Fletcher
   Two Noble Kinsman, The 93
Shoah 80
Sidney, Philip 59
sin 6
Sinfield, Alan 140
social class 23–4, 28, 30, 173 n. 11
society 19
   establishing 85
   Renaissance 58
sons 118–23
Sophocles
   Ajax 74
   Electra 60–1
Spain
   performance sites in 39, 40
   theaters 48–50

Spenser, Edmund
   Faerie Queene 73, 87
spiritual certainties 12
stage design 45–6, 47, 84
stage trapdoors 84
staging 40, 48–9, 51
Staley, Gregory A. 97–8
"stately Tragedy containing the ambitious Life and death of the great Cham the enchantments of Bagous the Brachman wth the straunge fortunes of Roxen the Captiuity release and death of his brother Manzor the Turchestan King and happy Fortunes of the Sophy of Persia with the loke of Bargandell his sonne, [a]" 137–8
Stern, Tiffany 135
Still, Melly
   Revenger's Tragedy, The 144
Story of Samson, The 50
Stow, John 25, 27
Strum, Johannes 36
Stuart, Elizabeth. *See* Elizabeth Stuart
Stuart, House of 71–4, 75–82
studiolo 33
subjectivity 142
suffering 72
Sulpizio da Veroli, Giovanni 31, 32, 35, 38, 39, 41
Sussex, Countess of (Bridget Fitzwalter) 51
Sussex, Earl of (Robert Radcliffe) 51
Sussex's Men 51

Talmy, Adrien 40
Tanner, Georg 60–1
Teatro all'antica, Sabbioneta 45
Teatro del Campidoglio, Rome 45
Teatro Farnese, Parma 45
Teatro Olimpico, Vicenza 45, 46
Telford, Kenneth
   hamartía 6
theatergrams 32
Theater of Marcellus, Rome 38
theaters 44–53 (*see also under individual names*)
   children's theater companies 67
   corrales theaters 48–9
   Cruelty 13
   design 51–2
   England 50–2
   France 46–8, 65
   Italy 44–6
   Jesuit schools 36–7, 70

Netherlands 52
Spain 48–50
special effects 23
stage design 45–6, 47
staging 40, 48–9, 51
touring companies 40–1, 47, 48
Thebes 104–5
Timoclea at the Siege of Thebes 50–1
Titian
    "Four Great Sinners" 18
    "Marsyas" 18
Torres, Bartolomé de 48
touring companies 40–1, 47, 48, 70
    English 50, 70
    national identities 58–9
Tourneur, Cyril
    Atheist's Tragedy, The 86–7
Tourneur, Cyril and Middleton, Thomas
    Revenger's Tragedy, The 83
tragedy, form of 1–2
tragic action 4
tragic complaints 22–3
tragicomedy 47
transgression 113, 123, 137, 141–2
    Edward II 140–1
    Hamlet 133
    Iocasta 129
    Othello 140
    Revenger's Tragedy, The 142–3
    "stately Tragedy containing the ambitious Life and death of the great Cham, [a] 137–8
translations 19, 60–2
transmedia storytelling 15–18, 23–30
transnational networks 58, 60 (*see also* touring companies)
Trauerspiel 74, 75, 76
traveling companies. *See* touring companies
Trissino, Gian Giorgio 63
    Sophonisba, La 19, 42, 63–4
true-crime 24–7
Tuccia, legend of 114
tyranny 98–101, 103, 104, 110

underworld 84
Urbino, Duke (Federico III da Montefeltro) 33

Valla, Giorgio 19
vice 137
violence 98–106
Virgil

    Aeneid 93–4
virginity 114
Vitruvius 44
    Architectura, De 31, 44, 45–6
Vondel, Joost van den 73–4
    Gysbreght van Amstel 52
    Mary Stuart, or Tortured Majesty 73–4
Vroye, Joost 31

Wakefield mystery plays 10–11
    Crucifixion 10, 11
    Mactatio Abel 10–11
Warning for Fair Women, containing the most tragicall and lamentable murther of Master George Sanders; A Yorkshire tragedie, Not so new, as lamentable and true 24–5
Wassenhove, Joos van 33, 34
Webster, John
    Duchess of Malfi, The. See *Duchess of Malfi, The*
    White Devil, The 83, 88
Western tradition 8–9
wheel of fortune 20, 21
widows 116–17
William of Moerbeke 19
Wilson, Thomas
    State of England, The 131
witchcraft 136, 137–8
Wolsey, Thomas (cardinal) 43
women (*see also* gender)
    as actors 62
    Antony and Cleopatra 137
    Arden of Faversham 115–16
    audiences 66
    Changeling, The 114–15
    controlling 112
    coverture, law of 111–12
    Duchess of Malfi, The 116–18, 145–6
    Edward II 140–1
    family position 111–2
    fidelity 123, 140
    hysteria 121
    marital status 113–14
    misogyny 123, 142–4
    mothers 118, 120–2, 132
    patriarchy, the 87, 90, 111–12, 114–5, 117–18
    promiscuity 141

Revenger's Tragedy, The 142–4
rulers 93–4
sexuality 113, 115, 116, 123–4
translating classical tragedy 61–2
virginity 114
widows 116–17
witchcraft 136, 137–8

York, Duke of (Richard Plantagenet) 22–3
Young, Julian
   Philosophy of Tragedy, The 72

Zeffirelli, Franco 170 n. 21
Zevecotius, Jacob 74
   Maria Stuarta 74